AF471029

# RED
# LETTER
# DAYS

# RED LETTER DAYS

## Fourteen Dramatic Events That Shook Arsenal Football Club

**Jon Spurling**

First published by Pitch Publishing, 2014

**Pitch Publishing**
**A2 Yeoman Gate**
**Yeoman Way**
**Durrington**
**BN13 3QZ**
**www.pitchpublishing.co.uk**

© Jon Spurling, 2014



A CIP catalogue record is available for this book
from the British Library.

ISBN 978 1-90962-639-3

Typesetting and origination by Pitch Publishing

Printed in Spain

# Contents

*For Mum, who didn't enjoy football, but quite enjoyed the swearing, x.*

*For Dad, who enjoys neither.*

# Acknowledgements

I'D like to thank the following for their help with this book: Sally Davis, for her excellent research into the life and times of Henry Norris; Tony Sandell and all his staff at the Arsenal Museum for making my time looking at the fascinating Catton archive so enjoyable and worthwhile; and to the staff at the Local History Archives Centre in Islington. The *Islington Gazette* – in all its guises – was a fantastic resource, particularly up to the end of the 1930s, and the archive was a real treasure trove of information, although my eyes were crossed after peering at all that Microfilm.

Thanks also to everybody at the Colindale Newspaper Library for their help and patience – just as their move across London was in the offing. I've never met Arsenal historians Andy Kelly and Tony Attwood, who write the Woolwich Arsenal blog, but I've found their work to be both informative and challenging, especially on the pre-Highbury era. Thanks chaps.

I'm indebted to John Harding, author of the excellent book on Alex James, and the late Brian Woolnough and Mike Langley for supplying me with cassettes of interviews they conducted with Tom Parker, George Male and Joe Hulme from the 1930s team. Hearing their voices was quite something, and I hope that excerpts from the interviews give the chapters on the 1930s a far more three-dimensional feel than they would otherwise have had. I'd also like to thank Alex Fynn for his sage advice down the years on football writing.

Thanks to the Arsenal players – past and present – who have contributed to the book, especially Frank McLintock, Perry Groves, Patrick Vieira and Gilberto, who went beyond the call of duty to unearth new contacts for me to speak to. Thanks also to fellow Arsenal writer David Tossell for lending me the Bertie Mee DVD and to Simon

Lowe, and his impeccable knowledge of all things Stoke City. And to all the supporters I've spoken to down the years for *Rebels For The Cause*, *Highbury: N5* and *Red Letter Days*, thank you for your time and your insight.

Down the years, Kevin Whitcher – *Gooner* editor – has always encouraged my (all too rare) pieces and remains a good sounding board for all things Arsenal. And to Ian Trevett – erstwhile of the now deceased *Highbury High*, thanks for printing my pieces. Thanks to Andy Exley at Arsenal for all the commissions and the assistance with the official magazine, the programme, and this book. Grateful thanks also to all the chaps at *FourFourTwo* over the last decade – Hugh, Hitesh, Nick, Gary, Andy, Louis and Dave, and Andy Lyons at *When Saturday Comes* for commissioning so many of my non-Arsenal pieces. Thanks also to Clare for lending me her Kindle. Thanks to everyone at Pitch for showing faith in the book, to Duncan Olner for the cover design, Derek Hammond for his work on the blurb and the jacket and sleeve, to Dean Rockett for his sensitive proofreading of the text, and to Paul and Jane for their encouragement and for not having a go at me because I was late getting everything done!

And to my agent David Luxton for 'closing the deal' – as they say these days. To Helen and Phoebe – both of whom I know are unlikely to stray beyond this line – thanks for your patience and 'hands off' approach to this project! The book is finally finished. X

Follow Jon Spurling on Twitter @JonSpurling1 (now that his nephews have shown him how to use it).

# Foreword

IN 1999, research by the *Independent* revealed that, based on league finishing positions, Arsenal were England's leading team of the 20th century with an average final position of 8.5. They narrowly pipped Liverpool to top spot, with Everton and Manchester United some way behind in third and fourth place. Factor in that since 2000, the Gunners' average league position has been 2.87, Arsenal remain by some distance England's most successful club. Apparently.

But in reality, what do these figures prove? That when it comes to the big picture, Arsenal have, broadly speaking, always been resolutely consistent and frequently in the running for glory. They also hint at the club's underlying conservative view, as espoused by Ted Drake, 'We have what we hold.' No prolonged periods in the lower-division wilderness for the Gunners, unlike many of their key rivals, including the Manchester clubs and Liverpool.

But the statistics mask Arsenal's colossal peaks and the deep troughs; the gluttonous bursts of success and the long periods of retrenchment and missed opportunities. In short, they do a disservice to the club's often turbulent history. *Red Letter Days* is an investigation of events which define an era, often marking the end of one historical cycle and the dawning of a new one. It is not an extended narrative of Arsenal's greatest games, or simply a paean to its epoch-defining individuals.

Arsenal's history – as with any club – can be broken down into thousands of game-changing, season-altering junctures. A crucial goal here. A dramatic save there. A timely piece of invective from the club captain, perhaps, signing the wrong man at the wrong time, a key team meeting or a tannoy announcement at the home of a deadly rival which acted as a spur to the visitors…a myriad of these moments are contained within the pages of this book. But equally well, there are a number of 'non-negotiable' events in Arsenal's rich and varied history. These form the overarching focus of each of the 14 chapters.

Rather than hone in on the fulminating climax to the 1970/71 Double season against Tottenham Hotspur and Liverpool, it's the story which sits behind the crucial FA Cup semi-final at Hillsborough against Stoke City which is the focus of attention because that was the timeline-altering clash.

Conversely, the 1930 'Zeppelin' final figures heavily because it symbolised the rise to power of Chapman's Arsenal. As a club, Arsenal are strongly aware of the role of individuals in mapping out their history, revealed by the deployment of the 32 cores on the outside of the Emirates Stadium and the statues of Chapman, Wenger, Bergkamp, Henry and Adams outside the ground. But such deification of Arsenal's historical figures is, to some extent, open to debate, and *Red Letter Days* – as well as looking closely at Arsenal's bronze icons – assesses the defining moments of others like Norris, Mercer, Mee, McLintock and Graham and assesses how what they did altered the course of the club's fortunes. It also suggests that the contributions of Rooke, Sexton and Rioch should be more recognised.

A note on the text. This book doesn't focus on Woolwich Arsenal's formative years, as the fledgling club began to take its early tottering steps. The reason for this is that, given the sporadic nature of newspaper reports, and the absence of any surviving eyewitnesses or visual evidence, there is a huge amount of conjecture about much of what really happened.

As one of the main drivers of the Arsenal History Project, Tony Attwood, commented on his blog, 'In the early days of writing histories of the club, people relied on their memories, or occasional comments from others. This built up a range of documentation all based on the flimsiest of evidence…later writers reprinted the story, and so it went on and on.'

A prescient example of this is the story which has been handed down over the generations recounting how, on 11 December 1886, a group of footballers from the Dial Square workshop in the Woolwich Arsenal crossed the Thames on the 'famous' Woolwich ferry, and walked to a piece of land which one of them had discovered on the Isle of Dogs. The boys from Dial Square, we were told, played on a rough and ready surface (club secretary Elijah Watkins commented, 'Talk about a football pitch! I could not venture to say what shape it was…I was going to say a ditch, but I think an open sewer would be more appropriate'), won 6-0 against the Eastern Wanderers, and then went back to Woolwich afterwards.

The historical waters are murky. Official histories have mentioned that there were other Woolwich Arsenal armament factory clubs which pre-dated Dial Square, but as no written evidence exists of their playing records, it seems to have been taken as read that Dial Square were the distant forefathers of Arsenal FC.

The fact that Dial Square also travelled to the Isle of Dogs (an arduous journey and a venue with precious little available municipal land) also seems curious given that there must have been some football pitches in nearby Woolwich. Additionally, there was no Woolwich ferry in operation until 1898, and there is no record anywhere of the Eastern Wanderers in 1886. Crucially, the evidence that exists of that first match hinges on the testimony of just one onlooker – Elijah Watkins, whose tale was published in *Association Football And The Men Who Made It* in 1906 – some 20 years or so after the event. The suggestion is that the dates, the venues and even the teams may well have become muddled over time. Much of the story may be apocryphal, distorted by smoke and mirrors; myth and legend.

Fascinating though these findings are, there are no documents – public or private – which could be described as 'a smoking gun' when it comes to the club's first match, and during the course of my research I didn't stumble across any further documentation which provides further information surrounding the club turning professional in 1891. The much reported 'boycott' of Arsenal by fellow southern clubs never happened, as the Arsenal History Project has proved, but further anecdotes and detail have not been forthcoming.

I was offered a diary by the great grandson of a former Woolwich Arsenal employee, and a couple of letters which their owners claimed would 'shed new light on Woolwich Arsenal'. Sadly, neither the diary nor the letters revealed anything revelatory. I hit a dead end so I've left the 'pea souper' fog-shrouded 19th century out. By the early 20th century though, the historical mist was clearing. *Red Letter Days* begins in 1910 with Woolwich Arsenal mired in serious financial trouble. The unlikeliest of saviours lay in wait.

Enjoy the book.

Jon Spurling, August 2014.

# Capital Gains

*'The little mind of Mr Norris is merely the little mind of a private gentleman thirsting for notoriety, and not much troubling how he gets it.' 'Chelstam' in the* West London and Fulham Times, *1905.*

*'The Manor Ground was a backwater really. An odd, out of the way place. Highbury on the other hand was in the centre of things. It had a real buzz and a real draw.' George Robertson, a regular at the Manor Ground and Highbury.*

BY January 1910 the executioner's axe looked set to fall on Woolwich Arsenal, who lay fourth from bottom in the First Division. At Woolwich Town Hall, a Voluntary Committee was set up to raise £1,000 to wipe some of the club's debt. Some of the novel fundraising schemes included a film show at the Woolwich Picture Palace and a whist drive. Such dedication from the core of the Woolwich Arsenal support appeared fruitless. The bottom of the barrel was about to be scraped. Woolwich Arsenal were knocked out of the FA Cup by Everton. The 5-0 shellacking meant that although the club received a share of the £842 gate money, there would be no more cup money for at least a year.

A friendly match against Fulham two weeks later altered the entire course of the club's history. The Fulham directors knew of Woolwich Arsenal's travails and had offered to send a team to play a friendly match in Plumstead to raise some much-needed income for the home club. It was an embarrassing day. It wasn't the result, a 2-2 draw, more the fact that a pitiful crowd showed up to generate just £35 of income.

In the Woolwich-based *Kentish Independent*, 'Inside Left' castigated the citizens of Woolwich as 'not deserving of a football team'. When just 4,000 turned up to see the league game against Manchester United on 12 March at the Manor Ground, George Leavey placed the club's limited company into voluntary liquidation. It was the only alternative to bankruptcy.

An owner of a gentleman's outfitters in Woolwich High Street, Leavey had worked like a Trojan to keep the club going. But he could only do so much. The meeting to wind up the limited company was held on the evening of Friday 18 March at Woolwich Town Hall. Fulham director William Hall tried to attend but was politely informed that it was for shareholders only. Before trotting back to west London though, Hall spoke to Leavey, leaving the Woolwich Arsenal man in no doubt that Fulham were willing to offer the club more financial aid. Hall missed out on a tense and bad-tempered meeting. Leavey revealed that the club was £900 in debt, and also owed a large sum of money to Archibald Leitch, designer of the grandstand at the Manor Ground.

Arsenal manager George Morrell ran the gauntlet of shareholders' frustrations. After spending nigh-on £1,000 on new players, the team's performances had worsened in 1909/10, not improved. In the *Kentish Independent*, Leavey claimed he was optimistic that the club could be saved, and over the next few weeks he attempted to form a group of local men who were willing to put themselves forward as directors of a new limited company which would buy the assets of the old one and reach deals with the creditors.

Rumours circulated in the press that the club was poised to move to Fulham's ground, Craven Cottage, and in May 1910 Leavey made the clarion call for a group of men to form a new limited company to take over the club. Leavey's plea was answered sometime in late April by three Fulham directors; William Allen, William Hall, and Henry George Norris.

Woolwich Arsenal would never be the same again.

·  ·  ·  ·  ·

He has been dead for 80 years, but Henry Norris continues to provoke controversy and divide opinion. He was a wealthy businessman and made his pile in the building trade. He was a football club director and a chairman. He was a vestryman in Battersea. He was a local councillor, Mayor of Fulham between 1909 and 1919, and Conservative MP for Fulham East between 1919 and 1922. He was a colonel in the army, although he never saw active service.

Norris was a high-ranking Freemason, married twice, had three daughters and was knighted in 1917 for services to Fulham and the war effort. He dabbled in football journalism and lived through libel writs and court cases. That is a lot for anyone to cram in to their 70-year life. But what Norris is – in equal measure – loved and loathed for, is uprooting Arsenal from Plumstead in 1913, bringing them to north London, and using his influence with the powers that be to ensure that Arsenal were promoted to the First Division in 1919. Described in his lifetime and after his death as little more than a cad and a bounder, Norris may well have been both of these things. Or perhaps neither.

He is arguably the most influential figure in the club's history. But there's no statue of him outside the Emirates Stadium, or a marble bust to sit beside those of Herbert Chapman and Arsène Wenger. Nor will there ever be.

He never wrote a journal or left a diary. He did write letters which were full of invective and sometimes found their way into local newspapers like the *West London and Fulham Times*. Norris lived in an age when it was extremely rare for leading football figures to give interviews. Snippets of his bluster remain, and are as resonant now as they were a century ago. He was an enigma.

As one frustrated music critic said of Mick Jagger in the 1960s, 'It's easy to get weary from chasing his mysterious soul through the mazes of fun-house mirrors he had built to protect it.' It is the same with Norris. Yet to fully comprehend Arsenal's fraught final days in Woolwich and their edgy early existence at Highbury in the latter days of the Edwardian era, his metaphorical coat tails need to be clung on to.

In the course of writing this book, and *Highbury: N5*, I issued several pleas for further information on him in various London publications. Some merely trotted over old ground. Others revealed just what a contradictory figure he really was.

Clive Edwards told the story of how his grandfather was forced to take respite from his job as a roofer after Norris took exception to the way he was tiling several houses in the Fulham area shortly before World War One. 'Norris hounded him, threatening to pay him less than the agreed price for the job, if he didn't complete the job to Norris's satisfaction.'

Eventually, Edwards's grandfather cracked under the strain, but returned to work two weeks later. Upon finally completing the tiling, Norris paid up in full, including a small bonus which wasn't part of the two men's initial agreement. Edwards also recounts, 'Norris would see to it that if any plumbers, or tilers were out of work, he'd do his best to ensure that he contacted other builders in the London area to see if they needed spare men.'

Islington resident Chris Carpenter informed me that his grandfather, who had been recruited into the army by Norris during World War One, suffered a shrapnel wound. Upon his return from France, Norris personally visited the soldier, and 'spoke to one of his Freemason friends to get him some temporary work in the plumbing trade in order that he could get back on his feet'. Norris gave another of his wounded comrades £5 from his wallet in order that 'he could get himself a decent meal or two'. Such personal anecdotes, and there must be dozens more which have disappeared into the ether down the years, give some hint of the man who was about to set Woolwich Arsenal on a different path.

Demanding, bullying, staggeringly well connected, philanthropic, civic-minded, sometimes generous with money and cavalier when it came to dipping into his own wallet, yet obsessed with driving the hardest of bargains…Norris is the most complex and contradictory of all Arsenal figures.

⌣ ⌣ ⌣ ⌣ ⌣

In May 1910, the big question was why the three Fulham directors decided to become involved in the affairs of the ailing Woolwich Arsenal. Despite much second guessing – there's even been a historical novel written on the topic: *Making The Arsenal* by Tony Attwood – there has never been a satisfactory explanation. Allen, Hall and Norris certainly never discussed it. Norris was not a sentimentalist, so the notion that he simply wanted to assist the good folk of Woolwich can be dismissed. There is a possibility that the three Fulham directors reckoned that Woolwich Arsenal could play their games at Craven Cottage and pay a tidy sum in rent to a club which had financial difficulties of its own. Perhaps they thought that if Second Division Fulham could gain a financial hold over Woolwich Arsenal, who looked like they might go out of existence, then a vacant position in the First Division might be going begging.

The Football League blocked Fulham's original plan to simply take over Woolwich Arsenal. There is a possibility that if Fulham had paid off the First Division club's debts, and then taken over its assets including the Manor Ground site, then the Manor Ground could have been sold for development. After all, Allen and Norris were housing developers. It appears likely that George Leavey blocked an alternative proposal that the two clubs share Craven Cottage.

In the end, the two clubs agreed that a new board of directors be formed (the third since the liquidation process began), with the caveat that Allen, Hall and Norris were to be members of the Woolwich Arsenal board in their personal capacity, and not as directors of Fulham, although they continued to act as directors for the West London club as well.

After the agreement was made, the three new directors agreed that football would continue at the Manor Ground for 12 months, before they decided upon whether or not to move the club elsewhere. It was hardly a satisfactory outcome. Fulham supporters reckoned their directors should have been concentrating on affairs at their first club. Allen, Hall and Norris were left tending to a very sick patient whose long-term prognosis was uncertain. Woolwich Arsenal's on-pitch fortunes were to worsen further.

Initially at least, the three men sought to inject stability to the club, confirming that George Morrell would remain as manager (there had been rumours in the press that Fulham's Phil Kelso would be sent in). Then the real problems began. The *Kentish Independent* informed its readers that 'promises have been made to strengthen the team'. If they were, they were broken. Quickly, Norris became spokesman for the rescuers, using the *Kentish Independent* as his mouthpiece. He didn't mince his words, expressing disappointment that only 520 shares in the new company were to be owned by Woolwich and Plumstead residents.

The rest would be controlled by Hall, Norris and Leavey. In order to save the local football team, 'there must be more local support', he insisted, before adding that Woolwich Arsenal must become 'self-supporting'.

There were to be no hand-outs of the kind that Leavey had freely indulged in prior to his arrival. The *Kentish Independent* was littered with letters criticising Norris for his tone. His answer was crystal clear. He invited critics to come forward before 17 June, and take over the club themselves. They didn't.

At a stormy meeting in a Woolwich hotel, set up to formally ratify the new limited company – Woolwich Arsenal Football and Athletic Company Limited – Norris was accused of wanting to get his hands upon the club's assets via loans to George Leavey. Leavey was forced to admit that the share issue had failed due to the apathy of locals, and Norris stated that the club wouldn't need to be moved if locals attended in sufficient numbers. By now though, Norris was likely pondering the club's escape to London, and over the next three years, the atmosphere of mistrust between Norris and any groups of supporters only worsened.

On Boxing Day 1910, the team lost 5-0 at Manchester United in front of over 35,000 fans, with the rampant Reds on their way to the league title. A meagre 7,000 saw the Woolwich reds face Bury just five days later at home. This was the grim reality of life at the Manor Ground, and all this at a time when both Norris and Hall had already put in £475 of their own money. Leavey had put in £234, and in a desperate effort to raise cash after Christmas, the club offered all its unsold season tickets for sale at half price.

In theory the three men were to be repaid in 15 years, but Norris and Hall made it perfectly clear that they had no intention of allowing their money to be tied up this way and a set of 5,000 shares in the club went on sale in the grim winter of 1910.

It was an unmitigated disaster. Only 50 shares were applied for. Norris resorted to desperate measures to attract new players, and end the catastrophic cycle of declining attendances leading to the best players being sold.

In early December 1911, word circulated that goalkeeper Leigh Roose was angling for a move away from Aston Villa. With the smart money on him moving to Fulham he unexpectedly ended up in Kent.

Roose was just the type of small-town personality the club needed. Woolwich Arsenal fans had always embraced colourful celebrities like the enigmatic forward Bobby Templeton and pugnacious full-back Morris Bates – nicknamed 'the iron headed man'.

Infamous for his scandalous affair with married music hall singer Marie Lloyd, Roose was the first goalkeeper to be described as 'mad' (by *Athletic News* in 1909) due to his penchant for chatting to the crowd during matches, and for originating the 'wobbly knees' act, later perfected by Liverpool's Bruce Grobbelaar when the opposition took a penalty.

Although it remained a secret for nigh-on 17 years, in his 1927 court case Norris admitted that he and William Hall had put up half each to pay a player £200 to sign for the club. The player was unnamed but the description suggested strongly that it was Roose. The player accepted the inducement, signed on the dotted line, and therefore all three men broke the Football Association rule that the maximum signing-on fee was a paltry £10.

Pitiful crowd figures appeared to have been the driving force behind Norris's decision to break the rules. Roose, although an amateur, was an international, and the crowd at the Manor Ground did increase for his debut, but it didn't last. Norris then sprung a trick he had used at Fulham. He doubled ticket prices from 6d to 1s for the Boxing Day clash with Tottenham. Arsenal won 3-1 but remained mired in mid-table. It wasn't the last time that Norris would spring a fiscal trick or two during his long association with the club, but not even this master of financial chicanery could conjure a solution to Woolwich Arsenal's travails.

The point of no return – the event which proved to everyone that the club had no future in Woolwich – came when centre-forward Andy Ducat was sold to Aston Villa for £1,000. He was unquestionably Woolwich Arsenal's jewel in the crown, aged 26 and in his absolute prime.

The evidence suggests that Ducat – also a fine cricketer who played for England – didn't actually want to go. He informed Jimmy Catton in *Athletic News* years later, 'I'd stayed loyal to the club throughout many hard times. I was very much at home down in the south, but it was indicated to me that a move to Aston Villa would be in everyone's best interests.'

In the short term, Ducat's sale certainly kept the wolf from the door. It meant that the club actually made a profit that season. But Ducat wasn't replaced. George Leavey had resigned from the board a few weeks before, suggesting that perhaps he knew Ducat would be sold, and at a stormy AGM in July, Norris's first as Arsenal chairman, he informed shareholders that 'crowd figures are enough to make any man go into mourning' and that was the key reason why Ducat was sold.

He also reminded his audience that he and Hall owned 50 per cent of the club's shares, and that they were unwilling to maintain the club at their own expense for the benefit of others for much longer. Although there was no explicit mention of relocation, Norris must have been delighted when Arsenal founding father Jack Humble stood up and announced that although he was a local, he would support a move away from Kent if it breathed new life into the club.

Ducat's departure triggered a cataclysmic decline in the club's fortunes. The 1912/13 season remains the club's worst campaign, ending in relegation to the Second Division with just three wins all season. The ever-shrinking support rounded on captain Percy Sands and there was incredulity at the club's failure to replace Ducat.

Following a terrible 4-0 hammering at Manchester City, future Gunners boss George Allison, writing as 'The Mate' in *Athletic News*, pointed out that the club had 'no one in the team who could be looked to get a goal'. Between August and March the team failed to register a single win. After a reverse against Blackburn, the match report in *Athletic News* stated there was no one in the team who could be described 'as even a passably good marksman'. A home tie with Liverpool in the FA Cup appeared to offer some respite, but the expected 20,000 crowd turned out to be less than half that.

Off the pitch, Norris was initiating some game-changing manoeuvres. By 1913, William Hall had become a member of the Football League Committee after Woolwich Arsenal nominated him as a candidate. Hall remained there until 1927, and as an insider on the Football League's governing elite he proved a key player for his club as Norris began to wield his influence.

He couldn't silence rumours circulating in the press though. In October 1912, *Athletic News* claimed that Norris had purchased a plot of land near Haringey Station. Another rumour suggested that a site in Battersea had been selected. But when the press confirmed in late February that Norris had identified a site owned by St John's College, an institution which trained young men for the church, at Gillespie Road, near Finsbury Park, his cover was blown. The revelation hit Tottenham and Clapton Orient firmly in the solar plexus.

Days after Norris suggested 'people should simply do what I always do with stories and ignore them', representatives from Tottenham and Clapton Orient went uninvited to the scheduled meeting of the Football League Management Committee to try and prevent any move by Woolwich Arsenal from going ahead.

The League agreed that such a move was highly unusual, but because of the high and dense population, considered north London well capable of supporting three football clubs. In other words, it proposed to do nothing to block any proposed move.

An *Athletic News* article (the publication was always very close to the League hierarchy and many of its members wrote in its pages) was remarkably pro-Woolwich Arsenal. Some have since suggested that the hand of William Hall, perhaps heavily guided by Norris, was responsible for a crucial piece which pointed out that crowds had been falling for years at the Manor Ground due to 'economic decline'. Later that week at the Connaught Rooms in Covent Garden, Norris held court with a gaggle of journalists to confirm that rumours of the proposed move were true.

The season had one final sting in its tail. Woolwich Arsenal showed late signs of a recovery in March and with Chelsea also slipping into decline, there were faint hopes that the team might just avoid relegation. Those hopes were extinguished when Chelsea went to Liverpool and won 2-1, confirming the Kent side's demotion. Norris watched the match and took Liverpool to task for their spineless display in the *West London and Fulham Times*, virtually accusing them of throwing the game.

The Football League investigation found Liverpool to have been 'spineless' but not corrupt. Norris was furious, remaining convinced that his team had been cheated.

The club's era at the Manor Ground ended in dismal circumstances. With relegation already confirmed, the team laboured to a draw with Middlesbrough. Even the farewell social evening was distinctly off key. Most of the squad attended, as did trainer George Hardy. William Hall and George Morell sent their apologies. Neither Henry Norris nor Jack Humble were even invited. Humble, one of Woolwich Arsenal's founding fathers, was snubbed because he had supported the move despite living in the area since the 1880s. A united camp it most certainly wasn't.

The *Kentish Independent* quaintly put it in 1906, 'The Woolwich boy believes in enjoying himself when he lets himself out for an airing.'

But the fact was that too few locals attended Manor Ground matches, particularly in the later years. By 1908, there were four other clubs in the top two divisions: Chelsea, Tottenham, Fulham and Clapton Orient.

Arsenal had originally been the first southern club to compete in the Football League, and then they could count on pulling in crowds who would be willing to travel to Plumstead. But much less so once there were other competing attractions in the metropolis. Plumstead, although close to London, was too much off the beaten track. The various train journeys down from London were notoriously slow and it took an extra 30 minutes to get to Plumstead by tram than it did to Millwall, the nearest other club.

The *Woolwich Gazette* probably made the correct call in 1906 when it claimed, 'The neighbourhood is solid for a six thousand gate at once.'

Although support was considerably higher than that initially, when the going got tough for the club, support regularly shrank back to that base level, sometimes worse. Had the club stayed in Plumstead they would most likely have morphed into an outfit of a size somewhere between Gillingham and Charlton, and averaged out as a struggling second-tier or high-achieving third-tier team. For Norris that was never going to be enough, and he couldn't wait to leave the Manor Ground behind. The almost unlimited potential offered by north London awaited. But so did an intimidating mob of local residents, not to mention the irate tenants at White Hart Lane.

Between March and September, those Islington residents who opposed the coming of Woolwich Arsenal waxed lyrical about the borough's respectability and urbaneness. Yet the pages of the *Islington Daily Gazette* and *North London Tribune* from that era reveal a melting pot of political intrigue with Progressives, Suffragists, Socialists and Liberals regularly going toe to toe in various halls and churches.

Fire and brimstone preachers forecast the end of the world, and numerous academic speakers warn of the powder keg situation in the Balkans. There are the usual stories of drunkenness, street brawls, traffic accidents, and lead thefts from church roofs. And, throughout spring and early summer, there are a growing number of stories about 'THE COMING FOOTBALL INVASION'.

There was already a thriving amateur football scene in the borough (several letters expressed concerns about the possible impact upon Tufnell Park – described in the *Gazette* as 'the Mecca of amateur football'), and there were lengthy reports on matches between other sides including Canonbury, Cross Street, the Casuals and St Peters. But Woolwich Arsenal's imminent arrival represented something else entirely.

The Highbury Defence League was formed by locals in mid-March. Councillor P.E. Inglis of Highbury was urged by others who attended that opening meeting on 17 March to 'try and do something to try and avert the calamity that would come upon the neighbourhood if the football club came into its midst'. Inglis, who was elected chairman of the group, claimed that property in the borough would depreciate by between 25 and 50 per cent and that the 'best class of resident will leave'.

The Defence Committee forced through a debate at an Islington Council meeting and the council confirmed that it would do its utmost to stop the 'interlopers' from coming to the borough. Henry Norris attended the council meeting, but records suggest that he didn't say a word. Not a single utterance from a man who prided himself on plain speaking and absolute directness. Perhaps his uncharacteristic taciturnity was because he knew that for all the opposition's bluster, their efforts would prove futile without support from the Football League. It demonstrated that the club had a consummate political animal fighting for it. The worst thing Norris could have done was to stir up a hornets' nest with his brusqueness when he didn't need to.

A general theme coursing through the pages of the *Gazette* in 1913 was the battle to preserve traditional values within the borough. There are arguments about 'decadent dancing in local halls', the 'lack of religious instruction within schools', the 'ever increasing hubbub of traffic on roads through the borough', the lack of affordable housing in the area, 'loud gramophones disturbing the peace' and, most intriguingly, ongoing debates as to whether residents should remove cockerels from their gardens because 'people should now awake to the sound of the alarm clock, not the chicken'.

Football was already heavily linked with a more secular, almost ungodly lifestyle in the borough. In two separate incidents, two groups of boys were fined for 'playing football and swearing in the street on a Sunday'. Benjamin Bradley of London Fields was fined £50 for running an illegal football betting house, and a brawl occurred after supporters of Tufnell Park got drunk on a pub crawl following their team's victory in an amateur league game.

The letters to the *Gazette* in connection with Woolwich Arsenal's impending arrival reflect the residents' fears about a huge increase in such sinful activities. Highbury Hill dweller T.E. Naylor, a member of the Defence Committee, was the first to protest about the gambling problem, writing, 'I object to this right being exercised on my doorstep, and on such a scale and in such a way to be a nuisance, if not an actual menace to my family.'

Mr Naylor urged the college trustees not to sign the contract to avoid 'holding a candle to the devil'. Arthur Read spoke of 'hawkers, litter, drunkenness and bad language and of fans arguing about the game at public houses'. Mr Read also discussed how football 'drives customers away from good businesses'. For this local resident, fearful that the increase in buses 'will shake down the ceilings of our houses', he really must have felt like the sky was falling in on his world.

Yet the response which the group received from the Dean of Canterbury, who was president of the council which controlled the affairs of St John's College, made it clear that he would not personally intervene.

Another recurrent theme running through the correspondence to the *Gazette* was a fear that the 'right sort of resident' would be driven out of the borough when Woolwich Arsenal set up shop. Concerns were raised about 'whelk stalls, fried fish stalls, jellied eel stalls' and 'intemperate types making a nuisance of themselves'. In other words, the move to Highbury would likely trigger a surge in the number of 'wrong-uns' flocking to the district.

In fact, attracting a more upwardly mobile type of customer was high on Norris's agenda. In order to attract large crowds to a stadium, cheap and reliable public transport was a must, and in a residential area where supporters could walk to and from the ground, so was a tube station. Finsbury Park was a focus of both the rail and tram systems in north London which, like the suburbs, were expanding. The area was slightly better connected than White Hart Lane and much better than Millfields, which was Clapton Orient's home ground. Norris later commented, 'If we had had the planning of the lines of communication ourselves, we couldn't have devised a better service.'

The type of football punter who travelled to Highbury was key to the club's future success. The *West London and Fulham Times* in March 1913 suggested that 'Central London workers released from toil on the Saturday afternoon' would likely fill the new ground. In other words, as Sally Davis points out, office clerks, of whom Norris had been one in the late Victorian age.

By 1912 and 1913 the type of that which largely dominated employment in London was office work, which had mushroomed as a result of the growth of empire, world trade and central bureaucracy. Offices were proliferating throughout the growing suburbs in Holloway, Finchley, Hendon, Barnet and Hertfordshire, which had excellent links to north London, and which have become huge reservoirs of support for the club.

Clerks were far less likely to be laid off due to economic downturns, unlike, say, the armament workers in Woolwich after the end of the Boer War. This class of supporter was more upwardly mobile than the archetypal Manor Ground fan. Just Norris's kind of man.

The club adopted a far more aspirational air and was as armour plated as any club could be against a major economic decline. When Norris made a bid for the land at Highbury, he timed his move perfectly as the small, privately funded college had been short of cash for years. It is hard to imagine a more astute political and financial networker in London during that era.

Ultimately, Norris and his other directors of Woolwich Arsenal had been unable to obtain the freehold to the site which they had craved, but due to their keenness to take the college's site they agreed to take a lease instead and abide by the covenants, which included an agreement not to play matches on Sundays.

The college drove a hard bargain over the financial guarantees it required from the lessees, leaving Allen and Norris personally responsible for around £50,000, the equivalent of an enormous £10m sum in modern figures. Norris felt the burden of being liable for so much debt and when World War One began in 1914, and football was suspended a year later, he must have felt the weight of the world on his shoulders.

To suggest that there was a general sense of doom at Woolwich Arsenal's arrival would be an exaggeration. A raft of shopkeepers and publicans appeared to strongly favour the move. Letters in the *Gazette* certainly reflect a sense of optimism from some local residents.

Donald Sutton wrote, 'Many people would visit Highbury for the first time, and would be so delighted with the pleasant neighbourhood that they would come and live here and fill up many of the unoccupied premises.'

Members of the Highbury Defence Committee are described in various letters as 'scaremongerers', 'busybodies' and 'do-gooders'. Lesley Anderson claimed in 1990 that Henry Norris had visited key shopkeepers and publicans to try to furnish them with key facts and turn the tide of public opinion in the local media. Given Norris's network of contacts, Anderson's claim is hardly an outlandish one.

One of the letters concludes, 'I think it would bring money into the neighbourhood if [sic] Woolwich team came to Highbury.' Another letter (sent by the 'Inquirer') asks, 'Is it not a fact that certain members of the Islington council who are so much against Woolwich Arsenal coming to Highbury hold shares, and are ardent supporters of the Spurs? Are they afraid that the dividends will decrease?'

A final anonymous letter, focusing on the economic benefits of the move, points out that the club would hire around 300 men during the building period. Well informed correspondents indeed.

'Highbury Arsenal', as one local resident described the new club, kicked off with a 2-1 victory over Leicester Fosse at its new ground on 6 September 1913. A few days later, the *Gazette*'s intrepid reporter 'Candid Critic' found Norris at his most truculent when he encountered him at the new ground, which wasn't completely finished. Perturbed though he may have been at the thought of meeting Norris, it at least gave the local hack a break from penning the poetry of which he was so fond. One verse in the *Gazette* after the Leicester Fosse game went:

'We're only second leaguers,
 can Chelsea really jeer?
At one time – late last April –
The Bottom they were near.
But with our faults admitted
We still remain the Reds.
Although we've quitted Woolwich,
We're not among the 'deads.'!

After arriving at the gates, no one was there to greet him. So he wandered around until he stumbled across Norris, William Hall, George Morrell and the site foreman wolfing down rock cakes and drinking tea. Amid a backdrop of hammering and crashing, Norris espoused his beliefs to 'Candid Critic', admitting, 'I don't personally believe in big transfer fees,' a view which coloured the club's transfer dealings for the next decade. Norris headed off controversy about the move to Highbury by claiming that manager Morrell had received 'quite a big bundle of letters from residents, who state that the coming of the club has been anything but a nuisance', and talked up the benefits of his club's new home, claiming that in due course, the new ground 'will hold some 90,000'.

Although new to the role, 'Candid Critic' did his level best to push hard and get Norris to say more, but after Norris insisted that the journalist 'was quite capable of judging' as to whether the team was strong enough ('I should tell you if I wasn't,' huffed Norris) he was whisked away in a fast car with Hall. The journalist's observation that Norris threw 'back his shoulders with the determined air of a man who is always doing big things, and not over fond of being asked to talk about them' was consistent with the general view of Norris as a grouch who kept his cards close to his chest. He didn't speak to the press for another nine years.

By then, Norris had been implicated in what has often been regarded as football's biggest scam. Whether his actions warrant him being held up as football's arch villain, despite what numerous histories have suggested, is open to debate.

The first act of the saga occurred 200 miles away in the north-west, at a First Division Manchester United v Liverpool game on Good Friday 1915. Those present at Old Trafford could tell that something was amiss. Flailing just above the relegation zone, United netted early on through George Anderson. Comfortably ensconced in mid-table, Liverpool were, blatantly, not trying. And when United went 2-0 up both teams simply strolled around for the rest of the match.

It was a blatant fix, or a 'squared match' as Edwardians called it. Around the country, bookmakers point-blank refused to pay out when eyewitness reports filtered in, and numerous bookies claimed there had been a flood of bets on a 2-0 United win. The FA found United's Enoch 'Knocker' West and four Liverpool players guilty of match-fixing and banned them all for life. United's George Anderson received an eight-month jail sentence when it was subsequently revealed that he had been part of a much larger-scale betting scam.

Norris, who had been so heavily censured two years earlier when he had lambasted Liverpool's players after their clash with Chelsea ('But if players play as some of the Liverpool players played in this match, they must expect to be criticised,' he had argued), fumed about the United–Liverpool fix for the next three years as the war brought an end to league football. Norris now knew that any chance he had of being repaid the money he had lent Arsenal would be put off until peace was declared. And he was still liable for damages to the ground.

He did his level best to secure a trickle of income for his club. In July 1915 at a meeting in the Holborn Restaurant on Kingsway between representatives of the Football League and the Southern League, Norris was elected chairman of the London Combination, a wartime league for clubs within an 18-mile radius of London. That way, Highbury could at least welcome a trickle of punters.

He was also busy raising an artillery brigade in Fulham. Norris responded to a letter from the War Office urging all mayors of

London boroughs to organise a troop of volunteers for their respective boroughs and rose to the challenge – even paying for all the expenses of the recruitment drive from his own pocket. But Norris's debts were going nowhere fast.

When the Football League met in Manchester in March 1919 to map out the post-war future of English football, it was proposed that the top two divisions (which previously consisted of 20 clubs each) both be increased to 22 clubs. The feeling among members was that Chelsea, who had finished second from bottom in the First Division ahead of Tottenham, be reinstated in the top flight without a vote.

The remaining First Division place did go to a vote. Tottenham stood against Arsenal, who had finished fifth in the Second Division in 1915. So did Barnsley and Wolverhampton Wanderers, who had ended up third and fourth respectively in the second tier. As did Nottingham Forest, Birmingham and Hull, who had all finished lower in the Second Division. Arsenal easily won, seeing off Tottenham by 18 votes to eight.

There are two theories as to how Arsenal returned so controversially to the top flight after a six-year absence. The first is that, being the master operator he was, Norris took advantage of the match-fixing scandal involving Manchester United and Liverpool in that last pre-war season. With the decision to expand the First Division from 20 to 22 clubs, Chelsea had been re-elected to the top tier partly because if Liverpool and United hadn't been in cahoots, they would have stayed up anyway. Tottenham were relegated because the scandal didn't involve them at all.

Norris agreed that Chelsea should be reprieved, and that the top two teams from the Second Division should also be promoted; Derby County and Preston North End. He then pointed out that United and Liverpool were not being punished for the 'squared game', and he wasn't prepared to accept this.

The jailing of United's George Anderson proved that match-fixing might well have been rife, and Norris threatened to force Government action against a corrupt Football League. With his extensive political contacts there seems little doubt that he would have carried out his threat. The League did not want to risk seeing two major northern powers demoted, so the hierarchy pushed through a secret deal.

Arsenal would be awarded the final place in the First Division and one new London club (West Ham United) would be elected to the Second Division.

Job done. It was hardly ethical, but pragmatist that Norris was, he figured that Liverpool's and United's collusion over results in 1915 was even worse, and they had gone unpunished.

The more conventional view (repeated in several official and unofficial Arsenal and Tottenham histories) is that Norris got to work on his contacts within the committee, secretly canvassing them in order to convince them that Arsenal deserved an unlikely promotion.

Norris had long since eulogised about Highbury's proximity to central London, which gave his club a distinct advantage over the directors of Barnsley and Wolves. Norris also maintained that Arsenal deserved their promotion due to their 'long service to professional football', and the fact that they were the south's first professional football club. On the face of it, this is an obscure argument. Promotions and relegations have never been decided upon longevity of service.

In the *Biography of Tottenham Hotspur*, a highly indignant Julie Welch points out that Arsenal had pinched the First Division slot that belonged to Tottenham. The place should really have gone to Barnsley, if meritocracy comes into play. She also describes Norris as indulging in 'the dark arts of bribery, inducements and cronyism'. It is almost certain that Norris did indeed collude with Liverpool and Football League chairman John McKenna – an old friend of his – and Norris's transfer track record proves that he was indeed willing to hand out inducements to get his way.

As for 'bribery' – it's never been proved. Norris was never found guilty of impropriety. The whole story was given added spice by Leslie Knighton's claim in his book that Norris had corresponded with 'a few financiers here and there'. Knighton may well have heard through the grapevine that money changed hands over Arsenal's promotion, but provides no supporting evidence for his claim. Perhaps the recipient of the 'sweetener' was still alive when Knighton wrote his book, and the former Arsenal manager feared receiving a libel writ. Perhaps his publishers told him to "sex up" his book.

In all likelihood, there are probably elements of truth in both theories. Arsenal historian Andy Kelly has offered £100 to anyone who can prove that Norris committed any wrongdoing in 1919. Andy will never have to fork out, because it's impossible to prove. But it's equally impossible to prove that Norris didn't offer bribes. Stalemate. It is hardly beyond the realms of possibility that a realist like Norris handed out 'sweeteners' here and there. Permanent residency in the Second Division would likely financially cripple him, and given Norris's willingness to dip into his pocket to secure the services of players, or fund his recruitment drive in World War One, we shouldn't get too indignant about claims that Norris may well have cut some financial corners.

That year, Conservative minister Stanley Baldwin described the House of Commons as 'a lot of hard faced men who have done well out of the war'. Norris, now elected MP for Fulham East, probably wouldn't have taken offence to Baldwin's claim. Norris knew the power of money, he knew what he wanted, and he knew when to take his opportunity. Yet politically, he remained utterly beguiling. He wasn't ultra-Conservative in his views, defending women's suffrage, claiming women could do a better job than men in several professions, and urging for equal pay. He also urged that ex-servicemen be taught a trade, and that disabled soldiers should remain in the state's care.

For years afterwards, ex-soldiers were offered free seats at Highbury on Norris's say so. Perhaps this reflected the fact that he wasn't from the old landed gentry, unlike so many members of the Tory party. He had worked his way up from a working-class background through bloody-minded determination, a hard-nosed approach to business and a willingness to maximise his potential. His club's move from Plumstead to north London was brashly innovative and speculatively self-improving. Now firmly encamped in north London, Arsenal were in many ways the embodiment of the upwardly mobile Norris, and vice versa.

Norris personally thanked *Athletic News* editor Jimmy Catton for writing positive articles arguing for Arsenal's promotion, and shortly afterwards, Norris made his maiden House of Commons speech. The whole promotion saga doesn't reflect especially well on Arsenal, the Football League, Norris, Liverpool or Manchester United.

One other previous episode is worth highlighting. Tottenham fans are very keen to remind Arsenal supporters that they gained First Division status by deceitful means, ignoring the fact that when they gained Football League status in 1908, they had just finished eighth in the Southern League (in the *Official Illustrated History of Tottenham Hotspur*, author Phil Soar admits, 'From a playing point of view, Spurs had little or no claim'), but still mysteriously gained promotion.

Julie Welch specifically mentions that in 1906/07, Tottenham appointed former referee Fred Kirkham as manager 'to grease the wheels of a renewed attempt to join the Football League'. All clubs in that era, to some extent or another, indulged in politicking and the dark arts. The story behind Arsenal's rivals' elevation to the Football League has never been properly explained, and is conveniently forgotten when the insults start flying around. Perhaps it's time for a sense of historical perspective all round.

Tottenham's parrot, given to them on their 1909 tour of Argentina and Uruguay, promptly dropped dead on the very day Arsenal were awarded the First Division place, giving rise to the 'sick as a parrot' phrase.

There had always been a tension between the two clubs. Even in the Plumstead days there had been some feisty encounters between Woolwich Arsenal and Tottenham. In 1900, an end-of-season minor match between the two teams was abandoned after 65 minutes when the referee took exception to the barrage of 'coarse chaff and vulgar rebukes' that the Spurs players were subjected to. Two years later, Spurs goalkeeper Charlie Williams was suspended for two weeks after punching a Woolwich Arsenal barracker in the face.

Matters worsened as time passed. In 1913, with his club poised to move to Highbury, Norris fanned the flames of enmity by memorably quashing Tottenham's directors' claim that there wasn't sufficient demand for another London club. In the *West London and Fulham Times* he claimed, 'It appears to me to be a foolish attitude, the population of the surrounding boroughs totalling up something like two million, but it is the old, old story. Some clubs want not only the earth, but a little bit of heaven and the other place as well.'

Norris, looking at the world through the lenses of his pince-nez, was often incredulous at the complaints of others towards Arsenal.

Although busy attending his myriad wine society, dining club and vintage car meetings throughout the capital, he'd made it his business to write to the *Gazette* back in 1913 and, through the medium of print, bark his astonishment that: 'a borough council should attempt to interfere with an owner letting his ground for purposes of sport – a sport witnessed by thousands every Saturday afternoon to their profit and pleasure.'

Tottenham were promoted from the Second Division anyway in 1920, and the next season finished they above Arsenal in the First Division and won the FA Cup in 1921. Yet even in the midst of triumph, Tottenham couldn't forgive their rivals for the 1919 affair. Spurs director Tim Peacock stood up at the FA Cup celebration dinner and announced, 'The Football League has allowed another club to come to North London and cut the main arteries to the Spurs ground.' And Henry Norris was the scalpel wielder-in-chief. In September 1922, Arsenal gained their first victory at White Hart Lane in highly controversial circumstances. Reg Boreham scored both goals in a 2-1 Arsenal victory but players from both sides clashed on several occasions, and the referee struggled to contain them. The *Sunday Evening Telegram* reported, 'Players pulled the referee, blows with fists were exchanged, and all the dignity that appertains in the referee was rudely trampled on.'

Even the *Gazette*, normally pro-Arsenal, noted, 'It was scarcely a nice game to watch. The "stop your man at any price" methods adopted by the Arsenal defenders caused bad feeling among the players and on several occasions greatly roused the feelings of the spectators.' Spurs' Bert Smith was found guilty by an FA Commission of using 'filthy language' at White Hart Lane. Arsenal's Alex Graham and Stephen Dunn were censured for their conduct.

The 'Woolwich Interlopers' had well and truly got under their rivals' skin. Arsenal were comfortably ensconced in their new home, and began to pull in the large crowds – especially against their London rivals – which Norris both craved and needed. One letter to the *Gazette* in 1921 stated, 'Success on the field of play is the only thing now needed to push the Arsenal into the front rank of the leading outfits.' It didn't happen immediately though.

# Box Office

*'Is it too much to hope that Buchan's example and success will induce other forwards to retain a measure of individualism and to blend the pretty art of dribbling with discreet passing?'* Athletic News, *1920.*

*'A footballer's career is relatively short – like the season of a seaside landlady. The man who does not look ahead must be short sighted.' Charlie Buchan – speaking in 1925.*

'STARS are what pull people into Picture Palaces, music halls and into sports stadia,' claimed Charlie Chaplin in early 1925. His words resonated through London during the roaring '20s. Revue impresario C.B. Lochran was hospitalised with stress in 1925 after Noel Coward initially refused to perform at the London Pavilion in Piccadilly Circus because he felt he wasn't being adequately remunerated. Lochran knew only too well that Coward's absence would mean 'paying customers would be far less likely to attend the opening night, or any other night'. Lochran paid up.

A year earlier, Wimbledon organisers fell into a state of apoplexy when French tennis star Suzanne Lenglen was forced to withdraw from the tournament after winning her quarter-final. 'Tennis fans come to see her, not the match,' claimed one irate official. And when Chaplin himself agreed to make a series of personal appearances at a string of top London nightspots in the 1920s, organisers ensured that the 'Chaplin tour' received maximum exposure in the press. 'We want the clubs full to the brim. People will pay almost anything to meet him,' claimed one. The message? Box office was king. Stars pulled in punters. The bigger the crowds, the more money could be made. In an increasingly visual age, with London's burgeoning tube network and a buoyant economy, the presence of top performers from all walks of entertainment in the capital created a unique buzz.

It is doubtful whether new Arsenal manager Herbert Chapman had Chaplin's comment in the forefront of his mind when he strode purposefully into Charlie Buchan's sports outfitters in Sunderland in the summer of 1925, but, as future Arsenal winger Joe Hulme (signed by Chapman from Bradford in January 1926) later explained, 'Chapman knew that football was all about entertainment, and that supporters like to see big names.'

Chapman informed the 33-year-old that he would not leave until he had signed for the underachieving London side, who had finished a dismal 20th in the First Division in 1924/25. A quick phone call from Buchan to Sunderland manager Bob Kyle confirmed the (almost) unthinkable – Sunderland were willing to let their prized asset go. It put into motion arguably the most talked about transfer of the decade.

Sir Henry Norris was unwilling to pay the required £4,000 fee in one lump sum (and equally reluctant to fly in the face of his *Athletic News* advertisement which had stated, 'Gentlemen whose sole ability to build up a good side depends on the payment of heavy and exorbitant transfer fees need not apply') and instead set up a deal in which Sunderland received £2,000 up front, and £100 for each goal Buchan scored in his first season in an Arsenal shirt. The deal would eventually cost the Gunners £4,100, once Buchan discovered his shooting boots.

Chapman had landed the club a player whom Hulme described as, 'The most tactically astute footballer I ever played alongside. Some players are just that – fine players – but Buchan was much more than that in the way he thought about the way the game was played. His logical brain was totally the equal of Herbert Chapman.'

Charlie Buchan only stayed at Highbury for three seasons and didn't win a trophy with Arsenal. He isn't one of the 32 greats whose images are posted around the exterior of the Emirates Stadium. Yet Buchan is surely the club's most important signing.

Everything changed at Highbury from the minute he first kicked a ball in an Arsenal shirt. The perception of Arsenal to the wider football world, the tactical changes, the club's eventual mutation into the 'Bank of England Club' and the modernisation of Highbury in the early 1930s – none would have been possible without the galvanising influence and razor sharp mind of Buchan. Chapman is rightly lauded as Arsenal's most influential manager, but the numerous biographies which have been penned about him don't give Buchan adequate credit for the foundations of success which were laid in the latter part of the 1920s.

On the face of it, Buchan's transfer south left him out of pocket. He bought a modest Islington semi, having previously lived in a well-appointed Sunderland townhouse. The north-south divide was pronounced even back in the 1920s. A crisis was brewing over house prices in the capital. The MP for Islington commented that £500 for an average semi in the area was 'far beyond the reach of an average worker, who has to live on an average of £2 a week'.

Added to this were Buchan's losses he suffered from giving up the running of his shop, although within the game, rumours persisted that Buchan had received a £2,000 'sweetener' to sign for Arsenal. His friend George Male recalled, 'His house was – by 1920s standards – really plush. He had a washing machine, a vacuum cleaner, an oven – all new.'

By Charlie Chaplin's, Noel Coward's or Suzanne Lenglen's standards at least, Buchan was criminally underpaid, but in the era of silent screen sirens there was no way that Buchan was ever going to be gagged. At a time when footballers were treated – and expected to behave – like ignorant serfs, Buchan bucked the trend, as his frequent clashes with managers and officials proved throughout his career.

At the age of 18, Buchan made his professional debut for Woolwich Arsenal in 1910, despite not having signed professional forms for the club. He had already endured a six-month injury layoff when, after making a slide tackle, he lacerated his leg on a piece of jagged metal embedded in the turf. Only a punishing fitness regime restored him to full health.

Desperately keen to impress, he paid his own way to games, but grew resentful of Woolwich Arsenal manager George Morrell's unwillingness to refund his travel expenses. The end came when Buchan presented Morrell with a bill for 55p. Morrell refused to reimburse the youngster's tram expenses, and Buchan left Woolwich Arsenal. The seeds of rebellion had been sown with Buchan arguing, 'From that point on, I decided never to duck an argument with an official. I'd been made to feel a thief, whereas all I wanted was my entitlement.'

Still a teenager, news of his expenses 'disgrace' spread rapidly through the football world and when Sunderland manager Bob Kyle signed him in 1911, the *Sunderland Echo* felt justified in labelling Buchan 'something of a rebel'. During a 15-year spell on Wearside he plundered 224 goals in 413 games, but as would happen under Chapman, he made a less than convincing start.

Weighing only 10st despite being 6ft 2in, and knocked off the ball with ease, he failed to make an impression in his opening three games and announced, within earshot of a journalist, 'I've had it with football.' His claim was splashed across the front of the *Sunderland Echo*, and the sports editor received sackfuls of letters describing him as a 'coward' and a 'traitor'.

The villain would soon become a hero when, after a punishing fitness regime and a steak and Guinness diet, he filled out to 13st. In 1920, *Athletic News* editor Jimmy Catton wrote, 'There is no other man of his mould and massiveness playing in class football that I know of.' In all sorts of ways, Buchan was quite literally head and shoulders above his peers.

Buchan never looked back. Like many of his England colleagues, he loathed the infamous selection committee, and fell foul of what he saw was 'petty bureaucracy' while visiting his cousin in Vancouver in the summer of 1912. Watching a local match, he was asked to play in the second half which he duly did. In the process he earned the equivalent of a week's wage back home. Unfortunately an eagle-eyed official, holidaying in Vancouver, took photographs of Buchan, presented them to the FA on his return to England, and Buchan was formally warned for his conduct, and forced to repay his match fee.

A year later, he made his England debut against Ireland but although he scored, the memory was marred by his spat with FA officials over his expenses. Rather than walk five miles from his home to the station he had dared to hail a cab. 'What's this for, Buchan?' barked an official, who refused to reimburse the cost. Within the FA, his reputation was further sullied, and despite the *Daily Mail* labelling his performance 'sensational', he wouldn't represent his country again for seven years.

George Male later recalled, 'They didn't like him, because he insisted they address him as "Mr Buchan" rather than simply "Buchan". He also made a point of not standing up or getting out of his chair when they came into the room. He saw them as parasites, who went on England trips to get stocked up on duty free whisky and cigarettes.'

As a member of the Grenadier Guards, he experienced the horrors of the Somme and Passchendaele in World War One before, in the latter stages of the conflict, dabbling in teaching history and physical education in tough north London schools. When league football finally resumed in 1918, the attitude among players was militant. Just as returning soldiers expected 'homes fit for heroes', footballers wanted a decent living wage, having seen four years of their careers disappear.

Buchan became a leading light of the Players' Union Committee, pointing out that the £9 per week maximum was less than many miners and shipbuilders were earning. He argued that with a large number of footballers killed in action there was a real shortage of quality in the First Division, and that simple laws of supply and demand dictated that players receive more.

FA official Henry Wright took exception to Buchan's suggestions, labelling them 'offensive and unnecessary', but with Buchan demanding strike action, the FA caved in and raised the level to £10. It was a small victory but Buchan had, once again, proved to be a thorn in the side of the establishment. Nor had he finished.

Proving that with a degree of imagination and hard work it was possible to circumnavigate the maximum wage system, he opened up his sports outfitters in Sunderland after World War Two, lamenting that it brought him greater financial reward than his footballer's wage. This brought him further castigation from the FA, who wrote to him and warned, 'Your business activities will not, we trust, affect your performances on the pitch.'

They didn't. Buchan juggled both successfully and began to dabble in journalism, where he expressed an opinion on virtually every topic under the sun. Corporal punishment? 'There's nothing wrong with boys receiving a good thrashing. It teaches them discipline.' Footballers hugging after scoring a goal? 'A disgusting show of emotion.' Smoking? 'Smoking causes bad wind and heartburn. Wait until you have laid the foundation of a good constitution, and then only take your pipe or cigarettes in strict moderation.'

Chapman was delighted to land his man. He had gained a highly experienced player, whose aura was quite unlike any other in the game. On the eve of his Arsenal debut, football writer Leo Munro wrote gushingly in *Athletic News* of Buchan's talents, 'He would stretch out a tentative leg, like a kitten not quite sure about a strange plaything, but the effect was almost always a pass, gentle, deft and sure, to a colleague in the exact position to carry on.'

This tactically astute individual also shared his new manager's belief that football needed to be reformed from top to bottom and rather than treating the players like mindless martinets, they should be respected and consulted about decisions at their clubs. Chapman and Buchan also saw eye to eye on the potential of building a football dynasty in the capital city. 'What a chance there is in London. I would like to build a Newcastle United there,' a thrilled Chapman told writer Ivan Sharpe in 1914 after an early visit to Highbury.

Joe Hulme recalled Buchan saying that although he had loved his long spell in Sunderland, he was 'looking forward to making a name for himself in London. In his eyes, there was simply nothing more thrilling.' Buchan also espoused the educational benefits of venturing 'back to town for the sake of my kiddie. Like any father, I want only the very best for them.' Upwardly mobile. A perfect marquee signing for London's most upwardly mobile club.

Buchan's baptism as an Arsenal player on the opening day of the 1925/26 campaign couldn't have been more high-profile. Arsenal would face Tottenham. The 53,183 Arsenal fans who streamed into Highbury to watch the north London derby saw the 'Gunners' – as they were now universally known – lose 1-0 under the scorching sun to a goal by Tottenham's Jimmy Dimmock, after Arsenal defenders Andy Kennedy and Billy Milne indulged in a spot of 'after you please', according to the *Daily Gazette*.

Arsenal regulars slipped away disappointed but they were aware of Herbert Chapman's advice to 'not expect too much in too little time'. Reports focused on the more defensive aspects of the clash. The *Daily Mirror* explained, 'Each defence outplayed the attackers, who seemed more content to hit the ball first time and let a team mate chase it rather than trying to create opportunities themselves.'

*The Sporting Life and Sportsman* referred to 'Arsenal's sturdy defence' but also paid tribute to 'the vim and determination of the home side, whose forwards gave a whole-hearted display that was in welcome contrast to so many of their unconvincing games last season'. Buchan's partnership with Jimmy Brain would prove to be one of the most durable and prolific of Chapman's era, but not on this particular occasion.

Perhaps both Brain and Buchan – as well as getting used to playing alongside one another – were also familiarising themselves with the freshly liberalised offside law. The law – unchanged since 1866 – decreed that, for a forward to be onside, three opposing players (normally a goalkeeper and two defenders) had to be between him and the opponent's goal.

Several clubs, most notably Newcastle United, had become so proficient at setting an offside trap that games would often be compressed into a narrow section either side of the halfway line. Attendances, and the average number of goals scored, were tumbling, and Joe Hulme recalled that at Bradford in the months leading up to the rule change, 'The play was almost suffocating. Attackers were very tense. It felt as if you couldn't move.'

During the close-season the ruling changed so that only two defenders needed to be between an attacker and the goal. *The Sporting Life and Sportsman* noted, 'Judging the game from the point of view of the average spectator, who wishes to see a non-stop match, there is no doubt that the alteration to the offside law must be rated a success, so far as Saturday's game proves anything. The stoppages were few in number and the offsides that were given were mostly following attacks on the goals when a player happened to be slow returning to his position.'

Previously, a side looking to spring their trap simply had to keep one full-back as cover. Once his partner stepped up the referee's whistle would invariably peep. The new rule change meant that a misjudgement risked leaving the forward through one on one with the goalkeeper.

Despite drawing a blank in his first four matches, the vibe surrounding Buchan was sensational and the press descended on Highbury to snap him in action for his new club. *The Times* was mightily impressed with the club's new striker, commenting, 'Some of his touches reveal the master mind of a great thinker.' Tellingly, *The Sporting Life and Sportsman* reported, 'The turnstiles were still clicking merrily, and later in the afternoon it was officially announced that the attendance was 53,000, a great send off from a financial point of view.' Even 90 years on, the sense of awe and wonder is visible on fans' faces on the photographs as the team's new talisman leads out his new team-mates.

'Whenever we stepped out into the streets near Highbury, supporters wanted to rub shoulders with Charlie,' recalled Joe Hulme. 'Whether it was to get his autograph, or simply take a look at him, he was the one that everyone wanted to see.'

It didn't stop the supporters criticising Buchan for his initial goal drought though – and he had to endure listening to their barbed criticisms of his lack of goals on the tube near the ground, but after he scored at home to Liverpool in September – his fifth game – he didn't look back.

His new team's form remained inconsistent though. After high-scoring wins against Leeds and West Ham in late September, Arsenal suffered arguably their most epoch-defining defeat – a 7-0 reverse at Newcastle United. The beginning of the season had been littered with freakish results (after the defeat at St James' park, the *Daily Gazette* noted, 'Old time form counts for nothing in the altered circumstances. Did not Aston Villa score ten goals in their opening match, and yet at the present time they only have three victories to their credit'), suggesting that some sides had adapted to the new offside rule better than others. Teams with pace in their side tended to fare better. As forwards now had more room in which to move, games became more stretched.

Short passing gave way to longer balls, and forwards with a spring in their step profited massively. Joe Hulme recalled, 'A lightning quick winger or forward could cause more mayhem under the new system than the old. If you could move the ball forward at great pace, you were very likely to be successful, up front at least. The other side of the coin was that your backs also had to have pace to counter the change.'

At St James' Park, the Arsenal defence crumbled under wave upon wave of Newcastle attacks and the Gunners were 6-0 down at half-time. The *Daily Gazette*'s special correspondent noted, 'Arsenal half backs… were bothered not a little by the erratic kicking of their backs, and this also put Lewis off his game. Under the new offside law the position of a goalkeeper is not to be envied. With a team of speedy sharpshooters playing on their toes Lewis had an uncomfortable time.'

The paper reported, 'The defence of Newcastle time after time held in check the determined rushes of Arsenal forwards, of whom Brain played as a hero, but it was easy to see where Arsenal failed. There were few, if any attempts to defeat [goalkeeper] Wilson by artistry,' is sketchy on the exact details of Newcastle's defensive approach.

As the game progressed, Newcastle centre-half Charlie Spencer remained in a very deep position and although he contributed little to the rhythm of his side's attacks, he repeatedly snuffed out Arsenal's attacks in their formative stages, allowing his side to dominate possession and control the whole tempo of the match. Hulme said, 'Charlie Buchan rated Charlie Spencer as a great player, and often spoke of his unsung quality of reading the pace and direction of the game.'

It was Spencer's display that afternoon which convinced Buchan and Chapman that the Gunners needed to radically alter their tactics if they were to survive in the late 1920s, let alone prosper. In his book *A Lifetime In Football*, Buchan claims, 'New methods were required and Arsenal were the first to exploit them.' One might suggest that Newcastle had clearly got their first with their use of Spencer as a deep-lying centre-half, but Buchan, we can only presume, is referring to tactics across the entire pitch.

Before Arsenal's tactical change occurred, Buchan blew his top. As George Male later admitted, Buchan 'possessed a quick temper, and a stubborn streak'. Hulme recalled, 'Charlie wasn't one to suffer fools or defeat, and was impatient to change things.'

Here was a man, after all, who threatened to walk out on the club on the first day when he found that his shirt was uncomfortable and that there was a congealed piece of Vaseline in his sock. Over-fussy he may have been, but Chapman admired his new signing's high standards.

Following the calamity in the north-east, Buchan informed Chapman that he would leave Arsenal and re-sign for Sunderland as he was 'clearly of no use to his new team-mates'. Yet Chapman calmed him down and asked him, at a team meeting at the Newcastle Hotel, to air his views. Buchan had been pressing for a change to the way Arsenal lined up since the beginning of the season, and now Chapman was ready and willing to listen to his ideas.

⌣ ⌣ ⌣ ⌣ ⌣

What happened next changed the fortunes of Arsenal, but perhaps not quite in the way many football writers have long suggested. Buchan's first suggestion was that a centre-half should be deployed to guard the edge of the penalty area. This in itself was hardly revolutionary. Chapman used Tom Wilson as a deep-lying centre-half in the 1922 FA Cup Final when his Huddersfield team beat Preston 1-0. Buchan himself wrote, 'It has many times been said that the change in law brought into operation the "stopper" centre-half, but there were many such "stoppers" long before that eventful day.' Crucially, Buchan's idea went a step further.

As Tony Attwood has pointed out on the Woolwich Arsenal blog, Buchan was inventing zonal marking for the centre-half, leaving the others free to cover the flow of play. Buchan also suggested that the centre-half should be 'a dominating personality around his own goal. And he should not be content just to get the ball away everywhere, but to send it, with head or feet, to the roving inside-forward.'

He was advocating that Arsenal should play a far more passing game. Buchan nominated Andy Neil – a player who could receive the ball with either foot and pass it quickly to get the counter-attack going. As Attwood points out, the zonal marking aspect of Buchan's suggestion has invariably been ignored, and the WM formation means more than simply pulling the centre-half back to play between the two full-backs. Other clubs – like Newcastle – had already started to do this. The impact of the new system was seen just two days later in an away match at West Ham in early October, which Arsenal won 4-0.

It would be an exaggeration to suggest that the team meeting after the Newcastle game appeared to be a definitive Eureka moment at the time. Buchan and Chapman's tactical change appeared to have gone largely undetected. It certainly escaped the *Gazette*'s 'Norseman', who understandably preferred to focus upon Buchan's artistry in the forthcoming weeks. He netted twice against the Hammers – the first a header from Brain's corner, and the second a rasping shot which sailed past goalkeeper Hufton. 'Buchan gave Brain a hearty handshake. "Pa" Buchan is a good father,' claimed 'Norseman'.

In referring to Buchan's paternal instincts, 'Norseman' identifies a key strength of Chapman as a manager. When he took over at Huddersfield in August 1920, one of the first things he did was to sign 30-year-old Clem Stephenson in a massive £4,000 move from Aston Villa. It was a controversial signing at a club where money had never been in abundance, and Stephenson became the fulcrum of Chapman's team as well as his manager's mouthpiece in the dressing room.

After Stephenson inherited the captain's armband from previous skipper Tommy Wilson, Chapman was moved to write a letter to the new leader, thanking him '…personally for your play, your wholehearted efforts both on and off the field. I have never had such confidence in any captain of a team I have been associated with.'

After Buchan's similarly-controversial arrival at Arsenal, Chapman showed sufficient confidence in the player – and his own skills in delegation – to allow the former Sunderland man to cajole the Arsenal players and put things in 'footballer speak'. 'In his early years at Highbury, Charlie did as much talking and was as much of an influence as Chapman,' claims Joe Hulme. 'He was a player whom Chapman knew would have the respect of all of us.'

By signing Buchan, he had already shown that he could persuade Henry Norris (who was still reluctant to fund a scouting network to match that of Everton or Sheffield Wednesday) that dogged parsimony in the transfer market was unlikely to result in glory on the pitch. Chapman had set out an ambitious five-year plan at Highbury and in Buchan, there was no one better to help him push through and hone those plans.

It was the ultimate meeting of minds, and the fact that Chapman got both the signings of Stephenson and Buchan so utterly spot on speaks volumes for his acumen when it came to signing the right kind of player. Hulme jokingly referred to Buchan's arrival at Arsenal as 'a Hollywood signing', but there was real substance to Buchan. Chapman and Buchan agreed upon the importance of letting footballers have their say. In a modern era of unprecedented player power, it seems almost unthinkable that team meetings were once frowned upon at many clubs back in the 1920s. But 90 years ago, Chapman appeared to be an exception to the rule with his insistence on whole group discussions.

Sunderland's Johnny Cochrane, a Scottish manager who led his team to the First Division title in 1934/1935, was notorious for his distaste for player gatherings, telling *Athletic News*, 'I do not believe in team meetings. Team tactics are overrated. In most cases they are only considered with a view to spoiling and stopping the opposition. That is not as I want to see football played.'

Legend has it that Cochrane would sidle into the dressing room 30 minutes before the game cradling a tumbler of whisky in his hand, and, whatever opposition Sunderland were playing, assure his players, 'Oh, we'll piss that lot.' Cochrane's *laissez-faire* approach was hardly unsuccessful, but as Tom Parker – signed by Chapman in 1926 – explained, 'It was often down to the experience of players in those days. Managers were administrators, and left the rest to players and the trainer.'

Joe Hulme claimed he 'rarely ever saw my Bradford boss. He was distant and addressed you by your surname only and spoke to you as little as possible.' Such coldness and lack of planning was the antithesis of the way Chapman worked.

After Chapman's death in 1933, Ernest 'Bee' Edwards wrote a gushing eulogy, 'Chapman got the lowly and the meek to talk…he arranged with some of the older members to lead the young lad up the garden path by saying something not entirely right, this encouraging the younger member to point out the error. Thus everyone joined in the great game of pre-playing the day's game.'

Often, testimonies such as these can be ridiculously rose-tinted. But Parker, Hulme and George Male concur that Chapman insisted on calling all players by their first names, and expected all to contribute. George Male, who made his debut in 1930, recalled, 'I'd just broken into the team, and we were having a conversation about what had gone wrong in a game we'd lost. The older players had their say, and Chapman, although listening carefully, was looking around the room. He turned to me, asking, "What do you think, George?"

'I think I blurted out something, but I remember two things clearly. One: all the players listened and no one laughed. Second: he looked me in the eye and nodded intently as I spoke. Then afterwards after the conversation had moved on, he glanced at me, nodded his head slightly and gave me faint smile. I felt on top of the world. The man knew how to manage players in every way.'

Chapman not only allowed his players to feel as if they were being listened to, he also allowed different players to lead discussions. Male explained, 'Tom Parker would often lead but others piped up about defensive or attacking points. He'd say to David Jack, "What do you think Davey?" And Davey, who was very articulate, would speak up.'

At other clubs, player meetings on tactics were common, but crucially the manager was rarely present. Chapman invariably was. He may have let Buchan or Parker speak, 'but nothing ever happened, tactically or otherwise, without his say so', explained Hulme. 'He was constantly looking for signs of leadership, or fear, or sloth, on the pitch or in the dressing room or in team meetings.'

Perhaps it was Buchan's initial idea to push on with the WM formation, but it was moulded according to Chapman's wishes. Buchan argued that withdrawing the centre-half would leave Arsenal short of personnel in midfield, and suggested he should drop back from his inside-right position which would have left a loose and unbalanced 3-3-4. Buchan was overruled because Chapman needed Buchan to score goals. Instead he gave the role of withdrawn inside-forward to Andy Neil, a third-team player, and described by Chapman as being 'as slow as a funeral', and by Buchan as 'slow as a post'.

Neil's newly carved-out role speaks volumes for Chapman's eye for the tiniest detail, and his ability to recognise which skills were needed where in the team. Chapman's argument was emphatic, 'He has ball control and can stand with his foot on the ball while making up his mind.'

With Jack Butler now in the deep-lying centre-half position, the classic Arsenal Mark 1 model under Chapman was born. After thrashing West Ham the team embarked upon an excellent run of form in the league, eventually finishing as runners-up to Huddersfield, who completed a hat-trick of championship successes. But for a spate of injuries around Christmas time the new tactics could even have propelled the team to the title, but Chapman would have to wait.

There is one further issue which needs to be addressed. Chapman and Buchan were both happy to take credit for devising the WM formation but the truth isn't perhaps as straightforward as has always been portrayed. In 2011, football writer Dave Juson discovered that on 3 October 1925, the same day on which Arsenal had been picked apart by Newcastle, a piece in the *Southampton Echo* penned by 'Cherry Blossom' pointed out that the Saints had been beaten at home by Bradford City '...by tactics. There is a lot of talk in dressing rooms at the moment over what is known as the W formation in attack to deal with the changed conditions of play. In this formation the centre forward and the two extreme wingers go well up the field – staying only a yard or so inside – and the two inside wing forwards remain behind, acting as five-eighths, or in other words operating in a sphere of play near the half backs and behind the three advanced forwards.'

'Cherry Blossom' adds, 'The goal scoring figures up to date go to suggest that this is the method mostly adopted,' implying that the use of the W system was already widespread. As well as urging Second Division Southampton to adopt the W formation that afternoon against Port Vale (which the Saints newly did), 'Cherry Blossom' also highlights Raith's Dave Morris as an example of the modern deep-lying centre-half, 'He positions himself a little in front of the backs and midway between them.'

These thoughts were penned with no knowledge of Arsenal's humiliation in the north-east, or the tactical change that followed. If teams as widespread as Southampton and Raith were deploying these tactics it suggests that it may actually have been a nationwide phenomenon to counter the new offside rule. What it does prove is that Arsenal weren't the first team to use the new tactics. Chapman watched a huge number of matches at all levels, so it's entirely possible that he saw the tactics deployed elsewhere and adapted them to Arsenal's needs.

Likewise, Joe Hulme explained that Buchan 'watched lots of games in the London area and was very well connected'. Perhaps, in the pre-TV age, Buchan and Chapman conjured up their scheme independently. What is true is that Buchan and Chapman had the foresight and the wherewithal to force the tactics through, and that by the time Tom Parker joined the club from Southampton in 1926, 'Everyone at the club was clear about how Arsenal played.'

In the league at least, Arsenal failed to push on in the 1926/27 season. Injuries to key players clearly affected the progress of the team but the general consensus was that teams had begun to exploit the fact that Jack Butler, the player who had been asked to check his creative instincts and play as the deep-lying centre-half, simply wasn't a naturally defensive player.

Arsenal suffered some horrendous reverses on the road, losing 6-1 to eventual champions Newcastle, 5-1 to Buchan's former team Sunderland, and most jarringly of all, 7-0 at West Ham. Arsenal conceded 86 goals that season, a high number even for those far off days, and although the Brain–Buchan combination was potent in the league (they netted 45 of Arsenal's 77 goals between them) Hulme claimed a further problem was that Arsenal lacked pace throughout the side. 'To play the type of counter attacking game we wanted required us to have speed right through the side. We didn't have that yet,' he admitted.

Despite the disappointing league finish, Arsenal fought their way through to Wembley where they faced Cardiff City, who had finished three places below the Gunners in 14th position in the First Division. Arsenal's key movers and shakers had enjoyed mixed fortunes when it came to the world's most famous knockout competition. When the Gunners knocked out Southampton in the semi-final at Stamford Bridge, Tom Parker, at least, was able to banish the bad memories of two years earlier when, as a Saints player, he had scored an own goal, missed a penalty and committed an error which led to Sheffield United's second goal in their 2-0 victory as they went on to win the final.

Even the *Daily Gazette*, usually partisan in supporting the Gunners, admitted Chapman's side had been lucky in their 2-1 win over the Second Division team with Southampton denied two clear penalties. The star man was Hulme, who scored the first and set up Buchan for a second. Parker recalled, 'Although I was sorry to see my old team go out, I was delighted personally, because that day a few years earlier was easily my worst in football.'

Chapman's memory of the 1922 Stamford Bridge final was distinctly bittersweet. Billy Smith's late penalty gave Huddersfield a 1-0 victory over Preston but the club was censured by the FA, which conveyed its 'deep regret' at the strong-arm tactics used by Chapman's team in the final. Many believed that Chapman himself was being admonished for his use of Tom Wilson as a deep-lying centre-half, prompting the *Huddersfield Examiner* to label Wilson as 'a great spoiler'.

Buchan's experience in the 1913 final, held at the Crystal Palace, would prove uncannily similar to what panned out in 1927. Targeting the 20th century's first Double, Sunderland lost to Aston Villa and a freakish Tom Barber headed goal. Buchan recalled, 'As our defenders stood apparently spellbound, the ball passed slowly between them into the corner of the net.'

Equally as prescient was Villa inside-left Clem Stephenson's comment to Buchan early on, 'Charlie, we are going to beat you by a goal to nothing, and Tom Barber will score the winning goal. I dreamed it last night.' Buchan didn't necessarily believe in fate or destiny, but 14 years on, Arsenal faced a Cardiff team convinced that fortune was about to favour them.

* * * * *

Cardiff had reached the final two years earlier where they had lost to a single Sheffield United goal at Wembley. It was an unremarkable game in most ways, save for three things. Firstly, the papers were universal in claiming that Cardiff had frozen on their big day with the *Daily Express* describing City's movements as 'jerk-like'. Secondly, Cardiff skipper and giant centre-half Fred Keenor was furious about the press criticism he received for his display, with the *Express* claiming that he had failed to deal with 'the wiles and stratagems' of Blades skipper Gillespie. As a group, the Cardiff players had been unimpressed by the English media's jingoistic reports after the match. 'Whenever scoffers point to our loss of prestige, we can still proudly declare that England has again won the England FA Cup,' commented *The Times*. 'St George succeeded in slaying the Red Dragon at Wembley,' proclaimed the *Express*, overlooking the fact that the Cardiff team was one of the most cosmopolitan of its day. Keenor vowed to 'silence those who mocked us in 1925'. On 23 April 1927 – St George's Day – Cardiff had another chance to become the first team to take the FA Cup outside England.

Both teams had five weeks to wait for the final after winning their semi-finals. It is fair to say that the Arsenal players found the wait to be a tedious one. Buchan claimed it was 'one of the reasons why the Wembley final so rarely produces a classic game'. Joe Hulme recalled, 'Players were put under pressure to lay their hands on extra tickets by anyone and everyone, it seemed to me.'

Buchan claimed the players received just two each. Hulme also explained, 'It was all anyone wanted to talk to us about for weeks and weeks. It got exhausting.'

The whole build-up took its toll on the Arsenal players. They rejected Chapman's suggestion that they enjoy some seaside training down in Brighton. 'A break might have done us some good,' admitted Hulme. Instead it was business as usual at Highbury with, as Tom Parker mentioned, 'Journalists clamouring to get words here and there.'

The *Daily Gazette* promised, 'The Arsenal, our very own north London team, will fight to the last ditch for the rose and the leek will have worthy representatives in Cardiff City.' But the normally partisan paper struck a note of caution, admitting, 'The [Arsenal] forwards, as a line are at times very good and at others very bad, as in the semi-final.' Particular criticism was aimed at Jimmy Brain, 'At his best he shoots on sight, at his worst he is miles off the target.'

Even the charabanc ride from Hendon Hall to Wembley sapped the players' nervous energy. With thousands of well-wishers lining the route, the half-hour trip turned into a two-hour grind and the players only reached the stadium with half an hour to spare.

Buchan especially found the whole ordeal stressful, confessing that he was nervous at the prospect of meeting King George V. The day before, he had spoken at length to radio broadcaster 2LO at Savoy Hill about the cup final and had been asked to stay longer than planned because Fred Keenor had been 'unable to make it'. Perhaps on this occasion Chapman had underestimated the fervour and the heightened sense of expectancy with Arsenal reaching their first cup final. Parker admitted to 'shaking like a leaf' and Hulme recalled 'feeling sick to my stomach'.

Cardiff players later recounted that they watched the Arsenal players 'march robotically' on to the pitch, looking 'terribly serious before the game'. A superstitious bunch, the City players drew strength from the fact that prior to the fifth round they had chanced upon a black cat, whom they named Trixie, wandering around on the Royal Birkdale golf course. Striker Hugh Ferguson, believing her to be a lucky omen, adopted the cat for the duration of the cup run and Trixie was present and correct in the Cardiff dressing room prior to kick-off.

If they actually needed any further incentive to win the FA Cup, Cardiff received it when their team charabanc was pelted with leeks thrown by Arsenal fans on the way to the ground. An estimated 22,000 had made the trip from Wales and, as in 1925, the *Express* noted that Lyons Corner House – a massive restaurant chain spread over four floors – opened its doors at 5am and was well prepared with 13,000 eggs, 6,000 rashers of bacon and 50,000 slices of bread and butter. The Cardiff fans were in great voice as the teams prepared for the pre-match pomp and ceremony.

This was to be a day of firsts. For the first time, community singing had been pre-planned and arranged by the authorities. A black platform – likened by *The Times* to 'a scaffold and an execution' – had been erected on the side of the pitch for conductor Thomas Ratcliff, who led the masses as they belted out 'Land of my Fathers', 'Pack Up Your Troubles', and for the first time, 'Abide With Me'. Beautifully sung, the community singing is preserved on vinyl as this was the first cup final to be broadcast live on BBC radio.

Hulme recalled, 'The sheer enormity of the occasion, and the noise level from the crowd, took my breath away. I quickly realised that although we had been installed as favourites, most of the Cardiff boys had seen and heard this before, which was advantageous for them.'

Some newspapers printed a grid with squares numbered one to eight so that listeners would have a clear idea of where the action took place. The rumour that the match gave rise to the phrase 'back to square one' is another urban myth.

The newsreel footage of the game, although short, does provide Sir Henry Norris with the briefest of cameo roles. Over the previous few years, Norris – no longer Mayor of Fulham or MP for Fulham East – had slipped out of the glare of publicity. His political career ended in controversy when he fell out with fellow Fulham Conservatives. Yet Norris was in trouble, and just a fortnight before the cup final he had endured a humiliating session with the Football League's Charles Sutcliffe where he had tried to explain how the £170 proceeds from the sale of the team bus had found their way into his wife's bank account.

Perhaps if he hadn't criticised journalists so heavily at an Arsenal dinner four years earlier, the press might not have begun to investigate Sir Henry's alleged financial improprieties with such relish. But grudges were held, and Norris was censured by the Football League for lending Henry White (signed in 1919) £1,000 after he signed from Brentford. Norris's past was about to explode in his face as the *Daily Mail* probed his financial history at the club. But not before his team received the kind of national exposure he had always dreamed of.

After leading out the team he met the King, and handed over the responsibility of introducing the players to the monarch to Buchan. On the jumpy film, Norris can be seen for roughly two seconds with his coat slung over his arm and his bowler hat in his hand, exchanging pleasantries with the Arsenal players as the King makes his way down the line. It is the only known visual footage of Norris, coming at a time when his authority over the club was about to loosen, especially as business partner William Hall had recently stood down from the board. 'I differ strongly from Sir Henry Norris on club policy,' he announced.

The match wasn't the best of spectacles. Early on Brain and Buchan were regularly caught offside, and Cardiff defenders Hardy and Watson kept Joe Hulme quiet. Arsenal's best early chances fell to Tom Parker, whose 30-yard free kick and dipping shot from outside the box forced

Cardiff keeper Farquharson to make two smart saves. Down the right, Hulme and Buchan threaded together some intricate moves but with no end product. Hulme claimed, 'We never really got started. Cardiff did well to stop us getting into our natural rhythm.'

Irish international Sloan gave Jimmy Brain a torrid afternoon. The *Sunday Pictorial* noted, 'The Londoner is frail of build and had not the physique to force his way past this resolute defender.' Buchan too was sent crashing to the floor following a couple of strong-armed Cardiff challenges.

City's Ferguson went close near half-time and the Gunners' Sid Hoar air-kicked when it looked like he might be in on goal. The half-time whistle went and *The Times* noted, 'A rather bored crowd settled down in silence to hope for better things to come during the second 45 minutes.'

Tom Parker recalled 'speaking to the team to try and get some urgency in the second half', and the Gunners appeared to have taken on board their skipper's advice. Brain headed just wide and after a great cross from Hulme, only a last-ditch tackle from Nelson denied him.

But, for Arsenal, the goal never arrived and City began to turn the screw. McLachlan and Curtis started to bomb down the wings and Ferguson narrowly missed the target with 70 minutes gone. Five minutes later, after receiving a pass from Davies, Ferguson tried a speculative shot from a tight angle. Due to the flickering newsreel footage it's hard to gauge the precise speed of events but what is clear is that Rhondda-born Arsenal keeper Dan Lewis went to ground and appeared to have the ball under his control. Like a slippery fish, it squirmed under his body, at which point he knocked the ball agonisingly over the line and into the net with his elbow.

Lewis blamed the error on his greasy new jersey, and more outrageous conspiracy theories claimed he took a bribe to support his fellow countrymen. Hulme offered a more realistic view, claiming, 'Dan's error symbolised what happened to us. None of us were moving quite right. We were tense and rigid.'

As if to reinforce Hulme's point, Brain and Buchan then remained rooted to the spot, leaving the ball for one another, as Arsenal had their best chance to equalise in the dying minutes. The ball rolled harmlessly away and for the only time, the FA Cup left England.

Fred Keenor had gained revenge on his critics and collected the trophy from the King. Hulme accepted, 'They deserved to win and shut us down in too many areas.' Nowadays, critics would suggest that Arsenal had frozen on their big day, and that nerves had got the better of them. Buchan was magnanimous in defeat, claiming, 'We were unlucky. When men do their best, they can do no more.'

In Cardiff, an estimated 150,000 ecstatic fans brought the city to a standstill as the team paraded the trophy in an open-top car.

The cold reality was that Chapman, having got Arsenal to their first final, had taken his Mark 1 team – shown up in the final as being too slow and constricted – as far as he could. The following season, Arsenal once again finished in a disappointing mid-table position and lost to Blackburn in the FA Cup semi-final. At the end of the campaign, Buchan – who confessed to suffering from terrible neuralgia due to 'my rotten teeth' – informed his manager that at the age of 36, he was retiring, and joining the staff of *Athletic News* to embark on a career in journalism, which culminated in his founding *Charles Buchan's Football Monthly*.

Over the next 30 years, Buchan's forthright views on the ills of English football continued to exasperate the authorities but his key role as Arsenal's first true superstar must never be forgotten. He had been an ideal sounding board, confidante, ally and dressing room leader for Chapman in his formative years at Highbury. Arsenal would not have gone on to dominate the 1930s without him.

As Buchan prepared to disappear into the sunset, Chapman informed him, 'It will cost £10,000 to replace you.' In fact it was £10,440. Ironically, when details of Buchan's transfer from Sunderland in 1925 were finally leaked into the public domain in 1929, the fall-out ended Norris's grip on power at the club and strengthened Chapman's.

# Power Shift

*'We had to learn from the mistakes we made in the 1927 final. We couldn't allow ourselves to lose at Wembley again.'* Joe Hulme.

*'It is the opening of a new era for London and the south… no club ever worked harder or more thoroughly deserved to lift the cup.'* Islington Gazette, *28 April 1930.*

ON 5 April 1929 the *Daily Mail* ran an intriguing story which virtually disappeared into the ether the minute it was printed, 'It has been reported that Mr Herbert Chapman, secretary manager of the Arsenal Football Club, has resigned and is returning to Huddersfield.'

The piece added that, although he was much sought after by other clubs, he had 'definitely decided to remain in London'. It concluded, 'So much of his time has been occupied by matters of an exceptional character that the record of the club can still be further improved.'

It is an extraordinary episode because the Arsenal players appeared not to have got wind of it – at least they never referred to it in interviews – and the story doesn't figure in Bob Wall's, Tom Whittaker's or George Allison's books from the era. The story slipped into a Bermuda Triangle of silence, but is well worth deciphering.

The reference to 'matters of an exceptional character' is surely alluding to the turbulent end of Sir Henry Norris's tenure as Arsenal chairman. Chapman and Norris had clashed for some time, and Joe Hulme told Brian Woolnough, 'We all knew that Chapman and Norris didn't get on. Norris was always quite affable when we met him –

he was as excited as any of us when we reached the first cup final in 1927 – but you hear things, and we knew that they disagreed over Chapman's staff.'

Hulme didn't name names, but he was most likely referring to the fate of trainer George Hardy, whom Chapman immediately demoted following Hardy's decision to bark instructions at the Arsenal players during a tense FA Cup clash with Port Vale in 1927. Incensed that Hardy had got ideas above his station, Chapman sent him back to the dressing room, at which point directors William Hall and Sir Samuel Hill-Wood were forced to intervene as Chapman and Hardy engaged in a heated row.

Chapman had long wanted Tom Whittaker to coach the first team and Hardy the reserves. With Norris away in the south of France, Chapman made his move and installed Whittaker as his first team trainer. It was a fait accompli. Norris later claimed that Chapman's reshuffle – supported by the rest of the board – had made his position 'untenable'. Unlike Leslie Knighton, who had claimed that Norris bullied him during board meetings, Chapman was more than capable of fighting his ground and indulging in his own brand of Machiavellian intrigue.

Norris resigned as chairman at the end of the season, ultimately outmanoeuvred by a manager who, as well as having the backing of several board members, also possessed the self-confidence, the aura and the wherewithal to push on with his five-year plan whatever the white noise in the background.

He remained a shareholder in the club and in late 1927, at the AGM, he delivered a personal attack on Chapman, accusing him of 'betrayal'. Chapman remained silent, and, thanks to the attitude of Norris's successor Samuel Hill-Wood's (his motto was, 'Why interfere when you've got experts to do the job?'), Chapman was allowed to control virtually all aspects of club policy, from training and fitness techniques, to transfer dealings. The club underwent an abrupt U-turn in policy in the late 1920s, and Hill-Wood's *laissez-faire* attitude – the direct opposite to Norris's approach – has underpinned Arsenal's management approach to this day.

Inevitably, Norris didn't go quietly. Joe Hulme recalls Norris 'passing on his good wishes to the team in person before and after the

1933 FA Cup Final', but by then his formal involvement in football ended in disgrace, after a series of *Daily Mail* articles alleged that Norris had made a number of illegal payments to Charlie Buchan following his move from Sunderland, and had personally 'overseen' the sale of the team bus, which raised a princely £125, the proceeds from which found their way into his wife's bank account.

As far back as 1921, Norris and William Hall had also been using Arsenal money to pay their chauffeurs, and in 1927 Norris also forged Chapman's signature on the endorsement of a cheque from the sale of the bus.

Questions were also asked about the signings of Henry White and Clem Voysey in 1919, and the knotty issues of illegal signing-on fees. In Voysey's case, Norris was alleged to have given him in the region of £200, in an era when the £10 limit still stood. As Norris pointed out to the FA enquiry in 1928, given the fact that he had pumped around £125,000 into the club, surely the payments to Ryder, his chauffeur (Gunners boss Leslie Knighton had warned Norris not to pay Ryder from the club's bank account), weren't so heinous. And as for under-the-counter payments, he argued that without them 'we should not have got the player'.

Norris tried to drag down Chapman with him, claiming he was aware of the payments to Buchan, and that Chapman had 'begged' Norris to do 'whatever it takes' to retain the player's services. Chapman, having been banned from football along with other Leeds City directors in 1919 for making illegal payments at the end of World War One, and aware that his career was on the line once more, totally distanced himself from Norris, and the FA enquiry deemed that he 'was not an accomplice' and was 'not involved in Norris's financial dealings'. The FA Committee banned Norris from football 'indefinitely', and he was forced to watch from the sidelines as Chapman steered the club towards glory in the early 1930s.

Although many football writers have claimed that Norris was a broken man after his life ban, Hulme recalled him as 'a jovial figure, whom we saw now and again in London and who always asked after the boys. It seemed like he was glad to be free from his pressures.' Doubtless, Norris's voracious social life and numerous business interests kept him occupied until his death at home in Barnes in 1934. Smart man though

Norris was, he struggled to grasp where the boundary lay between his own wallet and the club's assets. The balance of power within the club had irrevocably shifted in Chapman's favour, and yet, Chapman seemed to be in a quandary about his future in early April 1929.

Perhaps it was because nearly four years after taking over at the club, Arsenal were still a long way off the summit of English football. Chapman's aim to build a football dynasty in the south appeared to be little more than a pipe dream. Huddersfield (his former team completed their championship hat-trick in his first year at Highbury), Newcastle, Everton and now Sheffield Wednesday had won titles during Chapman's early years in north London, and the Gunners appeared to be in no fit state to wrest power south any time soon.

Chapman had spent a massive £10,400 on Bolton's cerebral David Jack as a star replacement for Charlie Buchan, but despite this no other big-name signings had been added. Crowds at Highbury crashed to their pre-Chapman levels in the latter part of the 1928/29 campaign. Just 21,000 turned out for the game at home to Newcastle and only 11,639 for the home win against Everton in mid-April. Chapman knew that such sparse crowds weren't going to fund the purchase of top talent, so perhaps his 'resignation' was a thinly-veiled threat to the Arsenal board that unless they sanctioned further high profile signings, he would leave. If it was a ruse, Chapman's ploy worked because within two months, Cliff Bastin and Alex James arrived at Highbury from Exeter City and Preston North End respectively.

There is another reason why Chapman may have been linked with a return to his former club four months into 1929. Hulme claimed that Chapman often spoke wistfully of his northern roots. A Yorkshireman born and bred, Chapman loved much of what London had to offer and the educational opportunities afforded to his children. But it didn't stop him, or several Arsenal players, missing home. Hulme recalls having conversations with Chapman 'about how big London could feel'. Hulme also claims, 'In the early days, many of us found the Arsenal crowd demanding and easily frustrated. They didn't behave as a "northern crowd" would.'

It is an intriguing point. In time, Arsenal would come to be seen as embodying London wealth, and yet few of the 1930s stars actually hailed from the capital. West Ham-born George Male, who made his debut in the late 1920s, recalled, 'Apart from Alex James, I wouldn't say that any Arsenal players lived the London life. We didn't earn the money! Some of the lads, like Jack Lambert, never really took to it, and he preferred the countryside.

'Many were overawed with London. They'd lived in mining villages and small towns all their lives. We had players, good players like Davie Halliday and Ray Bowden, who never settled. Davie, who was Scottish, used to say, "Get me back home" and he only stayed a year. Ray Bowden used to pine for the West Country. None of us really went to parties or premieres or chased women. We tended to keep low profiles, except for Alex. Chapman wouldn't have allowed us to live a party life.'

Male claimed that Chapman was wary of the pitfalls to be found in London, warning his players against 'schemers and money sharks'. In his autobiography, Cliff Bastin recalls his grandmother's warning about London. 'To her, the capital city was nothing but a Sodom or Gomorrah, full of snares and pitfalls for innocent young West Country lads, such as myself.'

After arriving from Bolton, Lancashire-born David Jack, labouring under the gigantic transfer fee, struggled to adapt to a more critical crowd, so much so, recalled Hulme, that 'none of us would have been surprised had David upped sticks and gone back home'.

It is not beyond the realms of possibility that the *Mail* story was based on a throwaway Chapman comment about his affection for his former club Huddersfield and he was indeed much sought after by the country's dominant teams, who were located in the north.

History shows that Chapman eschewed all offers from rivals and stayed put in 1929, determined to make good his promise of delivering success to Arsenal

⌣ ⌣ ⌣ ⌣ ⌣

Although league performances might not have been especially indicative of improvement, Chapman, one by one, solved the essential conundrums which lay at the root of Arsenal's underachievement. His unerring eye for detail saw him upgrade the team in several key positions. The first change he made, albeit in stages (Jack Butler retained his position in the team for some time) was to replace Butler with a £200 signing from Oswestry Town, Herbie Roberts. Joe Hulme recalled Butler's 'tendency to wander out of position, because his natural instinct was to go forward'.

On the other hand, Roberts 'would follow Chapman's instructions to the letter', explained George Male. 'He did as he was told, and had no wish to push forward like Butler did.' Gangling, awkward and red-headed, his job was to 'intercept all balls down the middle and either head them or pass them short to a team-mate'.

His low-key capture by Arsenal is a prime example of the manager's knack of slotting the right man into the right position, although it might not always have immediately seemed that way. According to Hulme, Roberts was 'almost automotive in his playing style, and was not very popular with the crowd who viewed him as being limited.'

Hulme's comment fits neatly with Bernard Joy's assessment of Roberts in *Forward Arsenal!* 'He was content to remain on the defensive, using his height to nod away the ball with his red haired head and he had the patience to carry on unruffled in the face of heavy pressure and loud barracking,' he wrote.

A vital cog in the machine had been added, but the machine still wasn't sufficiently oiled. Part of the problem was that inside-forward Andy Neil, who had done a sterling job in the role, simply wasn't quick or foraging enough. As the 1920s drew to a close, Arsenal were still too ponderous when the ball was played out of defence. When Preston North End put Alex James on the transfer list in the summer of 1929, Chapman fought off competition from Liverpool and Aston Villa to sign one of Scotland's 'Wembley Wizards' who had dazzled against England a year before. Ironically for a player who would soon become the fulcrum of the entire Arsenal operation, James initially appeared to be little more than an expensive spanner in the works.

James was 27 when he arrived at Highbury, and as the season got underway, the Gunners began well, winning four games out of five. There followed an almost catastrophic run of form which saw Chapman's team win just five matches between September and mid-February. This was relegation form and in the opening 14 games of the campaign, Chapman used 12 different forwards.

Just as Jack had run the gauntlet of abuse in the previous campaign, Alex James now bore the brunt of the crowd's frustration. Hulme recalled, 'Critics inside and outside the club suggested that Alec was too much of an individual to fit in with Arsenal's way of play. He looked very tense in his early months. He seemed to have lost the snap in his game, and because of the tension within him, he kept the ball for too long. So the crowd got on to him, and he tensed up.'

After yet another disappointing display in October 1929, the *Daily Mail* reported, 'The little man was too prone to keep the ball to himself until he was beaten by force of numbers. He would do well to remember there are four other forwards in the line.'

Chapman – whose success as a munitions factory manager in World War One and as Huddersfield manager had been forged through extolling the values of hard work and an adherence to a strict system of working, appeared to have landed Arsenal with a maverick individualist. No matter that the team was unsettled, that his team-mates hadn't yet become accustomed to his bluffing tactics on the pitch ('He'd call for the ball, but actually he wanted you to pass to someone else. It was all a ruse to trick our opponents, and that sort of scheme takes a while to get used to,' recalled George Male) or that his ankle was damaged, Chapman, it appeared, had bought a dud.

Arsenal weren't using James properly. Contrary to the claim that he was unwilling to carry out defensive duties ('Alec was excellent at harrying opponents and forcing them into losing the ball,' recalled Tom Parker) James was forced to play in a far deeper role than he expected. James was always clear that if he did hold on to the ball for too long, it was because there was simply no one available to pass to.

Through his newspaper columns, we can see just how focused and clear James was on his role in the team and what he was and wasn't prepared to do. In the *Star*, he wrote, 'The First Division inside-forward cannot possibly do all that is expected of him, ie donkey work, fetching and carrying, initiating all attacks, falling back and defending. Being human, and not a whirlwind, I say frankly that it cannot be done.'

As for his expectations, he was clear on how he expected them to operate, 'I always try to get somewhere clear of the opposition so that my colleagues are able to pass to me without interference. If they fail to do so, that's their funeral, not mine. I consider I have done my part of the job by getting into position.'

The most frequently quoted member of the 1930s Arsenal side, James's invective demonstrates a lively, confident, theoretical mind, which others took some time to adjust to. 'He was difficult to read, lived in his own world. These days [in the early 1990s], Alec would be labelled "mercurial".

'You had to get to know him, and that took time,' explained George Male. James kept his ongoing ankle injuries – a result of brutal treatment by defenders down the years – a secret with Chapman and Tom Whittaker, but the crowd grew increasingly impatient with him. Although James put a brave face on things, laughing with team-mates at some of the content of the critical mail he received (one fan sent him a battered old pair of kids' boots with a covering letter suggesting, 'You might try these') the pressure was growing on Chapman and his expensive band of underachievers. Dropped prior to Arsenal's crucial FA Cup third round clash with Chelsea, Chapman sent James home for complete bed rest.

What happened next represents arguably the most pivotal piece of man-management in Chapman's reign, and perhaps any era in Arsenal's history. The Gunners defeated Chelsea 2-0, and James, ordered by the club's physician to rest for a fortnight, listened on the radio as Arsenal drew their fourth round clash with Birmingham. Meanwhile, he had injections in his ankle.

Depending on which story you believe the syringe contained either painkilling fluid or water – and in a more relaxed frame of mind, James caught up on some sleep. The following morning, Chapman strode into his bedroom, instructed him to get dressed, and informed him that he would win the replay against Birmingham for 'the boys'. It represented a huge gamble for Chapman, who confessed, 'I did not know how we were going to get him back into the side.'

There is a rose-tinted view on what happened next. Hulme claimed, 'Alec played a marvellous game against Birmingham, and from that moment, he never looked back.' Similarly, Tom Parker explained, 'You could see the confidence return to his game, and suddenly everything clicked.'

The truth of the matter is murkier. James always claimed that his friend Phil Kelso had put the idea of arriving unannounced at the James residence into Chapman's mind. Although colleagues surrounded James like a returning messiah after the dour 1-0 scrap against Birmingham in a biblical downpour, the Scot wasn't fooled, claiming, 'It was another heartening stunt on the part of my colleagues…they knew as well as I that I hadn't done a thing.' And it took another massive Chapman gamble to finally discover the key which ultimately unlocked the Arsenal system.

Chapman realised that if James were to flourish in his role at Highbury, he required someone on the left to adopt both left-sided forward positions when the team attacked. James's role – falling back with a retreating defence – left the forward line a man short for much of the time. Hulme went as far as to say, 'Sometimes when we attacked, if felt as if we were hopelessly lopsided, almost a man down.'

Inside-forward Cliff Bastin was stunned when Chapman approached him in December 1929 and asked him to shift to outside-left. Bastin was persuaded by his manager that the move would benefit both the player and the club. Chapman had, by a mixture of bluff, shrewd judgement and persuasion sculpted the forward line which would ultimately bring the club so much success.

The Hulme–Jack–Bastin–James–Lambert formation was finally in place, but Chapman's machine continued to splutter horribly in the league as the 1930s began. The *Islington Gazette* liberally sprinkled words such as 'constricted', 'jaded' and 'fatigued' to describe Arsenal's league form. This was partly due to the fact that injuries and a flu virus laid low James, Lambert and Bastin at various times.

James always claimed never to have altered his style at Highbury, and that his resurgence in form was due more to Chapman switching Bastin's position and his own slow recovery from his troublesome ankle injury. Ultimately, Chapman must take enormous credit for this intervention, and the fact that James, after some serious palpitations, became the beating heart of this Arsenal side.

If Arsenal's league form was woeful at times, Chapman's boys certainly showed their fighting spirit in the FA Cup once they had disposed of Birmingham. Slowly but surely, James led the way. At Ayresome Park in the fifth round, James showed the type of form which later made him arguably the First Division's greatest attraction.

In the opening minute, he shrugged off the attentions of three Middlesbrough defenders, and squared the ball to Bastin, who narrowly put his shot wide. Two minutes later, James broke free again and slipped the ball to Lambert, who prodded home. A Bastin header gave Arsenal a comfortable 2-0 win with the defence soaking up plenty of Boro pressure after the break.

In the quarter-final, Arsenal swept aside West Ham with a fine display of counter-attacking play. A Lambert brace helped the Gunners to a 3-0 win and provided a welcome relief from their travails in the league.

Arsenal appeared to have luck on their side when they avoided Huddersfield and eventual champions Sheffield Wednesday in the semi-final, and instead drew Second Division strugglers Hull City. But as Hulme admitted, 'It was against supposedly inferior opposition that we'd often come unstuck.'

After 30 minutes at Elland Road, the Gunners were in deep trouble. A terrible clearance by Arsenal goalkeeper Dan Lewis saw him lobbed by Hull striker Howieson, and on 30 minutes Eddie Hapgood put through his own net. Early in the second half, Chapman got David Jack to swap positions with Jack Lambert. With the speedier Jack playing a more forward role, Arsenal gradually turned the screw. But with only 20 minutes left Arsenal seemed down and out.

Tom Parker recalled, 'Hull were rock solid. Their defenders were utterly impassable for so long.' But where there was Joe Hulme, there was always hope. On 70 minutes he galloped forward and sent a low cross into the centre where Jack steered the ball home. 'The only thing I had in my mind was that late on, my pace could do Hull some serious damage,' Hulme recalled.

Hulme, Bastin and Lambert then peppered the Hull goal with shots. Only six minutes were left when Bastin curled in an excellent shot from the edge of the box to pull the scores level at 2-2. 'The ball travelled so fast that the goalkeeper had hardly moved when it entered the net at about the level of his shoulder, and a finer goal than this was is seldom seen,' noted *The Times*. Speed and precision, two attributes which later defined Arsenal, had made the difference.

Arsenal's laboured performance prompted the Hull manager to claim, 'Arsenal in my opinion are an overrated side. They look to be some way off triumphing in a major competition to my eyes.' Bill McCracken's team showed no fear of their First Division opponents in the replay at Villa Park just four days later. Parker recalled it as being 'one of the roughest matches I ever played in for Arsenal'. *The Times* reckoned it was, 'one of the poorest semi-finals ever played. The tactics adopted by Hull City were entirely responsible for this and to crown a thoroughly unpleasant afternoon, Childs, the Hull City left-back, was ordered off the field.' His crime? 'A flying kick at James.'

Not all of the media believed the Hull defender deserved to be dismissed. The *Hull Daily Mail* reported, 'On the face of it the dramatic dismissal of the City centre-half suggested drastic punishment for sheer pertinacity and for the remainder of the game the official in charge got no peace from a crowd that obviously resented his notion. The City players had the sympathy from the bulk of the crowd.'

By the time Childs was dismissed, Hull were trailing 1-0 to a (soon-to-be) classic Arsenal move, albeit with one of the key components absent through injury. James seized on the ball in midfield but his raking pass down the right appeared to be running out for a throw-in. With Hulme injured, his deputy Joey Williams somehow kept the ball in, crossed low, and David Jack swept home. Against obdurate opponents, this was a game-changing, history-making moment.

In the face of brutal harassment from Hull, Arsenal squeaked through 1-0. The club's history is littered with examples of attritional victories where by hook or by crook, Arsenal somehow prevail. Similarly, there have been a raft of players like Williams who, in big matches, secure their fleeting five minutes of fame. After the Hull match, nothing would ever quite be the same for a club which, 44 years after its formation, still hadn't landed silverware. Now, they stood on the threshold of a monumental achievement.

- - - - -

Three years earlier, Charlie Buchan complained about the 'interminable six-week wait' for the FA Cup Final. This time, Arsenal played an incredible eight league games in 24 days. There were some eye-catching results like the 6-6 draw away at Leicester and an 8-1 home win over Sheffield United, and perhaps the busy programme kept Arsenal's players distracted. Up to a point, anyway.

One issue, again, was the ticket allocation. Ivan Gazidis registered his disapproval with the FA when Arsenal and Hull were awarded 25,000 tickets each in 2014 for the final, but in 1930 the allocation for the Gunners and Huddersfield was just 7,500 each. 'Every Man Jack wanted one,' explained Hulme. 'You couldn't move for everyone in the street asking you for one. But Herbert Chapman was adamant. There was to be no black marketeering among the players. I think we only got six tickets each anyway, which just about covered our immediate families. So there was no chance of selling them on.'

Tom Parker admitted that he was 'pestered by friends, family, fans and journalists for more. But I'd had that in 1927, when I'd hinted that "I'd see what I could do." It wore me out. This time, I just told them, "Sorry, I haven't got enough myself." They stopped asking then, and I hadn't given anyone false hope.'

Mindful of the angst-ridden build-up to the 1927 final, Chapman took his players to Brighton before the match three years later for a blast of sea air. A veteran of the Cardiff defeat, Hulme recalled, 'It was nice to get a change of scenery. It was much more relaxed this time. In Brighton, we enjoyed one another's company, and we had fun and some jokes. We played lots of golf. Chapman allowed the players to have a glass of wine or a beer, only one or two, and everyone had to be in bed by 10.30. He came around to make sure that our lights were out, too.'

The 'fun' and 'jokes' that Hulme mentioned probably refers to his wind-up of goalkeeper Charlie Preedy. Pretending to be a journalist, Hulme rang the bar telephone from the secretary's office in the golf club and asked for Preedy. Hulme promised Preedy £50 for a cup final exclusive and the goalkeeper asked Chapman's permission, which was granted because the Arsenal manager was also in on the joke. Preedy gabbled on for a few minutes before Hulme lapsed back into his Yorkshire accent and told him that he would see him in the bar for a drink.

Such three-dimensional insights into players' personalities from that era are rare and it demonstrates the level of team spirit Chapman had fostered within his players, and shows that he was not above sharing a joke with his players, too.

Hulme and Parker both admitted to 'tossing and turning' the night before the match but mercifully the coach trip to Wembley from Harrow this time was quicker, and Hulme recalled, 'Fans lined the route, but we got to the stadium with more than an hour to spare. Not too rushed and not too long to wait around and get nervous.'

Groundsman Bert Rutt played gramophone records in the changing room to drown out the noise from the crowd as Chapman's Gunners prepared to meet the mighty Huddersfield Town.

It is tempting to view the 1930 final (simply dubbed the 'North v South Final' by Pathe News) in purely black and white terms; the day on which the balance of power swung irrevocably from north to south. From Chapman's former club to the one he had headed south for. From Huddersfield to Arsenal.

There are certain aspects of the story which, broadly speaking, are correct, but in truth the two clubs had been travelling on increasingly divergent paths since 1926. Despite the hat-trick of titles won by the Leeds Road club between 1924 and 1926, the foundations upon which they had been built remained unsteady. In a predominantly rugby-supporting town they had been elected to the Football League in 1910, spent an incredible £25,000 on new players in just three seasons before World War One and narrowly staved off bankruptcy.

Chapman's arrival, and continued investment in the team, brought unprecedented success to the East Riding outfit, but at the height of their success, wrote Jimmy Catton in *All Sports Weekly* in 1926, 'The strain of endeavouring to be champions for three years without a break is enormous.'

Even the *Huddersfield Examiner* noted a sense of 'trophy fatigue' among the club's own supporters on the eve of the 1926/27 campaign. 'Never has the curtain gone up on the drama of the soccer season with less beating of drums and blowing of trumpets than it will do this year. One reason for the calm is the fact that the question "will Huddersfield Town win the championship again?" cannot arouse quite the same overpowering interest.'

Had Town supporters had any inkling that 1926 would be the last time Huddersfield would win a major trophy, they wouldn't have been so blasé. Amid managerial change, Huddersfield then finished as runners-up in 1927 and 1928, narrowly missing out on the Double, before finishing in disappointing mid-table positions in 1929 and 1930 as investment in the team and attendances at Leeds Road began to tumble. Sheffield Wednesday, champions in 1929 and 1930, were now the powerhouses in the north, but Huddersfield had helpfully removed them from the FA Cup equation by defeating them in the other semi-final.

Any clash with Huddersfield was a momentous occasion, as Hulme recalled, 'Chapman always reminded us that Town's achievements in the 1920s were what we should aspire to but he never blew his own trumpet about setting them on their way. He never needed to! Their blue and white striped shirts were famous right through the game.'

Tom Parker confirmed, 'Playing Huddersfield was the biggest game of all, but we were very confident that we would beat them. Neither team had had the best of league seasons, but I felt we would win.'

Huddersfield was already feeling the early impact of the Great Depression on its textile mills and surrounding coal mines. This was already driving down Town's attendances at Leeds Road. In contrast London, with its raft of consumer and service industries, was in a much stronger position to lead the way forward. The building industry continued to flourish in the capital. Suburbs sprung up along the newly extended tube lines, slum clearance continued apace, a record number of new houses were built in Islington alone, and the Piccadilly area was completely rebuilt. There were hardships due to the Depression in London, but as Hulme admitted, 'London and the north were like two different worlds, really.'

* * * * *

The teams emerged alongside one another in bright sunshine. Given the fact that Chapman had managed both teams, the FA decided that the Huddersfield and Arsenal players should walk out in unison. The Arsenal players may have cast a furtive glance at Town's Alex Jackson, nicknamed 'the Teapot' on account of his protruding ears, and widely regarded as the league's most dynamic winger. Or perhaps their left-half Campbell, who had already won the FA Cup with Blackburn.

Given both sides' inconsistent league form, it's hardly surprising that the *Daily Mirror* claimed, 'There never was a more open final. By no purpose of analysis is it possible to pick the probable winners.'

Parker explained, 'We were in agreement that we needed to make a positive, attacking start to the game.' His team-mates followed their captain's orders. The Arsenal fans fortunate enough to gain access to Wembley were in an ebullient mood and the *Glasgow Evening News* reporter noted, 'I met a flaming procession consisting of an Arsenal fan and friends covered in red from head to foot and carrying a copy of the cup in the same colour and half a hundred followers all similarly attired.'

They looked on as Arsenal set about putting Huddersfield under immediate pressure. Alex James seized the initiative on the big stage. Five minutes in, Arsenal won a free kick on the edge of the box, James shaped to take it, and left it to Parker who clattered the ball into Huddersfield skipper Tom Wilson's midriff.

A few minutes later, after weighing up his options, James delivered a defence-splitting pass that Jack Lambert latched on to but the Huddersfield goalkeeper pushed the ball wide. Then Bastin headed wide and Lambert headed fractionally over the bar. Joe Hulme recalled, 'I was confident that there would be no repeat of our seizing up against Cardiff in 1927. Alec loved the big stage and was like the conductor conducting the orchestra.'

It is supremely ironic that on the day Arsenal finally made their mark, and served notice that the tactical system they had spent nearly five years piecing together was a potent one, their first Wembley goal should come from a piece of off-the-cuff impudence.

With 15 minutes on the clock, James was fouled by Goodall and before he even heard the referee's whistle blow he nudged the ball on to Bastin, who scampered down to the corner flag, doubled back under Goodall's challenge and screwed the ball back to James.

Without breaking his stride, James hammered in a great shot past Turner with the outside of his foot. James later revealed that he had discussed the move on the team bus prior to the match with Bastin (the winger had laughed at James, reckoning that the Scot's goal-getting days were over) and that he'd had to think like lightning to outfox Turner.

He told 'Arbiter' of the *Daily Mail*, 'Turner had positioned himself so well that I saw that I could only hope to beat him by some deception. So I sliced the ball with the outside of my right foot and sent it swerving beyond the reach of the goalkeeper's left hand.'

James had been attempting lightning-quick free kicks all season, much to Chapman's annoyance, because the referee invariably made James retake it and by then Arsenal had lost their impetus. But when it really, really counted, James's improvisation had paid off.

Joe Hulme recalled, in an uncharacteristically colourful description, 'At that moment, Alec unlocked the door and opened up a new world for us. From that point on, the whole team relaxed, and confidence flooded through us.' Tom Parker was more concise, 'It was a goal which only Alec could score, but we still had a great deal of work to do.'

Just as the all-important tactical change back in 1925 had largely been Buchan's brainchild, James's spark of ingenuity was his own brainwave and as Tom Whittaker later noted, 'It is strange that he helped to win the cup by virtually disobeying an order from his chief.'

After the game, Hulme recalled Chapman, '…smirking at James with those twinkly eyes of his at the sheer cheek of what he'd done. He couldn't argue with James now, could he?' As Parker said, Arsenal still had work to do, but not before the mother of all distractions hove into view early in the second half.

Like 'a huge silver cigar' (*The Guardian*), the Graf Zeppelin, accompanied by a dozen aircraft, drifted over Wembley just as Huddersfield were about to place Arsenal under a period of sustained pressure in the second 45 minutes. Hulme recalled a 'droning sound which got louder and louder. I realised what it was, but I was so focused that I played on.' Parker was even more matter-of-fact. 'I glanced up, saw what it was, and didn't give another second's thought. I'd seen a Zeppelin over London before, anyway.' Parker might well have been referring to the R101 airship's maiden voyage in late 1929, which drew huge crowds as it passed over the capital.

The Zeppelin was in England on a publicity trip, and even at the time, its appearance was described by *The Guardian* as 'not graceful at all, but heavy, threatening, sullen, and creating a fearful din.' In various football histories, the 'Zeppelin Final', as well as heralding the emergence of Chapman's Arsenal, was also highlighted as an ominous warning of Germany's growing industrial might during the 1930s. Bernard Joy recounted in *Forward Arsenal!*, 'It cast a shadow of events to come, which were to be nearly disastrous for both the country and Arsenal.'

In fact, this was still three years before the Nazi party came to power and the purpose of the Zeppelin's flight that day, in the words of Home Secretary J.R. Clynes, 'is a symbol of how Germany and England can now work in harmony to ensure that both countries benefit from advanced aerial power.' After the enormous vessel eventually landed in Cardington, scientists from both nations met to swap aeronautic technology.

Inside Wembley Stadium, Arsenal fan Clive Evans, whom I interviewed in the early 1990s, was perturbed at the sight of the Zeppelin, 'During World War One, a young cousin of mine was killed during a Zeppelin raid in Leytonstone. We used to call them the "baby killers" because so many of those who were killed in the raids were young kids. So I wasn't happy when it appeared, and dropped so low over Wembley that you could clearly see the passengers waving to the crowd below.

'I thought it was in bad taste. Others didn't seem very pleased either, because the planes made a bloody racket, and the Zeppelin blocked out the light. The Arsenal fans around were booing and shouting into the sky for it to sod off and stop blocking out the light.'

The Zeppelin's appearance did arouse some controversy afterwards when it emerged that the skipper of the vessel, Captain Lehmann, had been one of the German captains heading up the Zeppelin bombing raids on London in World War One, but most newspaper reports suggested afterwards that the majority of the crowd (or those that weren't wedged at the back of the stands and therefore unable to look up into the sky) stared upwards and waved cheerfully at the passengers who waved at them 2,000 feet above their heads.

King George V seemed happy enough, raising his hat as the airship dipped its nose to salute him. George Male, 19 years old, pushing for a first-team place and looking on at Wembley, claimed, 'The appearance of the Zeppelin and the presence of the King, together with all the normal pomp and ceremony of the cup final, gave the 1930 final a sense of history. It was unique, because what happened was so unusual.'

Huddersfield certainly kept their concentration firmly on events at ground level, and laid siege to Arsenal's goal for all bar the final two minutes of the second half. This certainly went against Hulme's claim that the early James free kick had completely settled Arsenal's nerves.

The majority of Huddersfield moves were instigated by the Scottish outside-right Alex Jackson. Memorably, *The Guardian* reported, 'Jackson, instead of waiting Micawber-like as he had done in the first half, began to forage for himself.'

As Arsenal began to look fatigued, Bob John and Eddie Hapgood worked tirelessly to snuff out the threat from Jackson, and Alex James demonstrated his team ethic by dropping back to aid the defence and stifle Huddersfield as best he could. In the *Sunday Post*, 'Captain Bob' claimed, 'I have never seen a man so badly fouled and so frequently as was Alex Jackson.'

Hulme, who along with Bastin dropped back more and more as the half wore on, admitted, 'We had to keep our heads, and stop their key man – Jackson – however we could.'

Charlie Preedy, the Arsenal goalkeeper who had endured a nervy first half, managed to hold himself together in the second and Parker recalled 'a mass of our defenders every time Huddersfield attacked. Their winger, Smith, had an especially fine game.'

On several occasions, Smith sent over threatening crosses which were either nodded away by Arsenal defenders or put wide by Town forwards. Their skipper Tom Wilson headed narrowly wide on two occasions, and Raw was denied at point-blank range by Preedy. Huddersfield's best chance fell to Jackson, whose goalbound shot clipped Bill Seddon on the head and deflected just over the crossbar.

The Huddersfield skipper later commented, 'I remember two thrilling occasions in the second half when I said to myself, "Here's a goal."' But, thanks to last-ditch defending from Arsenal and profligate finishing from Huddersfield, Town couldn't convert any of their opportunities.

With 83 minutes on the clock Arsenal appeared ready to buckle. In the days before substitutions, David Jack was virtually a passenger, and Tom Parker had 'terrible cramps in both legs. I felt like I could barely stand.' But Huddersfield had virtually punched themselves out, and Alex Jackson hobbled noticeably after a robust challenge from Bob John. Try as he might, he had been unable to win the midfield battle against his fellow Scot James.

Then James intervened again. Decisively. Receiving possession in his own half, he 'held the ball long enough to make the halves and backs uncertain of his intentions. Then he pushed the ball straight down the middle where Lambert, between the two backs, could not be challenged promptly by either,' reported the *Daily Mail*.

Lambert looked up, briefly stayed on the ball, and as Turner committed himself, Lambert slipped it past him to make the score 2-0. It says much for Arsenal's general fatigue levels that when Lambert wheeled around to celebrate with his team-mates, he discovered that he was marooned way up the pitch. So he was left to applaud himself as he jogged back towards his own half. 'None of us had the legs to chase after Jackie,' admitted Tom Parker.

At long, long last, Arsenal had finally lifted silverware, and following in Tottenham and Chelsea's footsteps, brought the FA Cup south. Parker collected the trophy from the King and, half a century on, he reflected, 'I'm old now, and no one recognises me in the street which suits me. I'm not a vain man – modest in fact. But inside I'll always have the honour of being the first Arsenal captain to lift not just silverware, but the FA Cup. It's marvellous.'

Hulme was gushing about the performance of James, and the galvanising effect the victory quickly had on the club. 'Alec never looked back from that day, and neither did the club. Everything we achieved afterwards, including the way the two Highbury east and west stands were built, was because of winning the FA Cup in 1930.'

For Huddersfield, although they would remain a strong side well into the 1930s, the party was over. Arsenal's celebrations could finally begin.

⌣ ⌣ ⌣ ⌣ ⌣

At different times in the cup run Arsenal had been inspired, downright lucky, and relentless in the pursuit of victory. Critics suggested that Arsenal's football in the final, although effective, wasn't particularly inspiring. Such comments would soon become *de rigueur*.

Two days later the team was given a civic reception at Islington Town Hall, where thousands of supporters came to celebrate with the players. The cup was filled to the brim with champagne, and passed from player to player. Parker recalled, '…a wonderful occasion, when it felt like we could look our supporters in the eye'. The mayor,

Alderman W.E. Manchester, described the team as 'the pride of the borough'.

Aside from the minor irritation of losing 1-0 at Highbury in front of more than 35,000 spectators to Sunderland later that day in the league, the sky really did appear to be the limit for Arsenal and especially for Alex James.

Newspaper headlines in those far-off days tended to be rather reserved, but the press made an exception in James's case. Former Manchester United star Billy Meredith wrote in the *Daily Dispatch*, 'JAMES THE MAN WHO MATTERED'. The *Sunday Post* barked, 'Alec James The Wizard' and the *Daily Mail* announced, 'Magic Touch Of Alex James'. Perhaps the most perceptive and relevant headline of all was in *The Evening Times*, 'THE JUSTIFICATION OF ALEC JAMES: FAMOUS SCOT SCOTCHES HIS CRITICS'. With his entire reputation, as well as that of his manager and team-mates on the line, the Scot had proved to be Arsenal's alchemist.

The photograph taken of the victorious Arsenal team after the Huddersfield match shows Herbert Chapman looking wistful. Perhaps he was reflecting on Arsenal's ultimate 'sliding doors' moment. Had Huddersfield battered down Arsenal's defence in that fraught second half, James was in no doubt that Chapman would have dismantled the side and offloaded his midfielder, commenting, 'Chapman was never a man to give two thoughts to the fact that a player had cost many thousands of pounds to buy. If he did not make good, well, he was no use to Arsenal and would have to go. They paid £9,000 for me, but I tell you quite frankly, that if we hadn't won at Wembley, I am fairly certain in my own mind that Alex James would have been up for sale again.'

Hulme disagreed with James, claiming, 'Chapman might have sold some of the older players like Tom Parker and Bob John. Even by 1930, there was still grumbling among fans about David Jack, and he didn't have a brilliant game in the final. So perhaps he might have been sold. But I'm positive he'd have stuck with Alec and his group of youngsters like me, Cliff [Bastin] and Eddie [Hapgood]. As it was, he didn't have to change a thing.'

It is highly unlikely that a Samuel Hill-Wood-led board would have altered its *laissez-faire* philosophy and dismissed the manager or ripped apart the squad had Chapman failed to make good on his five-year plan. It simply wasn't the Hill-Wood style.

While the national dailies focused on details of the match itself, the *Daily Gazette* (as well as saluting the red-and-white-suited, bugle-playing, rattle-shaking 'Hi-Hi Boys' who had followed the club all over the country that season) viewed Arsenal's triumph from a broader perspective.

'St Ivel' wrote, 'Arsenal have spent money in prodigal fashion. Why? Because nothing is too good for their patrons. Was it wise? They have made a tremendous appeal to the public. The total receipts in League and Cup totalling £100,000.'

The ends, finally, were starting to justify the means. Chapman's post-match comments in the *Gazette*, in contrast to the frequently bland comments of his contemporaries, spoke volumes for his sense of business acumen, his broader economic understanding, and his awareness that stability, unity and patience were the key factors behind any successful organisation. He insisted, 'We showed the team spirit which is necessary to the success of any enterprise, whether sporting, business or municipal.'

He added, 'We commence our success in the boardroom. My directors have very great ideals on our great game and on the lives of the people. There is nothing too good for the Arsenal.'

Interestingly, 'St Ivel' described Arsenal as 'the Bank of England club' and reported that a gaggle of journalists had suggested to Chapman that he 'must have had a horseshoe in his pocket during the final'. The *Gazette* had picked up on the vibe. 'Lucky Arsenal' had bought themselves some silverware. The taunts became louder and more monotonous as the new decade progressed. 'The jealousy of other clubs sometimes frightened me,' admitted George Male. But Chapman stuck doggedly to his beliefs and his system, and would soon make Arsenal the most talked about team in world football.

# Bolts From The Blue

*'David beat Goliath. The match will go down in history as the biggest surprise ever, and a glorious Red-Letter day for Walsall.'* Islington Gazette, *January 1933.*

*'Many clubs have been jealous of Arsenal's rise. In their jealousy these clubs have forgotten what the Arsenal have done for the game.' Jimmy Catton, writing in* Athletic News, *1938.*

USING the FA Cup victory as a springboard, Arsenal surged to the league title during the 1930/31 campaign. They won their opening five games, came out on top in 25 of their 42 matches, gained a record 66 points and scored an enormous 127 goals. Bastin, Lambert, Jack and Hulme hit the back of the net a whopping 111 times between them. Arsenal hit their peak in November. Already top of the table, they ran out 5-2 winners over nearest challengers Aston Villa in front of over 56,000 at Highbury. Joe Hulme recalled, 'The way that Davie [Jack] and Jackie [Lambert] worked together, and used the space was so clever. And against a great team like the Villa too.'

A few days later, the Arsenal team flew over the Channel and they played Racing Club de Paris. The match was arranged to raise money for World War One veterans. It put Arsenal on the map. George Male recalled, 'Some of the boys weren't too keen on flying. Davie Jack didn't especially like it, and nor did [goalkeeper] Charlie Preedy. Herbert Chapman allowed them to have a drink or two to calm their nerves. Chapman always said that it would be a great opportunity for the team to see a different style of play.'

Soaring, soaring Arsenal crushed Racing 7-2 on a French public holiday, with Lambert netting four goals, while Chapman ran the line because the linesman fell ill. A gaggle of European journalists were present and correct to drool over the sheer potency of Arsenal's forward play. News of their successes spread beyond France in the 1930s.

The only downside of an almost faultless season came when the reigning FA Cup holders were dumped out in the fifth round by Chelsea at Stamford Bridge in front of over 62,000. It was one of the only times Chapman lost his cool. Hulme recalled, 'Chapman yelled and screamed instructions at us, but no one could hear what he was trying to say because it was so noisy. That meant that he got hotter under the collar.'

The Gunners bounced back almost immediately and thumped Grimsby 9-1, before finally securing the title against Liverpool in late April when goals from Bastin, Jack and Lambert enabled Arsenal to fight back from having been 1-0 down. To some, Arsenal's style of play was like football from another planet. Bernard Joy wrote, 'It was 20th century, terse, exciting, spectacular, economic, devastating.' Hulme looked back, 'There wasn't a better team than our 30/31 side. We were quick, fast paced, scored lots of goals…brilliant. What could be better?'

Hulme revelled in Arsenal's no nonsense style, but as Tom Parker explained, the Gunners' approach wasn't to everyone's taste, "Where are the dribblers Tom? Where are they? Where is the style and the grace?"' Parker would be asked. 'I'd get that all the time. Others in the game hated our lack of dribbling.'

Arsenal's critics suggested that they were too mechanical. Brian Glanville wrote that the team quickly 'approached the precision of a machine'. A *Daily Mail* article claimed that Chapman 'was the first manager who set out methodically to organise the winning of matches'.

Arsenal perfected the art of the 'ten-second goal'. George Male, who broke into the side in that first title-winning season reeled it off, 'Herbie Roberts would break down the opponents' move on the edge of the box. He'd push the ball forward to Alec [James]. Straight away, he'd look up and do his level best to find Joe Hulme, who'd sprint onwards, and get the ball to Cliff [Bastin] or Davie [Jack]. Or sometimes, Bastin himself would go down the other side of the pitch, and set up the forwards.'

Bastin later spoke of the utter simplicity of the system, 'Because of the passes of Alec James and David Jack, the ball beats the half-back and I merely have to collect it.' It was a slick, ultra-modern, art deco form of football.

Off the pitch, Chapman embraced change, invention, and creativity. Anything to give his club an edge. As the crowds poured into Highbury, gate money was reinvested in bricks and mortar and the construction of the east and west stands, which made Highbury the most modern stadium in the country, and attracted a more well-heeled punter (known as the Eton Set), who could afford to shell out for a spot of luxury in the cocktail lounge.

The Highbury clock was installed (although not the 45-minute model which Chapman had initially sought), white sleeves were added to red shirts in the belief that this improved players' peripheral vision, and new-fangled fitness facilities were bought to enable the Arsenal players to stay in peak condition. The rebranding of Gillespie Road tube station to Arsenal put the club on the map, quite literally, although whether Chapman – as had often been claimed – was directly responsible for the name change is open to conjecture.

On 10 December 1932 Arsenal hammered Chelsea 4-1 at Highbury, the day on which the East Stand was opened. Henry Norris had correctly predicted that the growing suburbs would continue to supply Arsenal with a constantly growing pool of support. Chapman suggested that even a 70,000 capacity stadium might be insufficient. Arsenal were reaching for the stars, and beyond.

In *Athletic News*, Ronald Allen wrote, 'Arsenal are on top of the football world because they have organized the winning of football matches down to places of decimals.' That applied to the tactics board, and the balance sheet. But Allen also warned of what might happen if Arsenal hit a lean spell. 'No club can put on West End shows for ever,' he warned. 'The club with the big banks might be better off than the club with the big stands.'

It was a prescient point, given this was the time at which the world's populace was suffering the fall-out from the Great Depression. What would happen if the Arsenal machine spluttered?

Chapman's team didn't always have things their own way. They lost the 1932 FA Cup Final to Newcastle, and were pipped at the death by Everton in the league. During that 1931/32 campaign, George Male recalled Chapman 'bellowing at us in the dressing room after we lost three games in a row in December. He told us that if we didn't work harder, he'd cancel our contracts. Then he stormed out and slammed the door, leaving us in silence. I'd never seen him so tense, before or since.'

The following January in the FA Cup third round, Arsenal suffered a setback which was the nearest thing to a catastrophe during Chapman's tenure. It happened at Walsall's Fellows Park.

On 14 January 1933, the day the Government warned of 'possible surprises ahead in the current climate of economic uncertainty', no one predicted the bolt from the blue which was about to hit Arsenal. The team travelled to the Midlands perched on top of the table, while their opponents languished in tenth place in the Third Division North.

The contrast between both teams couldn't have been starker. The Walsall team cost just £69. Arsenal's side was worth £30,000. Walsall hadn't won for a month and in their entire history had only once progressed beyond the third round.

Chapman rested Hapgood, John and Lambert. The official line was that they had flu. Joe Hulme, also left out, told Brian Woolnough, 'I'd been struggling with colds for some weeks. I was run down. Chapman thought that on this occasion, I could do with some bed rest. If it had been a higher profile match, I'm convinced that he'd have played me.'

Into the team came youngsters Tommy Black, Charlie Walsh, and Billy Warnes – all making their debuts – and Norman Sidey, who had made a solitary first-team appearance up to that point.

It was precisely the right time for Walsall to attempt to spike Arsenal's guns. Chapman's side had just lost back-to-back matches in the league to Sheffield Wednesday and Sunderland, and had seen their lead at the top of the table eroded from six points to two. *The Times* sounded a note of caution, 'They should beat Walsall easily, but when there are so many strange faces, one can never tell.'

Selected for the clash, George Male recalled, 'We hadn't been at our best for a few weeks. It had been a bitter winter. But I didn't sense us being especially nervous before the match. We still had James, Bastin and Jack playing. We were confident that we would win. Everyone tells the story of Charlie Walsh putting on his boots without his socks, but to be honest, he was nervous about making his debut, not nervous so much about facing Walsall. Either way, he seemed ok when we left the dressing room.'

Down the years, it has been suggested that Walsall indulged in a type of asymmetrical warfare against their First Division opponents.

It has been alleged that Walsall narrowed the pitch and flooded it, to forcibly create a more level playing field. Neither story is true. In the *Gazette*, 'St Ivel' conceded that the quality of the Fellows Park pitch was superior to the surface at Highbury. George Male recalled, 'It was heavy going under foot, but no worse than the kind of turf you'd play on in the First Division at that time of year.'

It was also suggested that the referee allowed the Third Division side to freely indulge in strong-armed combat against their illustrious visitors. 'St Ivel' noted, 'And their tackling! At half-time there was more blood running in the Arsenal dressing room than for many a day… Walsall knew they could not beat Arsenal at pure football level and their main objective was to tackle the man in possession hard and heavy.'

In his book, Cliff Bastin claimed the referee was 'curiously lenient' and that Walsall deployed 'crude tactics'. Male refuted that suggestion. 'They were no harder than any opponent we'd usually come across on a weekly basis. There were no complaints from us about the tactics they used.'

'St Ivel' also insisted, 'When there was the slightest panic, the ball was kicked into the crowd.' Male recalled, 'Walsall never even needed to panic, because we never placed them under any kind of pressure.'

One story that is true is that in the second half, as the ground continued to fill up (as with many other clubs of that era, Walsall allowed spectators in for free in the second half), several Saddlers supporters encroached on the pitch in the latter stages. That wasn't something which the Arsenal players would have been used to, but in fairness, neither was the Walsall team. By then, the crowd was in a state of ferment over what they were watching.

Tactically, Walsall were superb that afternoon, and probed for weaknesses in Arsenal's newcomers. Hapgood's replacement Black struggled to cope with the pace and directness of Walsall winger Coward. James and Jack made precious little headway against the resolute backline. Warnes and Sidey were subdued. Twice in the first half, homegrown hero Gilbert Alsop forced goalkeeper Frank Moss into smart saves. The Gunners appeared to pull their game together after the break as Walsh and Jack both missed good opportunities. But as *The Times* noted, the Walsall keeper was 'by no means overworked'.

With an hour gone, Alsop headed Walsall into the lead. He recalled, 'We had a corner and their full-back Black was marking me. He didn't get up. The ball was just a big plum pudding that day and I headed it off my forehead straight into the corner of the net.'

Five minutes later, Black yanked down the irrepressible Alsop in the Arsenal box and Sheppard made it 2-0 to the hosts. 'The crowd was wild,' recalled George Male. 'They could sense blood early on because we were very slow and laboured. I think that we missed Joey Hulme's pace. Walsall were always comfortable.'

When the final whistle went, the crowd invaded the pitch, and carried off their jubilant players shoulder high. Male recalled the Arsenal players being 'utterly silent in the dressing room. No one said a word. I think that we were in a state of shock.' None more so than Herbert Chapman.

When news filtered back to London about the defeat, Hulme recalled 'lying in bed for a few minutes, almost unable to comprehend what had happened'. Chapman acted swiftly and ruthlessly. Although couching his words carefully in the *Gazette* ('I was disappointed about the penalty'), he vented his fury at the miscreant – the reckless Tommy Black – on the train journey home, informing him that he wasn't welcome back in north London.

Within a week, Black was sold to Plymouth. Walsh was shipped out to Norwich within three weeks and Warnes went to Brentford during the close-season. Hulme summed it up, 'Chapman had high standards. He felt that those three hadn't met them, and that was that.' Intriguingly, Male commented, 'I don't know whether Chapman felt more annoyed at the team for losing, or himself for changing players around.'

Huge shock though it was, on the face of it the Walsall defeat didn't greatly change things. Arsenal, with their Fellows Park absentees immediately restored to the starting line-up, immediately regained their composure in the league and went on to secure their second title under Chapman. But the manager, perhaps concerned at the lack of depth in the squad, fearful that his team might suffer another Walsall-style giant-killing, or wary that both Jack and James were approaching their 30th birthdays, informed director George Allison, 'We must rebuild.'

Perhaps he feared that his team was lacking robustness. It is telling that the two players he earmarked for signing in late 1933 – Southampton's bullish striker Ted Drake and Leeds's 'iron man' full-back Wilf Copping – were known for their physical approach.

Drake, who joined the club in 1934, recalled, 'There was a definite sense among the players that it wasn't quite the same after Walsall. They'd made such rapid progress, and things had gone so swimmingly. Then they lost it [the match]. Alec James reckoned the Arsenal crowd had become spoilt by success, and expected more and more from the team. It was like Liverpool in the 1980s. Some years they'd win the league, but it wasn't seen as a vintage year. That was how it started to go with Arsenal. Perhaps the crowd thought that the big-name players like Alec weren't quite the force they'd been. Maybe they got a bit bored with the style of play. The Walsall defeat showed that the players weren't super humans after all. The crowd at home matches got more critical.'

So did the gentlemen of the press. Even before the Walsall defeat, their headlines had gradually become sharper and more cutting. The 'Lucky Arsenal' label became more firmly attached. By all accounts Arsenal had been fortunate to reach Wembley a year before, following a 1-0 win over Manchester City. The reports of the match were vicious. 'Did City commit any crime against football law that deserved this extreme punishment? Were they any less skilled in the finer arts of play than Arsenal? The answer of 40,000 of you is a most emphatic "no,"' wrote James Freeman in the *Daily Mail*.

The *Daily Express* suggested that the Gunners might now 'win the Grand National and the Boat Race' given the good fortune which came their way. Arsenal players grew more wary of the press. Male recalled, 'Some of us stopped talking to journalists. They were fickle. Talking you up one week, and putting you down the next. That, I suppose, was part and parcel of being an Arsenal player. But from what I gathered, no other club received such – well – aggressive headlines from football writers.'

The shockwaves from the giant-killing could easily have destabilised the club. This, after all, was the competition which had confirmed Arsenal's emergence as a major force in the game. Chairman Sir Samuel Hill-Wood told Jimmy Catton, 'There is a glamour about the cup which time, with all its change, has never reduced.' Tom Parker added, 'Lifting the cup is the most glorious moment any football captain can enjoy.'

Even the royal family looked on in fascination. At the 1932 FA Cup Final, the Queen asked the age of 'Boy' Bastin. When informed that he was only 18, the Queen responded, 'It is extraordinary that a boy so young should play so well.'

If the archived correspondence in the Islington Library is anything to go by, the club was inundated with requests from local dignitaries before cup finals for extra tickets, and requests to meet the players. In 1932, the Islington town clerk wrote several begging letters to the club requesting an extra ticket for the Mayor of Manchester.

Local officials used FA Cup Final tickets as personal leverage with the great and the good. Drake explained, 'You were massively in the public eye. Politicians, singers, actors, everyone wanted to make your acquaintance. It was probably because league games, compared to today, were so low-key. But the cup final was an international event. It gave players commercial opportunities.'

These were helpful to an Arsenal board stymied by the era of the maximum wage. Alex James worked as a sports demonstrator in Selfridges, rubbing shoulders with the likes of Suzanne Lenglen and transatlantic flyer Amy Johnson. David Jack received a tidy sum for advertising Afrikander Mixture (Flake or Shag) tobacco. Arsenal circumnavigated the maximum wage by setting up these kinds of opportunities for their players.

Losing to Walsall could prove seriously bad for business, so Chapman started looking at ways to construct a Mark 3 Arsenal team by putting tabs on Copping and Drake, even though his team won the league in 1933, and were top of the league by the following Christmas. But Chapman never had a chance to upgrade the squad because he died in early January 1934.

Already suffering from a cold, pneumonia set in after Herbert Chapman travelled to Guildford to watch the third team play. He died at 3am on Saturday 6 January, the day of Arsenal's home match with Sheffield Wednesday. It was so quick. So unexpected. The players, who had seen the boss just a few days earlier, were stunned.

George Male was walking to Upton Park station when he saw the newspaper billboard which read, 'Herbert Chapman Dead'. 'I just stopped and kept re-reading it. I couldn't comprehend it.' Joe Hulme recalled 'having the wind knocked out of me. It felt like the end of the world.'

Football rumbled on. As word spread among the supporters filtering into Highbury that afternoon, the 45,000 crowd became increasingly subdued. The players wore black armbands and four trumpeters sounded the 'Last Post' as the crowd stood to attention. Jimmy Dunne, one of Chapman's final signings, scored Arsenal's goal in a 1-1 draw which Male claimed to 'remember absolutely nothing about'. Chapman's favourite (football) sons – Jack, Hulme, Hapgood, Lambert, Bastin and James – bore his coffin at the funeral. The card on the team's wreath read, 'To the boss from the players. Our hearts are sad and hopes well-nigh shattered, but your inspiration, memory, and affection remain ours forever.'

Reserve team manager Joe Shaw was appointed as caretaker manager until the end of the 1933/34 season. Often airbrushed from history, the former Woolwich Arsenal player, who'd made over 300 appearances for the club and whom George Male remembered as an 'excellent organiser and an astute tactician', deserves enormous credit for stabilising the club as Arsenal went on to win a second title in a row. But despite Shaw's aptitude for the role, he was never going to be given it on a full-time basis.

Arsenal defeated Luton in the FA Cup and attracted a monstrous 68,000 crowd to Highbury that month for the north London derby.

They lost, and didn't win for the rest of the month. The club needed to stabilise. They appointed director George Allison to succeed Chapman. Allison's connections were mind-boggling. No wonder that arch networker Henry Norris admired Allison so much, but whereas Norris's contacts were mainly London-based, Allison's were national and international.

An acquaintance of US media magnate William Randolph Hearst (Allison had worked for him in the early 20th century), European royalty, Hollywood star Douglas Fairbanks Jr and music hall performer Gracie Fields, it was in no small part down to Allison that Arsenal's profile on radio and newsreel had been so high.

Male recalled, 'George was always bringing some famous person or another to the ground. I suppose it was quite a show business style of working for the time.'

When he was appointed manager, he said, 'I state frankly that I intend to follow his [Chapman's] principles as far as I can.'

Goalkeeper George Swindin claimed, 'What George [Allison] knew about the game, you could put on the back of a very small postage stamp.' But Allison was clever in other ways, adopting a largely non-interference policy, happy to build on Chapman's legacy.

He delegated the training and fitness to Tom Whittaker, who took care of the day-to-day management and welfare of the players, and trainer Joe Shaw. Allison also used the scouting network (constructed by Chapman after Norris's fall from grace) and his own contacts in the game and within the media to constantly monitor players whom Chapman had previously earmarked.

He proved an excellent and persuasive negotiator when it came to tying up deals for Chapman's targets. His first signing was Ted Drake, whom Southampton had refused to release until their promotion was guaranteed. Drake recalled Allison as 'a genial and charming man, who did an excellent sales pitch on Arsenal'. The defence was also in need of some urgent rebuilding. In came Jack Crayston from Bradford Park Avenue, and Leeds United's granite-hewn Wilf Copping.

Nicknamed 'Beauty and the Beast', they proved a potent and utterly reliable pair of full-backs throughout the rest of the 1930s. In Copping and Drake especially, Arsenal now had the harder edge which Chapman had targeted. It was effectively Chapman's Mark 3

Arsenal team. Except Chapman wasn't around anymore. Old soldiers faded out. Jack Lambert – Arsenal's most criminally underrated player of any era – departed. David Jack embarked on a management career.

Joe Hulme began to get injured more and more. 'I ended up playing less games every season,' he recalled. 'All those kickings down the years started to take their toll.' There was still Alex James though. Like Hulme, the little man's injuries ('Alec's ankles were permanently black. The only way anyone could stop him was by kicking him, and he didn't get the protection from referees,' explained Ted Drake) stacked up, but on his day, he could still weave his magic.

Allison was no pushover when it came to disciplining players. Drake recalled Allison threatening to drop him after he had scored a brace against Derby early in his career, because the manager felt he was too self-satisfied with his performance. Male said that Allison favoured 'pulling players to one side and giving them quiet reminders about their responsibilities to the club'.

Arsenal stormed to the title in 1934 and they completed their championship hat-trick in 1935. The fearless Drake scored a barely credible 42 goals that season. Against each of Birmingham, Chelsea and Wolves he scored four times as Arsenal finished four points ahead of nearest challengers Sunderland.

Bastin also continued to plunder goals with aplomb, and James pulled the strings in midfield. But more and more, the focus of attention shifted to Drake. In 1992 Drake told me, 'My job was to put my head where no one else dared to. My headache would be gone by the morning, but the memory of scoring the goal would live with me forever.'

It is a quotation which hopefully sums up Drake best, and is now preserved for posterity on the outside of the Emirates Stadium where Drake has taken his place as one of Arsenal's 32 greatest players.

Images from the time show Drake having sustained various knocks in the line of duty; gashes to his head, knee injuries, concussion, broken toes. 'Ted would get knocked about from pillar to post during games,' recalled Male. 'Normally, he'd just bounce off those kind of challenges, because he was built like a middleweight boxer. But not even Ted's head was made of concrete!'

Goalkeeper George Swindin explained, 'I loved Ted. He'd do anything to score, and secured my win bonuses on many an occasion. As a Yorkshireman who liked to watch his pennies, I can't tell you how good that made me feel. I even bought Ted a beer once, just to show him how grateful I was.'

In *Athletic News*, Jimmy Catton wrote, 'Drake's career is already a romance. In five months he has made a meteoric advance from what was obscurity to become England's centre-forward and one of the star players in the game.'

'But not everyone appreciated Drake's style at Arsenal – even on his own team,' explained Swindin. 'There were some – without naming names – who reckoned he was a bit of a brainless bull.'

Swindin is probably referring to Cliff Bastin. There was an enmity which existed between Drake and Bastin. When I interviewed Drake in the early 1990s, he mentioned that he and Bastin didn't see eye to eye, muttering that 'Cliff had said one or two things down the years'. Drake was presumably referring to comments in Bastin's autobiography, co-written with Brian Glanville in 1950. For its day it was hard-hitting. Bastin makes some occasionally withering assessments of former team-mates.

Alex James, readers were informed, 'hadn't made the best of educational opportunities which were afforded to him'. Bastin also referred to the Scot's 'aggressive self-esteem'. Hulme's tomfoolery 'was largely designed, I feel, to cover up and drive away his nervous misgivings'. Drake fared worst of all. 'I did not consider him as good a centre-forward as Jack Lambert. Jack was more of a footballer, and his style of play fitted in much better with my own than did Ted's. Ted, on the other hand, took the centre of the field as his lawful preserve. When he received the ball, he would charge straight down the middle, taking it, and often the attendant centre half, with him.'

In other words, Bastin considered Drake a 'crasher' – which was the popular phrase at the time – or the 'brainless bull' which George Swindin referred to. Worse, Bastin claimed Drake 'would take it [the ball] virtually off my foot as I was about to shoot'. Bastin's nose had been pushed out of joint by Drake's arrival and he believed the new signing's presence was – style-wise – a retrograde step for the team. Egos were easily bruised in the Arsenal dressing room.

In 1934, George Allison signed Bobby Davidson from St Johnstone, a stocky little winger nicknamed 'the new Alex James'. On the same day, James scored a hat-trick against Sheffield Wednesday, his only one in Arsenal colours. The story went (although it was denied later by James) that James strode into the dressing room afterwards and yelled, 'That'll teach them to sign anyone in my place.' Now in his 30s, time was ticking for the Scot, and supporters around the country did their level best to see him before the Highbury icon faded from view.

Record figures continued to pack grounds around the country when the Arsenal dream team came to town. In their natty, customised train carriage – complete with silver spoon waiter service and comfortable reclining seats – Arsenal players could relax in comfort as they travelled north. They often needed to be ready for the roughest of receptions. 'It could be difficult – especially at Middlesbrough, Sunderland and Newcastle,' recalled George Male. 'It was a jealousy thing. Our players would receive a terrible barracking.'

Drake explained, 'Some of the abuse we received, especially near the touchline, was quite alarming. There would be swearing, objects thrown at our players, and I think we showed admirable restraint not to wade into the crowd and get stuck in. Wilf Copping would sometimes suggest that the offending fan met him after the game outside the ground at a certain time. They never showed up. I think they were wise not to.'

Most isolated was goalkeeper George Swindin who, during the long periods of inactivity at his end, suffered endless verbal taunts. 'I found fans in Liverpool to be very sporting, but not those in Manchester or the north-east. "Get back to London, you flashy Cockney so and sos" was the general message. The others said it got worse after Chapman died. Perhaps it was because neutral supporters respected him in a way they didn't respect George Allison. I don't know, but even I noticed it got worse in the late 1930s.'

The Arsenal team continued to be the opposite of 'flash' and 'Cockney'. The new signings lived conservative lives. Jack Crayston carried the Bible around with him wherever he travelled, and Copping's only vice was to slip away from the team hotel on away games for a quiet Guinness. The verbal abuse was probably to do with Arsenal's style of play. More direct and abrasive than under Chapman, other sides had begun to copy Arsenal's Mark 3 style, except their variation wasn't as successful. Inferior copies looked ugly and crude, and Arsenal were blamed. This led to a vigorous defence in *Athletic News* from Jimmy Catton, 'Arsenal put football on the social map. People talked about going to see them play as they would about the Varsity Rugby match. They converted the crowds from rugby to soccer. Arsenal brought bright new moves to the field of play – or at least dished out old ones in a new way.'

The silverware continued to flood in and Arsenal's unparalleled ability to win when they had to was never better demonstrated than in the 1935/36 campaign. The Gunners trudged to their worst league position since 1930, ending up in sixth place, eight points behind champions Sunderland.

That campaign's most famous match came at Villa Park in front of 70,000 with Drake's seven-goal haul making headlines. 'Honestly – I was very lucky that day,' Drake told me. 'It's the kind of day that any striker dreams of, where your team-mates put chance after chance on a plate for you. And although what happened was – I suppose – noteworthy, I look back with only casual interest because we didn't win the league that season.'

Decimated by injuries and player fatigue, George Allison became the first top flight manager in years to be punished by the Football League for fielding an under-strength side as he rested stars including Drake (persistent cartilage problems) and Eddie Hapgood (thigh injury) in order to ensure they remained fit for FA Cup ties; the club's only chance of silverware that season.

James's position in the team was no longer certain as he struggled to overcome the rheumatism which sapped the energy from his legs. The Scot assumed the 'elder statesman' role but he didn't always set the team a good example. Drake commented, 'Alec had a great eye for the game, and when the mood took him, he could cajole the team, but he could also do the exact opposite, and retreat into his shell. In training, he liked to do what he pleased, and over the years, Herbert Chapman and George Allison indulged him in a way they wouldn't have with anyone else. That occasionally irritated the other players.'

During the 1935/36 season there was evidence that Allison was beginning to trust the Scot's eye for spotting players, and James was dispatched on a few scouting missions by the club. His Barnet home was also regarded as something of an open house by young players like the Compton brothers and he regularly asked his wife Peggy 'to cook the boys a steak', but in early 1936 he wasn't even assured a starting place alongside several of the club's emerging youngsters.

The team's goal supply began to dry up. Allison urged his Gunners to seek FA Cup glory and the Wembley trail began with a 5-1 hammering of Bristol Rovers in the ice at Eastville. James missed out, and Preston were linked with a move for their former talisman.

Three weeks later, as the team prepared to take on Liverpool at Anfield in the fourth round, Allison pitched him back in. James later admitted that if he hadn't been restored to the starting line-up he would have known his Arsenal career was over. It was a hugely significant moment and after knocking Liverpool out, the Gunners swept past Newcastle, Barnsley, and Grimsby (courtesy of another Cliff Bastin semi-final goal), with James receiving rave reviews for his performances.

On the morning of the FA Cup Final against Second Division Sheffield United, Allison made the shock decision to replace Eddie Hapgood with James as captain; a slight which Hapgood never forgot. Allison never explained or justified his choice to journalists (or the team, according to George Male), but it seemed to be a reward to James for his sterling performances on the Wembley trail.

It was perhaps a piece of James man-management similar to that used by Herbert Chapman six years earlier before the 1930 Birmingham FA Cup replay, where he had appealed to James's sense of duty to the team to bring him back into the fold. James's elevation to the captaincy appealed to both his ego and the 'aggressive self-esteem' which Bastin mentioned in his book.

The final against Sheffield United was a dour struggle, with the Blades on top for long spells. The decisive moment – and the only moment of real clarity in the match – arrived in the 70th minute as Drake sidestepped United captain Taylor to fire home the only goal. Drake – who was barely walking by that stage due to a cartilage problem – recalled hearing James bark, 'Go on Ted, bury it,' as he prepared to shoot. The captain's instruction worked, and James had the privilege of carrying the FA Cup around Wembley afterwards, to the delight of the Arsenal fans who stayed on to celebrate.

The party at the Café Royal that evening saw James at his ebullient best. Male recalled, 'All the players were there with their wives, and Alec was absolutely bubbling with enthusiasm.' But there was a poignancy to the party. The disappointing 1936/37 season, where Arsenal ended the campaign empty-handed, was to be Alex James's last year at the club.

The 1937/38 title season was arguably Arsenal's most remarkable success of that era. Male recalled, 'I did an interview at the start of the season, where I suggested that we were some way off winning the league. George Allison wasn't best pleased. He pulled me into his office and told me not to be so defeatist. But I just couldn't see how the team was good for much more, to be honest.'

There weren't even any major signings in the close-season to boost expectation levels. Youngsters including the Compton brothers, Reg Lewis, and Alf Kirchen were given their chance in the starting line-up but Drake explained, 'I didn't hold out any chance for us, not without Alex James in midfield. To my mind, the quality of player just wasn't there.'

But, in what proved to be a freakish First Division campaign where just 16 points separated top from bottom (the previous year's champions Manchester City were relegated), Arsenal prevailed despite losing 11 times that campaign, an unusually high number of matches.

After Arsenal went six games without winning in October and November, Charlie Buchan had written in the *Daily Mail*, 'Their decline is one of the surprise features of an amazing season and one that is most unwelcome. The game cannot afford to have a poor Arsenal because there is no other team capable of supplanting them just now.'

As if to confirm their fall from grace, Drake's list of injuries grew. He was hospitalised in October after being knocked out at Brentford. 'Drake has been so often in the Royal Northern Hospital that he almost needs a permanent bed there to use whenever necessary,' explained Allison.

The flesh may have been weak but the spirit was still willing. Arsenal clawed themselves back into the title race, eventually finishing two points ahead of nearest challengers Wolves, who had begun the season in magnificent form but fell at the final hurdle. The 40,000 who watched Arsenal's final home fixture knew that if the Molineux side won their match, they would secure the title. But when a steward at the front of the East Stand raised a white flag, Arsenal players dropped to their knees in celebration and were carried off the pitch. It had been a draining experience.

Drake explained, 'I didn't think I could play after that. We got through the latter stages of the campaign on adrenalin alone.' Cliff Bastin, already losing his hearing, confessed to needing further time off at the start of the following campaign, 'I needed to get away from the thought of football. It tires the brain. I suppose I'm not thinking quite so quickly as I was 12 months ago. It's not a question of losing interest in the game. It's a matter of snap.'

George Swindin remembered that Allison gave him three days off in the title run to 'go fishing in the middle of nowhere. The pressure of winning, as you live through it, can be enormous.'

'They have not always played like champions. They owe their success mainly to their wonderful defensive power and ability to keep the other fellows out,' concluded the *Daily Mail*. Arsenal couldn't have dug any deeper into their mental reserves. But all good things were about to come to a juddering end.

Arsenal's huge gates during the title winning campaign (they averaged over 50,000 per match) meant they generated a profit of £30,000 during the season.

The Bank of England club pulled out a gargantuan £14,000 wedge and spent big for one last time, securing the services of the Wolves midfielder Bryn Jones. Allison claimed his signature 'would fill the gap which we never filled after the departure of James. It will create a new future for the club.' Instead, it created a whole lot of trouble for Allison.

Jones's huge transfer fee was even discussed in the Houses of Parliament. Several leading journalists of the era claimed that the fee might never have been exceeded. In September 2001, the *Observer Sport Monthly* included Jones in their ten biggest wastes of money in football history list and calculated that, allowing for inflation, he would have cost around £28m in modern money.

A nippy, pacy player who had performed well in a decent Wolves side, the Welshman endured a rough first season at Highbury as his new club tailed off in sixth place in the league. He was in good company. Alex James and David Jack had also suffered from a loss of form in their first seasons at Highbury as they adapted to a new system and a demanding set of supporters.

Whereas Jack simply scowled his way through his bad spell, and James remained brazen and – at least outwardly – cheerful, Jones took things to heart. The Highbury crowd soon turned on him. George Male recalled, 'Bryn would come in at half-time or at the end of the match in his early days, and he'd be shaking. "They hate me, they hate me."'

George Swindin claimed, 'He was never comfortable with the fee. At Wolves, he was the lynchpin in their midfield, but with us, he needed to fit in to our style. I felt sorry for him, because George Allison needed to buy other players who could fit in with Bryn.'

Whereas Alex James had initially dwelt on the ball for too long, Jones seemed anxious to pass to a team-mate as soon as he received, and stopped making the incisive runs which had put him on Arsenal's radar in the first place. 'Bryn played hot potato with the ball,' recalled Drake. 'He stopped playing his natural game.'

Jones made all the right noises in his newspaper column, explaining how he had turned down an approach from Tottenham 12 months earlier to sign for the Gunners, and that, much as he respected James as a player, 'Don't expect me to do his tricks. They were his copyright.'

But the fans were unforgiving. Jones was dropped from Arsenal's first team in a bid to pull him out of the limelight. Expecting to run out in front of the proverbial one man and his dog at a reserve game, Jones was astonished to see that 33,000 had turned up – simply out of curiosity to see how the world's most expensive player coped in these surroundings. 'Bryn could never find a hiding place from the fact that he cost so much,' added Male.

Allison was unable to cajole the player through 'footballer speak' – as Chapman might have done. Neither did he restructure the midfield in order to maximise Jones's talents. The signing suggested that the Bank of England club had grown wasteful and careless with its considerable cash reserves. It lent further credence to the view held by Hapgood and Swindin that Allison had simply clutched on to Chapman's coat tails when he got the job, scooped up a few trophies, and trusted his luck, before the inevitable passage of time meant that the remnants of the Chapman era, player by player, faded away. Harsh though it may be (after all – who could replace Chapman?) there are several elements of truth in that appraisal.

It is ironic – although entirely apt – that the club's final public act of the decade was an appearance on the silver screen. Allison may have known precious little about football tactics but he did know how to garner publicity. In the 1930s, silent star Buster Keaton visited Highbury, as did music hall duo Flanagan and Allan. Thanks to Allison's Hollywood connections, Jean Harlow and Mary Pickford also met the players in the decade.

'Ah yes Mary Pickford,' laughed Drake. 'She was a real stunner, and when she came to Highbury she had some shots taken with the players. As I recall, she was quite taken with Eddie Hapgood.'

In 1938, Allison was approached by G & S Films to see if he was willing to allow the production company to come to Highbury to film *The Arsenal Stadium Mystery*, based on a novel by Leonard Gribble. Allison virtually bit G & S's hands off, especially when he realised that Inspector Slade – who finally cracks the case – was to be played by his old friend Leslie Banks. Several of the players were more interested in the filthy lucre on offer, and the prospect of working with Hollywood siren Greta Gynt.

Drake recalled, 'George called all of us into the changing room one day – he did have a lovely calm voice on him did George – and he said, "Now look chaps. We've had an offer from this film company who want to make *The Arsenal Stadium Mystery*. It's a nice little thriller, and there is an opening for any of you chaps who want to make a few bob over the summer." In those days, you weren't paid as much during the summer months as for the rest of the year. So we said, "How much, boss?" And he said £50 a week. Well – there was nearly a riot in there. The most any of us earned was £8 a week.'

The story was based around a mythical friendly match between Arsenal and the Trojans. One of the Trojans players is poisoned at half-time, and collapses and dies on the pitch. The culprit, as it turns out, is the Trojans manager.

Interspersed between the unfolding drama is bona fide football action. Visitors Brentford, who played their league game at Highbury on 6 May 1939, sportingly wore an unfamiliar black and white strip in order to simulate the Trojans. Alf Kirchen's and Ted Drake's goals, which gave Arsenal a 2-0 win, are therefore preserved on the film – a rare thing indeed for the 1930s.

Several scenes were shot within the marble halls and Highbury's dressing rooms, and the rest was shot at Elstree Studios. George Allison's acting was a bit on the wooden side but Bryn Jones was unable to escape the burden of his transfer fee, even on celluloid. 'He cost as much as the war,' claimed the voice which introduces the Arsenal players.

Arsenal's 2-0 win over Brentford, now part of celluloid legend, was the team's last first-class game for six years. After seeing their names up in neon lights throughout the 1930s the Gunners had now become box office themselves.

Arsenal had become respected, renowned and admired, but it would be an exaggeration to suggest they were universally loved. Their style, built on pace, power and clinical accuracy, scientifically boiled down winning to the absolute essentials. It wasn't graceful or aesthetic enough for purists. Chapman and then Allison had cut to the chase and hit their targets in what was Arsenal's most gilded era.

Three games into the 1939/40 campaign, league football was suspended as World War Two broke out and Arsenal's three victories were expunged from the records. By the time Arsenal next prepared for a league match, they were a far more down-at-heel operation. The Bank vaults were about to slam shut.

The age of austerity had arrived.

# Victory Through Austerity

*'They are said to be lucky too and it may well be that the mischievous imp who lives at Wembley will this time join forces with the south.'* The Times *assesses Arsenal's chances prior to the 1950 FA Cup Final against Liverpool.*

*'After the Burnley game, it was like everyone's legs had gone. We'd literally given everything we had to the season and to the club.' George Swindin, speaking about Arsenal winning the league in 1953.*

THE Arsenal players who regrouped in time for the 1946/47 campaign got a nasty shock when they received news about their salaries. George Male recalled, 'We were informed that our pay would be cut from £8 per week, the 1939 level – to £7 per week. So it was more than a ten per cent cut, and less than we were being paid six years earlier!'

It's fortunate that players from that era weren't overly money orientated. Financially, Arsenal were entering a period of retrenchment.

Highbury had been badly damaged during World War Two. Part of the Clock End terrace had been deemed unsafe after a German bomb landed on the adjoining practice pitch in 1940. At the opposite Laundry End, incendiaries had fallen through the roof and set fire to the tarpaulin sheets which lay beneath. The resulting blaze meant the roof was completely destroyed, and lay in a crumpled heap on the terracing below.

Locals, who had suffered damage to their houses during the Luftwaffe raids, mucked in to help repair some of the damage, but the Gunners were forced to decamp to White Hart Lane for a year and play their home games there. Starved of matchday income since 1939, the club was an estimated £150,000 in debt. Herbert Chapman's boast in the early 1930s of 'we can afford to pay £2,000 more for a player than any other club' belonged to a bygone era.

Several of the Arsenal players who returned from the war felt frustrated about missed opportunities. Ted Drake, whose career was in limbo following a spinal injury sustained during a wartime match, recalled, 'I knew many people who didn't survive the war and I'm grateful that I did. But it did stop my career in full flow. I was 27 when war was declared. I was in my prime. I'd scored 126 goals for Arsenal in around five years. I often wonder if I might have beaten Bastin's record if I'd been able to play in the early 40s.'

Drake never played again for Arsenal. Goalkeeper George Swindin, now in his early 30s, explained, 'I'd missed so much playing time. It didn't give me a lot of patience with time wasters or slackers.'

George Allison needed to rebuild his team. Urgently. When the 1946/47 season began, a 6-1 debacle at Molineux gave some indication that their eclectic mix of veterans like Male, Swindin and Bastin and youth team products (the Compton brothers and striker Reg Lewis) might struggle to acclimatise to the post-war landscape. The Gunners didn't win for five matches, and triumphed in just four of their opening 18 games.

An immediate post-war relegation appeared the grimmest of realities, despite the huge crowds which piled into the ground. Then Allison, ably assisted by his redoubtable right-hand man Tom Whittaker, pulled a masterstroke, signing a 32-year-old Everton centre-half whose career appeared to be over, and a 35-year-old striker from Second Division Fulham whose manager claimed it was 'about time he was put out to pasture with all the other old nags'.

Joe Mercer's creaking knees and Ronnie Rooke's hulking frame would save Arsenal from relegation in the 1946/47 season, and a whole lot more besides…

Mercer arrived in late November, following a 4-2 reverse at Anfield, in another defensive horror show. A title winner with Everton in the final season before the war, he had served as a sergeant major in the army before damaging his cartilage when resuming playing.

The player was forced to pay for the operation to remove his cartilage himself as Everton manager Theo Kelly refused to believe that Mercer was injured. Mercer approached Tom Whittaker after Everton had beaten Arsenal 3-2 at Goodison Park earlier in the season. After looking at the joint for a few seconds, Whittaker informed the Arsenal players that they had 'played against ten men', such was the poor state of the joint.

After a few months of covert negotiations, Whittaker convinced Allison that Mercer, his love for the game undiminished, could bring stability and organisation to Arsenal's frequently shambolic backline. For the princely sum of £9,000 (around £400,000 in today's money), Mercer became an Arsenal player. The final insult handed out by Kelly was to hand-deliver Mercer's boots to him at the station so that Mercer wouldn't need to bid his Everton team-mates farewell.

Mercer, widely considered to be the most even tempered man in football, barked, 'I'll prove you wrong Theo, if it's the last thing I do,' as he prepared to board the train south.

Kelly laughed contemptuously, informing the local press, 'Mercer's career is over. He won't last six months at Arsenal.' Mercer stayed at Highbury for nigh-on eight years. He made his debut in a 2-2 draw with Bolton the day after he signed for the Gunners.

Immediately, explained George Swindin, 'There was far more shape to the backline. Joe shouted at them. He encouraged them. He praised them. He cajoled them better than I ever could. He was the glue which stuck them together.'

Rooke lumbered into town a fortnight later. There are numerous colourful descriptions of the former RAF physical trainer by former team-mates. He looked like a gangster. He could easily have passed for the third Kray twin. He was at least two stones overweight when he arrived.

His glare could turn men to stone. He barely knew his own strength. George Male recalled, 'I didn't really think that Ronnie was Arsenal material at first. But the chap never stopped scoring.'

On his debut, Rooke stopped Arsenal's rot, plundering the winner on a quagmire of a Highbury pitch against Charlton to give his new side a 1-0 victory. The tide, and the mood of the club, had changed.

Mercer became one of the game's first 'commuter-footballers'. During those tense final few months at Everton, Mercer's father-in-law had brought him into his flourishing grocery business. It wasn't that he especially enjoyed the work (he had practically run out of the shop door at 2pm each day when his shift ended) but Mercer was convinced that his football career was entering its final phase, so he wanted a trade to fall back on.

George Allison allowed Mercer to keep a hand in on the Wallasey-based business — aware that without such an agreement, Mercer wouldn't have ventured south. It was another way of Arsenal getting around the maximum wage. Whittaker also agreed that Mercer could remain in the north-west during the week and train with Liverpool, joining his new colleagues for weekend matches and midweek clashes as required.

It seemed inconceivable that this part-time footballer would prove to be anything other than a short-term stop-gap for Arsenal but Allison's gamble paid off. When he was first introduced to his team-mates, Allison announced, to the amusement of the players and Mercer himself, 'Joe will usually join us only on a Friday for weekend games, as he is too old and past it to train all week.'

With rationing still in place for many items, Mercer occasionally treated his team-mates. Reg Lewis recalled, 'He wasn't a black market dealer by any means, but when it came to kids' birthdays, Joe could supply you with a sprinkling of sugar for cakes, and he could oblige special requests for scented soaps for wives' birthdays and things like that. Sometimes, he'd bring sweets with him.'

Players teased Mercer about his knobbly knees, and his bandy legs, which became even skinnier after muscle wastage following his knee injury.

After Tom Whittaker delivered the team talk prior to matches, Mercer reminded colleagues to 'enjoy themselves'. But underneath the jocular exterior lay a serious competitor and Mercer expected team-mates to give it their all once the game began. Defender Laurie Scott recalled asking Mercer how he stayed so good humoured as games approached, 'Joe looked me in the eye and said, "I lark about until the second I cross the white line on to the pitch Laurie. Then you will not meet a more focused footballer for the next 90 minutes. Then when I finish the game I go back to being my normal self. But never during a match."'

Male played alongside Mercer on a handful of occasions after he joined Arsenal. He recalls, 'Joe had an excellent understanding of the ebb and flow of matches. His pace had all but gone, and he admitted that he would hang back because he couldn't cover the grass like he used to. But that helped him read the game and assess what was happening.

'He was fantastic with chaps like Laurie Scott and Walley Barnes, always making sure that they held the line, and that they were a unit. On the pitch, Joe had a real temper on him. He took it personally if we conceded, and would have a right go at us, reminding us to "watch what we were bloody well doing". After the game, he'd pull people to one side and talk them through what they should be doing. He reminded me of Herbert Chapman and Tom Parker in that sense. He knew his job, and was top class.'

Mercer and Rooke were an unlikely comedy duo. Male recalled that Rooke regularly referred to Mercer as 'that bloody grocer' and mocked him for having 'legs like sparrows' knee caps'. Mercer would then suggest to Rooke that he needed to shed a few pounds, and that he had a 'big arse'. Reg Lewis revealed that mocking Rooke about his size wasn't always wise. 'Ronnie could have a good laugh, but he'd have ways of showing you not to push it too far. I called him "fat and slow" on the training ground once, so he grabbed me, got me in a headlock and rolled his knuckles round on my head until I was begging for mercy.' Rooke quickly shed two stones, and Lewis recalled him leaving 'a dent the size of a small melon in the punch bag in the gym. He was ferocious with it.'

Like Mercer, Rooke was a fearsome competitor, and an excellent leader of the forward line. Reg Lewis recalled, 'I could get lazy at times, and I was a bit of a goal hanger. The crowd used to get on my back. Ronnie had words with me, telling me to get moving during games. He reckoned that I gave the opposition defence too much time to move forwards and that I needed to prevent them launching an attack.

"You should be the first line of defence Reg," he'd shout at me during games. "Come on, get your bloody arse moving and get tight on those defenders," he'd scream.

'Ronnie and Joe soon became the leaders in the dressing room. They were very vocal. They'd both been physical training instructors in the war. He did a great job signing them, did George [Allison]. Hats off to him.'

The low-key, bargain basement signatures of Mercer and Rooke encapsulated the era. These were testing times for many supporters. Correspondence to the *North London Press* and *St Pancras Gazette* highlighted that many labourers hadn't worked since their release from the army, and that, in order to boost local children's vitamin C levels, 35,000 oranges were being shipped in from South Africa. Soup kitchens were set up throughout the winter of 1946 for the unemployed and the unhoused. These were hardly demob happy crowds.

There was also a sense of post-war faded grandeur about Highbury, with its (now) grubby East and West stands. Mercer and Rooke – Arsenal's shabby chic duo – were about to spearhead a title charge.

~ ~ ~ ~ ~

Tom Whittaker took over the reins from Allison in June 1947. He was conscious of 'the high standards which this club demands from everyone, including the directors, the manager, the players, and the backroom staff'. Whittaker admitted that with the money situation at the club, the Bank of England days were unlikely ever to return, although it's worth noting that by the early 1950s the £200,000 debt was repaid due to the huge crowds flocking into Highbury and the Gunners' parsimony in the transfer market.

Arsenal began the 1947/48 season in excellent style by winning all their games in August, the highlight being an excellent 4-2 victory at The Valley against Charlton, with 60,000 looking on. Unbeaten in September, Arsenal conceded just one goal. Rooke and Lewis made mincemeat of several opposition defences, including Charlton's (6-0) and Stoke's (3-0) as the Gunners surged to the top of table.

With skipper Leslie Compton absent due to cricket commitments, Mercer took charge at half-time against Bolton. Without the injured

Lewis and Fields, Mercer moved himself to centre-half and inside-forward Jimmy Logie was shifted to left-half. Rooke and Logie were both virtual passengers in the second half due to injury but Mercer's tactics paid off after the break as they held on to their lead.

Arsenal were undefeated in their first 17 games of the season, a run which ended at the Baseball Ground in a 1-0 defeat to Derby. Mercer was soon installed as skipper. It happened before a match at Deepdale against Preston. Reg Lewis recalled, 'Les Compton tossed the ball to Joe and told him that because he'd done such a sterling job in his absence, he deserved it. Les wasn't being flippant or sour or anything. He just knew that Joe was the right man for the job.'

In January Arsenal showed their true mettle. The month began with a massive FA Cup shock and a 1-0 home defeat to Second Division strugglers Bradford Park Avenue, with Billy Elliott volleying the winner. In the *Daily Mail*, Whittaker warned of the need 'for stout hearts and level heads. We have done everything as a team, and we shall not lose sight of that, I hope, in the next few games.'

In the race for the championship, Burnley and Preston were right on Arsenal's coat tails. So were Matt Busby's resurgent Manchester United, who had been runners-up during the previous season. Just two weeks after the FA Cup defeat, Arsenal faced Busby's team at Maine Road, which had been their temporary home since Old Trafford had been badly damaged in the war. It was the archetypal four-pointer, with United winger Johnny Morris claiming, 'Arsenal may be league leaders, but we believe that the FA Cup loss to Bradford has destabilised them. With Joe Mercer unlikely to play because of influenza, it is our time to take advantage of a chink in their armour.' Morris reckoned without Mercer's remarkable powers of recovery.

Mercer's wife Norah had even telephoned the club in midweek to inform them that Mercer, laid up in bed, was in no fit state to even train. After imploring the Mercers to be patient, Whittaker arranged for his captain to have no less than seven penicillin injections in a bid to get him ready. 'I saw Joe on the Saturday morning', recalled Lewis, 'and he looked grey and ashen and a bit unsteady on his feet. Tom gave him a nip of something or other in the dressing room, and the colour began to come back into his face, and he started to be more like the old Joe, encouraging us and telling us that we needed a big performance in the game.'

The game attracted a league record crowd of 83,260 to Maine Road. With the vast Kippax terrace unroofed, large portions of the crowd suffered a severe drenching (Lewis remembered, 'The ball felt like the weight of a lead balloon the longer the match went on') but the game made for scintillating viewing. United engulfed Arsenal in a maelstrom of attacking football in the first few minutes.

Goalkeeper George Swindin recalled, 'The sound was incredible, and United were outstanding early on. Charlie Mitten smacked me right in the midriff with the ball from point blank range early on, and I clawed a shot away from Johnny Morris, but then we hit them on the counter attack.'

From an Arsenal corner, the ball ran to Lewis who fired home through a gap between the United defenders. 'The crowd went absolutely silent,' recalled Lewis. 'It was a total smash and grab effort.' United's Rowley hit the bar, and then his deflected effort fizzed past Swindin to level the score ('He was a lucky bugger and I told him so,' Swindin claimed) before United again hit the woodwork twice in the closing stages.

In the dying seconds, Lewis contrived to hit the post from just five yards out before the final whistle went. 'There was a bit of needle afterwards in the tunnel,' recalled Laurie Scott. 'United knew that they needed to win that game. We dug in and escaped with a draw. I don't think I ever saw Joe Mercer shout as much as he did that afternoon. Whenever we started to get ragged at the back, he'd shout, "Keep your bloody position. Don't move." And he'd grab your shirt and pull you around, to keep you in place. He was frantic.'

Further up the pitch, Lewis had similar memories of Rooke's organisation, '"Keep those defenders busy Reg! Don't give them a bloody second." And he was strutting around, glaring at the United players, bawling at them to try and put them off their game. He was like a man possessed that afternoon. We did our job at Maine Road, and never really looked back after that, because we'd already beaten United at Highbury anyway.'

Arsenal suffered some grave news on the injury front when Lewis was ruled out for the rest of the campaign later that month due to an ankle injury. He had already netted 14 in 28 games. Tom Whittaker insisted that Lewis's injury wouldn't scupper Arsenal's chances, but it would certainly make their task more difficult. The Gunners drew a blank in their first league match of the month – a 0-0 draw with Stoke – but then rediscovered their goalscoring prowess, winning 3-0 at home to Burnley. The month ended with a 4-2 defeat at the hands of high-flying Aston Villa.

Arsenal closed in on the title, although their form began to stutter. Wolves were put to the sword at Highbury with a Rooke double setting Arsenal on their way. They followed this up with a comfortable 2-0 win at Goodison Park, and a 7-0 hammering of Middlesbrough at home. But there were also reverses at the hands of Chelsea and Blackpool. George Male recalled Mercer's calming influence with the younger players whenever form began to go awry.

The Gunners were able to celebrate in front of their own fans, with the final game of the season at home to long-since relegated Grimsby Town. It turned into a goalfest with Rooke plundering four (he netted a record 33 league goals in 42 games that season), Denis Compton scoring twice, and Forbes and Logie rounding off proceedings.

It gave Mercer an unexpected chance to score his first Arsenal goal. With the team awarded a penalty in the dying minutes, Mercer grabbed the ball as the crowd chanted 'We want Joe, we want Joe.' Rooke seemed to want to take it too before Jimmy Logie snatched the ball from Mercer to take it (and score) himself. Mercer simply shrugged at the crowd and ran back to his defensive position.

The Highbury supporters insisted that the champions did two laps of honour before they disappeared off down the tunnel. Male, the final link to the Chapman era, bade farewell at the end of the match. Arsenal had led the table from start to finish, rarely showing signs of faltering. Nearest challengers Manchester United finished seven points behind, and over two million supporters watched the Gunners secure their first post-war title.

It was the happiest of ships. From Rooke and Mercer's 'Punch and Judy' routine, to Leslie Compton's selfless gesture in giving Mercer the captaincy, this was a team of steady professionals (like dependable full-back Walley Barnes) who, although lacking the box office glamour of Arsenal's team of the early 1930s, led the table from start to finish.

They took their civic duties very seriously. The *North London Press* and *St Pancras Gazette* reported that former sailor Jimmy Logie had provided tickets for former shipmates who were unable to obtain them for important games. The team was particularly active with the Royal Northern Hospital, visiting sick children regularly throughout the year, and it was reported that new signing and keen bird breeder Freddie Cox, after he heard that a local widow had had her beloved budgerigar stolen, replaced it with one of his.

The team could laugh at one another. Although not as accomplished a footballer as brother Leslie, Denis Compton, the original 'Brylcreem Boy', notched up an impressive six goals during the season from his position at left-half. Compton's only weakness was his notoriously poor timekeeping, which occasionally incurred the wrath of Tom Whittaker.

It backfired on him one day when, after another tardy arrival to training, Compton realised he had forgotten his boots, hastily grabbed what he thought was a pair in the same size, and ended up playing in a pair two sizes too small for him. 'I remember Tom Whittaker giving him some plasters to cover his blisters afterwards, suggesting that he wouldn't be doing that again, and me and Laurie Scott pretending to limp like Denis. He wasn't very impressed with us,' recalled Reg Lewis.

The job specification for any great player is to make a difference when it really matters. Joe Mercer did just that. When asked by the *Daily Express* at the end of the season if he had any thoughts on Theo Kelly, Mercer responded, 'None at all. There can be absolutely no room for bitterness in football. The game's about putting a smile on people's faces, not scowls.' Mercer would be smiling even more broadly within a couple of years.

- - - - -

Arsenal were unable to follow up their title success the following season, ending up in fifth place, and bumbled along during the majority of the 1949/50 campaign too. Ronnie Rooke departed midway through the previous season, his place in the side taken by Doug Lishman. On the day he returned to former club Crystal Palace, Rooke sought out Lewis. 'Ronnie grabbed my hand with one of his crushing handshakes, looked me straight in the eye, and told me, "Now don't you go back to playing like a lazy sod, Reg." He winked at me, slapped me on the back, and walked out of the dressing room. He was a great fellow. What a shame he wasn't a few years younger. He was a cast-iron 25-goal-a-season player, at least.' Winger Freddie Cox arrived from Tottenham and, although never a regular in the team, added energy on the flanks.

Several veterans, aware that the clock was ticking on their careers, wanted to lift the FA Cup. Lewis was 30 years old. He remembered, 'I always felt that having not been able to really get going on my career until my mid-20s, I was fighting against the clock. I kept getting injured more and more. My ankles were black and blue. I'd been kicked to death in the line of duty! I'd put my feet and ankles in a bowl of water to keep the swelling down. It was unusual for a player back then to last much into their 30s. Ronnie and Joe were the exceptions. I'd won the league with Arsenal but I dreamed of landing a cup winner's medal.'

Jimmy Logie was 31. Denis Compton, who made it known to his colleagues that he would retire at the end of the 1949/50 campaign, was 32. It seemed to be now or never for Arsenal's gallant band of senior professionals.

At least one member of the squad was ultra-confident that it would be Arsenal's year. Prior to matches, Joe Mercer shared a room with George Swindin in the Northern Hotel. Before the third round draw was made, the Arsenal goalkeeper turned to his skipper and told him that the Gunners would be drawn at home four times throughout the competition, and go on to win the trophy at Wembley. 'I just had a really confident feeling about things. I was feeling bullish. So I told Joe about my premonition. His reaction was to look at me like I was some sort of nutter and laugh in my face. "I'll believe that when I see it George," he told me.'

Mercer became more and more incredulous as Swindin's bold prophecy came true. After defeating Sheffield Wednesday, Swansea, and Burnley at Highbury, Arsenal were drawn at home against Leeds in round six. 'I'll always remember Joe playfully punching me on the arm and telling the rest of the boys, "We'll discover that he can talk to the dead next." And everyone fell about laughing. Then Joe said, "Well boys, it looks like we're destined to win the cup then."'

By then, Arsenal had enjoyed so much good fortune in the competition that their name appeared to have been written on the trophy. Lewis grabbed the winner against an unlucky Wednesday side, which had been reduced to ten men after full-back Vic Kenny dislocated his shoulder early in the game. Second Division Swansea fought back from 2-0 down to grab what they thought was a deserved equaliser in the dying seconds only to see the referee judge that one of their players had handled the ball in the lead-up to the goal.

Lewis and Leslie Compton then scored both goals as Arsenal swept aside Burnley in the fifth round and Lewis grabbed the winner against Leeds in the sixth. 'Good grief,' recalled Lewis. 'Leeds threw the kitchen sink at us for the last 30 minutes. I don't think that Leeds could have tried any harder.'

In interviews, Mercer bristled when it was suggested that his team was 'lucky'. 'Don't forget that our defence is part of our side. People talk as if we are "Lucky Arsenal" because we've got a good defence. As if it were a sort of fluke we could rely on.'

The semi-final pitted Arsenal against Chelsea. With the Gunners 2-0 down at White Hart Lane to Roy Bentley's goals, Freddie Cox scored directly from a corner (the blustery wind played a crucial role) and Leslie Compton headed in powerfully from brother Denis's corner. Just as Alex James had disobeyed Chapman's instruction not to take quick free kicks in the 1930 final, Leslie ignored Mercer's insistence that he remain back in his own half.

Mercer was the first to congratulate Compton, and George Swindin recalled Mercer grabbing Compton by his shirt, and in mock fury, informing him he would 'be out of the bloody side if he didn't listen more carefully in future'. 'Les was laughing like a lunatic, pleading with Tom Whittaker not to drop him because he hadn't listened to Joe,' explained Lewis.

At the same venue four days later, Cox scampered into the Chelsea area and fired in the winner. As Arsenal fans swarmed on to the pitch to celebrate with their heroes, it was premonition time again. Cox's wife had been telling anyone who cared to listen before the game that she had dreamed her husband would score the winner and send his team to Wembley to face Liverpool, who had defeated Everton in the all-Merseyside semi-final.

The Chelsea players had become more than a little spooked about the 'lucky Arsenal' factor, and tried to fight fire with fire by having a rabbit's foot in the pocket of their shorts. It didn't work, but as Mercer freely admitted, 'All through the cup ties we only had to travel 13 and a half miles from Highbury to Wembley. Not only that. We were able to stick to our ordinary training. We could eat at home. We were never jolted out of our routine. Oh yes, we were lucky there all right.'

Such routine meant that Arsenal players became hooked on rituals and superstition. Alex James lent Alex Forbes his boots before the third round clash with Sheffield Wednesday. Forbes continued to wear them throughout the cup run, convinced that James's 'magic touch' was helping him. Leslie Compton insisted on cleaning the windows of his Hendon home on the morning of each tie. Lewis had porridge on every day of the week except for matchday. 'I put one teaspoonful of honey in it every day. I used the same teaspoon, of course. On matchday, I'd have scrambled eggs on one and a half pieces of toast,' he explained.

Old warhorses Swindin and Mercer got in on the act, insisting on having a shave from Dick, the Great Northern Hotel barber on matchdays, and walking down Euston Road until reaching a set of traffic lights outside the Hearts of Oak building. They would turn around and walk back to the hotel.

Mercer's routine was thrown off kilter by Arsenal reaching Wembley. Liverpool manager George Kay opted against allowing Mercer to continue training at Anfield until the final had been played. Instead, Mercer went running with his family's terrier – Taffy – near his house, or he trained with Tranmere Rovers. Two days before the match, Mercer was presented with the Footballer of the Year trophy and he went straight to the Great Northern Hotel to meet up with his colleagues.

The final was delicately poised with *The Times* concluding, 'Liverpool, more promising in attack, have the advantage of youth which on this rich tiring surface is a great consideration. But Arsenal possess the experience, the iron will power, a great tradition and a system.'

There was a deluge of rain before the kick-off and Lewis recalled, 'I liked heavy pitches. It sorted out the men from the boys – and in my case – fit and fast players from slow ones.'

The only selection issue Tom Whittaker faced prior to the match was whether or not to select Lewis, whose form had slipped, or Doug

Lishman, who had been playing well. It was rumoured that Mercer lobbied Whittaker hard to ensure that Lewis retained his place, a fact Whittaker always denied and which Lewis refused to discuss when I spoke to him.

Lewis was given his place and the Arsenal players discovered they would be wearing a fetching combination of gold shirts, white shorts, and black and white socks. Swindin wore a bright crimson jersey. He told me, 'I heard it said that Tom Whittaker made it that bright because he thought it would be a distraction for the Liverpool forwards. The thing was, I think it damned near put off my own defenders, it was that luminous!'

Laurie Scott feared Liverpool's Liddell and Payne the most. 'They were very quick and very clever. I knew that me and Walley [Barnes] needed to be on top form because they could kill you with one great ball to Albert Stubbins, who was a top player, and if you gave him an inch, he'd take a mile.'

Liverpool began like a whirlwind, forcing several corners and winning two free kicks in dangerous positions. Arsenal dug in. Forbes did a sterling job in tracking Liddell, thundering into tackles and giving him precious little space in which to operate. 'I have seldom seen a more devastating wing-half display,' commented Bob Wall in *Arsenal From The Heart*.

On 17 minutes, Lewis struck following a sublime move. Barnes flicked the ball to Jimmy Logie, who had begun to use his pace and trickery to good effect. At that point, Peter Goring made an excellent decoy run, pulling Liverpool's defence away from Lewis. Lewis tore into the gap, latched on to Logie's beautifully-weighted pass and slipped the ball past Sidlow to give his team the lead.

Forbes nearly put Arsenal 2-0 up before Swindin pushed the ball against the crossbar following Payne's effort, and dived on it before Albert Stubbins could latch on. 'Albert looked at me and called me a "lucky bugger,"' Swindin explained.

At the back, Mercer was marshalling the troops, barking at Barnes and Compton to 'hold your position'. George Swindin confirms that Mercer was even more fired up than usual that afternoon, 'He knew that this might be his last shot at the FA Cup. He was also performing in front of Liverpool folk, and against fellows he was used to training with. There were tears running down his cheeks at one point. It was such a big occasion for him.'

Seventeen minutes after half-time (Whittaker had ordered the largely ineffective Denis Compton to down a glass of whisky as he prepared to play the final 45 minutes of his football career), Arsenal grabbed their second. On the left, Peter Goring found Freddie Cox on the edge of Liverpool's area, and his neat flick enabled Lewis to run on to the ball and knock in his second goal. It was lightning-quick, reminiscent of Chapman's team at its most incisive.

Liverpool threw caution to the wind in the latter stages, hitting the bar, and forcing Swindin to make several fine saves, but it was too little too late. On the final whistle Whittaker recalled Mercer planting a kiss upon his startled manager's cheek, and Laurie Scott had to warn Mercer that he had tears of joy rolling down his cheeks, which Mercer hastily wiped away before being presented with the cup by the King. The Queen wrongly presented Mercer with a loser's medal before FA secretary Stanley Rous hastily called Mercer back.

Typical of Mercer's humility, he paid tribute to the Liverpool players, saying, 'No team should fade away into the lonely tunnel as Liverpool did.' At the Café Royal that night, Mercer and his team-mates hob-nobbed with 1930s legends including Jack, Bastin and James. Charlie Buchan, now editor of *Football Monthly*, was there too.

The headlines in the newspapers next day were magnanimous towards Mercer in particular. 'What a day for Joe Mercer, who once again proved that although he is thinking of retiring, he is still one of England's top-flight wing-halves,' wrote Jack Milligan in the *Daily Graphic*. The *Manchester Guardian* took note of Arsenal's fine tactics, 'Arsenal won by superior strategy. They took note of Mercer's ripening years and fading stamina and turned these into positive advantages. Mercer stationed himself well down the field, only slightly in front of Barnes and in close touch with Les Compton. This meant that Mercer could move quickly to Compton's aid, if danger threatened down the centre, or to Barnes's aid if Payne showed any signs of becoming troublesome on the wing.'

Lewis was a relieved man, believing that he had finally made up for all those lost years, 'I was delighted for the team and thrilled for myself after we beat Liverpool, because I'd lost so much playing time in the early 1940s, and now I'd won a league and an FA Cup medal. But really, I think the defence won it. Strikers have the easier task of just sticking the ball in the back of the net.'

Unsubstantiated reports in the media suggested that Mercer, granted the freedom of home town Ellesmere Port upon his return there following the cup final, had played his last game. But there was to be one last hurrah.

It just didn't seem possible for Arsenal, following two fallow seasons, to launch another title bid in the 1952/53 campaign. Newcastle had controversially beaten the Gunners in the 1952 FA Cup Final (even the curmudgeonly Stan Seymour, Newcastle's vice-chairman, told Tom Whittaker, 'Ours is the cup, yours the honour and the glory,') and Mercer claimed that captaining Arsenal that afternoon was the 'greatest honour of my career'.

Arsenal appeared to be up against it from the beginning of the new season. Walley Barnes, injured a few months earlier in the cup final, would miss the entire campaign. Also absent for the opening game against Aston Villa were forwards Jimmy Logie, Reg Lewis and defender Freddie Cox. Lewis didn't play again for the club. 'My body told me that enough was enough,' he explained.

Ominously, Tom Whittaker – not for the last time – spoke of the strain associated with being Arsenal manager, 'The pressures have grown massively over the last 20 years, as the game continues to become bigger and reaches a more and more global audience.'

Players later confirmed that Whittaker took to having rest periods after training had finished in order to combat the emotional and physical fatigue he was feeling. Winger Ben Marden confirmed that Whittaker 'regularly took naps in the medical room'.

Despite the troubled backdrop, the season began well with young Don Oakes scoring the winner at Villa Park in a 2-1 victory, and five days later he teed up Peter Goring to net the clincher against Manchester United at a packed Highbury in another 2-1 success.

Mercer was still present and correct, although at 38 years of age he couldn't prevent the onset of injuries curtailing his number of performances. In September, after defeats against Derby and Charlton, the team was booed by its own supporters and went scuttling down to seventh place at one point.

Goring went public and said, 'Perhaps the Arsenal fans, used to success down the years, have become a little spoilt. There have been a great deal of changes in the first team due to injuries, and they need to stick with us.'

The mood was lifted after wins against Portsmouth, and Tottenham at White Hart Lane. Goals from Goring, the fit-again Jimmy Logie and footballer/cricketer Arthur Milton helped give the Gunners a morale-boosting 3-1 win.

By December, Arsenal clambered up the table and had pacesetters Wolves in their sights. They drew with Burnley and defeated Aston Villa at home before playing out a remarkable 6-4 away victory at Burnden Park against Bolton on Christmas Day. The press dubbed it the clash between Nat Lofthouse – 'The Lion of Vienna' – and Cliff Holton, the powerful and dashing natural successor to Ronnie Rooke.

Although the press eulogised about the entertainment, and Holton's excellent double, Whittaker was less than impressed with his team's defending. Not for the last time that season he criticised the headstrong centre-back Ray Daniel for disobeying his instructions, and roving too far forward.

Goring recalled, 'Ray was incredibly strong willed, and was very confident. He was an outstanding defender, but Tom found it very hard to man-manage him. Joe Mercer was good with him, but even he couldn't stop Ray pushing forward and throwing the defensive shape out of balance on occasions.'

There was much to admire in Arsenal's play but at various intervals during the campaign, the press criticism stung. After a double defeat by Blackpool in February – in league and cup – the *Daily Mirror* noted, 'It was an Arsenal dream, the annual mirage of the double...but the dream is dead. It was slaughter on the south shore for Arsenal's ragged army...there was a clear suggestion of loss of control in the side.'

Even in victory, it seemed hard to please the press. Despite a 4-1 win over Bolton which sent Arsenal back to the top of the table, the *Daily Mail* insisted, 'Here was no championship form...there was much bad football on both sides.'

The occasionally negative headlines irritated George Swindin so much that he went to see Whittaker about it. Whittaker's response was, 'I'm surprised at you George, worrying about things like that. It's part and parcel of playing for Arsenal – always was, always is, and always will be George. I'd ignore it if I were you.'

The notoriously hard-to-please Arsenal crowd didn't always make life easy for the players either. Goring walked out of Highbury after the game, only to be confronted by a disgruntled fan. Goring recalled, 'This chap was completely drunk, but he started telling me that he'd seen the Arsenal team of the 30s, and we weren't fit to lick their boots… some of those Arsenal fans were very hard to please. We felt that they didn't know they were born.' One of Goring's team-mates snapped and told a *Daily Mail* journalist – anonymously – that he was 'ashamed of the crowd and considered them the most unsporting collection in the country'.

Arsenal hit a rich vein of form at precisely the right time, defeating Liverpool and Chelsea in early April. With further victories over Bolton, Stoke and Manchester City, Arsenal could have won the title at Preston with a victory on 25 April but succumbed to Tom Finney's excellence and lost 2-0 at Deepdale following goals from Finney and Wayman. *The Times* noted, 'Only one side wore the look of champions and it was certainly not Arsenal.'

With one match to play, the sides were level on 52 points. On 29 April Finney's penalty gave Preston the victory his side needed against Derby. Arsenal now knew that they had to beat sixth-placed Burnley two days later at Highbury in order to pip Preston to the prize.

- - - - -

Tellingly, Arsenal had garnered 52 points from 40 games, the lowest number any potential champions had gained at that stage of the season. George Swindin recalled, 'We were absolutely shattered going into the game, but we tended to play well on heavy pitches. It was a team which tended to play well on the big occasion, so I was confident, although not everyone was.'

That included the Voice of Arsenal column in the matchday programme, which noted, 'Preston beat us well and truly last Saturday and we may have to pay the penalty.' Team-mates noted that even Joe Mercer, normally the life and soul of proceedings, was noticeably quiet when the players ate their eggs on toast at Kings Cross station, surrounded by Blackpool and Bolton fans milling around because the FA Cup Final was being played the next day.

Ben Marden said with some alarm, 'There was barely a blade of grass in some areas of the pitch. Within minutes, what grass there was, was churned up. It was a quagmire from the start. It rained and rained, and the ball got heavier and heavier.'

The match kicked off at the early time of 6.30pm on Friday 1 May due to the absence of floodlighting at Highbury. Despite the teeming rain, 51,586 turned up to watch Whittaker's side's last stand. Doug Lishman remembered the Highbury din that night, 'The noise they made was unbelievable. It was really ear-piercing – enough to make the hairs on the back of your neck stand on end.'

The action was frenetic. After six minutes, Burnley's Des Thompson put his side ahead against the run of play. Midway through the first half Arsenal found their attacking rhythm. Alex Forbes – courtesy of a huge deflection – equalised, and two minutes afterwards, Jimmy Logie ducked out of the way to allow Lishman ('I just smacked the loose ball as hard as I could. It was the greatest moment of my life when it went in') to put Arsenal 2-1 up.

Just before half-time, amid another torrential downpour, Jimmy Logie pounced from five yards out to snaffle a poacher's goal. With puddles now visible on the Highbury surface, the Clarets' Billy Elliott pulled the score back to 3-2 five minutes into the second half.

The Arsenal players attempted to shut up shop – a risky strategy with 40 minutes left. Don Roper recalled, 'I noticed that Joe Mercer's legs had gone.

'Joe later admitted that they went for good that night. He reckoned it was the last time he operated as a top-class player. I had a knee injury, and at one point I thought I'd collapse with pain when the ball caught me on the side. It later turned out I'd torn a ligament, but these were the days before substitutes, so you had to carry on. Jimmy [Logie] and Pete [Goring] were virtual passengers by now. They could barely walk, and so we just stuffed them behind the ball. We had no option but to stand firm in the final half hour.'

Marden concurred, 'It was the football equivalent of the final scene in *Zulu*, when the soldiers stand firm in the face of the enemy charging at them. We stuck rigidly to our tasks. We had to concentrate and rise above the rain, the noise, the fatigue, and the pain.'

Whittaker couldn't stand the tension, walked down the tunnel and poured himself a double brandy. Late on, Roper caught Elliott in the box. The Burnley man stumbled and carried on. He told Roper, 'There are better ways of denying you the title than that Don.'

Finally at 8.10pm, the referee blew his whistle. The crowd invaded the pitch. Some threw their red scarves and rosettes into the air. Others carried the players around the pitch. Arsenal had won the title on goal average, by 0.099 of a goal. The rain stopped and the sun broke through. It was a red sky at night.

- - - - -

There were two hugely significant departures in the aftermath of the 1953 title victory. Centre-half Ray Daniel, almost ever-present that season, made the curious decision to depart to Sunderland, for a record £27,500. The Rokerites ended up in ninth position in 1953, and the allegation was that Daniel was tempted to the north-east by illegal payments. It didn't do his career much good. Sunderland narrowly avoided relegation during the following season. But Daniel's departure certainly destabilised Arsenal's often rock-solid defence.

The rot quickly set in. Marden recalled, 'The minute we won the league, it was as if all the ambition slowly seeped out of the club. The players that were brought in weren't really good enough, and Tom Whittaker just looked exhausted the whole time.'

Arsenal slumped into a mid-table position the following season, and suffered an FA Cup giant-killing at the hands of Third Division South outfit Norwich City.

Whittaker attempted to inject the glamour back into Arsenal by luring Blackpool's 35-year-old Stanley Matthews to north London in 1954. In his autobiography, Matthews claimed that Whittaker (in contravention of Football League regulations) offered to double Matthews's wages by arranging a secondary job doing promotional work for a London catering company. Matthews turned the Gunners down.

Whittaker did sign veteran Tommy Lawton in the 1953/54 campaign. The former Chelsea man quickly grew fed up with the presence of past legends, 'They'd hang around, and sometimes mix with us after games. That didn't go down too well with some of the lads. I remember Jimmy Logie asking why they couldn't "piss off down the pub".'

Whittaker couldn't mix the correct blend of ingredients to usher in a new era of success at Highbury. 'I don't know how many Arsenal youngsters were labelled the "new Alex James" or the "new Cliff Bastin" or whatever. It was a massive strain on them,' recalled Lawton.

Arguably, Arsenal's only top-class performer in the mid-50s was goalkeeper Jack Kelsey, who gained the number one spot at the expense of Swindin. Their most famous match of the late 1950s was a defeat – the epic 5-4 loss to Manchester United a few days before the Munich air crash in 1958. Like Chapman and Allison before him, the strain of managing Arsenal pushed Whittaker to an early grave and he died from a heart attack in 1956. Inevitably, the most poignant departure of all was Joe Mercer's, who bade the Highbury crowd farewell after breaking his leg in a home match against Liverpool in April 1954.

In the immediate post-war era, Arsenal's popularity had grown. Supporters' clubs sprang up across the world and the club worked tirelessly to ensure good links with local schools and hospitals. Their beaming, upstanding captain was invariably at the centre of any worthy cause or charm offensive, national or international. As Highbury crowds, a lot of the crowd were having a rough time of it, enduring the hardships of post-war rationing discovered, at least smiles and success weren't in short supply in N5 in the years that followed World War Two. Certainly not when Joe Mercer was around.

Mercer would claim that the celebrations following the win over Burnley in 1953 were the most enjoyable of his playing career. Hopefully everyone enjoyed themselves that night. There wouldn't be another Arsenal occasion like it for 17 long years.

# Playing The System


*'It's time that English coaches looked at coaching in a far more systematic and scientific way.' Ron Greenwood, Arsenal coach, 1958.*

*'The millstone had been lifted from around our necks. We believed this could be the start of something massive for Arsenal.' Frank McLintock, speaking after the Fairs Cup win in 1970.*


TRYING to bring success to Highbury throughout the wilderness years of the late 1950s and 1960s was arguably the toughest managerial assignment in football. Jack Crayston – Arsenal's elegant former centre-half from the 1930s – stepped up from the assistant manager's job in 1956 after Tom Whittaker's retirement but lasted just two years in the post. His main problem? 'I was never able to find the right system with the right players.'

Former Arsenal goalkeeper George Swindin took over in 1958. He reflected, 'I tried all sorts of new combinations on the pitch, and experimented with new systems, but I was always some way from the right mix.' Swindin embraced the progressive tactics which were espoused by his assistant manager and first team coach Ron Greenwood. In August 1959, both Swindin and Greenwood were interviewed in the *Observer*. Their comments appeared to usher in a new and forward-thinking era in Arsenal's tactics. 'We've got to change or be left behind,' explained Swindin. 'We've thrown away the defensive concept. To attract the public the game has got to be entertaining and in football, goals are entertainment.'

Greenwood spoke of 'the centre-half being much more mobile than he was. The halves must be the springboard of all your attacks. They must use all the space between them and the forwards so that by moving the ball intelligently they can dominate the field.'

Their Brave New World never came to fruition. Geoff Strong recalled, 'Ron was too hypothetical and couldn't man-manage. On one occasion he was talking to us about rotating positions and being clever without the ball. It got very, very technical and there wasn't the quality of player to run with what Ron said. Players kept being switched around too. It was chaos. I turned to young Gerry Ward and asked him if he grasped what Ron was trying to teach us. "Not a bloody clue," came Gerry's response.'

In the 1960/61 campaign, Eastham used 30 players in the league and FA Cup, an unwieldy number whatever the injury situation at the club. His final throw of the dice was to bring in George Eastham from Newcastle for a whopping £47,500 but he lost striker David Herd who, with an average strike rate of a goal every other game, was one of the best – if most underrated – players in the First Division. Herd exercised footballers' newly earned right to depart at the end of their contracts and went to Manchester United.

New signing Eastham turned down Arsenal's £30 per week offer in late 1961 only for the Arsenal manager to cave in and offer an improved deal. Swindin struggled to control events both on and off the pitch. Days after Tottenham completed the Double, Greenwood departed to West Ham as manager, and a year later Swindin was dismissed.

A missed opportunity to put Arsenal on a more creative and outward-looking path? Swindin claimed, 'Fans wanted a more attractive game, more like Tottenham's. Whenever I approached the board about signing new players who could play a more passing and expansive game, they weren't interested. They felt that sticking to tried and tested Arsenal methods was the way. One director told me, "Don't take too much notice of what Tottenham are doing George. We'll do things the Arsenal way." They were bloody-minded about it. I realised that what we needed was, first and foremost, a successful side and a winning one.'

In a break with tradition, Arsenal appointed Billy Wright as their new manager in the summer of 1962. He was the first 'outsider' to become manager since Herbert Chapman in 1925, and on the face of it he had all the credentials to drag Arsenal kicking and screaming into the 1960s. Before Bobby Moore lifted the World Cup some four years later, Wright – towering skipper of Wolverhampton Wanderers in their golden age – was the golden boy of English football. 'I want to bring trophies back to Highbury,' he announced in the *Daily Express* when he took over, 'and get people talking about Arsenal again for the right reasons.'

Wright, who won 105 England caps, arrived in an enormous wave of excitement, especially when he brought with him new signing Joe Baker, who signed from Torino for around £70,000. 'There will be more signings like Joe over the next few years who will make Arsenal fans' mouths water, and bring back the 60,000 crowds to Highbury,' promised Wright.

The Gunners began the 1962/63 campaign well, winning matches against Leyton Orient and Birmingham. Before game three, a Highbury contest with Manchester United, Wright walked down the tunnel, saw the expectant 62,308 crowd and returned to the dressing room, barely able to contain his excitement. Baker recalled, 'Billy told us, "This is what Arsenal is about. Packed crowds, sunshine, playing teams like Manchester United, and (he leant over and rubbed my sleeve between his forefingers) these lovely red and white shirts. Beautiful. Now go and win boys."' His team went down 3-1, and didn't win again for six matches.

The major drawback of hiring Wright as manager was his singular lack of managerial experience. He had served as a physical instruction teacher in the army but as a one-club man at Wolves, his knowledge of tactical systems and structures at other clubs was limited. Former Wolves team-mate Eddie Clamp, who scored Arsenal's consolation in the United match, reckoned his old skipper was more style than substance, 'Billy gathered the players together when he became manager, and you could have heard a pin drop. The players were so excited to have someone with his stature as their manager. He talked a bit about the Arsenal way, but his comments on what our style of play would be were just plain confusing.

'He spoke about passing the ball around, and defenders being more mobile and flexible. Then he talked about putting balls into channels – like we had at Wolves – and relying on Arsenal's traditional defensive strengths. It got really confusing. I was puzzled, because Billy must have learnt from Stan Cullis at Wolves that what players want is a clear structure and style right from the start. But Billy and his new coach Les Shannon never seemed to put their finger on what they wanted.'

Wright always hinted in the years after he left Arsenal – and the claims are repeated in Norman Giller's official biography *Billy Wright: A Hero For All Seasons* – that senior professionals including Eastham and Baker never fully pulled their weight. George Armstrong claimed that Wright's accusation was partly true. 'The forwards in Billy Wright's teams could, to the untrained eye, play fantastically well and grab the goals, but I only realised after I'd played in the Double side alongside Raddy [John Radford] and Ray [Kennedy] that there's more to playing as a striker than Joe [Baker] or George [Eastham] were prepared to offer. They were superbly gifted players, but strikers in great teams are actually the first line of defence, holding up the ball for team-mates, stopping opposition central defenders moving forward, and tracking back if necessary. We never got that from Joe or George.'

Baker admitted, 'I did my own thing up front, and the defenders did their job.' After a mind-spinning 5-5 draw with Blackburn, coach Les Shannon turned on full-backs Billy McCulloch and Jimmy Magill. 'He accused them of costing their team-mates and of not giving it their all,' recalled Baker. 'I'll never forget what happened next. "Flint" McCulloch turned to Shannon and said, "Well how about spending some time with us on the training ground to help us sort out the problems." Shannon's response was, "You're a professional footballer. You sort it." In my mind, that showed that he wasn't a top coach, and that Billy wasn't a top manager, who was prepared to iron out problems on an individual basis.'

Nicknamed 'the Laughing Cavalier', Baker scored a hugely impressive 100 goals in just 156 matches for Arsenal but decried the lack of leadership at the club in the mid-60s. 'Billy Wright often hinted that I should have been a better example to the others. I didn't always behave impeccably. Once, we were on tour in the West Indies and Billy went for me in front of the rest of the players. I'd had enough. I threw my boots at him and told him to shove it. It was disrespectful, but borne out of frustration at the fact no one was taking the club by the horns and dragging it out of the mire.

'Even worse after what happened that day was that Billy never asked me to apologise to him. Either he should have taken me to task, or sat down with me and discussed what was going wrong. Instead he just did nothing.'

Wright continued to give younger players first team opportunities. By the end of his second season in charge, John Radford and Peter Simpson had made their first team debuts and Jon Sammels also appeared regularly. The big-money signings continued. Dundee defender Ian Ure arrived for a whopping £62,500 in the summer of 1963 and 18 months later, Leicester's attacking midfielder Frank McLintock was signed for £80,000.

Both Scottish internationals made disastrous debuts for the club. Ure was all at sea as 50,000 watched him flounder on the opening day of the 1963/64 campaign against Wolves and McLintock made a similarly disastrous debut at home to Nottingham Forest, when his team were thumped 3-0.

McLintock remembers Ure, a player who struggled with knee injuries throughout much of his Highbury career, as 'highly intelligent and forthright, but prone to making horrendous errors at the back. Ian was a very skilful player, who had great feet, but was occasionally caught for pace, and used to lose concentration in the air as well.'

It was McLintock who struggled most of all when he arrived at Highbury, 'I wanted desperately to win, and because I could see weaknesses all over the pitch, I ran around like an out of control fire engine, trying to put out fires in defence and midfield. There's different types of indiscipline at clubs, but on the pitch anyway, I was probably the worst offender at the club. My entire body used to tense up in my first few seasons at Arsenal.'

Three months after joining, his new team crashed out of the FA Cup to Peterborough, after which Wright announced that he would take all the blame for the defeat, and that the side would remain unchanged for the Gunners' next match.

'Billy should have rung the changes after that,' claims McLintock. 'There was no real plan when we got on the pitch. Les Shannon was what I would call a blackboard coach – good in theory with some neat ideas, but our training sessions were too experimental. He'd do something new and a bit left of field, and then it would be a case of "Right, we've done that, now let's do something different." There was no continuity or repetition, which footballers need.'

As the 1960s began to swing, Wright struggled to control his vocal stars. In the post-maximum wage era Baker, Ure and Eastham regularly argued with their manager about their contracts, and on numerous occasions there were rumours that all three were poised to leave the club. Baker recalled, 'We knew what players were earning elsewhere. Johnny Haynes was on £100 a week at Fulham. The most anyone at Arsenal was on at the time was £30. Some of us felt that Arsenal were employing us on the cheap.'

McLintock exploded in rage at Shannon on a pre-season tour to Italy. Instructed before the game to rein in his attacking instincts, the Scot ventured too far forward for Shannon's liking and was chastised in front of the team. 'You're nothing but £80,000 worth of trouble McLintock,' screamed Shannon, to which the player responded, 'And you couldn't coach 11 fucking white mice.' Both were forced to apologise, although neither man really meant it. 'Another problem swept under the carpet,' mutters McLintock.

Peter Storey claims in his autobiography that Wright's reliance on alcohol accounted for his increasingly tetchy and erratic behaviour. On occasions he didn't watch Highbury matches, fearful of the crowd's reaction.

In the 1965/66 campaign, with Arsenal labouring above the relegation zone, the crowd's patience finally snapped. From March onwards, sections of Arsenal fans urged their fellow supporters to boycott games, and gathered outside the home team's dressing room chanting, 'We want a manager, we want a manager.'

Baker, who had scored 13 goals in 24 matches, was sold to Nottingham Forest, which only increased the home supporters' ire. Infamously, what remains Arsenal's lowest crowd of 4,554 turned up to watch the team lose 3-0 at home to Don Revie's emerging Leeds United on 5 May. Some of those present in the North Bank danced around a bonfire at the front of the terrace, and in the East Stand one bugle-carrying supporter played the 'Last Post'.

Six weeks later, after England's World Cup triumph, Wright was sacked. Wright's biographer Norman Giller claims that the former manager's 'fingerprints were all over Arsenal's 1971 Double team'. Radford and Sammels both recount Wright's decency and kindness to them personally as they began to make their way in the game. But it takes far more than the occasional kind word in a footballer's ear to make a great manager.

Wright – a whole-hearted, immensely gifted player to whom the game seemed to come almost naturally – simply wasn't attuned to the fact that players needed managing in different ways. He was one of a depressingly long line of lionhearted former England captains who failed to carve a career for themselves in football management. The team lacked unity, a clear tactical plan and direction. Arsenal were, to all intents and purposes, a laughing stock. Surely only a superhero could dig them out of the mire.

'Bloody hell Marj,' George Armstrong yelled at his soon-to-be wife, 'they've appointed the physio as our new manager.' After all the rumours that Don Revie would be appointed manager, Arsenal turned to their earnest physiotherapist Bertie Mee to lead them out of their miserable morass. He was hardly the high profile name which Arsenal players had hoped for. McLintock confesses to uttering numerous swear words when he heard the news, and remained sceptical as to whether Mee would have the managerial clout necessary to move the club forward.

Mee was the first Arsenal figure I interviewed, back in 1990. I had heard that he was a stickler for timekeeping, but for probably the only time in his life Mee was late, held up in heavy traffic outside Potters Bar. He was apologetic, slightly flustered, and a little on the back foot. Once he had settled down with a cup of tea, he was charm personified. The immaculately suited former Arsenal boss did nonetheless tell me that he didn't much care for my ripped denim jacket.

'How did being a physiotherapist prepare you for being the Arsenal manager?' 'In some ways, I was a confidante for many of the players. I knew what they thought of the training at the club under Billy

Wright. I knew the numerous quirks of everyone's character. It gave me a rounded view of the strengths and weaknesses of the players.'

'What did you feel were your main strengths as a manager?' 'Although I hadn't been in football management before, my roles in the army and as a physiotherapist in London helped me learn when to delegate responsibility, when to trust someone else with completing a task, when to crack the whip, and, most importantly, to surround yourself with men whom you know will do a fine job. The army also taught me that in order to be successful in any institution, you all need to be pulling in the same direction, and with a clear vision in mind.'

There, in a nutshell, was Mee's management philosophy, and within weeks of his appointment his clarity of vision was already being felt. 'Firstly, I wanted to ensure that the backroom staff was of the highest quality,' he explained. He installed Gordon Clark, who served the club for well over a decade, as chief scout, and admitted, 'Billy Wright already had a fine production line of young players in place. I tinkered slightly with the scouting network and expanded it. I knew that Gordon could head this up.'

Mee sold mercurial forward George Eastham – the man who once claimed to know within the first ten minutes of a match whether he would play well or not – to Stoke City. If there was one character trait Mee disapproved of most of all in footballers, it was a tendency to be mercurial.

Mee admitted that mastery of training techniques most certainly wasn't his strong point, so the appointment of the right first team coach was crucial. He plumped for Dave Sexton, who, while a West Ham player in the 1950s, was part of a group of young players, including Malcolm Allison, Noel Cantwell and John Bond, who spent hours discussing tactics in Cassettari's Café opposite Upton Park.

Throughout his spell at Arsenal, Sexton travelled up from Brighton to Victoria where, on the train everyday, he would draw up the training programme. After catching the tube to Cockfosters, Mee would give him a lift to the training ground. 'It was a great set-up,' recalled Sexton. 'I'd get my cup of tea on the platform and settle in my seat to think through what we would do that day. I had two hours of thinking time, and then Bertie and I could chat through my schemes and ideas in his car, away from interruptions.'

Sexton found the Arsenal players 'keen to learn, but a bit rudderless, because of the lack of clarity and vision they'd had over the past few years. Their sense of frustration and, in Frank McLintock's case, anger at the fact that Arsenal had underachieved for so long was apparent. They were a fine crew of footballers to work with. They literally gobbled up my ideas.'

With Mee's blessing, Sexton introduced a more harrying and pressing ten-man game, and a man-to-man marking system. Although the man-to-man marking would be dropped within a couple of years, the pressing game was the bedrock of everything which Arsenal achieved over the next few years. 'I regarded football coaching as a science,' Sexton told me. 'The most successful teams no longer played "off the cuff". On Sundays, I'd fly over to Italy and Spain and watch matches over there. The European teams were light years ahead of us in terms of spatial awareness and operating effectively as both a defensive and an attacking unit, so I worked on this with the team. That side needed relentless drilling. Their training previously had been all about a bit of jogging and a kick-about.'

Ian Ure recalls, 'Under Dave we had repeat sessions on shutting down players man to man. Defenders were told that if the player you were marking had the ball, you had to rush to within five yards of him and jockey him. I'd have to hustle him, trying to make him dilly dally on the ball in order that he should make a mistake. He'd then hopefully offload the ball under pressure, so I could intercept the pass, or be panicked so that I could tackle him.'

The Arsenal players then moved on to pattern plays – two versus two and three versus three. McLintock looks back, 'If the opposition's left-back had the ball, me, our outside right, and the right-sided centre-forward would form a unit against him.' Finally, Sexton worked with the Arsenal team on operating as a single unit in order to squeeze the opposition on the pitch.

'Dave played a massive role in Arsenal's revival,' recalls Bob Wilson. 'Now we finally had a team which operated as one. It was literally a case of "all for one and one for all".' Sexton relished working with players on an individual basis to eradicate mistakes and reinforce tactics. Mee also continued to weigh in with techniques by which players could remain fit. 'It was a great partnership with Bert,' recalled

Sexton. 'We saw things the same way, identified similar strengths and weaknesses in the team, and I was happy to leave it to Bertie to sign the players.'

In the first season under Mee and Sexton, George Graham arrived from Chelsea and Bob McNab came in from Huddersfield. 'At that time, Bertie had a fantastic eye for a new player,' explained Sexton, 'and he'd always give credit to the scouting team for the talent spotting.'

The Gunners finished seventh, but in October 1967 Sexton dropped a bombshell by walking out to replace Tommy Docherty as Chelsea manager. A disconsolate McLintock yelled, 'Fuck his canoe,' after Mee informed the players that Sexton needed to 'paddle his own canoe as a manager in his own right'.

'We were devastated when Dave left,' recalls Terry Neill. 'We really felt that under him, we were on the right lines and that with a few new signings, we could be successful.' Sexton recalls, 'I wanted to take the opportunity at Chelsea, and I like to think I was pretty successful, winning the FA Cup and the European Cup Winners' Cup. Who knows what might have happened if I'd stayed at Arsenal? Don Howe probably had more of a streak of ruthlessness and aggression in him which absolutely brought out the best in those players. I didn't have that. So it probably worked out best for everyone. That's the way I've always felt obliged to see it, anyway.'

Ure adds, 'Dave laid down the structure and gave us a team ethic from which Don Howe was able to build.'

Not that the Arsenal players – still smarting from Sexton's departure – made it easy for the newly-promoted reserve team coach. 'A few of us had played alongside Don when he'd joined us as a player from West Brom in 1964,' recalled George Armstrong. 'It's easy to subconsciously get a bit overfamiliar with someone in that position, and for a few days, we all moaned about Dave leaving.

'Don sympathised for a while, but after about a week, when he felt we weren't pulling our weight, he basically had a shit fit in front of all of us. He blasted his whistle and yelled, "I have fucking had enough of all of you. Unless you stop moaning, you can fuck off out of this club, and Bertie will sign some new players." He had our attention! From that point on, we were putty in his hands. Don was very tactically astute, and a superb coach.'

Howe soon abandoned Sexton's man-to-man marking system, introducing instead a zonal marking system which appeared to work better. 'It allowed us to use our brains slightly more, and wasn't as robotic as man-to-man marking could be, although we did sometimes deploy that technique if we needed to in some matches in later years,' explains McLintock.

Although Arsenal only finished eighth in 1967/68, the team reached the League Cup Final after a 16-year Wembley absence. Arsenal had only opted to enter the competition in 1966/67. Both Wembley experiences suggested that Arsenal, and particularly McLintock, were doomed to play out a Sisyphus-type existence. The Ephyran King was punished by the Greek gods and forced to roll a huge boulder up a hill, only to watch it crash back down, and to repeat this action for eternity.

McLintock had lost two FA Cup Finals with Leicester City in 1961 and 1963, and would suffer further Wembley heartache with the Gunners in the later part of the decade. Both League Cup finals against Leeds United and Swindon Town, horrendous in their own ways, proved to be the steepest of learning curves.

Don Revie's Leeds side was edging closer to silverware but, after finishing runners-up in the league in 1965 and 1966, and losing the FA Cup Final to Liverpool in 1965, some branded the players as 'chokers'. They had emerged victorious from all their encounters with Arsenal since their promotion from the Second Division in 1964, and had many of the components in place that would make them a formidable power in the years to come.

Leeds had nimble full-backs in Cooper and Reaney, a solid central defensive brick wall of Charlton and Hunter, and the steely midfield duo of Bremner and Giles. Gray and Lorimer added a shimmering of unorthodoxy to an increasingly well-oiled mean machine. 'Leeds were a couple of years ahead of us in their development,' admits Ian Ure. 'We saw reaching the final as a step along the way to our own development.'

For Leeds United, with so many near misses already under their belts, it was a match they simply couldn't afford to lose.

The profile of the final, played on a Saturday afternoon in the middle of a full domestic programme without live TV coverage, was distinctly low-key. That was probably no bad thing as the game, later described by Desmond Hackett in the *Daily Express* as 'a game so bad it was little short of scandalous', is commonly regarded as one of the most dismal ever played at Wembley. 'It was a car crash of a match,' admits Jon Sammels. 'It was like listening to two jagged pieces of metal grating and scraping against each other.' Ian Ure views it as 'being like a violent game of chess'. *Football Monthly* claimed both Arsenal and Leeds had 'a complete and cynical disregard for the £90,000 paid by real football supporters'.

Terry Cooper's superb volleyed goal after 17 minutes – a goal he dreamt of scoring on each of the three nights preceding the final – settled the game for Leeds. But it was a controversial effort because it came as a direct result of the pandemonium Jack Charlton caused by standing on the goal line in front of Jim Furnell for Eddie Gray's inswinging corner.

Charlton had suggested the idea to Revie in training and Revie duly sanctioned it. In its own crude way it was devastatingly effective, because although goalkeepers complained of obstruction Charlton was really only using his height. Ure recalls, 'Charlton was all over Furnell like he was a climbing frame. It was a level of ruthless professionalism we hadn't seen before in England.'

After Cooper's goal, Arsenal rarely troubled their opponents and Leeds were unwilling to gamble and risk conceding an equaliser in search of a second killer goal. A full-scale brawl broke out after McLintock charged into Leeds goalkeeper Gary Sprake.

'It was ugly and it wasn't worth the spectators coming to see,' admitted Bertie Mee. 'But I learnt that afternoon that tactically, we were a tight outfit. We harried, we pressed, and we made life difficult for Leeds. Physically, we matched everything that Leeds threw at us. I did make a mental note however, that we needed more striking options up front, as Leeds dealt with our forwards that afternoon rather too comfortably. We were merely average in terms of our attacking play.'

'We realised that if we wanted to be successful in that era, we'd need to copy some of Leeds' ruthless methods,' admits Ure. 'I would add that Arsenal never copied their more cynical elements. Bertie Mee and Don Howe would never have sanctioned it.'

It is worth noting that full-back Peter Storey, whom Giles and Bremner had unsuccessfully targeted throughout the final, was later deployed as a midfield 'enforcer' by Mee – so his manager clearly wasn't averse to copying one aspect of Leeds's dark side. Leeds had finally got their hands on silverware but the tone of future ill-tempered Arsenal v Leeds clashes had been well and truly set.

On the way to Wembley a year later, they had nudged out Tottenham over two legs in the semi-final. Arsenal put in a heroic defensive performance at Highbury with John Radford crashing home a last-minute winner before withstanding a Tottenham onslaught at White Hart Lane. Jimmy Greaves put the home side ahead before another late Radford header gave the Gunners a draw on the night which saw them win 2-1 on aggregate.

Greaves later explained, 'It was the first time I felt they were emerging from our shadow. Defensively, they could tie you up in knots and were a superb unit. Big Radford wasn't everyone's cup of tea, but he typified Arsenal. Strong, uncompromising, doing his job effectively. I didn't like the way Arsenal played, or Leeds for that matter, with so much emphasis on defence and organisation. That was how football was going in the late 1960s. Give me Spurs' style any day. But I can't disagree that in their own way, Arsenal weren't becoming effective'.

The final against Third Division Swindon Town seemed a formality but on a Wembley pitch turned into a quagmire by the previous autumn's Horse of the Year Show, and recent torrential rain, Arsenal crashed and burned.

'The reaction we received after losing the match was so bad that you'd think we should have packed up football and gone and played marbles or tiddlywinks instead,' admitted George Armstrong.

Desmond Hackett's infamous report of Arsenal's 3-1 loss to Swindon was eventually instrumental in spurring on the humiliated players, but at the time it seemed like Arsenal couldn't possibly go any lower. 'Look with admiration at these heroic athletes from the Third Division who reduced the traditions of Arsenal to a miserable myth… Arsenal betrayed the pride of London,' wrote Hackett. In case *Express* readers hadn't quite grasped the meaning of Hackett's report, it was headed 'THE SHAME OF ARSENAL'.

It was the most infamous Arsenal occasion since the Walsall defeat some 36 years earlier. Admittedly, the conditions were horrendous — the pitch had been reduced to an energy-destroying mixture of sand, mud and water, with hundreds of gallons of water pumped off in the days before the game, and eight Arsenal players had been laid low with a chest infection in the previous week — but there were no excuses.

Swindon goalkeeper Peter Downsborough played the game of his life, making several superb last-ditch saves, the best of which was a fine stop from Jon Sammels's volley. Ure's ill-judged backpass to Bob Wilson allowed Roger Smart to nip in and score the first. Bobby Gould grabbed a late equaliser and began to cry when he realised that his wife as providing a running commentary for his blind father up in the stands. Howe pleaded unsuccessfully with the referee to abandon the game as it went into extra time.

Don Rogers plunged the dagger into Arsenal's hearts in that torturous half-hour with a tap-in from a corner, and a quicksilver run from the halfway line, after which he drove the ball past Wilson from an acute angle. Arguably the most jarring image of the day was of a dazed and stunned McLintock wandering lost among the band of the Royal Engineers.

'At that moment, I was wondering if I was cursed, destined never to achieve anything of note in the game,' he admits. 'Luckily, I had a strong family around me to lift me, and I guess I had a mean streak inside me which meant I just couldn't give up.'

In London's Mayfair, comedian Bob Monkhouse had to alter his routine to reflect Swindon's unexpected success, and of course, Hackett busied himself writing his piece for the morning editions.

The day after the League Cup Final defeat, Mee spent Sunday at home with his family, 'gathering my thoughts and spending most of the morning fending off journalists who wanted to speak to me'. His policy was to avoid speaking to tabloid hacks in the aftermath of matches, which explains the singular lack of explosive Mee quotes in the archives.

On the Monday morning, Howe and he met with the deflated Arsenal players, and in time honoured Mee fashion, delivered a 'let's get on with it' type of speech. 'I told them that the team spirit we'd nurtured would not disintegrate, rather that we would gain strength and come back from adversity. I looked into the eyes of all my men, and although I saw disappointment and hurt, I also saw hunger and desire, none more so than in the eyes of Frank McLintock. I thought that if he, after all he'd been through, remained strong, then this team would stay resolute.'

Bob Wilson recalls, 'We could have gone home, gone to bed, pulled the covers over ourselves, and stayed there. Instead, we came out fighting.'

The players immediately looked on the only positive they could draw upon from the whole experience. There was still a Fairs Cup place up for grabs if they could finish in the top four in the league, which remained a distinct possibility if they could stabilise quickly.

Howe and Mee then made two key tactical switches. George Graham, who had been a substitute at Wembley, was asked by Mee and Howe to play in the number six shirt as an old-fashioned left-half, who could play in midfield and ghost into the box to score some goals. His relaxed skill on the ball – hence his nickname 'Stroller' – made him a fairly obvious choice for the role. More unorthodox was chief scout Gordon Clark's suggestion that McLintock could be converted from a high-energy, occasionally rash midfielder, into an effective centre-back. It meant the beginning of the end of the error-prone Ure's Arsenal career.

McLintock's move to central defence wasn't made permanent until midway through the following season, but the player – in his own words – 'had a go in the role and felt like it could work for both me and the team. It meant that as captain, I could now see the game from the back, which changes your whole perception of the game. There was no guarantee it would work. Bob McNab reckoned it would be a bloody disaster, telling me that I lacked the discipline to do it. But it paid off, and without wishing to blow my own trumpet, the team now had strong leadership on the pitch, which it hadn't always had in the past.'

One of the features of Mee's emerging side was the players' constant cajoling of one another. 'We became a very vocal side, and the most vocal were Frank and Bob [McNab]. You should have heard what Frank called George Graham, who could be a bit casual at times,' recalled

Ure. 'I'd call Bob a "wanker" and worse, and he'd come back at me with worse and worse! I often clashed with George about his work ethic on the pitch. My prime aim was to keep the shape and balance of the side right. Bob McNab and I used to dish it out to each other and everyone on the team, but I like to think we could take it back and there would be no recriminations.'

'We were a tough, tough side, driven on through adversity,' explains McLintock. There were also feisty team meetings in the Halfway House – a poky room half way down the tunnel at Highbury – where players would vent their spleen at one another on a Monday after a match, and then take it out on one another in five-a-side matches. 'There was no quarter given,' recalls Wilson. 'The air was usually blue, but people took it and learned from it.'

Arsenal somehow roused themselves and finished fourth to qualify for the Fairs Cup, but Mee conceded that he still needed more options up front. He warned journalists that he would avoid waving the chequebook around, telling the *Daily Mirror*, 'As all keen-eyed Arsenal fans know, I've got a couple of excellent young strikers in the reserve side, of whom we all have high hopes. Their names are Ray Kennedy and Charlie George. I'm planning on using them next season. They'll be vital to us.'

The Gunners' domestic form throughout the 1969/70 campaign was poor. By the time the clocks went back in November there were press rumours that Mee might even lose his job. At the end of home matches against Leeds and Sheffield Wednesday, the Highbury crowd slow-clapped the team off, chanting, 'We want football.'

There was a huge churn of players due partly to injuries (23 were deployed that campaign), and also because Mee and Howe decided that the likes of Robertson, Court and Gould were now surplus to requirements. Always keen to promote from within, young full-backs Rice and Nelson made their first team breakthroughs, and the precocious talent of Charlie George began to emerge.

It wasn't always a pleasant atmosphere for the newcomers. Several Arsenal players went public and asked the crowd to lay off Jon

Sammels and John Radford, who bore the brunt of the frustration. Mee put up a sterling defence of the club's reluctance to spend money on new players (Francis Lee, Allan Clarke, Mick Jones and Derek Dougan were several players whom Mee had been linked with) at the AGM in October 1969. It showed that he was at least willing to meet his detractors face to face, but it was the European run that kept the malcontents at bay.

Arsenal disposed of Irish part-timers Glentoran, Sporting Lisbon, Rouen and Dinamo Bacau before facing the much-fancied European Cup finalists from the previous year – Ajax – in the semi-final. The previous ties hadn't entirely captured the imagination of Arsenal's fans but a clash against the team containing arguably Europe's brightest talent – Johan Cruyff – certainly did.

The first leg at home drew over 50,000 to Highbury and for the first time in perhaps a generation, all the key components – tactical adeptness, robust leadership on the pitch, and a shimmering of skill – fused to produce an unforgettable night at Highbury. It remains a largely unheralded and forgotten victory but it gave the first bona fide hint that Mee and Howe might have finally sculpted a side with real potential.

Ajax goalkeeper Gert Bals recalls, 'Arsenal came at us with phenomenal intensity and pace. They started so quickly that we were looking at each other saying, "What's this all about?" They were a classically English team but with some unpredictability in young Charlie [George]. I also liked the play of Sammels. Very assured and cool on the ball. I'm sure that he should have been born Dutch or French.'

It was McNab who went close early on with two rasping efforts, before George rifled home on 17 minutes. 'I didn't even see it,' recalls Bals. 'It flashed past me with virtually no backlift.' George's unerringly accurate passing – often delivered with the outside of his foot – even had Cruyff drooling. He later claimed, 'Charlie can become as good as Di Stefano.'

Cruyff threatened Arsenal on several occasions and Ajax looked potentially devastating on the counter-attack, but Peter Storey, revelling in his designated role of keeping the Dutchman quiet, stuck closely to him. Sammels's display confounded the barrackers, 'Against

Ajax, I rediscovered my best form. We upped the tempo, and Ajax continued to play their tried and tested game, which afforded me a fraction more time and space than I was used to in Division One matches.'

It was Sammels who bundled in a crucial second late in the game, at a time when it appeared that Arsenal might buckle. Mee made a crucial substitution when he withdrew young winger Peter Marinello from the action and replaced him with George Armstrong, who proved to be a thorn in Ajax's side late on. When Graham was hacked down in the area, George grabbed the ball from McNab and said, 'All right, give it here Nabbers,' and thumped the spot-kick past Bals into the net to make it 3-0. 'We came of age that night, in many ways,' explained Armstrong. 'The leadership of Frank, Peter Storey playing the enforcer role in midfield, and Charlie's talent shining through was there. For me, it was a massive night, because many people automatically assumed that Peter Marinello would permanently oust me from the team, but after this, Bert stuck with me.'

Despite the distraction of the Apollo 13 saga, and terrorist threats from neo-Nazi groups to Ajax, a club with strong Jewish connections, Arsenal stuck doggedly to their task in the second leg. Cruyff showed his full repertoire of skills. 'He was such a beautifully balanced player. So quick to read the game, and move like lightning to exploit space. I'd describe playing against him as a retrospective pleasure, because I was so concerned at that time what damage he could inflict on us,' recalled Armstrong.

Thanks largely to Wilson and Peter Simpson, the Dutch side failed to build on Muhren's 17th-minute goal and the Gunners' rearguard action in keeping the score down to a single 1-0 defeat – and hence a 3-1 aggregate victory – ranks as one of their finest European displays.

For the third time in three years, the Gunners were in a final and would face Anderlecht, conquerors of Inter Milan in their semi-final. In front of 30,000 Belgian fans at the Parc Astrid Stadium in Brussels, the McLintock curse looked to be crossing into another decade. After a good start by the Gunners an uncharacteristic error by Simpson allowed striker Johan Devrindt the chance to give his side the lead. On 30 minutes, Devrindt set up Jan Mulder who made it 2-0 from a half-volley.

'I didn't even think we'd played that badly,' recalls Sammels, 'but the passing interchanges between Devrindt and Mulder were absolutely superb. One would pull our defenders away with a decoy run, and the other would exploit the gap. Frank McLintock said that Mulder was the best he'd ever played against. His pace could kill you.'

With 15 minutes remaining, Mulder appeared to have killed the tie when he blasted home a third. The klaxons inside the ground were absolutely deafening. As a last throw of the dice, Mee hauled off a tiring George and brought on 19-year-old Ray Kennedy. 'Anderlecht might have switched off a bit. They struggled to cope with the high balls that Geordie [Armstrong] and Jon [Sammels] started to pump my way. They were old-fashioned English tactics. They didn't like it,' recalled Kennedy.

On 82 minutes, Kennedy powered home a header from Armstrong's cross. The late consolation goal did little to ease Arsenal's pain at being picked apart for much of the game by Anderlecht's lattice-work passing.

Armstrong recalled, 'As we trooped in at the final whistle, I don't think any of us said a word. The young lads – like Charlie and Ray – looked shell-shocked – and the older players like me, who'd been in the teams which had lost to Leeds and to Swindon, we just thought, "Here we go again."'

There was one Arsenal player who felt his side still had hope. McLintock may have been devastated by the loss but he recalls, 'I was in the shower, and I thought to myself, "I'm not having this shit anymore. I had all that bad luck in the 60s, and I'm not having that happen to me in the 70s too!" So I came out shouting [McLintock demonstrates – punching the air and banging his fists], "Come on you lot, get your heads up, 'cos we aren't finished yet. We'll do them at Highbury! We'll get at them! We'll go for it. An early goal, and you'll see them start worrying." I went on like that for some time, shouting and screaming.'

Mee recalled, 'Sometimes, it's time for a manager to let his captain do the work, and cajole and inspire. Frank [Mee looked at me for a while and paused] was an inspiration to those men.'

A crowd of 51,000 packed Highbury for the return leg. By now, 17 painfully long years had passed since Arsenal lifted a trophy – and didn't the players know it. McLintock recalls, 'You'd play your game, and all the guys from the 30s and 40s would be there afterwards. You know – the Mercers, the Drakes, the Comptons. All Arsenal legends. And it made you feel inadequate, to be honest. They'd won things. And we'd won nothing. And you'd think to yourself, "Christ – this isn't good enough." You'd see picture of the 30s side all around the stadium, and it would fill me with this feeling, "We've got to strive to equal what they did." Some people suggested taking the pictures down, but Don Howe always argued that we had to be aware of their achievements, in order to try and match them.'

Added impetus was given by UEFA's ruling just a few hours prior to the second leg that in the event of a tie, away goals would count double. Arsenal knew that a 2-0 win would suffice, not that such a score would be an easy task. For 25 minutes Anderlecht backed off Arsenal, threatening briefly when Jan Mulder and Paul Van Himst ventured forward. McLintock recalls, 'You had to keep Mulder under guard all the time, as he could – in the blink of an eye – make runs off you and drop deep. One touch – and bang – he could make the passes or hit you with a great shot.'

Arsenal exploded into life on the half-hour. From a Sammels pass, Eddie Kelly sidestepped his marker and smashed an unstoppable shot past Anderlecht keeper Trappeniers. 'Although we were halfway there,' recalls McLintock, 'I said to the lads at half-time to keep it tight, and keep hounding the Anderlecht players.'

As the Arsenal players jogged back on at the start of the second half, the captain decided to take matters into his own hands. 'I ran over to the North Bank, and did this [at this point, McLintock jumps up from his chair, and starts thumping his fists together – his leadership skills just as potent 35 years later]. "Fucking sing up, come on" I was shouting at them.'

In the 70th minute the non-stop chanting finally paid dividends as a mud-splattered Radford headed in an Armstrong cross. Two minutes later, Sammels blasted home a third.

Forty-three years later Van Himst still marvels at Arsenal's ferocity at Highbury. 'They hit us with a whirlwind. McLintock and McNab – I remember them. They were like dervishes. Screaming, yelling, fists pumped. They never got suckered in, thinking they could match us for skill, but their pressing game, their constant harrying and their sheer – well, British approach – of guts and determination beat us.'

It was claimed that the Anderlecht players had suggested that their British counterparts must have taken stimulants to have played at such a tempo, but Van Himst insists, 'We didn't say that – it was the British press trying to provoke some anti-Belgian feeling!'

Although Mulder skimmed the post with a late volley, the referee blew his whistle after four minutes of injury time. The scenes were astounding. For Bob Wilson, the memories of that evening remain as fresh as ever, 'All that pent-up frustration in the fans and players was gone in flash. If you think about some of the older members of the crowd, they had seen the great sides of the 30s and 40s, and finally the slumbering giant had awoken. All the crowd – it seemed – came over the barriers at the final whistle, and the police knew that it was a friendly pitch invasion. So they turned a blind eye.'

The sense of relief felt by Arsenal players was unbelievable. How did McLintock feel in the aftermath of the Fairs Cup victory? 'Like I wasn't jinxed anymore. Like I'd delivered, and that my team had finally delivered. Now I could finally look people like Joe Mercer in the eye.'

Mee recalled, 'It was hugely satisfying. The team had tough moral fibre, a marvellous sense of responsibility to one another, and clear leadership. It was a superb blend. We had a system which worked, and which we could now take forward. Everyone was working towards the same goal.' From a complete systems failure throughout much of Arsenal's colourless 1960s, Bertie Mee and Don Howe now had a blueprint which would take them to the greatest domestic achievement of all as the Technicolor Age dawned.

# Semis Detached

*'I looked down the pitch as Peter Storey stepped up to take the penalty. I could barely contain my nerves. It didn't occur to me to wonder how he must have felt!' Bob Wilson.*

*'He'll be eternally damned for that afternoon. Someone's always got to be the fall guy when a team loses. On this occasion, it was Jeff Blockley.' Alan Ball.*

ON 30 September 1970, in front of just 18,000 at the Victoria Ground, Stoke City appeared to be laying waste to Arsenal's title pretensions. The unbeaten Gunners travelled north in fourth place, tucked in behind Leeds, Manchester City and Tottenham. They had defeated Lazio in the Fairs Cup just three days earlier but the Gunners' impressive form counted for nothing in the Potteries.

Bertie Mee's team was destroyed by Tony Waddington's red and white candy-bar-striped team. Peter Dobing and the hugely skilful Jimmy Greenhoff and Terry Conroy had run rings around a sluggish Frank McLintock on the edge of the Arsenal box. The muscular striker John Ritchie gave the Arsenal defence a torrid afternoon.

'At half-time, I looked around the dressing room, and everybody looked spent,' recalled George Armstrong. 'We were very quiet, lacked any real spark, and we were 2-0 down. Normally, we were able to rouse ourselves. But on this occasion we completely collapsed in the second half.'

Soon after the game resumed, a scintillating move saw the pacey Irish forward Terry Conroy crack home a third before, with Arsenal's defence in disarray, Greenhoff and Bloor scored Stoke's fourth and fifth goals.

McLintock recalls, 'We were routed. Completely humiliated. It was as bad as it could possibly get. I was furious about what had happened. The good thing – retrospectively – was that we all were. We didn't afford them enough respect and we deserved everything we got.'

The reaction from the press towards Arsenal's shellacking was vicious. 'Bloody Desmond Hackett came up to me a couple of days later,' recalled Armstrong. 'He said, "You'll never win the league George. You're too slow at the back, McLintock is over the hill, you're ponderous in midfield, and Radford and Kennedy are like statues up front."

'I quite liked Desmond actually, but on that occasion, I could willingly have shoved that bloody bowler hat of his up his arse. And I thought, "I'll bloody show you." I told the rest of the boys what he'd said, and it acted as a real fillip. We were good at coming back from big defeats.'

Ray Kennedy recalls, 'Desmond Hackett liked to write controversial headlines, and he was often saying we were a bit dull. When things didn't go our way, we got tense and could grind to a halt.'

Mee and Don Howe ripped into the team privately but Mee insisted that his players would get the defeat out of their system quickly, and in by now time-honoured fashion he allowed the players to deal with the thrashing at the Victoria Ground themselves.

The Halfway House meeting was at its most vitriolic on the following Monday. As usual, McLintock chaired proceedings, 'I freely admitted that I'd been utterly useless in the game. It was a case of "You're not fucking doing it, and you're not fucking doing it either." And they came back at me and said, "Well Frank, you didn't fucking do it either, did you?" And I couldn't argue with that! We sorted it out, and bounced back.'

Kennedy recalls, 'The players didn't go easy on me because I was a youngster. They told me and Raddy after the Stoke game in no uncertain terms that we hadn't contributed enough, and hadn't tracked back when Stoke went at us. It wasn't easy for me to hear, but at Arsenal you either sank or you swum. I dealt with it. Bertie Mee kept me in the side, and we all moved on to the next game.'

The Arsenal players never forgot that dismal afternoon at the Victoria Ground. It was a chastening experience for the Fairs Cup winners, none more so than Bob Wilson. Already enjoying a burgeoning TV career, Wilson offered to talk viewers through the Stoke debacle on BBC's *Football Focus* on the following Saturday.

Wilson recalls, 'Bertie wasn't too pleased about me breaking confidences. With hindsight, I was naïve. He was right to build that fortress mentality. Us against them.'

Two decades after the incident, Mee explained, 'After that Stoke defeat, I realised, as with the Swindon defeat, and the loss to Anderlecht, I'd see what kind of a reaction my team had within them. I was always confident they'd come back stronger, and they did.'

Arsenal hammered Ipswich 4-0 in the League Cup, put six past West Bromwich Albion in the league game at Highbury, with Kennedy netting five goals across both games, and went on a 14-match unbeaten run in the league.

Arsenal would next encounter Stoke City in the most dramatic circumstances, in an FA Cup semi-final at Hillsborough. It would prove to be arguably the most epoch-defining Saturday afternoon in Arsenal's recent history.

In a 2011 poll among Stoke fans, over 60 per cent of the 1,800 who voted cited Arsenal as their least favourite rival. In part this was a reaction to the controversy surrounding Ryan Shawcross's tackle on Aaron Ramsey – which resulted in the Welshman breaking his leg, and the mutual antagonism between Arsène Wenger and the then Potters boss Tony Pulis, which revolved around the clubs' contrasting playing styles.

Yet for many Stoke fans of a certain generation, their dislike of Arsenal is borne out of events in the early 1970s. Ironically, given Wenger's lambasting of Pulis's sides' playing styles, it was Tony Waddington's team who looked down on Arsenal's yeoman style.

In 1970, Stoke boss Waddington had described Arsenal's tactics in a league game – won 1-0 courtesy of a John Radford goal – as being similar to those of '11 navvies'. A characteristically terse Mee responded in the *Islington Gazette* by saying, 'We use the tactics which we believe will win us the game. Football is about results. At least it is at Arsenal.'

Whether that was a dig at Stoke remains unclear, but the perception within the game as the 1970s dawned was that Waddington's side was 'soft'. Much was made of former Gunner George Eastham's decision to leave for South Africa – in protest at referees' *laissez-faire* approach to the tackle from behind – as evidence of this.

By the 1970/71 season, Stoke had toughened up. McLintock recalls, 'John Ritchie was a highly effective target man, and with Denis Smith and Alan Bloor in defence, they suddenly had a much meaner look about them. Jimmy Greenhoff and Terry Conroy up front were really skilful forwards who would keep anyone busy. And with Gordon Banks in goal, it gave them massive confidence going into any game.'

Buoyed by their 5-0 victory over Arsenal, and a 3-0 win against Leeds, the Stoke players believed they had the tactical nous to cause leading sides problems every time they faced them. 'Tony Waddington was a great tactician,' recalled John Ritchie. 'He always tried to point out two or three weaknesses in any teams we played; something we should aim to do in the game. Against Arsenal, there were two things in particular. Firstly, place two midfielders as close to Radford and Kennedy as possible – to cut off their supply line. I always remember Waddo saying, "Do that and they'll be toothless." And secondly, use pace to go straight at McLintock. Waddo always reckoned he was a good player but a bit pedestrian.'

'Stoke were well balanced and could mix it if they wanted to,' shrugged Armstrong. 'To be honest, I think we always found them a bit of a pain in the arse to play against,' he admitted, 'because they could vary their tactics.'

When Arsenal were drawn to play Stoke in the semi-final, the league-leading Gunners were unsurprisingly installed as hot favourites to win. Yet Mee's team was entering a pivotal period of the season. Three days before the Stoke game, the Fairs Cup holders had been knocked out by Cologne after some highly controversial refereeing decisions in the second leg in West Germany. Mee, who had delivered a rousing speech just a few weeks earlier urging his team to seize the opportunity to compete for three trophies, began to feel the weight of expectation upon his shoulders.

'By the time you get to late March, and you're still competing in the big competitions, you start to become aware that there can be little room for error,' he explained. 'Even after we lost to Cologne – unfairly – I still believed that we could bounce back against Stoke. I could feel the pressure, and I began to appreciate why some teams seize up when the finishing line is in sight, but I tried my best not to transfer that to the players.

'Arsenal hadn't played in an FA Cup semi-final for – what was it – 19 years? Scandalous, for a club of Arsenal's stature. And then you think, "We have to win this, otherwise the entire season might grind to a halt." I tried to banish those thoughts from my head, and as the game approached, I was absolutely convinced that we'd progress.'

Several of the articles written in the lead-up to the game were a tad patronising towards Stoke. The *Daily Mirror* reported that whereas Arsenal players enjoyed specially selected pre-match meals prior to games, Waddington made his lads ham sandwiches when they ventured to away games.

Likewise, when the Gunners ventured home by coach, they could tuck in to smoked salmon, chomp away on cigars, and drink the finest liqueurs. Stoke players had to make do with fish and chips, and a crate of beer. The same applied to the clubs' staff roster. The Victoria Ground had one groundsman whereas Highbury had several employees responsible for the general upkeep of the stadium.

'The media portrayed it as a David v Goliath style encounter,' explained Armstrong. 'We certainly weren't thinking like that. We were really annoyed at how we'd lost to Cologne, and we just couldn't afford to lose this one. Some in the game reckoned that Stoke might have a psychological edge because of what they'd done to us back in August.'

One Arsenal player who certainly wasn't underestimating Stoke was midfielder Peter Storey, who had revenge on his mind. 'A defeat like that is a blot on our record this season and we will be determined to rub it out,' he told the *Evening Standard*. 'One thing's for sure. We will be mentally prepared for them this time. We will be treating them just like Leeds.'

Storey had already scored coolly from the spot in both FA Cup fourth round matches against Portsmouth. Pompey goalkeeper John

Milkins recalled, 'Jesus – when Arsenal screamed "Penalty!" it was something else. Frank McLintock charged like a lunatic after the referee, with Bob McNab and Peter Storey right behind him, pulling his shirt and pointing to the spot. They were seriously aggressive, especially Storey. They were right in a referee's face when they felt that they'd been wronged. All you could see was their tonsils, and all you could hear was their swearing at officials.'

'Nothing would give me greater pleasure than to stick one [a penalty] past Gordon Banks in the semi-final,' Storey told the *Standard*. 'That would really be something, wouldn't it?' They proved to be prophetic words.

The Arsenal v Stoke clash reunited former Leicester City team-mates Frank McLintock and Gordon Banks. Despite the longevity of his career, World Cup winner Banks only had the 1964 League Cup to show as tangible domestic success while the Scot was keen to add to his Fairs Cup medal from a year before. There was a groundswell of popular opinion for the amiable Banks to add the FA Cup medal to his collection, especially given the fact that he was now 33. He had also been made Stoke City skipper, and despite the fact it was only nine months since his remarkable save from Pele at the 1970 World Cup, his form had slipped below his normally ultra-reliable best.

Ritchie explained, 'I'm never convinced that goalkeepers make the best captains. They're too far removed from the action for long intervals, and Gordon, possibly feeling that he had to intervene and fight his team's corner with officials, began to get a bit tetchy and irritable. He started to make a few mistakes.'

Wilson, who had watched his boyhood idol play for local side Chesterfield, commented in the matchday programme, 'We goalkeepers look to his conduct as the target for our own standards. We can only hope to achieve a greatness like his.' The lines between hero and villain status soon became blurred.

Hillsborough was regarded by Arsenal players as the most atmospheric of all FA Cup semi-final venues. Armstrong recalled, 'I loved the scale and the drama of the place. Highbury is a compact and tight venue, but Hillsborough always was so spacious.'

Arcing upwards in the sky and framed by trees on the hills above Sheffield, 25,000 Arsenal fans crammed the Spion Kop terrace on a bright and breezy afternoon, with Stoke supporters shoehorned into Leppings Lane.

Wilson recalled, 'The moment of truth was approaching. Even though we prepared for the game as we would any other, we all knew that this was a match of seismic proportions for the club. Bertie had talked to us a few months before about going for a trophy Treble, but now we had to focus our minds on a Double. Somehow I always thought that this game could make or break us.'

Waddington instructed his players to pressurise the Arsenal defence which he believed could be caught square. For the first 20 minutes of the game, the teams indulged in a phoney war; playing keep-ball and knocking the ball around in neat triangles. Then, on 20 minutes, Stoke drew first blood. Wilson turned Jimmy Greenhoff's effort around the post, and from Harry Burrows's corner, Stoke centre-half Denis Smith nudged it on. Arsenal half cleared their lines but the ball only rolled back out towards Smith, with Peter Storey the last line of defence in front of Wilson.

In the unforgiving code of 1970s hard men, Smith has reiterated his belief down the years that Storey 'bottled it'. Smith slung out his left foot to block the ball and alleges in his autobiography that Storey pulled out of the challenge. '"Interesting," I thought. "A 50-50 with Peter Storey and he's just disappeared."'

On the footage of the game it's true that Storey is a fraction of a second too late in making his challenge, as if he's disoriented by the pinball movement of the ball. He toe-pokes the ball against Smith's ankle, and watches on in horror as it balloons upwards and loops over Wilson into the top right-hand corner of the goal.

Nine minutes later, things got worse. Burrows flicked on a long ball from defence, which was intercepted by Charlie George midway inside his own half. Controlling the ball on his chest, he opted to pass back to Wilson. It fell agonisingly short and John Ritchie nipped in, took the ball around Wilson and slotted it in to the empty net in front of the ecstatic Stoke fans who were packed in to the Leppings Lane end.

It was 2-0 to Stoke and Ritchie's celebratory run down the left of the pitch, his arms raised aloft in celebration, is now preserved in stone outside the Britannia Stadium.

The big striker, who died in 2008, remains Stoke's record scorer, and he recalled, 'I was so convinced that we had Arsenal by the nuts. I literally thought about them, "Is this all you've got?" Remember that we'd beaten them 5-0 at the Victoria Ground, and now we were 2-0 up within half an hour. I'd say that the football we played in the first half-hour in the semi-final was the best period of play I ever saw from a Stoke team.'

Football history, of course, is about what was, not what might have been. But as a shell-shocked Arsenal limped towards half-time their Double dreams hung by a thread due to a fractionally mistimed tackle by Storey and a moment of recklessness by George. History could have turned out so differently and cast those two Arsenal players in an entirely different light.

Had John Mahoney, who ripped through a frighteningly square Arsenal defence early in the second half courtesy of Jimmy Greenhoff's splendid through ball, slotted his shot past Wilson to make it 3-0 rather than driving it straight at him, there could have been no opportunity for late redemption at Hillsborough and therefore no *Jesus Christ Superstar*-style celebration by George at Wembley.

Mee grimaced at the thought of the counterfactual scenario where Mahoney made it 3-0. 'There would have been no comeback from us if that had happened,' he admitted. 'And it's true, Charlie would be remembered perhaps only as the young hothead who made a defensive error. But then, [Mee threw his arms out expansively], what if Ray Kennedy hadn't scored that late consolation in the away leg against Anderlecht a year before? Would you and I be talking now at all? It's interesting what you say, but I think that if I'd thought about what might have happened at the time, I'd have driven myself into an early grave.'

More infamous than Mahoney's squandered opportunity is Greenhoff's moment that might have been. Twisting and turning on the halfway line with Arsenal players committed up front, Greenhoff surged beyond McLintock and, with his blonde hair fluttering in the wind, bore down on Wilson's goal. He could have attempted to take the ball around Wilson but instead opted to blast it from just inside the box. Taking a crucial bobble at point of impact, the ball ballooned into the Kop, much to Greenhoff's despair. 'It still keeps me awake at night occasionally,' he later admitted.

It was Stoke's last chance to hammer the final nail into Arsenal's coffin. Arsenal's best first-half chance came after an elaborate string of dummies saw Kennedy's drive parried wide by Banks. His fine save followed an extraordinary sequence of events where Banks had dropped the ball in his box, and thundered a clearance against the back of Radford.

'It was a bit unusual, to see a top goalkeeper behave like that,' admitted Kennedy. 'It was a high-pressure situation, but this was a guy who'd won the World Cup and had made that save from Pele less than a year earlier in Mexico, so it was a bit unusual to see him shouting at pretty much everyone.'

'It's true that of all the Stoke players, he was the least calm. I think Gordon was desperate to win the FA Cup, and as captain, he felt he had to fight our corner if things got tight in the game. It just got to him a bit, but he wasn't fully in control that day,' recalled Ritchie.

The Stoke skipper and England number one was powerless to stop Arsenal clawing their way back into the match shortly after Mahoney fluffed his golden opportunity. A throw-in from Armstrong was hooked onwards by Kennedy, and the ball was nodded clear to the edge of the box where Peter Storey was lurking with intent. The Arsenal midfielder cracked his shot on the half-volley and it took a slight deflection as it rocketed into the net past Banks. It was a sublime finish.

Minutes later, Greenhoff blasted his shot high and wide. On such contrasts in fortune hinge semi-finals. Ritchie recalls, 'Even then, I still felt that we were in control, and as we ran down the clock, I didn't really feel that Arsenal had enough left in the tank to salvage the tie.'

With 90 minutes up, referee Pat Partridge added two minutes of injury time. It proved to be the most critical 120 seconds in the Gunners' modern history. With the Stoke fans urging Partridge to blow the final whistle, Armstrong chipped the ball into the box and as Banks prepared to gather it, George Graham barged into him and Banks sent the ball spinning out for a corner.

A furious Banks hounded Partridge, claiming that Graham's shoulder charge meant he had been impeded. And yet what Partridge clearly hadn't seen, and what has not been mentioned in any Arsenal histories since, is that immediately after Banks dropped the ball, Stoke centre-back Denis Smith clearly nudged it away with his left hand, a fact he openly admits in his autobiography.

Stoke striker Ritchie recalled, 'In that era, I'm not entirely sure that George Graham's challenge should have been treated as a foul. I scored plenty of goals by being a damned sight more physical than that. I know that's almost a form of heresy from a Stoke player, but Smithy's handball is more clear cut than George Graham's shoulder barge.'

With the game in its death throes, Armstrong floated over a corner which McLintock nodded powerfully towards to the left of Banks, who couldn't get near the header. Instead, Mahoney dived to push the ball away with his hand. 'I wish I'd scored that goal,' admits McLintock wistfully, 'but it would have taken away from the sheer drama of the whole occasion.'

Substitute Jon Sammels recalled, 'We knew that it was a penalty straight away but just in case Pat Partridge had forgotten, we all screamed in his face at top volume, pointing to our hands.' This time, Partridge hadn't missed the handball by a Stoke player, and pointed to the spot. Banks later talked of a sense of 'fatalism' washing over him.

The pendulum had swung. Armstrong recalled, 'I don't think any of us had any doubt that we were about to claw it back. Well maybe Peter Storey did but he never showed it! I felt Banksy lost the plot that afternoon, really.'

As the Arsenal players hugged one another in celebration at the penalty being awarded, Storey knew that he still had his job to do from the spot. Having been given the midfield 'enforcer' role, he was now the designated penalty taker ('I always got the nasty jobs') with George having been substituted. 'It was one of those defining moments which I sensed would live with me forever,' he later recalled. 'Miss and Arsenal would be out of the FA Cup and I'd never hear the end of it.'

Storey has had many dubious nicknames and labels affixed to him in the 43 years since that momentous afternoon at Hillsborough, in no small part due to his brushes with the law since he retired from the game. George Best claimed Storey was 'a joke', although in his final years on the after-dinner speaking circuit Best actually admitted on several occasions that Storey was his most obdurate opponent.

Chelsea skipper Ron Harris described his fellow 1970s hard man as 'the bastard's bastard'. Twelve years ago, *Match Of The Day Magazine* put Storey at the very top of their Shifty Fifty list. In *Rebels For The Cause*, I compared him with one of Alex's sideburned droogs from *A Clockwork Orange*.

In his no-nonsense autobiography, Storey says of the 1971 Hillsborough semi-final, 'Me? I'll always have Sheffield.' The Steel City was a suitably raw and unvarnished venue for the player his team-mates labelled 'Cold Eyes' to stamp his mark indelibly in Arsenal's long and rich history.

It all came down to a highly disputed penalty deep, deep into injury time. Storey skipped slightly as he approached the ball and drove it straight down the middle to Banks's left as the England keeper shifted his body weight to the right. Framed by the Spion Kop behind him, Storey immediately stops dead as he dispatches the ball, throwing his hands into the air. 'Whenever I see the penalty on TV, my heart is still in my mouth,' recalled Kennedy. 'It wasn't a great penalty. If Gordon had stayed still, he could have just kicked it away. But he didn't and so it was Peter's moment.' It was 2-2. Somehow, Arsenal had saved themselves and forced a replay.

The contrasting fortunes of football were never better illustrated in the seconds that followed. Wilson offered up a prayer in thanks, Radford and Kennedy embraced, and in the dug-out, Mee 'realised that I had a bad stomach ache. The tension had been building all game. In fact it was so bad I was almost bent double for a few minutes before the relief washed over me.' Such was Mee's sense of relief that he later told the *Sunday Times*'s Rob Hughes, 'I feel like I have won the FA Cup itself after today.'

Banks lashed the ball away in a fit of rage as the recriminations began in the Stoke defence and Ritchie reacted most violently by butting Frank McLintock on the bridge of his nose. 'It was a fit of temper, and it was inexcusable. I couldn't believe what had happened. I felt such a pent-up rage. We'd had the tie in the bag and blown it. I just thought, "Piss off Frank." And I nutted him.'

Banks spoke confidently afterwards about finishing the job at Villa Park in the replay three days later and Mick Bernard talked about how easy it had been for him to mark George out of the game. 'But we knew that we had them,' claimed Kennedy, 'and I think they did too.'

At Villa Park in front of 60,000, one of the first acts of the game was George's backpass to Wilson – 'just so I could get myself settled for the match' – and a header from Graham and a tap-in from Kennedy (Banks barely moved for either goal) meant that Arsenal went to Wembley to face Bill Shankly's Liverpool.

Down the years, Storey has downplayed his role in the semi-final, insisting that he simply did his job. The drama of the events at Hillsborough led to some memorable headlines. In the *Sunday Times*, Brian Glanville claimed, 'Arsenal's penalty unmakes history.' Other newspapers preferred to focus on the hero of the hour's surname. 'It's Storey, Storey hallelujah!' and 'A Storey Book Ending' were two of the most popular.

Arsenal's team ethic that season was phenomenal, and even now players confirm that 'no one was bigger than the team'. But in individual games that campaign, different players came to the fore at different times, meaning that certain matches were destined to become their signature 90 minutes.

Just as the August thrashing of Manchester United was notable for Radford's hat-trick on *Match Of The Day*, and the derby win over Tottenham at Highbury became famous for Armstrong's double, so Hillsborough rightly belongs to Storey. Even the man himself, known for his efficiency and insistence on getting on with the task, admits in his book, 'It can be all too convenient to claim you win as a team and lose as a team. That way of thinking can soften the blow for a player who has cocked things up. Yes, it is a team game, but sometimes individuals must show bottle.'

Armstrong recalled, 'That team will always be regarded as one which didn't have sufficient flair or personality, except perhaps for Charlie. Yet we had players like Peter who showed different qualities, like nerveless penalty taking, and a willingness to step up to the plate. Here was a guy who, because he wanted to play for the club, didn't kick up a fuss when Bertie converted him into a midfielder. You need that kind of selflessness, and I think he deserved his day at Hillsborough.'

Stoke visited Highbury for a league match just a few weeks later. Due to a spate of injuries, Waddington flooded their midfield in order to try and gain a point. They came within three minutes of grabbing a 0-0 draw before Eddie Kelly toe-poked the winner past Banks as the Gunners closed in on the title.

Having recently seen at first-hand Arsenal's steadfast refusal to lie down and die, the Potters discovered that Arsenal – who won ten league matches by a 1-0 scoreline – were the ultimate flatline bullies. 'We rarely gave away a lead,' explains McLintock. 'For us, it was all about the bottom line – winning. It's not to everyone's taste – that kind of attitude – but it worked.'

Kelly's winner was no less dramatic or vital than George's dramatic intervention against Newcastle a few weeks earlier when the score was 0-0. Stoke players quickly grew to despise Arsenal. Although they lifted the League Cup in 1972 – courtesy of former Gunner George Eastham's winner – players of that generation look back with bitterness on what happened in 1971, and a year later, when Stoke faced Arsenal again in the FA Cup semi-final. This time Radford scored the winner in the replay from a clearly offside position. The referee had mistaken one of the peanut sellers at the side of the Goodison Park pitch for a Stoke defender.

Even to this day Denis Smith switches off his television whenever Arsenal's name is mentioned, and two former Stoke players point-blank refused to speak to me, describing the Arsenal games as 'nightmares'. Ritchie explained, 'I thought that Arsenal were lucky, and helped by the officials. Perhaps it's just a case that when push came to shove, they simply had more bottle than us. Maybe they just wanted it fractionally more.'

Occasionally, Arsenal players have pondered what might have happened had Storey not completed his task. McLintock explains, 'It would have shaken us, because we'd already gone out of the Fairs Cup earlier that week, but even though we might have wobbled, I still think we'd have won the League.'

If Arsenal had wobbled by a fraction after Hillsborough in such a tight title race, it would have proved fatal to a team which only nudged out Leeds by a point and goal average. Mee had a different point of view, 'It's the match at Hillsborough that I think about the most, because that's the sort of occasion where champions are made. Or destroyed. You find out just how much mettle your team has. That Stoke match was the moment of truth for the team. Everything we achieved afterwards stemmed from that.'

The title clincher at White Hart Lane, where Kennedy's soaring header won the league, is regarded as one of the great Arsenal occasions. So is the FA Cup Final against Liverpool where George's stupendous finish and *Jesus Christ Superstar* celebration on the Wembley turf won the Double and afforded him instant cult hero status.

But those games weren't historical game-changers. The Hillsborough semi-final was. Misty-eyed purists will never view the Stoke game with any affection after Mee's team clawed their way back from the abyss against more aesthetically pleasing opponents. If ever a match embodied the 'Arsenal spirit' it was this one. It was the day that Arsenal came through with flying colours after their credentials, quite literally, were put on the spot.

Having secured the Double, Mee accepted that in order to earn himself a place in the pantheon of great Arsenal managers his team would need to win more silverware during the 1971/72 campaign. It was always going to be a tall order. Coach Don Howe departed to manage West Bromwich Albion a few short months after the Double was won ('It was an occasion of me going when I really should have stayed,' he admitted years later) and even though Steve Burtenshaw was a fine replacement, 'he wasn't able to kick us up the arse and bollock us like Don did,' explains McLintock.

Another issue was that several players soon slipped below the highest standards they had achieved in the previous campaign. 'Eddie Kelly and Ray Kennedy put on some weight,' recalled Armstrong, 'and they weren't as sharp as they had been. Little things like that weren't picked up on quickly enough. I don't think that Don would have allowed Ray and Eddie to get into that situation. He'd have bawled at them in front of the team, told them to stop eating chips or burgers or sinking the beers or whatever, and put them on a fitness drive.'

The outlawing of the tackle from behind also curtailed Arsenal's combative approach in the early weeks of the season. 'You could see from our early games that the defence and midfield was a fraction less tight on opponents that they had been in 1970/71,' explains Wilson. 'One of our strengths had been that we'd never allowed opponents a second on the ball. With the rule change, we lost a little of our combative side.'

Mee felt the loss of Howe keenly, explaining, 'Don and I had a fine professional relationship, and we respected one another's views on the merits of respective players. Things weren't ever quite the same again after he left the club.'

The most pressing issue to face Mee was how to freshen up and add some depth to a small squad. In December 1971 he shelled out a British transfer record £220,000 on Everton's World Cup-winning midfielder Alan Ball. If Mee had previously been criticised for being too conservative and low-key in the transfer market, the capture of Ball appeared to signify a sea change in thinking at the club.

Arriving at Highbury with his father Alan Ball Senior, the Preston North End manager, Ball – resplendent in his double breasted suit – held court in the boardroom with a gaggle of journalists as he outlined his hopes for the future. Described by Frank as 'a strutting peacock', Ball would soon be photographed in tabloids in his Triumph Stag (the Holy Grail for many 1970s footballers) and discussing the London casinos he liked to frequent. A 'branded player' – one who made his name and reputation elsewhere – Ball was something of an anomaly. Not since the 1930s had the Gunners imported a star talent of such luminance.

Ball made his debut in the league match with Nottingham Forest in late December, and the official programme for the Arsenal v Everton game on 1 January described his first outing in almost reverential terms, 'His debut at Nottingham was as we all imagined it would be…. Of course it will take time for him to bed down, but that he will in due course is inevitable for a player of such skill.'

Ball's signing didn't work out tactically. There was also dissension in the ranks when news filtered out about his estimated £10,000 a year wage. 'Some of the homegrown lads like John Radford and Charlie George found out – via a journalist,' he told me in 2005. 'They were massively pissed off. I got on well with the Arsenal lads, but the issue of money unsettled a lot of players, and it started to break down the unity of the squad. It led to bickering and a bit of jealousy.

'One day in the Halfway House, we had a team meeting and although it was supposed to be about that weekend's game, it went on to be about money. I'd say five or six of them really turned on me. I stood my ground. I said to them, "It's not my fault, don't blame me." But it wasn't ideal and I could understand that they'd seen me come in, get a signing-on fee and a big wage, and ask, "Who the fuck does he think he is?" Some of the players went to Bertie demanding a pay rise, questioning why they weren't earning what I was earning. You know what he said? "Because Alan is a superstar, he's a World Cup winner." It's like, "Oh thanks a bloody bunch Bert." That really helps the situation!'

Armstrong recalled, 'The issue of money was there. The club paid its youth graduates less than the going rate. It was kind of forgotten during the Double season. Everyone pulled together. Was it a major issue in the years that followed the Double? Well put it this way. When you're young, you don't think so much about cash, but as you get older, have a family, and hear what new guys like Bally are on, it becomes an issue. I don't feel we were always looked after that well. Some of the lads like Charlie [George] and Eddie [Kelly] blamed Bert for not taking care of them, but maybe the board was also at fault.'

Ball's signing also created a tactical dilemma for Mee which was never resolved. His first three games for the club ended in disappointing draws against Forest, Everton and Stoke. Ball sought out McLintock and expressed his frustration with what had happened. 'I said to Frank that the team had made me look like a prat. Frank and "Stan" Simpson carried on playing like they'd always done; dropping balls on to the head of Kennedy and Radford. But I wasn't seeing enough of the ball. I felt that in order to get the best out of me, they needed to channel the ball through me, so we could push on and build the attack more slowly.

'Frank was great with me, saying, "But we can't change things just like that. You'll have to be patient." Problem was, that situation was never resolved in my four years at the club. Never. It needed someone – probably like Don Howe – to say, "Right, we'll change the tactics and use him as the fulcrum for our attacks" – or just say, "Right, this isn't working. Sell him and get in top players who do fit this system." Someone needed to be brutal and take the bull by the horns. But no one did, so it all fell between two stools.

'If we're being honest here, I was an expensive misfit at Arsenal and Bert would have been better off telling Kennedy and Kelly to stay off the pies and ale and bringing in a couple of players – £100,000-type players who were more Arsenal's kind of thing – who could inject a bit more pace into midfield and the attack. That would have suited them better.'

Painful viewing though it is, the 1972 centenary FA Cup Final against Leeds United is a microcosm of the 'falling between two stools' approach which Arsenal, who ended up finishing fifth in the league, had begun to pursue. Ball cuts a frustrated figure, often drifting aimlessly around while McLintock and Simpson, increasingly pinned back by Leeds forwards, resort to type and pump the ball long to an isolated Radford. George, apart from hitting the bar, looks exhausted, and the entire team lacks pace, eventually succumbing to Allan Clarke's headed winner. It was a dismal encounter.

Two months earlier, Arsenal had been knocked out of the European Cup at the quarter-final stage by Ajax. After losing 2-1 in Amsterdam, George Graham's own goal consigned Arsenal to defeat at Highbury and led Ajax trainer-coach Stefan Kovacs to describe Arsenal's style as 'robotic and predictable'. Johan Cruyff turned the knife, claiming, 'There is more to football than hitting high balls into a crowded goalmouth.'

A year earlier, *Goal* editor Alan Hughes had described Arsenal's FA Cup Final against Liverpool as 'without doubt the worst for years. Many more like that and the distribution of cup final tickets shouldn't be a problem. Only the fans of the two teams will want to go.'

Mercifully, Hughes kept his thoughts on the 1972 final to himself. Mee was disappointed by the criticisms made by journalists of his team, and some Arsenal histories have since claimed that such a chastening experience against Europe's finest proved to be the catalyst behind his side's brief flirtation with a more expansive passing game in the 1972/73 campaign.

Mee explained, 'It had always been my aim to evolve the playing style. My view was that first we needed to win silverware, and then we look at the style, because I accepted that we are in the entertainment business and we have a duty to our fans. But there's a fine line between entertaining and winning. Sometimes you can't have both.'

In the excellent *Bertie Mee: Arsenal's Officer And Gentleman*, coach Steve Burtenshaw differs slightly with Mee's views and tells author

David Tossell, 'Bertie wanted a more Total Football-type team because he was very impressed with Ajax. He felt that Arsenal should be innovative. I warned him it would not come quickly or easily. I said we needed to show more restraint.'

But come August 1972 the Gunners played with a great deal more flair, went seven games unbeaten, and prompted Peter Batt to write in *The Sun*, 'I saw enough here to convince me that these new style Gunners really can lead English soccer out of the dark age.'

Ball cut a far happier figure, recalling, 'It was like the pressure had been lifted. More was now channelled through me, and we injected some pace in the team with Peter Marinello coming in and doing well. But I knew that many of the players weren't comfortable and I realised quickly that if this was going to be a long-term sea change, then Bertie would have to buy in newer, fresher players who could fit in with the system.'

Within the space of five days in late November, Arsenal were thrashed 5-0 by champions Derby and hammered 3-0 at home by Norwich at Highbury in the League Cup. Enough was enough for Mee. He went back to basics, instructed his team to 'harass and squeeze opponents', and Arsenal proceeded to go 11 league games unbeaten, and stay on leaders Liverpool's coat tails.

In early 1973, Mee shelled out a whopping £200,000 on Coventry City skipper Jeff Blockley. With the exception of Gus Caesar there hasn't been a more derided player in Arsenal's history. Blockley was signed by Mee as a long-term replacement for McLintock, and his arrival made serious waves within the club.

Armstrong recalled, 'As Frank went on to prove, he had a few good years left in him at the top, and Jeff's arrival unsettled us. You felt that Bertie was about to dismantle the team, but he never communicated to us what his plans were.'

McLintock explains, 'I'd been dropped from the team in the New Year, and was none too happy about it. We were right behind Liverpool in the title race. I really did feel that we could win it again. Jeff's arrival made it clear that Bertie thought my time was almost up. He never talked things through with me.'

Blockley's arrival did add a level of competition to the squad, which had been lacking, and McLintock was suffering with a leg injury throughout much of the campaign but when Blockley made his debut against Sheffield United in October 1972 he replaced the injured Peter Simpson, and the new man himself was forced to play on with a calf injury. Perhaps if he had been eased into the team alongside McLintock, who could have guided him through the formative stages of his Arsenal career, things might have turned out differently. Arsenal players from the era, a tough crew when it came to accepting outsiders, remained unconvinced.

Ball recalled, 'The squad had been together so long that when a newcomer arrived, they weren't always welcomed with open arms. I found that. When Jeff came, there was speculation about the money he was on, and his signing-on fee, and I did get the feeling that because of the players' loyalty to Frank, it was never going to be easy for him.

'I remember his early training sessions. When a new boy arrives, the others test him out. Geordie Armstrong and Peter Marinello ran rings around him. They were nutmegging him, making him look a fool. He came in when Simpson and McLintock were injured, and there was no time for him to settle. Bertie Mee had to pitch him in straight away. At a top club, you have to show straight away that you're a swimmer and that you've got a big game appetite. Football is cruel, but this was Arsenal.'

By early April, Arsenal were neck and neck with Liverpool in the title race and when they were drawn against Second Division Sunderland in the FA Cup semi-final at Hillsborough, the venue for that epic fightback against Stoke two years earlier, a third consecutive final appearance seemed more than likely.

A biting wind sliced across Hillsborough on 7 April, making it an uncommonly chilly spring afternoon. On top of the main stand, a flag with the Sunderland crest fluttered around playfully in the wind, while an Arsenal flag became wrapped around a pole and remained unmoved for the duration of the match. It was a poetic image.

The travelling Sunderland fans occupied the entire Kop as well as half the giant cantilever stand and the main stand. There were even Sunderland fans in with the Arsenal fans at the Leppings Lane End.

Estimates suggested that Sunderland followers outnumbered Arsenal's by roughly 2-1. Armstrong recalled, 'We ran out and the sound was absolutely deafening. It was like a home game for Sunderland. I always felt that because they occupied the Kop — it gave them an advantage.'

The key difference with the 1971 semi-final was that McLintock was absent for Arsenal due to injury. Blockley had also been missing from the team for nearly six weeks, but after passing a fitness test two days before the match he told Mee that he felt ready to play and replace McLintock. Blockley's inclusion (he was partnered alongside Peter Simpson) proved disastrous.

Sunderland, displaying the self-confidence which had seen them knock out Malcolm Allison's Manchester City in the fifth round, took the fight to Arsenal from the first minute. Early on, midfielder Mickey Horswill's spectacular 25-yard half-volley was tipped away spectacularly by Wilson, before disaster struck after just 20 minutes.

A speculative through ball from Horswill rolled through to Blockley, who faced the seemingly simple task of knocking the ball back to his goalkeeper. But with the barrel-chested Vic Halom breathing down his neck, Blockley chronically under-hit the backpass and Halom nipped in, rounded Wilson, and sidefooted home.

Halom recalls, 'Before the game, we'd been so wrapped up in our own bubble that I couldn't have cared less whether Jeff Blockley or Frank McLintock played. In fact, I might have preferred to have faced Frank, because Blockley was a big, big fella. But I quickly saw that Blockley wasn't on his game, and so I targeted him. As a striker, you have to exploit every weakness you can in your opponent. I could sense his hesitancy. I could tell he was nervous.'

Armstrong's deflected effort — tipped away by the excellent Jim Montgomery — was Arsenal's only effort of note in the first half. Halom had the chance to double Sunderland's lead when he barged Blockley out of the way and shot, only to see Wilson tip his effort away in front of the Kop.

Wilson recalls, 'The noise was absolutely deafening. I can remember it to this day. The longer the game went, on, the more confident Sunderland and their supporters became.'

Arsenal's players trooped in at half-time in desperate need of a tactical team talk and an analysis of what had happened in a poor first half. Wilson claims, 'We were used to Frank cajoling, but he wasn't there. In the Double year, Don Howe would have had his say too, but he'd gone too. We missed the impact of a half-time bollocking. The leadership we'd been used to was lacking.'

It seems odd, given the vocal nature of players like Ball and Bob McNab, and the big game experience of Arsenal's side generally, that that should be the case. Ball recalled, 'Everyone was very quiet. With respect to Bertie Mee, I thought that occasion showed his lack of tactical acumen, because he added nothing to the conversation other than to say, "Get tighter, keep doing the basics and things will come right." We needed a bit more than that.'

After one more slip early in the second half by Blockley, Mee replaced him with Peter Storey. Minutes later, a long ball into the Arsenal box was headed on by Dennis Tueart and Billy Hughes's flicked back-header looped over the back-pedalling Wilson to make it 2-0. Ironically, Blockley's presence on the pitch might have prevented this goal because Storey's lack of height gave Hughes an advantage he would otherwise not have had.

Sunderland carried on coming at Arsenal in waves before, with 85 minutes gone, Simpson foraged forward down the left, crossed the ball low, and Kennedy just failed to connect with the ball. Lurking with intent though was George, whose scuffed shot crept through Montgomery's grasp and rolled into the empty net.

Yet again the Gunners, playing in their yellow and blue away kit against a less fancied team clad in white, found themselves 2-1 down at Hillsborough in the semi-final. This time though, there was to be no epic comeback; no last-minute heroics.

Arsenal did drive forward in the dying seconds only for Armstrong's cross to be headed away for a corner. As Radford and Armstrong dithered over who should take it, the referee blew the final whistle. The Gunners players – many of whom had helped guide the team through the last 12 semi-final ties over the previous five years successfully – ran for the sanctuary of the dressing room as Bob Stokoe and his players took the applause of their 35,000 travelling supporters.

'The noise of the Sunderland supporters will always haunt me,' explains Wilson, 'because it symbolised the end of an era really. I remember someone coming into the dressing room afterwards and telling us that Liverpool had lost at home to Birmingham in the league, meaning that we now had the advantage in the title race. But it meant nothing, and we were unable to get ourselves together enough to put pressure on Liverpool.'

It was Shankly's team who won the title that season – despite Arsenal's splendid 2-0 away win at Anfield in February – and Liverpool, not Arsenal, dominated the 1970s.

Players and fans played the blame game in the years that followed Hillsborough. The loss of Howe as coach has been cited as a key reason, as have Mee's damaging fall-outs with George and McLintock. Perhaps the truth is that when it came to recruiting key players to improve and develop the team, Mee spent £520,000 on three players – Marinello, Ball and Blockley – who in their different ways never fitted the jigsaw.

Arsenal finished as runners-up in 1973 but McLintock had already played his last game for the club. He was sold to QPR in the summer and admits, 'Bertie Mee broke my heart.' The Metropolitan Police, meanwhile, investigated claims that death threats had been made by Arsenal fans against Blockley.

'In many ways, it wasn't fair what happened to Jeff,' recalled Armstrong. 'But there are certain games which define you and which can make or break you. That Sunderland game broke him.'

The two Hillsborough FA Cup semi-finals were the pivotal matches for Mee's side in the early 1970s. The fall-out from the Sunderland defeat was – by Arsenal's standards anyway – catastrophic. It was Mee's Waterloo. As Britain entered an era of power restrictions, the three-day week and Glam Rock, Arsenal would face only relegation scraps and early cup exits.

# The Rise And Fall Of The London Irish

*'I'm very confident that young Liam Brady will emerge as one of the best midfielders in England over the next few years.'* Bertie Mee, October 1973.

*'And it's su-per Ars-enal [clap, clap, clap, clap], super Arsenal FC, and we'll win the world over, and champions we'll be…' Arsenal FA Cup Final record 1979, to the tune of 'The Irish Rover'.*

IF MASOCHISTIC Arsenal fans wish to identify a date which offered irrefutable proof that Bertie Mee's Gunners were headed for a dramatic fall from grace, they should circle 2 October 1973, the night their team lost to Third Division Tranmere Rovers in the League Cup.

At 7.59pm exactly, Rovers striker Eddie Loyden controlled a cross and steered the ball home. It was the only goal of the game. Alan Ball was stretchered off with ten minutes left and at the final whistle, the paltry 20,337 crowd sportingly applauded off the victors before venting their fury on their own players.

With no major summer signings, Arsenal appeared leaden-footed and predictable. Mee insisted, 'By then, the board had decided that they would prune their spending and place their faith in the players we now had in the youth team.'

Long-term salvation lay just four days after the Tranmere debacle. Fifteen minutes into a dour scrap with bottom-of-the-table

Sir Henry Norris – the man who brought Woolwich Arsenal to North London in 1913, and whose political manoeuvrings helped gain Arsenal a Division One place after World War One.

Charlie Buchan leads out Arsenal at Aston Villa in 1926. He was the club's first true box office star, and crowds flocked to see him play for Herbert Chapman's new team in the mid-1920s.

The Arsenal team pictured with the FA Cup after their 2-0 win over Huddersfield Town in April 1930. Chapman's classic Mark 2 Arsenal team, including Alex James, David Jack and Cliff Bastin, are present and correct.

*Arsenal manager Herbert Chapman pictured in 1931. He was in the process of turning Arsenal into the most talked about club in world football.*

*Fearless striker Ted Drake tries to get the better of Charlton goalkeeper Sam Bartram in April 1938. Drake's arrival at Highbury signalled the move to a more physical and direct approach to the game by Arsenal.*

*The victorious Arsenal team hoist skipper Joe Mercer aloft after their 2-0 win over Liverpool in the 1950 FA Cup Final. Mercer had trained with the Merseyside outfit until just days before the final.*

*Arsenal coach Dave Sexton instructs Frank McLintock, Bob McNab, Peter Storey, Jon Sammels and Terry Neill in August 1967. Sexton laid down a tactical blueprint which Don Howe later adapted, with great success for the club.*

*Skipper Frank McLintock celebrates with Arsenal fans after the team wins the Fairs Cup in 1970. It brought to an end a 17-year barren run for the club.*

*The moment of truth at Hillsborough, March 1971. Deep into injury time, Arsenal's Peter Storey (obscured by Stoke City's Gordon Banks) levels up the FA Cup semi final at 2-2. Banks admitted a 'sense of fatalism' washed over him as Storey stepped up.*

*Alan Sunderland celebrates scoring Arsenal's dramatic late winner against Manchester United in the 1979 FA Cup Final with Pat Rice (left) and Steve Walford (right). It was the only trophy which Terry Neill's team won.*

*David Rocastle drives home a dramatic late winner for Arsenal in the 1987 Littlewoods Cup semi final replay against Tottenham at White Hart Lane, watched eagerly by Martin Hayes (left). Rocastle's goal swung the balance of power in North London, and ushered in a prolonged era of success under George Graham.*

*King George with the Bonnie Prince. Hardly a marriage made in heaven, but Charlie Nicholas's two goals in the 1987 Littlewoods Cup Final against Liverpool delivered George Graham his first trophy as Arsenal manager.*

*Michael Thomas scores Arsenal's decisive second goal at Anfield in May 1989. By the late 80s, George Graham's team possessed the tactical nous required to defeat Kenny Dalglish's Liverpool.*

*Always a big player on the big occasion, Arsenal's Alan Smith celebrates winning the 1994 Cup Winners' Cup Final. It proved to be the last hurrah for Graham's Arsenal.*

*Dennis Bergkamp scores against Manchester United in February 1997. The Dutchman's arrival gave Arsenal a new sense of identity, and by the late 90s, Alex Ferguson admitted: 'Arsenal have the firepower to damage us.'*

Following a calamitous error by Manchester United goalkeeper Fabien Barthez, Arsenal striker Thierry Henry grabs a third in a season-changing 3-1 victory at Highbury for the Gunners in 2001/02.

Patrick Vieira scores the decisive penalty against Manchester United in the 2005 FA Cup Final. It was his last kick of the ball for the club. His departure signalled the end of Arsenal as a credible title threat.

Theo Walcott drives his shot past Tottenham's Brad Friedel during Arsenal's 5-2 win in February 2012. It was Arsenal's ultimate 'house of cards' match.

*Eagerly pursued by Kieran Gibbs and Jack Wilshere, Aaron Ramsey celebrates scoring Arsenal's winner in the 2014 FA Cup Final against Hull. The nine-year trophy drought was over.*

*The victorious Arsenal team throw manager Arsène Wenger high into the air at Wembley in May 2014 and drench him in champagne. Is the FA Cup win a springboard for new glories, or simply a one-off?*

Birmingham City, Jeff Blockley sustained an injury and was replaced by young Irish midfielder Liam Brady. The *Islington Gazette* reported, 'Brady's arrival came like a breath of fresh air. Just by his presence he seemed to inject a little extra interest in the outing.'

It was Brady who began the move which saw Ray Kennedy thump home John Radford's centre, enough to grind out a grim 1-0 win for mid-table Arsenal.

Later that week the *Islington Gazette* reported that for the Republic of Ireland's match with Iceland in October 1973, a record five Arsenal players – David O'Leary, Noel O'Brien, Liam Brady, Frank Stapleton and John Murphy – were selected for the squad.

Arsenal chief scout Gordon Clark had a network of spies across the Irish Sea to rival any Cold War espionage unit and he was mining a rich seam of talent which would, in time, dig Arsenal out of an enormous hole. But this was no short-term fix. Brady flitted in and out of the team in 1973/74, Stapleton wouldn't start appearing in the first team until the tail end of the following campaign and O'Leary wasn't pitched in until the execrable 1975/76 campaign. By then however, the club had done an admirable job in tearing itself apart.

❧ ❧ ❧ ❧ ❧

Despite finishing as runners-up in the league in 1973, Arsenal had been denied entry to the UEFA Cup because under FIFA rules, only one club from each city could qualify and precedence was given to a team if it had won the League Cup so it was Bill Nicholson's Tottenham who gained the berth.

Don Howe's successor Steve Burtenshaw had been removed by Mee in a footballing equivalent of a *coup d'état* at the start of the new campaign. A delegation of players, including Bob McNab and George Armstrong, went to Mee early in the new campaign after a series of ponderous displays saw Arsenal mired in mid-table and Mee promptly removed Burtenshaw with due haste.

Kennedy recalls, 'The feeling was that Steve was too soft. It wasn't nice, what happened. You could say that it was sign of good management that Bertie listened to the players and moved quickly. Or a sign of weakness that he'd been aware that things weren't quite right earlier, and had reacted in a knee-jerk way in the face of player power.'

New first team coach Bobby Campbell's bullishness ('I don't mess players about and I don't expect to be messed about') and Mee's increasing distance from first team matters made the situation at the club worse. Campbell, who came in from QPR, took an aggressive approach, telling each and every one of the players that they'd gone 'too soft since winning the Double'. Armstrong recalled, 'I knew that Bobby was trying to shake us out of our lethargy. But I thought he was just a bit too aggressive really.'

An air of tetchiness surrounded the entire club, which had declared war on illegal burger sellers outside the ground ('The smells are obnoxious,' insisted Islington MP Michael O'Halloran), and on motorists who parked their cars too close to Highbury on matchdays. General manager Bob Wall stopped fractionally short of an evangelical rant in the club programme about why Arsenal wouldn't be playing Sunday games in the era of energy cuts and the three-day week. Fans asked why none of the photographs on the front of the programme were actually taken at Highbury (it was the club's 60th anniversary at the ground) and why it was nigh-on impossible to keep hold of one's cup of tea at games on account of how piping hot it was.

Everyone, it seemed, had the hump, although Mee comforted himself with the opinion that up to five of his team would travel to West Germany for the World Cup as part of Alf Ramsey's squad.

Opportunities for the young Irish contingent seemed sparse, particularly after Campbell told a pack of journalists immediately after arriving, 'I'm only interested in today. The future will take care of itself.'

Armstrong claimed, 'Many of the younger players reckoned Bobby was a smart arse, who could be cruel to them.'

Brady confirms, 'Bobby could be talking perfectly civilly to older players, and then when, say Frank or I arrived, he would shout at us and try and make us feel small. It wasn't a pleasant atmosphere to be in.'

The Gunners ended the season in tenth place, and Kennedy moved to Liverpool in the summer as Bill Shankly's final signing at the club. It was a damaging public relations exercise; Liverpool went on to dominate the rest of the 1970s with Kennedy playing a starring role.

Mee was surprisingly candid about potential signings in the *Islington Gazette*. A trawl through the archives makes painful reading, revealing several missed opportunities.

Sunderland's central defender Dave Watson – who had just won the FA Cup? 'He's no better than any of the central defenders we have on our books.' Fellow Mackem Dennis Tueart? 'He doesn't match up to our requirements.' Celtic striker Kenny Dalglish? 'I have never put in an offer for him, nor will I be.' QPR skipper Gerry Francis? 'He's not an Arsenal type player.' And finally – Stoke goalkeeper Peter Shilton to replace the retiring Bob Wilson? 'He's contracted to Stoke and will remain there.' A few months later, Shilton joined Leicester City.

Equally as revealing was Arsenal's attempt to sign Oldham's Alan Groves and Ayr's John Doyle, neither of whom were exactly household names. Yet Mee baulked at the £100,000 asking price for the Oldham winger, and Doyle ended up at Celtic with Mee claiming, 'So few Scottish players seem to want to play in England any more.'

Mee admitted, 'Perhaps we could have been more aggressive in signing new players, but spending money for players whom we considered to be overpriced just isn't the club's way. I did regret selling McLintock. He had several good years left in him.'

A story has done the rounds over the years that Mee attempted on more than one occasion to sign West Ham's Trevor Brooking, and that both times Brooking and his representative simply failed to show up for talks. Mee denied this rumour when I spoke with him 20 years ago, though he admitted there was 'one big, big star – as big a name as Alan Ball whom I was convinced I'd persuaded to join us. But it wasn't to be.'

Instead an outlay of £25,000 brought in QPR veteran – and honorary Irishman – Terry Mancini. Mee justified the signing, and his decision not to move for Dave Watson on the grounds that signing the Sunderland man 'would have blocked the progress of David O'Leary. We needed a short-term stop-gap to play alongside Peter Simpson, while David was allowed to develop in the reserves.'

For a time, Eire international Mancini, who stayed for two years, was the most high-profile Irishman at Arsenal. An occasional guest presenter on LWT's *The Big Match*, along with London football mates

Rodney Marsh and David Webb, the bald Mancini arrived in October 1974, with the team mired in the bottom three.

He said, 'I knew that I was no world beater, and that under normal circumstances, I'd never have been an Arsenal player. But I quickly realised that my main role at Arsenal was to act as a mentor for David [O'Leary] but I did try and put a smile on everyone's faces too. Arsenal could be a bloody miserable place, at that time.'

His most important intervention for the club came with just four games left of the 1975/76 campaign in a home match against fellow relegation strugglers Wolves, when Mancini connected with a corner to nod home a vital winner in a 2-1 victory. Arsenal avoided relegation that season by six points having survived by just four in the previous campaign. Mancini reflects, 'David O'Leary was now firmly established in central defence, where he remained for about 100 years!'

By the time the Eire international departed Highbury, the Republic triumvirate of O'Leary, Brady and Stapleton were firmly established in the first team. But the manager who gave them their break had resigned.

Once Arsenal's First Division status had been confirmed, Mee told the players that he wouldn't be with them for the following campaign. 'I was tired and mentally drained. It needed a fresh face to take the club forward. I was finding it harder to motivate those around me. At the time I blamed the increasing amount of money in football, and the increasing affluence of footballers, but it was also down to me.'

There was civil unrest in those uncertain weeks that followed Mee's resignation. In their autobiographies Brady, Stapleton and O'Leary allege that Ball and Mancini, probably keen to secure coaching positions within the club, lobbied the players to give their backing to coach Campbell to become the new manager.

'Alan Ball was very vocal about wanting Bobby as the new boss,' recalls Brady. 'He was trying to maintain the status quo, because a new manager from outside would most likely come in and make drastic changes and cull them.'

Mancini denies the suggestion that Ball and he attempted to coerce team-mates into backing Campbell, though he admits, 'I think Bobby would have been a good manager at that time.' Ball bristled at my suggestion that he was the ringleader in the 'pro Campbell' movement. 'That's total crap. Never in a million years would I have tried to pressurise the players into supporting my scheme, and I didn't try to pressure the chairman or anyone else into appointing Bobby Campbell as manager.'

Ball's version of events wasn't supported by his team-mates. The three Irishmen point-blank refused to support Arsenal's senior professionals, and when Ball did take his opinions to the boardroom he was told to keep his nose out. Campbell informed the backroom staff that he wouldn't be needing them for much longer, only to be reminded by a furious Ian Crawford, 'You haven't actually got the fucking job yet Bobby.' After the final game of the season, as Stapleton and Brady headed out of Highbury to the airport, Campbell asked them where they were headed. 'Back to Ireland,' came the response. Stapleton recalls a hostile Campbell insisting they return at the end of the week to pick up the offer of their new contracts. Stapleton and Brady headed home regardless. It was the last time they would see Bobby Campbell at Highbury.

To the surprise of many, former Arsenal skipper Terry Neill was appointed Gunners manager in the drought summer of 1976. The Ulsterman's references for the job at Arsenal were mixed, to put it mildly. After playing 241 matches for the Gunners in the 60s he left Highbury in 1970 to embark on his managerial career at Hull City, and by the mid-70s he had been appointed Tottenham boss.

It was a jarring sight to see Neill's Tottenham and Mee's Arsenal ensconced in relegation battles and although Tottenham didn't fall through the trapdoor until a year after Neill departed, he was often accused of being the root cause of Spurs' demise.

In many ways Neill, naturally outgoing and always willing to talk to journalists, was a welcome contrast with the increasingly austere Mee, but he belonged to the same age group as some of the Double-winning dinosaurs whom he had once played alongside, like Storey and Armstrong. Armstrong admitted, 'I didn't always make life easy for Terry. I wanted out of Arsenal by then, and I didn't have the best of relationships with him.'

Much the same can be said of Ball, who admitted, 'We'd heard rumours that Dave Sexton, whose coaching skills were respected throughout the game, might take over, but he stayed at QPR instead. Then there was talk of Milan Miljanic taking over, but he stayed at Real Madrid. That would have been a really bold move by Arsenal, a sign that the club was willing to do something out of the ordinary.

'But instead Terry took over. I didn't think that was an especially ambitious move by the club, and when he brought in Wilf Dixon as coach, whom I'd worked under at Everton, I wasn't happy. Nice man that he was, I didn't think that Wilf had a sodding clue.'

Ball's departure to Southampton in December 1976 caused consternation among some players, notably Neill's new signings Alan Hudson and Malcolm Macdonald. Hudson believed that he would play alongside Brady and Ball; Neill believed that if Arsenal were to prosper, Brady, not Ball, needed to be the fulcrum of Arsenal's attacks.

Macdonald, the eye-catching £333,333.33 signing from Newcastle, recalls, 'I was very impressed with Liam Brady. He was such a graceful and intelligent player. For me, there was no one in the country better in his position. I couldn't wait to play with him, and then there was the promise of David O'Leary as well. I saw them as the backbone to the side in the future.'

History could easily have turned out differently. O'Leary was tapped up about a possible move to Manchester United by manager Tommy Docherty, and initially Neill didn't believe that Stapleton had a future at the club. Only a late hitch stopped him departing to Luton Town for a measly £60,000.

After a disappointing defeat to newly-promoted Bristol City on the opening day of the season, with the Radford–Macdonald partnership spectacularly misfiring, Stapleton was slotted in up front alongside Macdonald as Radford departed to West Ham. With Neill as manager, Northern Ireland full-backs Rice and Nelson, Pat Jennings arriving on a free transfer from Tottenham, John Devine in the wings and the Eire trio mainstays in the first team, it's easy to see why unwitting observers believed an Irish Mafia existed at Highbury.

Brady is quite insulted by the claim that they were a clique, 'I always found it odd that people thought I would naturally socialise with David and Frank simply because they were Irish. It's not like the rest of the team didn't speak the same language!'

Jennings recalls, 'You'd get people coming up to you suggesting that we spent the whole time arguing about politics or religion, but the fact is we never discussed it. Sammy Nelson is a Unionist and proud of it. Frank Stapleton is a Catholic. Others have their own beliefs and opinions. It was a good example of how men from different backgrounds can mix. Footballers often aren't all that interested in current affairs.'

O'Leary admitted, 'Frank, Liam and I never really socialised together at all. Frank was teetotal and kept himself to himself, Liam's best mate at the club was Graham Rix, and I was good pals with Pat Jennings. The "London Irish" thing mattered more I think to outsiders than it did to any of us.'

As the Neill era began, the soundbites emanating from O'Leary, Brady and Stapleton were revealing. O'Leary claimed, 'I can never see a day when, as a footballer, I won't be playing for Arsenal.'

Brady admitted, 'I'm hungry for silverware. Arsenal needs to win things quickly. I'm impatient for a crack at the title.'

Stapleton claimed, 'As a footballer, you have to evaluate the situation you find yourself in at the end of each season. I've learned already that you have to fight your corner and take care of yourself.'

Lines were already being drawn in the sand. O'Leary; loyal to Arsenal almost to a fault. Brady; a passionate lover of the club but fiercely ambitious to play in a team which could genuinely challenge for the title. Stapleton; hungry for success yet something of a lone wolf.

It wasn't the Irish contingent which concerned Neill when he took over, rather a glut of increasingly disenchanted Englishmen. New signings Hudson and Macdonald were soon at loggerheads with Neill over their contracts. The swashbuckling Macdonald, who netted a highly impressive 29 goals in the frequently chaotic 1976/77 season, describes the campaign as 'a hotch-potch of half-baked ideas, with players coming and going through a revolving door'.

Neill labelled his side 'a bunch of morons' to journalists after a terrible day at Middlesbrough, and Brady recalls, 'In those early days, Terry didn't do himself many favours. It's pretty much okay to say anything you want to players within the confines of the dressing room, but if you just go around shooting your mouth off to journalists about your own team, you're asking for trouble.'

Arsenal's infamous tour to Australia and the Far East in the 1977 close-season – where Hudson and Macdonald were sent home for flaunting Neill's drinking ban – was close to outright civil war. 'The tour was about taking the piss out of Terry Neill,' recalls Hudson.

Among the tabloid hullaballoo, former coach Don Howe slipped into Highbury virtually unnoticed, and introduced a far stricter training regime. His first job was to try and mould a more rounded team, one which didn't solely revolve around the formidable firepower of Macdonald, whose single-minded mantra during games was, 'Get the ball, turn and shoot.'

Howe cracked down on Macdonald's lateness to training, and urged him to track back during games. But it wasn't always an easy task. Central defender Willie Young, who had joined from Tottenham the year before, recalls, 'Malcolm was such a dominant personality, that it was almost impossible not to channel the play through him. When he was on form, he was devastatingly effective.'

There was no more thrilling sight in English football at the time than the swashbuckling striker showing defences a clean pair of heels and bearing down on goal. He was also a magnificent header of the ball and played the assisting role in many of Stapleton's 26 league goals in the two seasons they played up front with one another. Howe was able to pitch in the emerging Graham Rix, who complemented the left-footed Brady, and with youth team product David Price's robust approach in the centre of the pitch the Gunners had a backbone in midfield which they had been lacking in recent years.

In 1977/78, Neill's team finished fifth in the league – clear evidence of genuine improvement under the new manager – and reached the semi-final of the League Cup, where they were ousted 2-1 on aggregate by Liverpool after largely dominating the first game at Anfield. Having scored early on, Macdonald twice hit the woodwork, before former Gunner Kennedy netted the winner. Arsenal had so nearly reached Wembley again after a six-year absence but fans and players didn't have too much longer to wait as the Gunners went all the way in the FA Cup.

At Wrexham in the quarter-final, the Welsh club gave Arsenal a scare before a late Willie Young effort saw off the Second Division outfit in a 3-2 win. It was a significant day in the towering Scot's development at the club. 'I'd come from Tottenham, so the fans weren't too sure about me,' he recalls. 'But it always helped your kudos in those days if you got a winner in a tough game like that. Liam Brady was astonishing in that FA Cup run. He knew exactly how to take the sting out of the game and buy us some time.'

The *Daily Mail* described the Irishman's performance at the Racehorse Ground as 'sublime…like the most articulate and soulful of Irish poets'. Young laughs at such a description, 'I always saw Liam and the other Irish lads more as Arsenal born and bred, not Irishmen.'

The Gunners coasted to a semi-final victory against Orient at Stamford Bridge with Macdonald credited as scoring both even though they took hefty deflections off opposing defenders. He spent around an hour after the game arguing with journalists who claimed both should go down as own goals. Rix added a late third, ghosting through the opposition's tired defence to slot home.

The club was keeping quiet about Macdonald's physical condition. 'By now, I was barely able to get through games. Terry Neill would say, "I just need you for the next round. Get through that." But there was pressure on me to keep playing'. His knee was locking at regular intervals during games, forcing him to waggle his leg around to unlock the joint.

Arsenal faced Bobby Robson's emerging Ipswich Town in the final but their two most influential players, Macdonald and Brady (with an ankle injury) were palpably unfit. Neill's side began well with Hudson especially incisive early on but Brady lacked the urgency he had displayed earlier in the campaign, and Macdonald's knee – in full view of millions of TV viewers – ceased to function. 'Liam put several balls my way in the Ipswich danger zone,' Macdonald recalls, 'and each time I just couldn't go. My knee was shot.'

Brady beat himself up for years about the fact that he'd declared himself fit to play at the expense of midfield comrade Rix, describing the match as 'The biggest disappointment in my Arsenal career. The sense of guilt I felt about playing when not fully fit was enormous. I felt like I'd cost my team-mates.'

Roger Osborne's second-half winner was enough to take the trophy to Suffolk, and Neill declared, 'We'll be back next year.' Neill later hinted that he and Howe still believed the team was far too one-dimensional from an attacking point of view.

Four matches into the new season, change was foisted upon them at a packed Millmoor in a League Cup third round match. Clean through on goal, Macdonald's cartilage ripped to shreds as he prepared to pull the trigger, his football career to all intents and purposes over.

The next day's headlines may have been all about Arsenal's defeat to Third Division Rotherham but Neill and Howe realised that they would have to find a way of coping with the long-term absence of their star goalgetter. Not for the first time in Arsenal's history, salvation lay within. Alan Sunderland, an attacking midfielder signed from Wolves the previous season, was pushed up front alongside Stapleton, and one of Arsenal's most popular partnerships was born.

Known for his assured first touch and his phenomenal ability to deliver killer passes, Sunderland brought a new deftness to Arsenal's attack. 'I was a good foil for Frank and we had a great understanding. I linked well with Liam Brady and Graham Rix and tried to bring them into play as much as possible. I thought a lot like a midfielder, so I could anticipate what Liam and Graham might do before they actually did it. Liam and I occasionally rotated our positions just to keep defenders guessing.'

If any player epitomised why Arsenal were mutating into a great cup team, but never seriously challenged for the league title, it was Sunderland. In 1978/79 he netted eight league goals. Two of them came at old Trafford in Arsenal's smash-and-grab 2-0 raid, and he plundered a hat-trick in his team's famous 5-0 Christmas win at White Hart Lane. The plaudits went to Liam Brady for his iconic curled shot which curled past Mark Kendall, and which epitomised the Irishman's almost laconic skills, but Sunderland's goals, all delivered after quick bursts forward, also highlighted Arsenal's ability to break at speed away from home and punish the opposition.

But the moustachioed forward was regularly taken to task by Neill and Howe about his tendency to drift in and out of matches. He was maddeningly inconsistent, and often virtually anonymous in 'run of the mill' matches.

It was the Sunderland–Stapleton partnership which steered Arsenal through some testing FA Cup challenges. Sunderland's goal saved

Arsenal in the opening round of their five-game marathon against Jack Charlton's Sheffield Wednesday, and a brace from Stapleton saved Arsenal's blushes in a tempestuous 3-3 draw with the Owls at Filbert Street. It was the Irishman's first which saw Wednesday's resistance finally crumble in the fourth replay and helped his team ease to a 2-0 win. Their finest cup performance came in the fifth round at league champions Nottingham Forest. Clough's side, who had been unbeaten for nigh-on two years at the City Ground, threw everything at Neill's team on a bog of a pitch. McGovern and Robertson had shots which were tipped against the woodwork by Jennings and Garry Birtles hit the bar from five yards out.

The Gunners' defence remained resolute and, on 79 minutes, after Viv Anderson had chopped down Sunderland on the edge of the box, Rix floated a free kick towards Stapleton, and the Irishman twisted in mid-air and bulleted a header past a stationary Peter Shilton into the top corner of the net. It was a magnificent, if largely forgotten 1-0 victory against a team which went on to win the European Cup three months later.

Two elegant Sunderland strikes saw off Southampton in the quarter-final and at Villa Park, Arsenal's strikers grabbed a goal each as the Gunners eased past Sunderland's former club Wolves. The victory was achieved without the injured Brady, who was replaced by David Price.

Arsenal's push towards Wembley scuppered any chance of winning the league. They won just four of their final 18 games, although two of those were well received home wins against Chelsea and Tottenham. Brady recalls, 'The expectation in those days was that players would play in every game, but we had seen at the end of the previous season how several of us were playing after pain-killing injections. It was the same in 1978/79, with tired players struggling on. If we'd had just a sprinkling more of players – 17 or 18 like Liverpool rather than 14 or 15 – it could have made the differences. We ended up 20 points behind Liverpool. Way off.'

For the time being, Brady's focus was firmly on making up for the disappointment of the previous year and defeating Dave Sexton's

Manchester United in the FA Cup Final. This time Arsenal utilised the assessment skills of 1930s star George Male, who travelled to United games throughout April and early May and reported that Sexton's side had a major weakness. 'I noticed that their full-backs Jimmy Nicholl and Arthur Albiston got careless on crosses. They drifted out of position on frequent occasions,' he explained. Male was spot-on in his judgement and it proved to be United's Achilles heel.

Outside the ground, 'London Irish' scarves sold like hotcakes, and on a scorching hot day several fans received medical treatment after fainting in the heat. The bleached-out turf proved to be an ideal platform for Brady to develop his stellar skills. After ten minutes he broke from just inside his own half, shrugged off the attentions of three United defenders, nudged the ball to Stapleton on the right, and Stapleton fed the marauding David Price whose run drew United keeper Gary Bailey away from goal. As Price cut the ball back, Sunderland and Talbot arrived at the same time to slam his shot home. Although the goal is credited to Talbot, replays still suggest that both players hit the ball at the same time.

Joe Jordan and Jimmy Greenhoff went close and Gordon McQueen had his goal struck off for handball but Arsenal's midfield pushed and probed while at the same time shackling Macari and McIlroy.

With just two minutes remaining of the first half, Brady glided past United skipper Martin Buchan and then Arthur Albiston, looked up, and delivered a perfectly weighted cross to Stapleton on the far post and his fellow Irishman nodded past Bailey. United's marking was non-existent, as Male had predicted.

Willie Young recalls, 'You never take anything for granted, but United looked phenomenally tired. Out on their feet. It wasn't even the case that we felt we should ease off. We felt that if we carried on playing the way we had been, we could score more.'

Time and again, Brady pushed forward and kept United pegged back. On the hour his pass to Rix found its way to Stapleton on the far post, and only a desperate Bailey save kept the ball out. With five minutes remaining, central defender Steve Walford replaced the tiring Price.

Within three minutes United, somehow, were inexplicably level. McQueen stabbed home after a Jordan pass and then McIlroy seized on Coppell's long ball, squirmed past O'Leary and Walford, and tucked home.

It was all Walford's fault, apparently. In his book, David O'Leary said, 'A centre back replacing a midfield man and it upset the balance of the team.' Sunderland disagrees, claiming, 'I never thought it was a case of a lack of balance, more the fact that we all switched off. Jimmy Nicholl had so much time to pick out Steve Coppell for Sammy's goal that it was ridiculous. I think the heat caught up finally. We were done in.'

Young backs O'Leary's view, 'It was a daft bloody move. Pricey had been superb all game. Second only to Liam. Sure, he was tired, but so were United's forwards. We had to do some unnecessary shuffling at the back and I thought it had cost us. I wanted to vomit.'

'In the blink of an eye I thought we'd had it,' admits Sunderland.

But where there was Brady there was always hope. He tore into the United half, slipped a ball out to Rix on the left ('I just wanted to get the ball into their half because I was convinced United might score again') and Rix looped over a cross which soared above Bailey and dropped invitingly for Sunderland, who poked in Arsenal's dramatic late winner. 'I can't remember exactly what I said as I ran away after scoring,' he admits, 'but it was pretty much every swear word I knew. It was such an explosion of relief.'

'We thought that Arsenal were on their knees and that we'd hammer them in injury time,' admitted Sammy McIlroy, 'but we forgot to keep our eyes on the ball after we equalised. We let them off the hook.'

Arsenal's players were slightly stunned afterwards, struggling to come to terms with the game's dramatic death throes. Sunderland's memorable celebration – as his blue butterfly collars flapped in celebration – remains one of Arsenal's most iconic images. In an era when players swapped sweat-soaked shirts after the match, it was ironic that only Brady and Stapleton should end up cavorting around Wembley with the FA Cup wearing opposition shirts. Omens, omens.

After the match he joined his colleagues at the Grosvenor Park Hotel, where he sang 'Irish Eyes Are Smiling' lustily for the benefit of radio. The next day, on a Belfast radio station, several listeners rang in and claimed that if only all Irishmen (at some time or another, all Arsenal's Irish players expressed the wish that one day, a united Ireland international team would take to the pitch) lived their lives like the 'London Irish' then the ongoing troubles would be a thing of the past.

Arsenal were immediately linked with a £400,000 move for Dutch star Johann Neeskens and Brighton's central defensive prodigy Mark Lawrenson. 'We now have to aim for the title,' Neill claimed in the tabloids. But there never was a nod towards Total Football at Highbury; Neeskens headed to New York Cosmos. The Irish contingent didn't grow either and for the time being, Lawrenson remained on the south coast. Arsenal's only summer signing was John Hollins for £50,000, and Malcolm Macdonald officially retired.

Worse, just a few days after the 'Three-Minute Final', Brady casually mentioned to the *Islington Gazette*'s Ken Burgess, 'I fancy playing in Europe like Kevin Keegan. Everyone needs a change. If I stay another one or two years, I'd still like to give it a go.' Brady had just handed in his notice.

Decades later, Brady remained frustrated about the situation at the club after the FA Cup triumph. 'We had a superb backbone of young talent who would be the core for many years at Highbury. But to win the league we needed more of a depth in the squad. Here was a real chance to push on. The club signed John Hollins but after our cup runs there was enough money in the bank to have signed someone like Bryan Robson and absolutely gone for it. We never did. What I wanted was Terry to sit down with me and discuss his vision for the future, but he didn't. I felt like I was being taken for granted.'

The Brady situation was an uncomfortable backdrop to Arsenal's epic cup exploits in the 1979/80 campaign. The semi-final with Juventus in the European Cup Winners' Cup whet the appetite of all Arsenal players, who'd had their fill of matches against Eastern European sides including Magdeburg, Lokomotiv Leipzig and Hajduk Split over the previous months.

The Turin side, in their classic zebra tops, conjured up images of efficiency, elegance and brutality in equal measure. 'The Old Lady' possessed three world-famous stars; goalkeeper Dino Zoff, midfielder Marco Tardelli, and silver-haired striker Roberto Bettega, the golden boy of Italian football. Twenty minutes into the first leg at Highbury, Bettega lunged at O'Leary with both sets of studs up ('I reckon David might still have a couple buried in his leg somewhere,' winces Terry

Neill) and the defender left the field to be stitched up. The crowd was in uproar but Juve dealt a serious blow to Arsenal's chances when Talbot hacked down Bettega and Cabrini smashed the rebound past Jennings after the keeper saved the first effort.

The Juventus backline kept Brady and Rix quiet, and Stapleton's battering ram approach bore no rewards. Five minutes remained when Young nodded down Brady's cross, and the ball went in off Bettega. Justice of a sort, although as Clive White commented in *The Times*, 'They (Juventus) are capable of murdering Arsenal 0-0, you would say, for this is all they need to go through after the 1-1 draw at Highbury. And 0-0 are the most popular figures in Italian football.'

Although Neill had appeared on Bettega's chat show the night before in an attempt to defuse some of the tension between the two sides after Bettega's tackle on O'Leary (Neill had been outspoken in his criticism), a huge banner which read 'NEILL THE DOG' could clearly be seen through the purple, orange and red smoke from the Roman candles.

In the stands was Tardelli, who recalls, 'Liam Brady and Graham Rix orchestrated everything for Arsenal that night. They knew precisely when to hold on to the ball and when to release it. They seemed almost to have a telepathic understanding of where each other would be. Stapleton had two half-chances after Rix and Brady put him in. My heart was in my mouth, but I thought we were going to survive.'

Juventus had never lost at home to an English club in Europe, and hadn't lost at the Stadio Communale for the best part of two years. A stalemate suited the home team perfectly. The home crowd got steadily louder. 'All you could hear was "Juve, Juve", but we kept going,' recalls Young. 'Juve never pushed for a goal, which would have killed us off, so there was always a chance.'

With 15 minutes to go, Young clattered into Juve 'enforcer' Scirea ('He'd taken a few liberties, and I reckoned I owed him one,' chuckles Young), leaving the Italian requiring treatment. It gave the players time for a breather and Neill brought on Hollins and Vaessen for the tiring Talbot and Price. Tardelli recalls, 'Both those two guys were classic English midfielders, and when Arsenal brought on Vaessen, whom none of us had heard of, I was convinced that their engine had gone. Stapleton and Sunderland looked particularly tired. I don't know how much ground Talbot and Price had covered. I thought the game was up.'

With two minutes to go, Rix flighted a beautifully weighted cross which sailed over Zoff's head. Paul Vaessen's point-blank header slipped past the goalkeeper. Vaessen later recalled, 'Immediately I saw their players put their heads in their hands and collapse to the turf. I was engulfed by team-mates. It was just the best night.'

Tardelli says, 'The deafening whistles in the stadium stopped. All I could hear was a group of Arsenal fans going mad and I saw their players hugging one another in the distance. Nothing else. The lights had gone out on us. Everything had gone to shit.'

On the touchline, Juve coach Trappatoni slumped in disbelief and a raft of missiles rained down on the travelling support.

Back in England, Arsenal's FA Cup marathon against Double-chasing Liverpool gave Alan Sunderland another opportunity to demonstrate that he was Arsenal's ultimate thrill-seeker. The first match at Hillsborough ended goalless after Brian Talbot's lob came back off the crossbar, and in the first and second replays Sunderland's high-calibre goals – an outrageous chip and a quicksilver burst and finish – were cancelled out by Kenny Dalglish's improvised finishes.

The FA decided that if the third replay ended level there would be a penalty shoot-out. Despite a Liverpool onslaught and McDermott, Souness and Dalglish all going perilously close, Talbot's thumping close-range header settled the tie.

Brady recalls, 'In the space of a fortnight, we'd pulled off two of the greatest ever results in the history of the club. It seems remarkable, given just how many games we ended up playing that campaign (a then-record 67 matches) that we were still so fresh and energetic against Liverpool.'

Only the briefest of highlights are available of the two matches against Juventus, and there is no footage at all of the first three games against Liverpool in the FA Cup. It is sad but at least the freeze frames of a wide eyed Sunderland outfoxing Clemence in the Liverpool goal, and Brady, doing battle with Juve's finest at Highbury, have retained their sense of aura and mystique.

There was no opportunity for Arsenal players to bask in the glory of their semi-final conquests as they were still chasing UEFA Cup qualification. Neill had already awarded Davis and Vaessen their league debuts in an Easter victory against Tottenham (Vaessen also scored the winner against Coventry away from home) which meant a brief respite for Sunderland and Stapleton, but the season had caught up with the players.

'It's one of those times I look back and I wish we'd had a bit more in reserve,' recalls Sunderland. 'Vaessen, Davis and McDermott were starting to break through, but they were just kids. We'd all lost a few yards of pace. Even Brian Talbot, the fittest player at the club, was complaining about his back and his knees.'

In an FA Cup Final where, as the *Sunday Times* memorably put it, 'the bookmakers made West Ham so much the underdog that there was a danger of somebody calling in the RSPCA', Arsenal's top dogs suddenly pulled up lame.

The Hammers' midfield trio of Brooking, Devonshire and Allen pressed and pressured Arsenal's fatigued rearguard for the entire match. Brooking's header deservedly won the day for the Hammers but Young's ('I thought, "Son, you've gotta go"') infamous professional foul on Paul Allen remains the only other stand-out memory of a desperate Arsenal performance.

The image of a crestfallen Pat Rice, sitting disconsolately on the turf with his head in his hands, his blue socks rolled down, told its own story. Behind the scenes, Arsenal's players questioned the logic of nominating left-back John Devine as a substitute, rather than Paul Vaessen. 'John Devine did later come on, and a few of us thought it would have been a far better and bolder move to throw on Vaess later on,' recalls Sunderland. 'Fresh legs, something different. Young. No fear. On top of the world after his goal in Turin. You think, "Why not?"'

The Cup Winners' Cup Final at the dilapidated Heysel Stadium in Brussels four days later was virtually the beginning of the end for the 'London Irish'. Neill's team was unable to go through the gears, although O'Leary superbly man-marked Argentinian World Cup winner Mario Kempes out of the match. Brady's effort was blocked and Arsenal were unable to throw off Valencia's smothering defensive blanket. The match drifted towards a penalty shoot-out, which in those far off days was a gut-churningly new experience.

Brady missed his effort and ultimately it came down to Rix, freshly shorn of his curls, to keep his team in with a shout. Rix's daisy-cutter was easily saved by Carlos Perreira. All that was left was for Brady to guide the tearful Rix around the pitch and convince him that Gunners fans wouldn't hold a grudge against him.

Two days later the team was back in Wolverhampton, somehow grinding out a 2-1 away win, but then the wheels came off in the season's final denouement when Arsenal were thrashed 5-0 by Middlesbrough in the last game and missed out on UEFA Cup qualification.

After the Gunners' Herculean efforts they hadn't even managed to earn a place in Europe. 'It was just an awful way to finish at the club,' recalls Brady. 'There was champagne on the flight on the way back from Middlesbrough. The chairman insisted on bringing it out. Everything was a bit flat.'

The summer of 1980 was a time for superglued smiles at Highbury. Arsenal were linked with St Etienne star Michel Platini, emerging Dutch midfielder Ruud Gullit and Danish forward Frank Arnesen, but the deals were never concluded. Old soldiers Pat Rice and Sammy Nelson departed, and the Gunners finally knocked on the padded doors of the lunatic asylum and spent a cool £1m on Crystal Palace left-back Kenny Sansom, having initially signed QPR's emerging striker Clive Allen, and then swapped him for Sansom after just 60 days at the club. It gave rise to multiple conspiracy theories, most of which should probably be ignored.

Sunderland recalls, 'The issue was that Clive was a six-yard box striker, a poacher, and Arsenal have never been in the market for that type of player. To accommodate Clive, who was a great player, Terry would have needed to have altered his tactics, which he wasn't prepared to do.'

So despite huge amounts of media speculation, Arsenal ended up only signing a replacement left-back – albeit an excellent one. Not enough to get Arsenal fans salivating, or make up for the fact that, despite numerous tabloid stories suggesting he'd had a change of heart, Brady departed to Juventus for just £600,000. Under UEFA rules that was the maximum fee that a player moving abroad, who was at the end of his contract, could fetch.

It was a drawn-out divorce. At least he hadn't departed to Liverpool or Manchester United, as had been predicted, but initially at least, Neill didn't even try and replace Brady. The Gunners' midfield, consisting of Price, Talbot and Hollins, took on a distinctly blue collar veneer. The buck stopped mainly with Terry Neill, who later described Brady's departure as 'a tragedy for the club of monumental proportions'.

Brady later reflected, 'Football wasn't big business then,' although he adds, 'It never stopped Liverpool or Manchester United paying out big money when they needed to.'

In March 1981, Arsenal invested £500,000 in Crystal Palace's doughty Welsh midfielder Peter Nicholas. He wasn't the last midfielder to feel the wrath of the fans simply because he wasn't Liam Brady.

Arsenal ended up finishing third in 1980/81, but the balance of power had begun to shift in north London with Tottenham winning the FA Cup. Although Stapleton was their top league scorer with 14 goals, the tabloids were rife with rumours that he was about to follow Brady out of the club. 'Frank was my strike partner,' recalls Sunderland, 'but he kept any dealings with the club completely to himself. None of us knew what was happening until he was about to go.'

The tell-tale signs had been creeping in. He threw his hands up in the air when the service from midfield wasn't quite right and he went on several barren runs throughout the campaign, in which he and Sunderland scored just 21 league goals between them. 'We should probably have signed both Clive Allen and Kenny Sansom,' muses Sunderland. 'We had the money, and ended up just seven points short in the league. Clive could have been the difference.'

Belatedly, when Stapleton did start to talk to Arsenal about the possibility of him staying, the board made him an offer that would have made him the best-paid footballer in the country. It was too late. He had already made a gentleman's agreement with Manchester United boss Ron Atkinson and departed for £900,000, the fee set by the transfer tribunal. 'Scandalous really,' sighs Sunderland. 'Steve Daley cost Manchester City £1.5m, the combined amount Arsenal got for Liam and Frank. How does that work? If any players in England at that time were worth £1m it was those two.'

As the economic recession kicked in in the early 1980s, Arsenal found themselves in a negative downwards spiral. The team's fortunes waned. Cup runs were curtailed. Eighteen months after leaving Highbury, Stapleton returned in a Milk Cup semi-final with United, scored, and seemed to stick two fingers up at the crowd which had been goading him for much of the game.

Attendances tumbled from the 40,000-mark to nearer 25,000 or worse. Pat Jennings is adamant that, despite the recession, Arsenal's selling of their two most bankable assets was sheer folly, at a time when Neill repeatedly claimed, 'The transfer market is dead.' 'They should have tied them down,' claims Jennings. 'Crowds want to see stars, and the minute Frank and Liam went, you could see the gaps appearing on the terraces. Lower crowds mean you can't invest more in star players, so you don't have the cup runs or go for it in the league and it goes on and on. Spiralling downwards...you have to speculate to accumulate.'

Neill tried to fill the gap left by Stapleton. 'Ray Hankin, John Hawley, Lee Chapman...not really up to the mark, were they?' Jennings sighs. 'Tony Woodcock was a great player. He came in for £500,000 from Cologne, but never quite fitted into the Arsenal style like Frank. Charlie Nicholas was a goal machine for Celtic, but couldn't lead the line like Frank.'

Neill spent around £1.5m in the three years after Stapleton left, trying unsuccessfully to replace the departed Irish striker. 'It's Arsenal's way,' explains a puzzled Willie Young. 'They have a sudden burst of success, then seem to rein everything back in and become overly cautious and conservative, like they want to start again from a blank canvas.'

Neill pinned his hopes on a new generation of youth team talent in the early 1980s. But with the exception of Paul Davis – who took several years to mature into a top performer – the likes of Vaessen, Meade, Madden, Kay, McDermott, Hill and Whyte fell by the wayside. Rix was never quite the same player without Brady alongside him.

'It was grim trying to come into the team and fill Frank or Liam's shoes. The crowd was so down on everything,' recalled Vaessen. 'It could literally do your head in and send you over the edge.' As Stewart Taylor's excellent *Stuck In A Moment: The Ballad Of Paul Vaessen* shows, that's exactly what happened to the Bermondsey-born striker, who died after years of heroin addiction in 2001.

The era of the 'London Irish' fizzled out and Neill was sacked just before Christmas in 1983. 'I couldn't find replacements who were a patch on Liam or Frank,' he shrugs. Within two years, O'Leary was the final member of the original gang left at the club, and he recalled Stapleton calling him a 'mug' on several occasions for opting to stay at Highbury. Ironically, O'Leary was the only one out of the three Republic of Ireland stars to win a championship medal in England, when he lifted the title with Arsenal at Anfield in 1989.

In one sense, it was a case of the best things coming to those who wait. But Neill's team should have won more than a solitary FA Cup Final. The fact that O'Leary didn't play in a title-winning Arsenal team until he was 31 – apart from speaking volumes for his loyalty – also demonstrates how the club missed an incredible opportunity in the late 70s and early 80s to create an era of success as gilded as any other in the Gunners' history.

# The Court Of King George

*'Nobody's been doing it around here for years.'* George Graham, May 1986.

*'Arsenal are back, Arsenal are back, whooah, whooah.'* Arsenal fans, Wembley, 1987.

ARSENAL directors always claimed to have been 'keeping tabs' on their former Double winner George Graham, once nicknamed 'The Stroller'. In fact he was only formally approached after both Alex Ferguson and Terry Venables turned down the job.

Barcelona boss Venables preferred to stay in Spain – reportedly unimpressed with the Gunners approaching him while Don Howe was still in post, and Ferguson – still with Aberdeen but caretaker Scotland manager in the wake of Jock Stein's death – wanted to assess his options after the 1986 World Cup.

So the Arsenal board summoned Millwall's promising manager. His appointment was greeted with a polite murmur of approval rather than a fanfare of trumpets, but Graham's conservative management style struck a chord with a board which had become exasperated with the string of drink-driving charges, marital bust-ups and cup giant-killings that beset Arsenal in the early part of the decade.

It is hard to imagine the expansive and indulgent Venables having the same effect at Highbury as his former Chelsea team-mate. In Graham, a dour Roundhead had arrived to curb the playboy instincts of the Gunners' band of underachieving cavaliers; at least it's tempting to look at it that way.

'George Graham may have been nicknamed "The Stroller" in his playing days,' wrote Brian Woolnough in *The Sun*, 'but as he's shown at Millwall, any Arsenal player falling below the high standards Graham sets is likely to be in for a nasty shock. He will take a hatchet to Highbury, and wield it immediately.'

No Arsenal fans were in any disagreement that the hatchet approach was desperately needed. Arsenal's matches at the tail-end of the 1985/86 campaign had more than a touch of farce about them. At Highbury in April, every Watford attack had been greeted with ironic cheers as Graham Taylor's men, prompted by former Gunner Brian Talbot, eased towards a 2-0 win. The May home match against relegated West Bromwich Albion was played out in front of the lowest home gate for 20 years; 14,486, and in the final pre-Graham match, relegation-haunted Oxford United confirmed their First Division status by hammering an inept Arsenal team 3-0.

It was a grimly fitting end to a season of botched tactics and false dawns. Never have Nick Hornby's words in *Fever Pitch* rung so true, 'That Arsenal team – full of cliques and overpaid, over-the-hill stars – would never be bad enough to go down, but never good enough to win anything, and the stasis made you want to scream with frustration.'

Football in general seemed to be under attack from both the Government and its own fans. In the wake of the riots at the Heysel Stadium, St Andrew's and Kenilworth Road, Parliament debated prohibiting the sale of alcohol at games, a move which was estimated to be likely to cost clubs up to £4m a year.

Mr Justice Popplewell had published his report in July 1985 which suggested banning away fans from matches. The TV blackout for the first part of the season summed up the horrendous mess English football found itself in, although at least no evidence remains of Arsenal's dismal goalless draw at Highbury in December against Birmingham, regularly voted the worst ever Arsenal match by more seasoned supporters.

'It was bloody awful to play in. I can't even guess what it was like to stand in the cold and watch it,' explains Charlie Nicholas. These were dark times for the sport and for Arsenal, but Graham would quickly show there was light at the end of a long tunnel.

His managerial manifesto had been laid out in black and white for some time. Graham's most revealing interview in his pre-Arsenal days was with James Mossop in 1985. Graham spoke of his belief of 'living within one's means' and 'not spending more than one has', by-products of being the youngest of six children in a family where his father had died when Graham was just two months old.

At Millwall he had undergone a crash-course in the grim realities of 1980s football. He had witnessed the 1985 riot at Luton first-hand, when Millwall hooligans ripped out seats at Kenilworth Road and used them as frisbees. As a result of tumbling crowds at The Den, he was forced to balance the books and sell striker John Fashanu to Wimbledon to make ends meet. 'I suppose they [the hooligans] represent that degree of open lawlessness that exists in Britain today,' Graham told Mossop.

He also spoke passionately of the overriding need for 'professionalism' and 'discipline', and in the precious little spare time he had he was a regular visitor to Companies House, where he familiarised himself with accounts. 'It's essential if I'm going to trade in the transfer market,' he explained.

It certainly would be at Arsenal, who were around £1m in debt, and with the ban on English clubs playing in Europe there was no immediate possibility of filling any coffers. Graham was pragmatic about Millwall's style of play, 'I had to shelve my principles because I like to play creative, entertaining football…but we had to play hard, uncompromising football. We needed fighters. In the end, winning is all that matters,' he explained, and he would stick rigidly to those underlining values throughout his eight full seasons at Highbury.

Not for nothing would he soon gain the nickname 'Gadaffi' among his players. Some football writers even suggested there were certain parallels between Graham's style of management and that of Margaret Thatcher.

Graham was portrayed as a reincarnation of Bertie Mee; a younger member of the Puritanical 'club blazer and tie, short back and sides' brigade. In a crisply-ironed white shirt, his early clarion call to disaffected Arsenal fans and players now appears as 'holier than thou' as Thatcher's reciting of St Francis of Assisi's poem on the steps of Number 10 after she became Prime Minister in 1979.

'In society, standards are falling. Now if that's a problem of society, I'm gonna try to make sure it's not gonna be one of Arsenal's problems in the future. I want ambitious young men with the right attitude. Allied with skill, I think that would be an ideal combination.'

On a London radio show, Mike Langley described Graham as 'one of a new breed of manager inspired by Thatcherite attitudes and new right economics. No nonsense, uncompromising, willing to ruffle feathers, convinced they're always right…always aware of the balance sheet and the bottom line – that football is about winning matches.'

Graham already had the inside track on the infamous Arsenal drinking club, which certainly didn't pack up and go home after half a shandy at The Orange Tree in Totteridge on a Saturday night. Nicholas recalled that Graham would often pop in for a drink after a match when he was Millwall boss. 'He would always tell me that Arsenal wasn't the right club for me. He said, "Arsenal's strength is built on defence and teamwork." He knew all about Arsenal's tradition. So when he became manager, I thought to myself, "Oh Christ, here we go."'

Midfielder Paul Davis relished Graham's arrival, 'Under Terry Neill and Don Howe training wasn't serious enough because no one was taking any responsibility. The players weren't conducting themselves in the right way. It was like a casual jog. George Graham had real clout though, and was mentally strong, right from the training ground to players' contract negotiations. He made it clear that the joking was over.'

Graham claimed his main inspiration to be former American football coach Vince Lombardi. 'Occasionally, he'd quote Lombardi to us,' explained David Rocastle. 'One of George's favourite Lombardi quotes was, "Confidence is contagious. So is a lack of confidence." Another one was, "Show me a good loser and I'll show you a loser." Sometimes, quotes like that can get a bit cheesy and a bit hammy. But for younger players, what he said when he arrived made perfect sense.'

Lombardi also claimed that cliques were the most damaging cancerous growths within any institution, and Graham approached the job with scalpel in hand. Within days of his arrival, Tony Woodcock and Paul Mariner, both of whom had laboured horribly during the 1985/86 campaign, were dumped on slow-boats to Portsmouth and Cologne respectively.

Graham fired a poorly disguised parting shot at the pair after their release, insisting that players would have to 'earn the right to play for Arsenal'. He also served early notice of his parsimonious attitude to transfer dealings and contracts when, after refusing to allow Martin Keown an extra £50 a week, the defender was sold to Aston Villa for £200,000.

'I refused to pay him more than the likes of Tony Adams and David Rocastle, and so he was off to Aston Villa,' Graham later wrote in *The Glory And The Grief*, although he admitted it cost him ten times more to bring him back to Highbury in 1993.

The sale of Keown was controversial, especially as Tony Adams had spent much of the last two seasons in and out of the side. 'Keown looks a more polished performer than the occasionally cumbersome Adams,' wrote David Lacey in *The Guardian* after the former's excellent performances against Liverpool and Manchester United in December 1985. Brian Woolnough recalled, 'Most journalists at the time who watched Arsenal reckoned Keown was the better long-term prospect. He seemed to have more attributes. He was a better passer of the ball and certainly quicker than Adams.'

Gunners coach Steve Burtenshaw had once told Adams and Keown that it would be nigh-on impossible to play both defenders together given that David O'Leary was a fixture in the side. 'It surprised me when Martin left,' admitted Davis. 'It did seem odd, given that he had been a revelation when he'd broken into the side. The thing is, Tony Adams was vocal and was a born leader. At that age, Martin was quiet. I would say it was George's first big decision.'

Graham was already wielding the 'hatchet', as Brian Woolnough predicted, eliminating the old guard and the dissenters. He promised, 'Eventually it will be my squad at Highbury but for the moment I'll wait to see how things develop'. The tabloids linked strikers Kerry Dixon, Tony Cottee and Danish forward Preben Elkjaer with a move to Highbury, but Graham's first foray into the transfer market – the signature of Perry Groves – was as low-key as it gets.

Groves recalled, 'When I arrived at Highbury, I was taken upstairs to George Graham's office. It was like a headmaster talking to a pupil, even down to the fact that he was in a big chair and mine was a smaller one. There was no negotiation over terms or anything, and there were no agents in those days. At least – I didn't have one. It was a case of, "Here's your contract – sign it." I did as I was told.'

Groves's arrival sent out a clear message to the squad. 'I bowled up to my first training session in my knackered old car which had steam pouring out of the engine because I'd pelted down the M25. Guys like Viv Anderson – who were driving BMWs and Mercedes – were looking at me as if to say, "Who the fucking hell is this?"' Low budget, distinctly blue collar, keen as mustard, malleable; the Colchester man's arrival was an early example of the Grahamite philosophy at its most extreme.

Graham's training routines were a culture shock to the squad. 'There was George, ready with his clip board, ready to get us moving,' recalls Nicholas. 'There was a sense of urgency – he wasn't the old "Stroller" anymore. I remember he had a go at Kenny Sansom when he called him "George". He told Kenny to "call me boss" or "Mr Graham". There was a different atmosphere around the place. He wasn't revolutionary in his training methods. He put an emphasis on the right things, encouraging the older players like Viv and Kenny to lead by example, bigging up Tony Adams, and playing to traditional Arsenal strengths – keeping it tight at the back and instructing midfielders to protect the back four with their lives.'

There was genuine apprehension before the first match of the 1986/87 campaign. The forward partnership of Niall Quinn and Charlie Nicholas rarely inspired confidence but was symptomatic of the tactical fad to pair a big man and a small man up front. 'Lots of teams did it,' recalls Nicholas. 'Everton played Graeme Sharp with Adrian Heath. But Niall and I weren't quick or mobile enough to stay as a partnership.'

Graham played down Arsenal's prospects with the media, insisting that a top-five finish and a 'decent run in one or more of the cups would be a more than decent start to my time as a manger here'. A 41,000 crowd filled Highbury for the opening-day fixture against Manchester United. The 'tough spine' which Graham craved was already in place; Lukic, Adams, Robson and Quinn, although two of the vertebrae would later be surgically altered.

Arsenal weren't inspiring against United but that wasn't the point. The defence operated as a solid unit, which hadn't been the case for a number of seasons. 'Players were talking to each other on the pitch more,' explained Nicholas. 'Defenders yelled at one another, and the midfield.'

In the *Daily Mirror*, Joe Melling noted how 'midfielders Stewart Robson and Graham Rix squeezed their United counterparts effectively, not giving them time to breathe'. Nicholas grabbed an uncharacteristic poacher's goal in the dying minutes to win the match and the score of 'one-nil to the Arsenal' was a prophetic one.

Over the next seven league games, Arsenal won just once – against Sheffield Wednesday – and lost three times. 'The quality of football was just as bad as it had been under Don Howe, if not worse,' recalls Nicholas. In the *Daily Telegraph*, Frank McGhee described a goalless draw with Tottenham at Highbury as, 'underwhelmingly tedious'. Steve Jones described the goalless draw away to Luton as 'like one of those existentialist novels in which nothing much ever seems to happen'.

At the end of another blank scoreline against Oxford United, sections of the North Bank chanted, 'What a load of rubbish' and sang 'Georgie, get your chequebook out'. Only 20,000 came to watch the home matches with Sheffield Wednesday and Oxford; 5,000 below Arsenal's 'break-even' figure. The message? Punters in N5 were yet to be convinced.

'Arsenal are big and growing smaller – certainly in the minds of their fans. It's time George Graham listened to the Arsenal fans and spent some money,' insisted Stuart Simons in the *Daily Mail*. 'I'm not going to panic, and I'm not going to waste money either,' Graham countered. 'We'll get this right together. My feelings about the Oxford and Luton games? We didn't lose.'

He wheeled out his stock phrase, 'I will buy the right player when the time is right for Arsenal'. Not for the last time, luck was about to intervene on Graham's behalf. Some of Arsenal's old guard were about to fall victim to 'natural wastage'.

With the team labouring in tenth place, Stewart Robson's groin injury flared up once again during the Tottenham game, Rix pulled a hamstring against Oxford and Nicholas suffered a deep gash to his leg away at Nottingham Forest. Graham brought Martin Hayes, Perry Groves and Steve Williams in to the line-up, which meant he had almost stumbled upon a far more quicksilver team. The injuries also meant he wasn't seen to be 'dropping' established crowd favourites which would have been a brave decision indeed in his early days at the club.

Nicholas recalls, 'During the couple of months I was out, the team won eight out of ten matches. George realised that Arsenal could play well – perhaps better – without me in the team.' Robson never played for Arsenal again after he was substituted in the Tottenham match.

The Graham–Robson partnership was destined to be dysfunctional from the minute Graham arrived at the club. On the face of it, Robson seemed ideal for the new Arsenal – his youth and energy seemingly a prerequisite on any Arsenal player's CV under the Scot. Yet Graham harboured deep-rooted suspicions of Robson, commenting in *The Glory And The Grief* that neither he, nor 'any of the coaches could communicate effectively with him'. Graham was also resentful that in an early meeting, Robson's father insisted that his son should play in a central midfield position only.

Robson alleges, 'Early in the season, I was called into the England squad for the game in Sweden and there was a dinner for the players which I attended. I had to withdraw due to injury, but George met with my father and I where he began to question my loyalty to the club. I couldn't believe what I was hearing. When I had my hernia operation and came out of hospital, George said in the press, "He's part of our future, no question. We'll offer him a new contract." In reality, he cold-shouldered me. Then West Ham came in. I didn't want to go, but it was clear that George didn't want me at Arsenal. Once, I'd been a role model for emerging Arsenal stars. Now I was out.'

Such cold-shouldering of crowd favourites became a familiar Graham ploy and would eventually backfire on him eight years down the line, but the Scot insists that in the case of Robson unpleasant means justified glorious ends. His subsequent career was to be blighted by injury at West Ham and Coventry, and the £700,000 West Ham paid for him almost wiped out the club's debt in a stroke. It was all about the bottom line.

Arsenal were about to show their full potential under the new manager without Rix, Robson and Nicholas in the team. By the time his side took to the field at Everton in early October, his favoured Mark 1 Arsenal line-up was complete, save for Nicholas replacing Groves when he regained fitness: Lukic, Sansom, Anderson, Adams, O'Leary, Davis, Williams, Rocastle, Quinn, Groves, Hayes. The total cost of the team was around the £1.7m-mark (Sansom alone cost £1m). Cheap and mainly homegrown; just as George Graham liked it.

One of the prime exponents of the Graham effect was Steve Williams, whose contribution had been fitful to say the least since he had arrived from Southampton in 1984. Linked with a move to QPR, Williams seemed set to be the first casualty at Graham's Arsenal but flourished during the 1986/87 season.

'He did in six weeks what Don Howe had failed to do in about three years of trying. He got people playing for each other, not just operating as individuals. George gave everyone a chance – no matter who you were. He understood what made a team tick and how it interlocked. "Steve – you need to defend the back four," he'd tell me. He understood that if you didn't concede, you weren't going to lose. And that was the bottom line.

'Everyone at the club was crystal clear about that. He worked on set pieces, which became a major strength of all his sides. He drilled the defence, telling them to work on the linesmen when it came to the offside trap. He told Viv and Kenny to bark at the linesmen. He reckoned linesmen dozed off in games. He also worked with pairs of players. Rocastle and Anderson were a good partnership on the right. He spent a lot of time with those two. He did the same with Paul Davis and me in midfield.'

After four games without a win, Graham called for greater commitment and effort at Goodison Park. The team produced a backs-to-the-wall performance and beat Everton 1-0 with Williams scoring direct from a corner. That victory proved to be the springboard for a monumental two-month charge up the table. Arsenal found their shooting boots, putting three past Chelsea, Watford, Manchester City and Luton. By the time they defeated Tottenham at White Hart

Lane in early January, there was clear daylight between them and the Merseyside clubs at the top of the table.

Arguably the unlikeliest of Arsenal's emerging young players at the time was Martin Hayes, whom Graham planned to sell to Huddersfield in October for a paltry £20,000. Nicholas's injury presented Hayes with his chance. Between them, Hayes and Niall Quinn netted 18 goals in that three-month spell.

The jury always appeared to be out on the pair; one Arsenal fan at the time told ITV Sport, 'They look like a couple of teenagers who've pinched their dad's credit card, gone on a spending spree, but know they're about to be caught out.'

Hayes speaks positively about Graham's impact on the club's emerging youngsters, 'I generally went around with Niall, Rocky, Mickey Thomas and we had our own taste in certain things. Everyone at the club got on, but you also had the big star element and they went around together like Charlie, Graham Rix and Kenny Sansom. Two different worlds really.

'What George did was slowly shift the balance, so that the young-sters ruled the roost. That's how he wanted the club to go. He gave us youngsters the confidence to play without fear and allowed Perry, Rocky and me off the leash. As a kid you just wait for the next game. George took the pressure off us. We just got on with it.'

Groves concurs, 'George told us forwards to play our natural game. He had to be very flexible with his tactics, and that suited Martin Hayes, Rocky and me, because none of us were out and out wingers or midfielders. We could mix things up. I think that's why we did so well for those two months before Christmas. We had the element of surprise, and defences didn't quite know what to do about us. George gave us that confidence. He kept our feet on the ground, and we never got cocky – he'd never have let us.'

The transformation in Arsenal's fortunes was a revelation for a generation of Gunners supporters who had been used to bleak winters. Some of the team's displays were breathtaking. David Rocastle's performance in the 3-1 home win against Chelsea was exquisite, and Hayes and Groves caused Doug Rougvie no end of problems. The 3-0 victory against Manchester City was due in no small part to the pace of Hayes and Groves as well. 'The one thing central defenders like me struggle with,' recalled City skipper Mick McCarthy, 'is real pace. You can use your positional sense and employ all the tricks [McCarthy winded both Hayes and Groves during the game] but sometimes, that just isn't enough.'

All the time, the Highbury crowds slowly increased, and the encounters with West Ham, Chelsea and QPR were watched by 30,000-plus attendances. By the time Arsenal trounced Aston Villa 4-0 away from home amid a tornado of attacking wing play the tabloids suggested that Graham's boys might even be title contenders. But already, football journalists were forming their own opinions on Graham's team, and not all of them were complimentary.

In November, the often combative Mike Langley asked Graham if he really thought the forward triumvirate of Quinn, Groves and Hayes were the right trio to steer Arsenal to the title – in that or any season. 'I've never said we'd win the league this year,' countered Graham. 'For now, those three are playing their socks off for me.' 'But they're hardly Dalglish and Rush, are they?' Langley countered. 'I've always said that I'd build my own squad, and we'll see how things pan out,' the Arsenal manager concluded.

There was already a feeling that change was likely to occur and the pugnacious Langley insisted, 'Those three will run out of steam any time soon. I can feel it.' Graham was also pragmatic about tactics. 'I've seen it written that we play a rather dull 4-4-2 formation, but I would argue that when Rocastle, Groves, Hayes and Quinn are firing, it's more like 4-2-4. I want versatility and creativity – I think the 4-4-2 label straitjackets what we're doing unnecessarily,' he claimed.

Some journalists were beginning to apply the clichéd, military-styled descriptions to Arsenal which became commonplace in the latter years of Graham's time in charge, and which invoked the spirit of the 'Bertie's Bores' headlines from the early 1970s. It was partly because the Gunners' defence was proving adept at soaking up punishment for long spells and then hitting back on the break at lightning speed. Chapman's teams in the 1930s were famous for playing in a similar style, and were dubbed 'lucky' and 'boring' by detractors. History was now beginning to repeat itself.

'These Arsenal stormtroopers rallied to General George Graham's demands,' wrote Bill Day in the *Mail On Sunday* after the Chelsea win. 'General George has marched the Gunners to the top of the hill,' claimed Ken Montgomery after a win against Southampton in December which kept them top of the table.

Brian Woolnough admitted, 'Certain stereotypes remain attached to some football clubs whatever happens, and football writers are prone to resort to clichés. Arsenal played excellent football in that spell, and most of us felt that George Graham deserved credit for turning their fortunes around so rapidly. But not everyone liked George Graham, or Arsenal. They were an acquired taste.'

Graham sometimes played up to the stereotype that he was obsessed with a mean defence. After a 4-0 away win at Southampton, where the Gunners only scored after Tim Flowers was replaced in goal by striker Colin Clarke, he claimed, 'Arsenal has the best back four in the country, but they did not look like that today,' and after the 3-1 win against QPR, Graham lambasted the defence for nigh on an hour after they conceded a late goal.

Arsenal began to run out of steam in the league in the early part of the New Year. As Mike Langley predicted, the Groves–Hayes–Quinn forward line began to lose shape and creativity, and the return to the team of Nicholas couldn't stop the slide in form.

'I think defences began to find us out,' admitted Groves, 'and the weekly grind of league matches started to take its toll. It was a phenomenally young team, and we were due a reality check.'

Symbolically, the final hurrah in the league came at White Hart Lane, where goals from Adams and Davis put Arsenal five points clear in the title race. The lead quickly evaporated, but by mid-January, the Gunners were already in the Littlewoods Cup semi-final with the old enemy from the other end of Seven Sisters Road lying in wait.

~ ~ ~ ~ ~

Tottenham Hotspur; an unforgiving barometer of Arsenal's fortunes throughout the early and mid-80s. Spurs had often been present and correct to rub salt into Arsenal wounds on a regular basis. Now and then Arsenal had shown glimpses of what they could do, usually with Nicholas orchestrating things.

'I always felt revitalised when it came to north London derbies,' he explains. 'It's probably because I grew up on the Glasgow derbies, and felt a huge sense of expectation when these games came around. I loved that "do or die" feeling.' In the 1983/84 season, Nicholas starred at Highbury and at White Hart Lane as the Gunners won 3-2 and 4-2 respectively.

But Tottenham had won two FA Cups and the UEFA Cup. They had glamorous foreign signings in Ossie Ardiles and Belgian Nico Claesen, whom they had captured after the 1986 World Cup. They had built a new stand in the early 80s which comprised executive boxes, floated on the stock exchange, and England stars Glenn Hoddle and Chris Waddle had branched into the pop world with 'Diamond Lights'.

Their home match with Nottingham Forest in September 1984 became the first live league match broadcast on national TV and shortly before Graham took over at Arsenal, Tottenham announced that White Hart Lane would host the Joe Bugner v Frank Bruno fight.

Arsenal used to pioneer those types of activities – but not anymore. Tottenham's increased commercial awareness wasn't to everyone's taste – departing manager Keith Burkinshaw famously said, 'There used to be a football club over there,' but it was in stark contrast with Highbury, which had one tiny commercial outlet, where Gunners fans could well be served by former goalkeeper Jack Kelsey, who ran the shop with his wife.

Given Arsenal's league form since the game at White Hart Lane – they had drawn 0-0 at home to Coventry and lost 2-0 at Old Trafford in a fractious encounter – and Tottenham's fine track record in cup competitions, they were slight favourites to win over both legs of the semi-final. At Highbury in the first leg, Arsenal malfunctioned badly.

The usually accurate passing moves sparked by Davis and Williams went awry (Williams spent most of the match barking at the referee and Ardiles) and Hayes, Quinn and Davis all missed good chances to put the Gunners 1-0 up. Badly missing the Rocastle–Anderson combination down the right, Arsenal were generally toothless.

Nicholas was probably most disappointing of all. In his tight 80s-style top and micro shorts, the mulleted Scot looked slow, chunky and cumbersome, and apart from the odd fancy flick he contributed little. Nicholas already believed his cards were marked, recalling, 'The week before the Tottenham game, I'd scored an excellent goal in the FA Cup against Barnsley. George told the press I was "lucky". At that point I knew my days at the club were nearing their end. Because if he couldn't praise me after a goal like that, he never would.'

Clive Allen's 34th goal of the season gave his side the advantage in the first leg, but it could have been far worse with Hoddle, Waddle and Allen going perilously close to adding to Tottenham's lead. Graham expressed disappointment with Arsenal's display. 'We just banged aimless balls forward in hope more than expectation,' he claimed. 'However, I remain convinced that we'll play far better in the second leg.' It took them a further 45 minutes to spark into life.

At White Hart Lane, Allen put his side 2-0 up on aggregate and missed three gilt-edged chances to put Tottenham out of sight. Arsenal looked jaded. Nicholas's opportunist lob which clipped the crossbar was the Gunners' only real chance. The doubts which had been raised about Arsenal's ability to win 'big' matches over the last few weeks appeared to be coming true. David O'Leary and Viv Anderson aside, no Arsenal players had won silverware during their career.

At half-time in the dressing room, the mood among the players was one of concern. Nicholas recalls, 'We knew that we faced a tough task to get back into things. I don't know what George was thinking privately, but he remained calm with us, telling us not to panic, to keep things tight, to maintain the belief that we could turn back the tide.'

What happened next acted as a bolt of electricity for Arsenal's jaded players. Tottenham's stadium announcer informed Spurs supporters that tickets for the Littlewoods Cup Final would go on sale within the week, and in order to add to the party mood he played Chas and Dave's 'Spurs Are On Their Way To Wembley' hit over the tannoy.

Nicholas explains, 'Suddenly our heads went up, and we just stared at each other. No one said anything. Everyone, including George, just glanced from face to face in disbelief. Maybe it's a bit simplistic, but I do think the true Arsenal spirit awoke there and then. Suddenly everyone was on their feet, ready to go out for the second half. They were taking the piss out of us, and we wanted to make them pay.'

Davis says, 'George gauged our mood perfectly. Under pressure, he always knew what to say. Anfield 1989, the points deduction in 1990, Parma 1994…that was one of his strengths as a manager. He told us that we would keep our heads, and that we would put away our chances this half.'

The roar from the supporters at the Paxton Road End which greeted the Gunners players as they ran out for the second half was huge, and one of the greatest of all Arsenal fightbacks was about to unravel. Yet it wasn't quite as straightforward as some Arsenal histories have suggested.

Kenny Sansom claimed, 'It was obvious to me as we trotted out that Arsenal were not going out of the competition.'

The truth was that Tottenham could easily have buried the tie within 30 seconds of the second half starting as Allen skewed his shot an inch wide, and when Arsenal did score, 'We were dead lucky,' as Nicholas admits. A long throw from the right by Rocastle found Quinn, who flicked the ball towards Anderson. The right-back took full advantage of hesitancy by Mitchell Thomas and keeper Ray Clemence to scramble the ball home. Anderson later admitted, 'Clem should have done better with that. I was surprised to see it go in, really. He wasn't at his best by then, I don't think.'

Allen's uncharacteristic profligacy (he fluffed two one-on-ones with John Lukic) also kept the Gunners in it. 'Yes, we rode our luck,' admits Paul Davis. 'When he [Allen] went through on John [Lukic] you think, this could it be it...but sometimes, when the opposition blows chance after chance, you start thinking, "This has to be our day." But what we did was exploit their weak right-hand side through Viv and Rocky.'

It was a Rocastle burst down the right that set up Quinn to slide in the Gunners' second goal in the 64th minute, and Nicholas might even have won it outright at the death but Clemence saved his shot.

After extra time the teams were tied up at 2-2. David Pleat and George Graham gauged their sides' respective nervousness at home by admitting that playing away from home in the replay might just be preferable for both teams. But Pleat had little option but to call 'home' when he won the toss. The scene was set for the most pivotal north London derby since Arsenal won the league at White Hart Lane in May 1971.

The match was even throughout the first half. Quinn and Hayes went close for the Gunners and Allen did likewise for Tottenham, who were without the injured Hoddle. On 60 minutes Allen put Spurs 1-0 up and Nicholas was stretchered off after a heavy tackle from Richard

Gough. When Ian Allinson, who had barely figured in the first team that season, was thrown into the mix by Graham, it hardly appeared to be a tactical change which was going to turn around Arsenal's fortunes.

Here now, when it really counted, Graham's refusal to purchase a top-class striker seemed likely to cost the club dear. Through necessity, Graham 'told us to play 4-2-4,' recalls Davis. 'He told Rocky to move forward and support Hayes, Quinn and Allinson.'

With 25 minutes left, Allinson snuck in a soft equaliser, his shot squeezing between Clemence and the post. The scorer looked delighted but surprised; Clemence was horrified. Allinson, who had almost ended up at Arsenal by accident in 1983 – a clerical error at Colchester United meant his contract expired – was the first of a string of unlikely heroes who played their part under Graham. The impact of this unassuming player's strike was seismic.

'I looked at experienced players like Gough and Waddle,' recalls Davis. 'In that split second, their heads were gone. They had nothing left.'

Finally Arsenal squeezed the life out of their rivals. The reaction from Arsenal supporters after Allinson's goal was telling. 'We were literally bouncing up and down with sheer unbridled excitement at the Paxton Road End,' recalls Gunners fan Matthew Yates. 'I've followed Arsenal for a long time, and you only get that kind of feeling once in a blue moon…that the whole thing is coming together in front of you. You get a sense of enormity about the whole thing. It's an intoxicating feeling, but that night more than any other, you knew that the players were feeling the same way.'

Arsenal's winning goal was classic early Graham. A direct free kick by David O'Leary was flicked on by Quinn to Allinson, who tried his luck from just outside the box ('What the bloody hell was he doing having a go from there?' laughs Hayes) and the ball ricocheted loose to Rocastle, who galloped on to slip his shot low under Clemence's body. 'Arsenal are through to Wembley!' barked ITV commentator Brian Moore. Two minutes later, they were.

Direct football, a stroke of luck (Arsenal scored four times and Clemence was at fault on three occasions) and the boundless energy of youth; Graham's team had delivered. The pattern of the match –

'One-nil down, two-one up, we knocked Tottenham out the cup' – was telling. Graham said afterwards, 'This result shows that my team will never roll over for anyone.' It also spawned the name of the fanzine which was founded in 1987.

Steve Williams recalls, 'So many of us at the club were also Arsenal fans. That night meant the world to everyone.' At the final whistle, the entire Arsenal contingent – players, substitutes and the management team – milked the applause in front of the supporters, with a gaggle of snapping cameramen present.

The most poignant image of the night is a picture of a beaming Rocastle being hugged by Graham. 'George let his guard down a bit,' explains Davis. 'He was still the stern father figure, but he congratulated every one of the players. That night was the spiritual regeneration of the club. You can never underplay the significance of the semi-final win over Spurs. It was the stepping stone for everything which George achieved.'

'GLORIOUS GUNNERS RISE FROM THE DEAD', claimed *The Sun*. A month later against Liverpool at Wembley in the Littlewoods Cup Final, the club's resurrection under Graham would continue at pace.

⌣ ⌣ ⌣ ⌣ ⌣

Sunday 5 April 1987; a day packed with omens and symbols for the rest of the decade. Raw Wembley nerves were a new experience for so many connected with the club. It had been seven years since Arsenal last played there, and as Graham reminded his players, 'Playing here is a luxury. Make sure that you soak up and enjoy the experience.'

The whole package was breathtakingly fresh and thrilling, all played out in glorious red and white Technicolor. It was to prove the ultimate white knuckle ride for players and fans. Arsenal fans – booming out 'Que Sera' and 'Yellow Ribbon' – were off to watch 'Georgie Graham and his red and white army' face Double winners Liverpool.

Slaying Tottenham, who'd had the psychological advantage over the Gunners for much of the decade, was one thing but defeating Liverpool would be quite another. Always a keen observer of club history, Graham pointed out to his players that historically Arsenal had the edge over Liverpool in big matches, defeating them in both the 1950 and 1971 FA Cup finals.

That didn't cut too much ice with the media, which unsurprisingly honed in on Ian Rush's imminent departure to Italian club Juventus. 'It would be the perfect end to Rush's glorious Anfield career,' claimed *The Sun*, 'if he could grab a piece of silverware just once more before he swaps a plate of Scouse for a bowl of pasta.' In the *Daily Mirror*, columnist Terry Venables scored both sides equally except for up front, awarding Walsh and Rush 9/10 and Quinn and Nicholas 8/10.

Whereas Venables described Rush as 'the outstanding striker in Britain', he said of Nicholas, 'Too many times nibbling at the edge instead of biting a bigger chunk.' Since defeating Tottenham in the league on 4 January they had scored just once in nine games, and tumbled out of the FA Cup to Watford in the quarter-finals. It was the Littlewoods Cup or bust for Graham's Gunners.

Then there was that hoary old Rush statistic; he had scored in 144 Liverpool matches and his team had never lost when the Welshman had found the back of the net. 'Anyone who claimed they were unaware of it or reckoned they could ignore it are kidding themselves. We took the view that Rushy's record had to be broken at some time,' explains Steve Williams.

For the first 20 minutes, under glorious blue Wembley skies, Jan Molby's passing threatened to slice Graham's team apart like a roast. 'There seemed only one possible outcome, for at that stage Arsenal looked as though they were asking permission to play,' wrote David Lacey in *The Guardian*. 'Liverpool strolled into the Arsenal half of the field and drove through their defence like farmers considering their next crop rotation, unperturbed by a few stray bullocks.'

Rush rounded off a slick Liverpool move in the 23rd minute after an excellent interchange of passing between Molby and Steve McMahon. 'It's such a familiar sight,' exclaimed an almost weary-sounding Barry Davies on the BBC, after which Liverpool proceeded to play keep-ball for the next five minutes.

But Liverpool had a couple of telling injuries. Centre-back Mark Lawrenson had already sustained the Achilles injury which ended his career a few months later, and they also missed the drive of Steve Nicol in the centre. 'We weren't 100 per cent stable at the back,' recalled Alan

Hansen, 'and we lacked pace in midfield and at the back too. Even when Rushy gave us the lead, Arsenal's heads didn't drop.'

Nicholas recalls, 'For a couple of minutes, you think to yourself, "Oh Christ, Rushie has scored, that's it." But we had that inner mental strength which we'd developed from coming back from the dead twice in the semi-final. There isn't the time to worry. You have to believe in yourself and the team, and get on with things.'

Six minutes after Rush gave Liverpool the lead, Nicholas poked home Arsenal's equaliser after Liverpool's defence failed to clear Davis's free kick effectively. Despite being nearly throttled by Adams in the ensuing celebrations, Nicholas recalls, 'It was back to the Tottenham scenario again. We were thinking, "We'll break this Rushie hoodoo, and we'll do it now."'

Much of the rest of the match was constricted to 20 yards either side of the halfway line, and balanced precariously on the 'knife edge of midfield chessplay', in *The Times*'s David Miller's words. Williams and Davis's midfield partnership proved an equal match for Jan Molby's ball skills, and while the Rocastle–Anderson combination caused Liverpool problems down the right Arsenal's winner came from a move down the left.

Graham substituted the labouring Quinn for Groves, who was about to plunge 'his pace like a dagger into Liverpool's defence', as Patrick Barclay wrote in *The Independent*. Within minutes of coming on, Groves latched on to Kenny Sansom's pass, slipped the ball under Gary Gillespie's sliding challenge, scampered forwards and passed to Nicholas. The Scot's weak shot to Bruce Grobbelaar's left took a hefty deflection off Ronnie Whelan, wrong-footed the Zimbabwean keeper, and crept over the line to the right.

The supreme irony of the match lay in the tale of the substitutes. Dalglish brought himself on in the 73rd minute but could only stroll around morosely, unable to impose himself on the game. At the final whistle he booted the ball away, and later refused to attend his scheduled press conference. Bargain-basement signing Groves, on the other hand, had swung the match in Arsenal's favour.

'George just told me to wreak havoc down the left,' Groves explains, 'so I did just that. I just ran at a tired defence. I could see the fear on their faces, and I knew that Gary Gillespie was knackered. I think that

George maybe thought the game would go to extra time, but we killed it earlier than he thought.'

Graham's reactions after the final whistle are a fascinating combination of pride, irritation, and unbridled ambition. Clad in immaculate blue blazer and grey flannels, he hugged his victorious players but bristled when confronted with the claim that Arsenal's winning goal simply gave more fuel to that 'lucky' tag. 'There's nothing lucky about what we've achieved. Our success has come through hard work.' Later he added, 'I'm thrilled that we've won a trophy in my first season, but I still plan to make several additions to my squad.'

Nicholas, who had 'mugged Ian Rush on the way to Italy' according to Alex Montgomery in *The Sun*, felt uneasy in the days and weeks following the final. 'I was "King Charlie" at last, apparently. The "Bonnie Prince had delivered". Finally. Charlie had "hit the jackpot". They were great headlines, and I was thrilled with the win on the day, but George wasn't convinced,' he laughs.

'I remember afterwards one of the newspapers quoted me as saying, "Sell me if you dare" to George. They were mischief-making. I'd never have been so stupid as to say anything like that to him. He awarded me a one-year deal, which was a "wait and see" set-up at best.' *The Times* had it spot on, 'Charlie the prince for one glorious day'.

His Arsenal career was almost over but Charlie had at least set off one spectacular flare from his sinking ship.

- - - - -

Losing the Littlewoods Cup Final certainly didn't signal the end of Liverpool's dominance, and Kenny Dalglish's side captured the title with ease during the 1987/88 campaign. Yet Arsenal had got under Liverpool's skin – not for the last time in the 1980s.

They were far from perfect, as their New Year league form demonstrated. Hayes and Quinn were already being booed by sections of the Arsenal support and Gus Caesar's displays had been desperately poor when he was called upon. Crowds once again tailed off to below 20,000 for several sterile league matches, and after 0-0 draws with Oxford and a 1-0 home defeat against champions Everton in April, fans once again chanted, 'What a load of rubbish,' only weeks after seeing their team win the Littlewoods Cup.

But the Wembley win gave Graham the kudos, the leverage and the funds (the domestic cup runs and improved league form before Christmas brought much needed revenue into the coffers and meant that Arsenal had made a £2m profit in Graham's first season) to sculpt and shape the squad as he wished. In March he signed Leicester's Alan Smith for £700,000 and a month later, brought Wimbledon full-back Nigel Winterburn to Highbury for £400,000. Two more pieces of his jigsaw were in place. Graham also blooded young striker Paul Merson.

No manager in the 1980s, not even Howard Kendall at Everton, had made such a seismic impact at their club so soon after taking over. It was certainly a happy camp at the end of Graham's first season in charge – the most crucial Gunners campaign in 15 years – and Groves even caught his boss humming Sinatra tunes to himself one day at training. 'Any particular favourite?' I ask Groves. '"My Way", of course,' comes the response.

# Anfield (Acts 1, 2 and 3)

*'The Highbury side dipped into the transfer market to buy defender Steve Bould but they still lack the firepower up front to make any significant impact. A place in the top six will be the best they can hope for. Verdict: sixth place.'* Shoot! *August 1988.*

*'The Liverpool players looked at one another after "Smudger" scored. They didn't seem to know what to do next.'* Perry Groves.

THE Gunners had invariably been swatted away like flies throughout the 1980s whenever they faced Liverpool in their own city. George Graham had been criticised for not pursuing the signature of Watford's John Barnes, a player who had expressed a wish to remain in London (the satirical Arsenal fanzine the *Arsenal Echo Echo* ran a headline 'George Graham spends £5. Interpol alerted'), and his arrival at Anfield in July 1987 seemed to herald the start of another long period of Liverpool dominance.

Graham insisted, 'I feel confident that within a year or so, we'll be seen by the football world at large as legitimate contenders for Liverpool's crown.' It appeared a wildly optimistic claim. Liverpool cruised to the title in 1988, losing just two matches all season.

Less than 18 months after their chastening 2-0 defeat at Anfield in January 1988, with Barnes the tormentor in chief, Graham's team somehow stormed Fortress Anfield. Arsenal were about to knock Liverpool off their perch.

Despite slick hammerings of Bayern Munich and Tottenham in the pre-season Makita Tournament, with Alan Smith, Paul Merson and new signing Brian Marwood bonding well as an attacking force, the signing of prematurely-balding centre-back Steve Bould from Stoke's reserve team for £390,000 did not seem to be the catalyst which would inspire an assault on the league title in 1988/89.

The last of the old guard were ruthlessly discarded. Graham Rix departed to French side Caen, and Steve Williams went to Luton. Kenny Sansom also finally fell victim to Graham's purging and although he remained at the club until December, he was frozen out and sold to struggling Newcastle. With only Davis, Adams, O'Leary and Lukic remaining from the Neill era, Graham's assurance that 'within two years this will be my Arsenal team' had come shockingly true.

The squad could best be described as raw and wafer-thin. It seemed a tall order to ask Nigel Winterburn and Lee Dixon to immediately work in tandem, although the settling-in period George had granted the pair in the previous campaign turned out to be an inspired decision.

The palpable weakness appeared to be in central defence, traditionally a bulwark of successful Arsenal sides. Adams's performances at the European Championship made him a subject of ridicule after Dutch striker Marco Van Basten's performance in the group stage clash against England left him looking bereft of any form or confidence. There was also concern over David O'Leary's Achilles tendon injury which had ruled him out of the tournament. At 30, who was to say that his best days weren't behind him?

In midfield there was a vibrancy about the pairing of Rocastle and converted right-back Michael Thomas, but after Williams's departure the only creative option lay in Paul Davis. As for the front line, there remained doubts about Alan Smith's ability – he had looked laboured and a little cumbersome on occasions during his first season at Highbury – and Paul Merson's likely longevity in the team. The jury remained out on Marwood as the three games he had played at the tail-end of the previous season had provided insufficient evidence of whether he could really feed the often goal-famished Smith.

Tabloids suggested that the Arsenal camp was unsettled. Graham's failure to lure West Ham's Tony Cottee to Highbury in the close-season prompted Alan Smith to admit, 'If we'd signed Tony, our prospects might have looked a little brighter.' As for Smith, allegedly unable to settle in the south, he was allegedly pondering a move to Aston Villa or Derby.

Graham realised that if his team were to win the title after an 18-year gap they would, sooner or later, have to start getting the better of Liverpool. It wouldn't be an easy task.

In 1998, Rocastle recalled, 'You'd climb off the team coach outside Anfield, and there would be the Liverpool scallies. "Y'alright there Rocky la'?" they'd say in their broad Scouse accent. They had a swagger and they'd smirk at you on the way in as if to say, "You're in for it today."

'You didn't get that anywhere else. The "This is Anfield" sign was hugely symbolic. It was a warning. You'd always feel that 50-50 decisions would go their way. I remember a year earlier we'd played really well there, and lost 2-1 in a close game. Right in front of the referee, Tony Adams jumped against Kenny Dalglish, and Kenny literally smacked him in the solar plexus. And he got away with it! He got a free kick!

'Tony would never ever let on that he was injured if he could avoid it, but on this occasion, he was doubled up, and gasping for breath. They had the cunning and the know how to beat you.'

Perry Groves was even more succinct, explaining, 'You went there in the knowledge that you wouldn't see the ball for long periods of time. So we had to find a way of stopping them from getting it, and making sure that we kept it more.'

Graham reckoned his side possessed the tactical nous to start making life difficult for the champions. Groves recalled, 'We had a formidable unit. The back four protected the goalkeeper, the midfielders protected the back four, and the strikers – Smith and Merse – also had a defensive role to play. It was about trust, and counting on your team-mate to support you. George spent a long time on the training pitch getting "Smudger" to operate between the right-back and the right centre-half, and Merse, to work between the left-back and the left centre-back.

'George would go nuts if either striker allowed their central defender to ghost in between them. The strikers had to harry and close down their man, just as everyone else did on the pitch. "Alan, Merse, you're the first line of defence. Push, squeeze and don't give them a minute," George would say.'

Groves explains how Graham instructed his defence to deal with Barnes, who had been in majestic form. 'He'd tell us that on no account should we allow Barnes to go down the outside. That way, he'd skip past you and run riot, and the entire pitch would open up because he could kill defenders with his pace.

'We were told to jockey him inside, so if he got past Lee Dixon, who was always excellent at closing Barnes down, then Rocky or Tony Adams would deal with him next. You knew that on most occasions, someone would be waiting for him. That was the strength of that Arsenal team. We had a very disciplined and rigid approach to matches under George.'

Remarkably, the two sides clashed on six occasions that season – and five of the meetings came before Christmas. In September, Arsenal defeated Liverpool in the Mercantile Credit Centenary Trophy semi-final at Highbury. The tournament was arranged to celebrate the 100th year of the Football League and in an era when English clubs were banned from Europe, it was meant to be a coffer-filler for top clubs. Over 25,000 turned up to see the Gunners take on Kenny Dalglish's side and found the visitors in a state of disarray.

Although unbeaten in the league, injuries were disrupting the flow of a team which had glided almost effortlessly to the title just a few months earlier. Bruce Grobbelaar was in hospital suffering from meningitis and skipper Alan Hansen had been out injured since the beginning of the campaign. A defence consisting of Gary Gillespie and Barry Venison, with midfielders Steve Nicol and Ronnie Whelan helping out, gave Liverpool a jittery look. Up front, the returning Ian Rush – who had been re-signed after a difficult season with Juventus – had been suffering from a virus since August. Dalglish had attempted to play Rush alongside lookalike John Aldridge, but Rush wouldn't score in the league until late October and Liverpool didn't win a game in which the pair started together until the middle of that month.

There was a sense that Dalglish had tampered with a winning formula and that although Aldridge was considered a more 'bread and butter' player than the pacy and stealthy Rush, he could play the role of target man perfectly (he had netted 26 league goals in the previous campaign) and dovetail better with Barnes and Beardsley. Dalglish tinkered with his team selection and for the first time in a generation, with several key players ageing, Liverpool were in the early stages of flux.

In the Mercantile Credit match, Groves poked in the opening goal before Steve Staunton grabbed the equaliser after a dreadful backpass by Thomas. Late in the second half, Thomas made amends by chipping a great pass into the path of Marwood who cracked in a superlative volley past the despairing dive of Mike Hooper.

Although Liverpool rested Barnes and Beardsley, and the pace of the game was hardly ferocious, Graham said afterwards, 'It's always good for any team to beat Liverpool. It breeds confidence. We need to make that a habit on bigger occasions.'

Liverpool promptly lost in the league to Luton and Nottingham Forest and were booed off at Anfield after a tedious 0-0 draw against Coventry. In the league, the Gunners took advantage of Liverpool's uncertainty by pulling five points clear of them by early November.

*     *     *     *     *

Liverpool and Arsenal met in the Rumbelows Cup third round at Anfield on 2 November. The match has largely been airbrushed from history. The highlights can only be located on (in my case anyway) an increasingly clapped-out VHS tape of the season. The team's display is the forgotten gem of that era.

Roared on by a 4,000-strong following – a large turnout for a midweek match in the late 1980s – Arsenal took the match to Liverpool from the outset on a night when Graham's side showed the potency of their counter-attacking. After just a few minutes Thomas nudged a pass through to Marwood, whose goalbound shot deflected off Nicol's heel for a corner. Midway through the half, Thomas twisted and turned on the edge of the Liverpool box and knocked the ball wide for Marwood. His cross was met with a cracking left-footed volley which

Hooper acrobatically tipped over the bar. From the resulting corner kick, Bould's flick was met by Adams and his header was scrambled away by the Liverpool defence.

The half-time whistle was greeted with relief by the home crowd but Arsenal maintained their onslaught after the break. Venison gave the ball away to Marwood midway in his own half, and after galloping forward Marwood's shot was tipped around the post by Hooper. Then another Marwood corner, another Bould flick-on, and this time Adams's header was headed off the line by Venison. Marwood recalls, 'It was our best sustained display of counter attacking that season.'

Massively against the run of play, Liverpool took the lead after Barnes slalomed between Dixon, Bould and Adams to plant the ball past John Lukic in front of the Kop.

Arsenal were level within minutes. In a sublime move, Winterburn launched the ball forward to Smith, who controlled on his chest and slotted a pass to Thomas. Thomas's neat pass found Rocastle on the edge of the box, and he evaded Barnes to rifle in a thunderous shot from just inside the area. Crisp, clean and clinical, it encapsulated the growing maturity of the team.

Bizarrely, the goal doesn't appear on the official club history released in 2003, although Brian Moore's original commentary had been overdubbed on to Rocastle's more scrappy effort against Charlton some months later.

The travelling Arsenal fans, who had largely outsung a rather subdued Anfield crowd that evening, urged the team onwards. In the dying minutes, Marwood poked the ball into the net but the goal was disallowed for an apparent Smith foul on Hooper. Denied a late winner, the aggrieved Gunners protested in vain.

'That game took away a lot of our fear of playing Liverpool,' recalls Groves. 'I felt that we were chipping away at them bit by bit, slice by slice. Normally after a game, George would pick up on a few things, and say, "You could have done better on this", or that, but on this occasion, he just told us we had played well, and we got on the coach and went home. I could tell that he was chuffed to bits.'

Arsenal were turning into a frightening proposition on their travels. They had already thumped FA Cup winners Wimbledon at Plough Lane on the opening day of the season (5-1), and won at Tottenham

(3-2) and Nottingham Forest (4-1). 'We had the pace and the drive to exploit teams' weaknesses away from home,' explains Davis. 'We could squeeze and squeeze them, soak up pressure, and get the ball out of defence quickly down the channels, so that we could open up teams.'

By now, Davis was banned for nine games following his infamous punch on Glenn Cockerill which broke the Southampton player's jaw, meaning that midfielder Kevin Richardson gained a regular starting berth.

The Anfield match confirmed several things. Arsenal's back four, which had had a drastic makeover during the last two years, was solid, and Bould and Adams posed a growing threat to sides from set pieces. Thomas and Rocastle were already screening the back four highly effectively, Marwood was proving to be an inspired purchase by Graham and was dovetailing excellently with Smith, who was now mutating into arguably the most accomplished target man in the First Division.

In the Highbury replay, Arsenal tangled Liverpool up in a spider's web of defensive play, springing the offside trap with mind-boggling regularity to frustrate Beardsley and force a 0-0 draw. It was a dire spectacle, yet from a defensive angle it was an utter triumph of organisation and doggedness. 'We didn't concede,' shrugged a defiant Graham after the match, 'therefore there has to be an element of satisfaction even though we could do without another replay at Villa Park in the middle of such a busy schedule.'

Arsenal's replay performance was insipid. Merson's excellent tight angled drive gave them a first-half lead and prompted a fan sat near the dugouts to throw a cheese and tomato sandwich at Kenny Dalglish, which the Scot threw back.

In the second half, Liverpool turned on the style and midfielders Steve McMahon and Ray Houghton provided a masterclass in possession football. By contrast, Thomas gave the ball away early in the second half and McMahon delivered a cracking drive from just outside the area to tie up the match.

Late on, a Houghton cross was met by an Aldridge header and it was enough to give Liverpool a 2-1 win. Arsenal followed their defeat at Villa Park with another 2-1 loss away at Derby County in the league, courtesy of a late Phil Gee winner. The *Sunday Times* immediately cast doubt on their title challenge. 'Arsenal's credentials to assume Liverpool's mantle are under the microscope. Kenny Dalglish had warned that the test of nerve and personality is staying on top once you get there. And after his own Reds brought the first doubts about Arsenal on Wednesday, Derby yesterday doubled them.

'Next Saturday the Gunners face Liverpool again, and the following week they visit Norwich, the league leaders, who certainly do not pale by comparison with anything offered at the Baseball Ground.'

It was a remarkably open title race by the time Arsenal took on Liverpool at Highbury in the league on 4 December. Norwich led the table with Arsenal three points adrift while Liverpool, level on points with newly-promoted Millwall, lay fourth. Derby and Coventry were just a single point further back.

With the game broadcast live on ITV's *The Match* a disappointing 31,000 crowd turned out, adding further fuel to the prevailing view in the late 1980s that live football would have a detrimental effect on attendances.

It wasn't the best of spectacles. Arsenal struggled to keep Dalglish's men at bay as Aldridge struck the bar in the first half. Arsenal's best chances in the first 45 minutes both fell to Smith, who headed over inside the area. The one player to step out of the morass was Barnes and it was he who gave Liverpool the lead after a stupendous dribble took him through the defence to plant his shot past Lukic.

With Liverpool looking to extend their lead, Barnes curled one of his trademark free kicks against Lukic's crossbar. But Arsenal continued to push and hustle and when Rocastle crossed the ball into the Liverpool box with 20 minutes left, Smith bundled the ball over the line for his first Arsenal goal against Liverpool.

In the dying seconds, Aldridge missed a straightforward header and the match ended 1-1. 'It turned into a bit of damage limitation,' recalls Marwood. 'In the end, I think that they were more frustrated than we were, so in one sense at least we'd done our job.' Victory for Norwich at Anfield a couple of weeks later prompted another crisis in confidence in the red half of Merseyside and Arsenal finally hit top spot after winning at Charlton on Boxing Day.

Liverpool continued to nag away at Graham. 'The fewer points Kenny collects before he gets his injured players again, the better chance for the rest of us. I learned the hard way that it doesn't matter who are top at Christmas. That's where Arsenal stood at this time two years ago but we still didn't win the title,' he told the *Daily Mail*'s Jeff Powell. He later added, 'I still believe that whatever Liverpool's current form, Liverpool will be neck and neck with us when we play them towards the end of the season at Anfield.' By then though, English football had changed forever.

Football reached a watershed in this final full season of the 1980s and the winds of change were beginning to gust into the game. At the apex of the cyclone lay the power of TV. By late 1988 David Dein, now seen as the bright young thing of English football, and spokesman for the 'Big Five' of Arsenal, Tottenham, Liverpool, Manchester United and Everton, was busy constructing the framework of a brave new TV world. Chairmen had negotiated a £44m TV deal with ITV while at the same time proposing a Super League of around 12 clubs. It was clearly a precursor to the Premier League which kicked off three years later.

Late-1980s Arsenal, overwhelmingly blue-collar with their collection of youth team products and bargain buys from lower division sides like Stoke and Colchester, encapsulated the tradition of English football's past with their direct and uncompromising approach. It was a team lacking in box office talent, a point acknowledged by Graham, 'We haven't got stars in our team in the sense that Liverpool have Barnes and Rush or Tottenham have Gascoigne or Waddle, but we prefer to nurture our own, and in my mind, players only become true stars when they consistently win trophies.'

A quarter of a century later, Arsenal's style appears robotic and often crude. The state of the Highbury pitch – memorably described as being like a 'winkle pickers' paradise' by Marwood in the *Evening Standard* – added a primitive feel to many of the home games that season.

Narrow victories against Luton and West Ham were notable for the fact that most players' kit was completely soiled within about 20 minutes of kick-off. 'It did make it difficult for us to string too many passes together,' recalls Groves. 'You'd get teams coming to Highbury to camp out in the mud. They'd come for a point and just sit, and sit, and sit.'

Arsenal also endured a public relations own goal. In February, ITV broadcast a *World In Action Special* entitled 'Offside'. Referee David Elleray was connected to a microphone for the full 90 minutes for a fiery London derby between Millwall and Arsenal at The Den.

O'Leary, Richardson and Rocastle questioned the referee after decisions were awarded against them, and regular use of the f-word was bleeped out. In the second half, when Adams squeezed the ball over the line but Elleray deemed that it hadn't gone in, Merson and Richardson harangued the Harrow schoolmaster with Adams's high pitch screaming at top volume, 'It's our goal, it's our goal. That is over the line.' Adams was booked for shouting 'fucking cheat' at Elleray.

That footballers used the f-word was hardly revelatory and the Arsenal team saw the amusing side, with Groves describing Adams's protestations as sounding like 'a cross between Orville and Donald Duck'. But it didn't reflect well on the club, even though the players were unaware that they were being taped. There was a depressing backdrop to the programme. The chant of, 'You're going home in a fucking ambulance' rang out loud and clear from Millwall fans. Supporters were penned in by wire cages topped with barbed wire. There was a huge police presence. This was late-80s football at its bleakest. Arsenal were right in the thick of it.

By mid-February the Gunners stuttered after facing a string of teams containing at least one tabloid cartoon football villain from the era. In a dreadful 0-0 draw at Loftus Road, QPR's 'mad' Mark Dennis was substituted after 55 minutes to avoid him being sent off, and a few days later Coventry's Brian 'Killer' Kilcline slammed home a penalty to send Arsenal scuttling to defeat at Highfield Road.

At home to Millwall in early March, Smith and Merson were unable to escape the attentions of Keith 'Psycho' Stevens and Terry 'Wild Man' Hurlock. At precisely the wrong time of the season Arsenal were starting to run out of steam.

On 2 April, a week after the team's morale-boosting victory over Southampton at The Dell and a few days after Celtic striker Frank McAvennie opted to join former club West Ham rather than Arsenal, the Gunners faced Manchester United at Old Trafford.

In a surprise move, Graham – in football speak – 'changed horses' by ditching his tried and trusted 4-4-2 formation and deploying a sweeper system with a back three of O'Leary, Bould and Adams. That was how he opted to spin it. Full-backs Dixon and Winterburn were now playing as 'virtual wingers' (Graham-speak) but in reality it was more a 5-3-2 formation. It was certainly a bold tactical move, especially at that time of the season.

The reasons behind the switch have never been satisfactorily explained, least of all by Graham himself. 'I introduced the system because we had two excellent full-backs, and I would have introduced it sooner if Steve Bould hadn't been injured. Unfortunately, when you play that way somebody has to drop out up front, but it all fitted to plan because Brian Marwood got injured badly.'

Yet when Graham unveiled his 'master plan' against Alex Ferguson's team, Marwood was still in the team and remained so for the next two matches. Rocastle recalled, 'We all thought he was mad when he told us what he was going to do. I always thought it was a more defensive move than anything else, whatever George says. Merse had been struggling for a bit of form and Brian had been looking a bit tired, before he got injured. It was as if George was saying, "Well we're looking a bit knackered so rather than outscore other teams, we'll have to outdefend them." I wouldn't say it worked perfectly though, because at Old Trafford I felt we should have gone for it more and won.'

On a sodden Manchester day, Arsenal drew 1-1 at Old Trafford with Adams scoring at both ends. Arsenal were now just three points ahead of Liverpool and Dalglish's men had a game in hand. In *The Independent*, Patrick Barclay likened Graham's new formation to 'pleading guilty to passion killing'.

On close inspection, Ferguson outfoxed Graham by quickly withdrawing Brian McClair into midfield, leaving three central defenders to take care of just Mark Hughes; a serious case of overkill. Late on, when Arsenal pushed forward for a winner against a mediocre United team which limped home in 11th place, there simply wasn't enough in the tank and Graham was forced to substitute an attacker for an attacker when Merson entered the fray to replace the jaded Marwood.

After a rather fortuitous win at Highbury against Everton, Brian Glanville was even more scathing of Graham's use of O'Leary as a sweeper in *The Sunday Times*, commenting, 'It depends on who your sweeper is, and O'Leary, for all his poise and perfection, is essentially a defender…they should not adopt very late in what could be a championship season a strategy they are not equipped to play…leaving out Merson is absolute folly.'

Graham pursued his 'libero' experiment against Newcastle (the day of the Hillsborough disaster), Norwich and Middlesbrough and enjoyed three straight wins with no goals conceded. In the penultimate Highbury league game against Derby, with the Rams already 2-0 up, the back three was simply unable to cope with the small and fast Dean Saunders, who worked superbly in tandem with Paul Goddard.

'I've got enormous respect for all three of their central defenders,' explained Saunders, who scored twice, 'but I felt out there that there were too many marking me. Maybe attacking us would have been their best form of defence.'

Smith's late goal couldn't stop Arsenal plunging to a seemingly catastrophic 2-1 home defeat. For all Graham's tactical experimentation, perhaps he had inadvertently scuppered any chance his team had of winning the title. Ahead of the final home game of the campaign against Wimbledon, Graham announced that he would jettison the sweeper system, reverting to 4-4-2 with forward Hayes in the team instead of Bould. Graham was defiant after the Derby game, claiming that Arsenal, now needing to win both their final matches against the Dons and then Liverpool at Anfield, 'will complete the job'.

One member of the Arsenal team who has contributed to this book comments, 'There was an overwhelming sense of sadness; a sense that football was irrelevant. You couldn't think anything else, really. Journalists wrote things like, "Well, the league doesn't matter this year." And I could see what they meant, but as professionals, we all knew that we had a job to do. We had ambitions to win the title. We owed it to ourselves, and to the fans who paid to watch us. I think that's how we all felt, and the Liverpool players also felt they owed it to their supporters, so we still felt that a cracking end of season was in prospect.'

The Hillsborough disaster and subsequent postponements meant that Arsenal's match at Anfield, originally scheduled for 23 April, was moved to Friday 26 May. Even though Liverpool had two games in hand, Arsenal's eight-point lead over Dalglish's team appeared to give them enough of a cushion to approach the end of the season with massive confidence. Until, that is, the loss to Derby and the agonising 2-2 draw with Wimbledon appeared to leave Arsenal with no hope.

A day after the Arsenal players had gone on a thoroughly depressing lap of honour following the Wimbledon match, FA Cup winners Liverpool crushed West Ham 5-1 to send the Hammers down. On this occasion, the Rush–Barnes–Aldridge triumvirate clicked perfectly. The Gunners were three points behind and needed to win by two clear goals to lift the title.

Newspaper headlines in the lead-up to 26 May have become almost as famous as the match itself. The *Evening Standard* conceded, 'Barring a miracle Liverpool now look certain to end this harrowing season with a record 18th league title as a memorial to those who died at Hillsborough.'

The *Daily Mirror* was even more emotive, screaming, 'You Don't Have a Prayer Arsenal', and in light of the Gunners' Highbury meltdown, *The People* claimed, 'George Graham tried to put on a brave face and even forced a weak smile. But behind it was the haunted look of a man ready to reach for the cyanide tablets.'

It was *The Sun*'s heading 'MEN AGAINST BOYS' which became the most infamous of all the tabloid assessments of Arsenal's chances. Former Liverpool star Graeme Souness said, 'The November night I watched Liverpool beat Arsenal in the Littlewoods Cup at Villa Park also told me who would be champions. It was a case of men against boys and my old Anfield team were the gaffers for the whole 90 minutes. For me they are the BEST – mainly because they have the BEST players.'

Liverpool had gone more than 20 matches unbeaten and no team had won by two clear goals at Anfield for three years. Graham's ultra-optimistic 'all is not lost – it can still be done, and I believe that we will complete the job' seemed to be an extreme case of whistling in the dark.

But there were a number of things which were overlooked; Arsenal had been formidable on their travels that season, and *The Sun*'s article neglected to refer to that initial Littlewoods Cup clash at Anfield, where Arsenal dominated proceedings.

The 3,000 supporters who travelled north on the late morning of 26 May boarded the coaches and trains more in hope than expectation. Even the normally optimistic London newspapers appeared to have given up the ghost on Arsenal's title challenge. Gunners photographer Doug Poole was the only London-based snapper to venture to Anfield.

Liverpool had gained in strength over the passing months with their injured cohort restored to full fitness. Skipper Alan Hansen had returned with two months of the campaign left. Hansen said, 'After what has happened in the last six weeks, it would in many ways be a fitting end to the season if we were to lift the title. But football doesn't work like that, and Arsenal will come at us. They'll still fancy their chances.'

The Arsenal players were far more taciturn. 'George told us not to stoke the fires beforehand,' recalls Groves, 'because he knew there was already a lot of emotion surrounding the game. He told us that he would handle the press in the lead-up, and that we were to focus only on the game.'

They enjoyed a full and relaxed series of training sessions that week and Graham informed them that he would revert to the sweeper system for the Liverpool match. 'I was a bit surprised,' recalls Smith, 'but he justified it by explaining, "We have to prevent Liverpool scoring, because if they get one we then have to score three or possibly four at Anfield, so we'll play three at the back, keep it tight, and see what happens."'

At their team hotel following a pre-match meal, Graham asked the staff to vacate the room and he proceeded to deliver arguably the most prophetic speech in English football history. After directly using to the 'men against boys' article (the players claim this was the only time he referred to a specific article in front of them), he set out his grand vision for the game. 'Be patient, we don't want the game won in the first five minutes. If it's 0-0 at half time I won't mind. Score early in the second half and Liverpool won't know whether to go forward or defend and then the next goal will come. You've got nothing to lose. Go out and play and don't be frightened.'

When the Arsenal players – average age 21 – ran on to the pitch, each of them carried sprays of red roses and laid them in front of the Kop in memorial for the Hillsborough victims.

On a calm summer evening, the early stages were something of a phoney war, with both sides probing one another for weaknesses. When Liverpool ventured deep into Arsenal territory it was Barnes whose powerful runs caused most problems for O'Leary and Adams, and Rush who had the best chance to score when he cracked in a shot from outside the box which flew over Lukic's crossbar. Almost immediately, Rush was substituted for Beardsley.

Bould's early header was destined for the net until Whelan nodded over the bar. Liverpool looked serene and assured, with no pressure on them to go for broke and score. Arsenal trudged in at half-time defiant and unbowed. Smith recalls the atmosphere in the dressing room, 'We were confident and relaxed. Tony Adams was urging everyone on and George Graham was reminding us not to panic, and that he was confident we would score early in the second half.'

With 52 minutes elapsed, Arsenal were awarded a free kick just outside Liverpool's area. The home side appeared unsure about what to do. Grobbelaar was unable to bellow instructions to his defensive wall over the din. When Winterburn curled in an indirect free kick, Smith glided in to guide the ball into the bottom corner of the Liverpool net. Time froze as the importance of the goal sunk in. The Arsenal players' reaction was to gallop to the goalscorer while the Liverpool players surrounded the referee, insisting that he talk to his linesman because they were convinced that Smith hadn't made contact.

The scorer recalls, 'I never knew why they appealed. I still don't, to be honest. We just stared at them and hoped, because at Anfield, 50-50 decisions tended to go their way. I was thrilled when it stood because you never knew how many chances we'd get.'

On the bench, Groves looked on. 'The Liverpool players looked to Dalglish, and he didn't seem clear on what to do. You could sense the panic. Stick to a 1-0 defeat to win the league, which just wasn't their way, or push forward, try for a 2-1 win, and risk losing it all? They never did work out what their best course of action was.'

A wave of confidence swept through the Arsenal players. Achieving the seemingly impossible was now a definite possibility. Liverpool tried again to score the killer goal. A blistering Houghton effort whistled inches over the bar, before they dropped deeper into their own half to defend a 1-0 defeat. Thomas – so long in the doldrums in the New Year and described by Brian Glanville in the *Sunday Times* in January as 'exactly what he is, a muscular, adventurous full-back converted to midfield', probed for weaknesses in Liverpool's backline.

Rocastle pushed further and further forward. The bite offered by Richardson in midfield was never better illustrated by his tackle on Houghton late on, which signalled aptly how Arsenal's midfield had been on top for much of the match. It was Richardson who delivered the coolest of through balls to Thomas in the 86th minute but the midfielder hurried his weak shot and Grobbelaar smothered it easily. 'It was there and gone in a flash,' recalls Thomas. 'Put it this way, I'm glad that miss is largely forgotten. It wasn't my best moment on a football pitch.'

Although, to all intents and purposes, Thomas's miss appeared to have signalled the end of Arsenal's title challenge, Smith doesn't remember feeling that way, 'We knew that time was moving on fast, but we just had to plod on.' Three minutes later, time was officially up. The Red Empire looked to have withstood a mighty onslaught. ITV commentator David Pleat spoke of 'poetic justice', Steve McMahon gave his team-mates the 'one minute' sign and, perhaps symbolically, Richardson slumped to the turf, writhing in agony from cramp. For all of Arsenal's gallant efforts their brave battlers were, at the last, falling. Or not, perhaps.

As Barnes slalomed his way into the right-hand side of Arsenal's penalty area, Richardson ('He'd moan about everything – his breakfast, his lunch, his dinner, the weather – but he was a great competitor,' recalls Groves) rose from the dead to dispossess the Liverpool winger and tapped the ball back to Lukic. Grit and determination had won out over pure skill.

In a scene which is now part of cinematic history, Lukic threw the ball out to Dixon, and his measured pass found Smith. For so long castigated as a typical Arsenal buy – safe and unadventurous and described harshly by a tabloid hack as 'a man with the charisma of a regional sales manager from Slough' – Smith truly came of age that night at Anfield. He chested it down and knocked the ball on to the galloping Thomas, who moments earlier told Richardson that he was 'going upfield to see if I can grab us a goal'.

Despite being surrounded by a pack of Liverpool defenders, a lucky break off Nicol's legs put him clean through against Grobbelaar, face to face with Arsenal immortality. Thomas waited for the Zimbabwe stopper to commit himself. Everything stopped. The Anfield crowd, whistling for the end, fell into silence. Grobbelaar moved low to his right, and Thomas, dropping his shoulder, flicked the ball to the goalkeeper's left and scored.

As Thomas performed his somersault on the pitch, and the Arsenal fans ('A mad sea of blue and yellow bobbing up and own in the far corner' recalls Alan Smith) celebrated, the camera panned to Dalglish, slumped against the dugout and scarcely able to take on board what he had just witnessed.

There, in the eye of the storm was Graham himself, telling the substituted Merson and the unused Quinn to 'calm it down' as they jumped for joy on the touchline.

Thomas remains remarkably lucid about his date with destiny, explaining, 'I didn't think about what rested on that shot. All that was in my mind was Bruce Grobbelaar. I waited for Bruce to make the first move and he took such a long time making up his mind whether to come out or not. I knew that Liverpool couldn't come back. There wasn't enough time.'

The tabloid headlines – 'KING GEORGE!' (*The Sun*), 'MICKEY TAKERS! BY GEORGE THEY'VE DONE IT!' (*Daily Star*) And 'MIRACLE MEN' (*Daily Mirror*) were simple and predictable enough, but what was lost in the immediate aftermath was the fact that Graham's predictions about the match had come startlingly true. 'I was sat with Steve Bould afterwards,' explains Groves, and I said to him, "Everything turned out the way George said it would."'

Even in the midst of triumph, Graham knew that the levels of expectation among supporters had risen. He said, 'They'll sing themselves hoarse for a few days and mob the team's open top bus and then they'll start telling themselves, "Really great clubs win the league twice not once. That Herbert Chapman won three in a row, so get on with it George."'

Smith recalls, 'George knew that if the club was to be viewed in the same light as Chapman's teams – and as importantly if he was going to be seen as a top manager – we had to repeat what we'd done in 1989.'

But in the close-season there were no significant additions to the squad, and they tailed off into fifth place in the following campaign with Liverpool once more strolling to the title by nine points. It seemed almost inconceivable in the summer of 1990 (in *The Sun* Emlyn Hughes predicted, 'Kenny's boys will run away with the title as usual. No doubt. No contest. It's all over before the first ball has been kicked,') that Liverpool would fail to win the title for 24 years, but despite a long unbeaten start to the 1990/91 campaign, there were ominous signs that the edifice was about to rupture.

Dalglish replaced the retiring Alan Hansen with Swedish centre-back Glenn Hysen. He wasn't in the mould of the former skipper and with Peter Beardsley in and out of the side, Liverpool were again unsettled.

In contrast, Graham upgraded his squad in the summer of 1990. The outbound Marwood was replaced by Anders Limpar. Arsenal had signed a prodigiously gifted player. Thomas recalls, 'In training, Tony Adams and Steve Bould would always try and kick anyone who was new as a "Welcome to Arsenal" initiation ceremony, but they couldn't get near Anders. It was hilarious watching them trying to catch him.'

Limpar was the most rampantly destructive attacking force in the First Division before Christmas and he developed an excellent rapport with Smith and Merson. David Seaman, signed from QPR for £1m, also settled in to the team well, and the Gunners' defence was even meaner than it had been in 1988/89.

Arsenal had to overcome several self-inflicted problems during the campaign. The first was the two-point deduction following the fracas at Old Trafford, after which Graham was fined £10,000 and Limpar, Rocastle, Davis, Thomas and Winterburn £5,000 each. The effect? It bolstered Arsenal's siege mentality even more and they had won a crucial match 1-0 thanks to Limpar's opportunism. The second was skipper Adams's spell in prison between December and February.

The Liverpool games proved decisive. In December, unbeaten Arsenal prepared to take on the unbeaten league leaders Liverpool at Highbury. It hadn't been the best of weeks for the Gunners. Trounced 6-2 at home by Manchester United in the Rumbelows Cup, they went into the game trailing the Anfield side by a massive six points. O'Leary had commented in the *Daily Mirror*, 'They might as well hand the title to Liverpool on a plate.'

Graham's tone was anything but defeatist. Limpar recalls, 'The way in which George used the events of the week to our advantage was him at his best. He told us that we owed it to ourselves and the club to come up with a massive performance against Liverpool. I'd never seen him so impassioned. He said, "We're playing Liverpool, and we all know of their reputation. But I think we've got the measure of them. They think they've already got the league won. They think we're down and out. Subconsciously, they feel we've relaxed. We've been hammered by the tabloids all week, so now you boys need to go out and hammer Liverpool."

'When we walked out for the start of the match, the fans made an unbelievable noise. Even their chants had a "fortress mentality" spirit about them. Especially the one which even some of the players began to sing, "You can stick your fucking two points up your arse." It was a fantastic atmosphere in which to perform.'

Smith recalls, 'My abiding memory of that period is of the fans chanting, "You can stick your two points up your arse." It was our mantra. It was a two-fingered salute to the rest of the world.'

The Liverpool game is surely the high point of 'Grahamism'. Even though it was only December the match already had the air of a title decider. Broadcast live on ITV's *The Match*, it signified a fundamental power shift away from Liverpool, permanently. Merson squeezed home the first after his half-volley was adjudged to have crossed the line before Venison desperately tried to clear. Midway through the second half, Dixon scored from the penalty spot after Limpar was brought down by Gary Gillespie. The Swede received criticism for the way he went to ground but Limpar argues, 'That's nonsense. Gillespie caught me with his trailing leg. TV rarely conveys just how fast the attacker is running.'

There was a spectacular finale. With Arsenal pushing forward for a third goal, Merson backheeled the ball into the path of the onrushing Smith, who smashed his shot past Grobbelaar. 'It was probably the best goal I scored that season,' confirms Smith. 'It was a fantastic team goal, and as others have said, destroying Liverpool so convincingly – and on telly too – sent a hell of a message out to other teams.

'As footballers, you rarely think about what ifs, but if Liverpool had won that day, they would probably have cruised to the title. They would have been nine points clear at Christmas, which would have been very difficult for us to chip away at. As it was, the lead was cut to just three.'

The gap had been narrowed to three points and it would be Arsenal who would seize the initiative from then on.

Graham had outwitted Dalglish tactically. Rattled by his team's shambolic defensive display at Anfield a week before – they had drawn 2-2 against Manchester City and been lucky to grab a point – Dalglish was uncharacteristically cautious at Highbury, replacing Houghton, Beardsley and McMahon with Nicol, Molby and Venison. Their line-up contained no less than six defenders and Beardsley wasn't even on the bench. 'It struck me that Liverpool came for a point, which surprised me,' recalled Limpar.

Once again, Graham had opted for the sweeper system in the wake of the midweek Rumbelows Cup debacle, selecting O'Leary, Adams and Bould at the back, and they comfortably dealt with the lone threat of Rush while keeping Barnes isolated on the left.

The year of 1990 had a decidedly *fin de régime* feel to it; out-of-touch Eastern European despots were toppled, Margaret Thatcher was ousted by her cabinet, Presidents Bush and Gorbachev officially declared the end of the Cold War, and Nelson Mandela's release from prison signalled the dismantling of apartheid. And now at Highbury, the old order had been – at least partially – dismantled. Liverpool were never quite the same again after that defeat at Highbury. At Anfield in March, Arsenal would deliver their knockout punch.

Between January and March, Liverpool won just two league games. Dalglish resigned after an FA Cup defeat to Everton. The Gunners and

Graeme Souness's Liverpool were neck and neck when the two sides met at Anfield on 3 March. Adams had recently been restored to the starting line-up after his release from prison. The match began with wave upon wave of Liverpool attacks raining down on Seaman's goal. Beardsley and Rush had crisp shots turned away, and Seaman made an excellent save from a trademark curling Barnes free kick. In one of his first – and finest – matches for the club, David Hillier stifled Jan Molby's creativity, but opportunities were thin on the ground.

Liverpool finally cracked early in the second half when Merson picked up Beardsley's stray pass. He played a sublime one-two with Smith and galloped forward. Merson waited for Grobbelaar to commit himself and nudged the ball gently to the goalkeeper's left before running to the Arsenal fans and flashing them his toothy grin after making it 1-0.

From then on the Gunners did not relinquish their lead in the title race and, with Kevin Campbell and David Hillier becoming regulars in the starting line-up in the New Year, they also had a depth to their squad which had been absent before. Eventually they won the title by a comfortable seven points as Liverpool uncharacteristically crumbled at the death. Not as dramatic as two years before, certainly, but in Graham's eyes it had been a more polished season with his 'Rolls-Royce team'.

There is a lingering feeling that Arsenal never received the credit they deserved for their monumental victories over Liverpool in 1989 and 1991. Perhaps it's because, for all his side's doggedness in the first of those seasons, Graham's side will always be regarded as the 'spoilers' who took advantage of Liverpool's emotional grief following the Hillsborough disaster. It might also be because the late drama of that season outweighed the actual quality of Arsenal's overall play – especially at home. Dalglish once claimed, 'They play in a certain way which is not my way.'

Or perhaps – as the graininess of the action from that night proves – it's because it happened in the pre-Sky era and therefore isn't afforded the same gravitas as the dramatic season finale to the Premier League in 2012. In the midst of his barely coherent 'cuddles and love bites' stream of consciousness after Sergio Aguero scored Manchester City's winner at the Etihad, Sky pundit Paul Merson, present and correct in May 1989, claimed, 'I've never seen anything as dramatic as this.' Surely Anfield must run it close?

For all Alex Ferguson's claims that his greatest achievement as Manchester United manager was 'knocking Liverpool off their fucking perch', Arsenal got there first, not once but twice. Such rewriting of history occasionally rankles the Arsenal stars from that era. Limpar argues, 'Has anyone ever challenged Ferguson on this? [Author's note – No Anders] In 1989 United were miles off [25 points away in fact] and in 1991 they finished sixth. They just weren't a threat in the league at all. And yet he's said it again and again down the years.'

The Gunners' league double over Liverpool in the 1990/91 campaign was arguably even more epoch-defining because it definitively ended the era of Liverpool's league dominance, whereas after 1989, Dalglish's side came back once again.

But it's true to say that having created a vacuum, and with Graham vowing that his side 'will dominate football for ten years', they failed to replace Liverpool on their (fucking) perch. The reasons? Graham wasn't perhaps as all-knowing as Arsenal fans thought.

# The Wars Of Attrition

*'Paul Davis could well be the player who makes the crucial difference for us in Europe this season.' George Graham, speaking prior to Arsenal's European Cup campaign, 1992.*

*'Congratulations to Arsenal, because they deserved to win. But I'm glad I'm not an Arsenal fan, if they have to pay to watch that each week.' Faustino Asprilla, speaking after Arsenal won the European Cup Winners' Cup, 1994.*

IN September 1991, as Arsenal prepared to embark on their first European Cup campaign in 20 years, a bullish George Graham said, 'It's going to be a major test for me and the players, coming up against different characters and different systems. But we are not frightened. It is English teams who have always been feared – and rightly so.'

Arsenal crushed first-round opponents Austria Vienna 6-2 on aggregate then faced Benfica. In the Estadio da Luz, Kevin Campbell's excellent angled shot equalised the bearded Marques Isaias's opener. Arsenal spent much of the match struggling to contain the Brazilian, who was only denied further goals thanks to last-ditch David Seaman saves and the post.

Graham singled out Paul Davis for special praise after he dropped back in the second half to quell Benfica's lively midfield. The manager said, 'Paul sacrificed his attacking urge for the team. He understands what you need to be successful in Europe. One ill-thought-out move can prove disastrous and give your enemy the advantage.'

Davis recalls, 'It's ironic that George said that about me, given what happened next. We were a bit lucky to escape with a draw. Steve Bould hadn't played since the start of the season. That had really disrupted the defence and it showed in our league form. Tony Adams played on with a groin injury and that made it difficult for whoever was alongside him, like Andy [Linighan] or Colin [Pates].'

On a night of incredible intensity in the second leg at Highbury, Paul Merson's early shot was tipped away by Neno and Campbell's header hit the bar before central defender Colin Pates grabbed his five minutes of fame, swivelling and crashing home the opening goal.

From that point on, Arsenal performed like startled rabbits in the headlights. The midfield duo of Rocastle and Davis appeared listless, unsure whether to sit deep or press forward, and were powerless to stop Isaias grabbing an equaliser before half-time.

Arsenal's second half tactics were as chaotic and confusing as their acid house style away shirts, which UEFA insisted they wore for the home leg. The defence resorted to pumping long balls forward to Campbell and Smith but Benfica's defenders held firm. Perry Groves replaced the largely ineffective Limpar in the 75th minute and recalls, 'Sven-Goran Eriksson had them really well drilled. They didn't panic and as the game wore on, they were one step ahead of us. We looked one-dimensional in comparison to them. The European ban meant we hadn't played in the UEFA Cup after the Littlewoods Cup win or in the European Cup after Anfield 1989 and that showed.'

In extra time Arsenal launched another aerial bombardment. A half-chance fell to Smith, who shinned his effort over the bar, and minutes later, Tony Adams sliced his shot against the post from only five yards. Kulkov then slipped in between Adams and substitute Bould and fired Benfica into the lead before Isaias galloped forward and scored. Arsenal were out.

According to *The Guardian*, 'They didn't understand the body language of continental football when they met it at the highest level…they ended up tongue-tied and left the arena looking more than slightly dumbfounded.' In public, Graham claimed Arsenal had been 'Unlucky. We should have won it in normal time, but Benfica ran away with it in extra time.' There was some truth in what he said, but Arsenal's naivety had ultimately been their undoing.

In private, he vented his fury. 'He said we'd played too fast and loose,' recalls Limpar, 'and he made no bones about telling me how poor I'd been. I wasn't at my best, but that went for several in the team. Something changed inside him after that defeat. The emphasis was on an even more resolute defence, a tight midfield, and one main outlet up front – Ian Wright. That approach might work on big nights in Europe and one-off cup games – but it wasn't going to win Arsenal the league under Graham again.'

Apart from missing out on a £2m windfall for qualifying for the European Cup's group stages, the ramifications for the club were huge. Deploring the 'helter skelter' football which typified Arsenal's display in the closing stages on that turbulent evening, a seething Graham retreated into his defensive bunker in the years that followed, stripping the team of its creative edge. Behind the scenes and in the stands, players and supporters grew disaffected, despite continued success in cup competitions.

With hindsight, the Benfica match at Highbury proved to mark the beginning of the end for Graham. Conversely, it also marked the origins of Arsenal's remarkable European Cup Winners' Cup triumph against Parma in 1994. As the ancient Chinese proverb says, 'Sometimes, victory can actually be a defeat in disguise.'

Limpar remains his former manager's biggest critic, recently telling a Swedish newspaper that playing under Graham was 'like living under Saddam Hussein in Iraq'. Yet his views on the impact of the Benfica defeat have been paraphrased numerous times by team-mates down the years. Graham's Arsenal were never quite the same again after the Benfica loss. The first immediate casualty was Davis. A few days before the match at Highbury, Graham described him as 'our best player this season'. Davis recalls, 'George had asked me more and more to track back and close down space, which I'd done in Lisbon. He asked me to do the same in the return, but I never felt that I was playing to my strengths by playing that way. He said I'd pushed too far forward against Benfica at Highbury. We argued about it and I was dropped. If you stand up to him, you have to be prepared to face the consequences.'

The 'consequences' were that over the next 18 months, Davis was frozen out. He would make only two league appearances and the Gunners were left with a midfield of an increasingly overburdened David Hillier and David Rocastle, now pushed into a central midfield slot.

Sven-Goran Eriksson was customarily polite about Arsenal after the match, although he did raise a question as to the whereabouts of Michael Thomas. 'It was a surprise not to see him alongside Davis and Rocastle, because I believe he is fit to play,' he said. 'Thomas is a player I admire.'

Thomas made his final appearance in an Arsenal shirt against the Hammers a week later. It was a wretched display in a 1-0 home defeat, coming just a week after he had told *The Sun* about 'MY HIGHBURY HELL'. His performances had been inconsistent since his signature goal at Anfield in 1989 and the oasis of surging runs that characterised his early years at Arsenal had long since dried up. Thomas blamed Graham, saying, 'I'm fed up with watching the ball sail over my head all the time. I feel that the midfielders just don't see enough of the ball.'

He later told me, 'George often said that the defenders would play until they were 40-odd, and the midfielders until they were 30-odd. Never was a truer word spoken. In fact it was more extreme. We did all their running for them, and Rocky and I had had our best seasons in football by the time we'd reached our 23rd birthdays. That is down in no small part to George's tactics.'

He admitted that he felt let down over his wages. By 1991, Thomas and other homegrown stalwarts from the 1989 side remained – according to reports – on a basic £800 a week. 'We felt like George was playing us on the cheap. Then you heard what the new boys who'd been signed by George were pulling in, and it annoyed us.'

History was repeating itself. Twenty years before, the stability of Bertie Mee's side had been undermined by youth team products Charlie George and Eddie Kelly questioning their pay. By December, Thomas was appearing in the red of Liverpool after Graeme Souness splashed out £1.5m to take him to Anfield. It was a jarring sight. His disenchantment at Highbury proved to be the thin end of an increasing wedge of discontent among the players, heightened by a shock 2-1 defeat at Fourth Division Wrexham in the FA Cup third round.

In *Addicted*, Tony Adams claims, 'I believe it [the Wrexham game] was the match that turned us into the side we were to become over the remaining seasons of George's management of the club,' but by the time the Gunners faced Wrexham, the die was cast anyway.

Graham had admitted to Martin Samuel back in November that he was not going to encourage his side to play a more expansive, passing style, insisting, 'We can win the European Cup playing our way. To attempt a change would mean trying to copy the skill factor of the continentals. They have had a head start on us in that and would probably do a lot better.'

The goals for Merson and Limpar had dried up since Wright's arrival in October, and Smith, winner of two Golden Boots in the previous three years, was struggling to find the net.

He explains, 'When Ian arrived, he wanted the ball all the time, and it made us far too one-dimensional. The effect on my game was immediate. I'd always scored lots of goals, but they dried up. My strength was holding up the ball, and allowing others to run on to it. But now, I saw less and less of the ball. Subconsciously, I think that many players from the era believed that if they gave the ball to Ian, everything would work out fine, which is hardly healthy for the team ethic.'

The full impact of the 'Wright effect' wouldn't be fully visible until the following year but by the time his team reassembled in August, titanic wars of attrition were about to become the order of the day.

* * * * *

In June, Graham sold Rocastle, who had pushed Wright close for the supporters' Player of the Year award, to champions Leeds United for £2m. It seemed a bizarre decision given that Rocastle returned to his best form after February in the previous campaign. Graham has always hinted that Rocastle's knee was permanently damaged, a fact the player always denied. 'The players missed Rocky when he went to Leeds,' admits Perry Groves. 'The close atmosphere which George had at the start was gradually fading. It didn't feel as much fun anymore.'

In place of Rocastle came Danish midfielder and European Championship winner John Jensen, whose spectacular goal against

Germany in the Euro 92 Final fooled many into believing that he was a gritty, box-to-box sharpshooter. His limpet-like close marking and short passing game made him invaluable in one-off cup games, but he was hardly a glamour signing.

On the eve of the season, Ladbrokes installed Arsenal as 5-1 favourites for the title but by the time the domestic cups gathered pace in the New Year they were floundering in mid-table, struggling for goals and creativity with Jensen, Hillier and Morrow labouring in the middle. Graham was regularly playing Campbell and Merson on the wings, meaning that an increasingly fractious Wright was often isolated up front on his own.

A visible cult of personality was developing around Wright. Nike's marketing men turned him into football's anti-hero. He starred in adverts to the backdrop of Lou Reed's 'Walk On The Wild Side', pointing to his boot and goading supporters. The arrogant image he presented in the 'Gary who?' commercial shifted public opinion against him. As Lineker headed for the J League, Wright taunted him with 'Sayanora, Lineker san' after pinching the Golden Boot from him on the final day of the previous season.

Behind the scenes at *Friday Night's All Wright* in the late 1990s, he confessed, 'Those Nike ads made me appear something I wasn't, and I had a great deal of respect for Gary Lineker. I would never have sneered at him. George turned me into the main outlet up front. It was a bit of a pressure cooker.'

The disciplinary points piled up. At a time when Manchester United signed Eric Cantona to boost their attack, Graham shelled out a hefty £2m (£800,000 more than Cantona cost United) to bring back Martin Keown to Highbury. His stockpiling of central defensive lieutenants – Keown, Adams, Marshall, Bould, O'Leary, Linighan – appeared excessive, especially when he occasionally fielded up to four in one game. United swashbuckled their way to their first championship in 27 years; Arsenal fought and clawed their way to Wembley on both fronts.

In the FA Cup semi-final against Tottenham at Wembley, Adams ended Venables's side's resistance with a towering header from Davis's free kick. There was precious little *joie de vivre* about Arsenal's victory; Dixon and Edinburgh snapped at one another like tetchy velociraptors and Arsenal 'parked the bus' before the phrase was even coined – but that didn't matter. It was all about the bottom line; reaching the FA Cup Final.

Where Gascoigne and Lineker had subtly unpicked Arsenal two years earlier, the Gunners suffocated their rivals in 1993. Within a fortnight Arsenal defeated Sheffield Wednesday 2-1 in the Coca-Cola Cup Final. Steve Morrow drilled in the Gunners' winner but his joy didn't last long as Adams threw the young midfielder over his shoulder and lost his grip. As Morrow lay stricken on the turf with a badly broken arm, Merson – unaware of his team-mate's plight – made his infamous lager-swigging gesture to Arsenal fans.

Merse was about to become a (sometimes) unwilling regular in *Loaded*'s Platinum Rogues Gallery as the lads' mag phenomenon exploded in the UK. That afternoon simply gave more credence to the view that Adams and Merson were just too boozy and boorish for their own good.

Arsenal hadn't finished with Wednesday. On Thursday 20 May, with most Premier League footballers sunning themselves on the beach, the two sides did battle one last time in the FA Cup Final replay after the first match ended 1-1.

It didn't go down too well with neutrals. In the *Daily Star*, Bob Driscoll described the match as, 'turgid…with its sneaky, spiteful fouls – mainly off the ball'. In *The Sun*, Brian Woolnough spoke of 'outrageous thuggery' and 'ugly combat'.

Early on, John Jensen fouled Chris Waddle and then Adams removed him from the equation again. Mark Bright's flying elbow broke Andy Linighan's nose and the Gunners' central defender broke two fingers as he landed. Waddle then blatantly dived, clutching his face after Winterburn caught him in the chest.

With the scores tied at 1-1, the referee had the whistle in his mouth to signal the end of extra time – and a penalty shoot-out – when Merson's inswinging corner was headed goalwards by Linighan and it spilled through Chris Woods's grasp, before Phil King, trying to salvage the situation, blasted the ball into the roof of his own net.

'We were absolutely exhausted and could barely lift our feet off the ground at the end,' explains Davis. 'We'd scrapped and fought for our lives. We'd now won five trophies in seven years. It was a better return than any other team in the country. George would always say, "You've won medals which you can show your children and your grandchildren." I saw his point, but is was a gruelling way for a team to operate.'

Arsenal had virtually changed out of all recognition since the first Wembley triumph in 1987. Only Davis and Adams survived from that Liverpool final; O'Leary was about to disappear into the sunset. The post-match chant, 'No one likes us, we don't care,' was revealing; proof that Arsenal had mutated into a wealthier and more successful version of Millwall, Graham's first club.

It was strangely befitting that Morrow and Linighan should end up physically damaged in their respective glory games – these were the most attritional of times for Arsenal after all. Graham said prophetically afterwards, 'There's only Europe left for us to conquer now.' In truth, his team had nowhere else to go.

The European Cup Winners' Cup had always been regarded as the weakest of the three continental competitions, but Ajax, Atletico Madrid, Torino and Paris St Germain were all lurking. So were holders Parma, who had swept aside Antwerp at Wembley in majestic fashion.

The contrast in styles was marked. In *The Guardian*, David Lacey suggested, 'It is hard to believe that next season Arsenal will be playing on the same planet, let alone the same competition as Parma.' Graham consulted a public relations firm in an attempt to rectify his dour public image but the advice he received didn't appear to be especially helpful. He became even more stubborn, criticising 'prima donnas' and reiterating that he mistrusted star players, telling Joe Lovejoy that Eric Cantona 'would always let you down at the highest level'.

With a manager sending out such unequivocal signals, it was hardly surprising that the Gunners were unable to sign the star midfielder that Graham reportedly craved. He informed Melvyn Bragg that he'd had a t-shirt made with the slogan, 'I'm trying to sign a quality midfielder' but he certainly wasn't in the market for the country's hottest midfield prospect, Roy Keane, who chose to sign for Manchester United. According to the press, Keane's wage demands were double the going rate Arsenal were prepared to pay. Instead of the complete midfielder, Graham signed Eddie McGoldrick for £1m, a cut-price utility man from Crystal Palace. For the first time, there was audible grumbling among supporters about Graham's transfer dealings.

Considering the money raked in from two successful championship seasons, and the domestic cup runs, a more affluent and critical supporter base – some of whom had splashed out £1,500 on a club bond – rightly asked serious questions. The board had categorically stated two years earlier that 'turning Highbury all-seater will not hinder George's attempts to purchase new players'. Fans would never have openly turned on Graham – he had been too successful for that and they owed him too much – but he was becoming a victim of his own success. Tony Francis wrote in the *Sunday Times*, 'He wants expressive football – it's time for him to put his money where his mouth is.'

In the *One Nil Down* fanzine, editor Tony Willis also questioned the Wright effect, but in mitigation the striker was winning games almost single-handedly at the start of the 1993/94 campaign (his superlative lob over Everton's Neville Southall in September in a 2-0 win being the prime example) until his goal supply dried up in October.

The Gunners misfired miserably, drawing four consecutive blanks against the likes of Oldham and Norwich. Graham rested some of his stars, confessing after the Oldham match that he considered the game 'less important' than the upcoming Cup Winners' Cup tie with Odense.

It was the first time Arsenal supporters had really seen squad rotation in action – especially at such an early stage of the season. Davis recalls, 'He was basically admitting that we weren't going to win the league.'

Average ticket prices at Highbury were now £15 – considerably above the national average – and a clump of fans unfurled a cryptic banner at home to Norwich in the 0-0 draw, 'Give the suckers their money back'. A few weeks earlier, chairman Peter Hill-Wood had allegedly labelled the bond-holders as 'suckers'.

The natives – many of whom watched from the high-tech, all-singing, all-dancing, all-seater North Bank – were getting restless. It wasn't supposed to be like this. Not from the team which seemed to have the world at its feet in 1991. At least there was still the European adventure – which Limpar describes as 'Graham's Holy Grail'.

It really was the Cup Winners' Cup or bust. Arsenal beat Odense then Standard Liege, whose manager Arie Haan described the Gunners as 'grim and functional'. At Highbury, Wright's stealthy header and crafty chip, together with Merson's delightful curling free kick saw the home side win 3-0. In Liege, with Wright rested, Smith notched a goal after just a minute which extinguished any lingering hopes the Belgians had of fighting back, and then the Gunners went on the rampage to win 7-0 on the night and 10-0 on aggregate.

The humiliated Haan resigned shortly afterwards, and Arsenal had reached the quarter-finals where they would meet Torino. The message? Write off Arsenal at your peril.

Graham continued to bemoan his side's lack of creativity, admitting, 'We lack something in the final third of the pitch.' Kevin Campbell, who notched hat-tricks that season against Ipswich and Swindon, seemed in constant awe of strike partner Wright. Increasingly, Graham played Campbell wide on the right, and when Campbell did move inside he snatched at chances. It wasn't the only thing to irritate supporters – Winterburn's obscene left-footedness, Merson's laziness and Parlour's maddening inconsistency also grated – but Campbell's decline in form was alarming. If Campbell's Arsenal career was on the rocks, then Limpar's relationship with Graham was headed straight for the divorce courts. Limpar's final Arsenal appearances were in away matches at Ipswich and Southampton as Arsenal ran out 5-1 and 4-0 winners respectively, with Wright grabbing hat-tricks both times. Wright reflected, 'Anders was the architect behind those wins. He was a funny little fella, but man – could he play.'

Limpar signed for relegation-threatened Everton for £2m later that week. In his autobiography, Graham claims the Swede slowly lost the confidence of his team-mates due to a lack of application.

There are some grains of accuracy in what Graham says. Limpar didn't exactly prove Graham wrong after he departed Highbury, and failed to shine in the 1994 World Cup. Yet his cards had been marked for some time. At the start of the campaign, Graham told journalist Joe Lovejoy, 'Limpar doesn't work hard enough,' adding that although he could be the star turn against the likes of Ipswich and Southampton, he wasn't capable of making the difference in tight games against more astute opponents.

Smith comments, 'George could still squeeze the maximum out of mediocre players,' but not – it appeared – out of Arsenal's two most naturally gifted stars – Limpar and Merson. Add that to his cold-shouldering of Davis and one could present a fairly watertight case that the key reason Arsenal were floundering was Graham himself. Limpar remains bitter about his final days at Highbury, 'Graham stopped communicating with me. He couldn't man-manage creative players. That's why he couldn't take Arsenal any further.'

⌣ ⌣ ⌣ ⌣ ⌣

Graham's team headed for Europe's glamour parks in the spring. Torino were in a horrendous internal mess as Arsenal faced them in the Stadio delle Alpi in the first leg of the quarter-final. Allegations of Mafia connections, bribing referees, crippling debts and an unexpected relegation dogfight meant that only 32,480 fans turned up to watch in a ground which could hold nearly double that number.

Graham was in his element. 'George watched them a few times in the flesh, and several times on video. He knew them inside out,' recalls Davis. 'In fact, I thought he went a bit overboard, because he really hyped them up and actually when it came to it, they weren't exactly world-beaters. Maybe he was trying to get a reaction from us, because this was now our only chance of silverware.'

It was the first competitive game an English side had played in the city since the Heysel Stadium disaster nine years earlier. Offic-ially, the Gunners played a 4-5-1 formation in Turin, but when 'wingers' Merson and Campbell fell back to assist Jensen and Hillier in the middle it was almost 9-0-1 with Smith struggling manfully up front.

Arsenal literally strangled the life out of Torino, and ITV couldn't even muster five minutes of highlights for viewers later that night. The only fireworks exploded off the pitch with Italian fans detonating smoke bombs and purple flares. David Hillier clung tight to Venturin, Torino's playmaker. Starved of the ball, the Uruguayan Enzo Francescoli and a teenage Benito Carbone barely figured. The home crowd howled in frustration at the end of the goalless match, burning their flags and raining missiles down on the pitch. Graham claimed to be satisfied, mysteriously adding that he had told his team 'to go out and express themselves'.

Over 34,000 packed into Highbury to watch Arsenal, with Graham's instructions to 'squeeze them and harry them' ringing in their ears, move in for the kill. Jensen and substitute Ian Selley once again shackled Venturin and Francescoli, and Arsenal relied upon their tried and tested dead-ball routine to plunder the decisive goal.

In the 66th minute Davis floated his free kick towards Adams, who steered home his header. The goal was further evidence that Davis – brought back in from the cold – was the only Arsenal midfielder with the guile to unlock Fort Knox defences in Europe. He recalls, 'I liked the pace of European games. I always felt that my game was suited to that tempo. The Torino game was like a chess match, and our goal was really the only chance we had. We had to battle against the urge to throw everything forward, otherwise Torino might well have punished us, like Benfica had.'

On 'a night for men', as *L'Equipe* described it, Graham opted for a 4-3-2-1 formation as the Gunners faced eventual French champions Paris St Germain in the semi-final first leg at the Parc des Princes. Smith was the main spearhead with Wright and Merson out wide, tucking in behind. Graham's flexible tactics worked well with Wright grabbing the vital away goal shortly before half-time, after latching on to yet another floated Davis free kick. Although the extravagantly gifted David Ginola equalised in the 50th minute, the home side rarely threatened again in the 1-1 draw.

At Highbury, Arsenal scored a vital goal early with Campbell glancing Lee Dixon's cross past Lama after just five minutes, and the remaining 85 minutes were largely about Jensen and Selley keeping Valdo and Ginola quiet. Arsenal lived right on the edge – and with five players going into the game on a yellow card, including Adams, there was virtually no room for error. Ginola spurned PSG's best chance, blasting wide from close range after wriggling free of Dixon's attention, but the Gunners held on.

The tabloid headlines were dominated by Wright's yellow card and subsequent ban from the final after fouling Alain Roche in the first half ('Crying Shame' blasted *The Sun*) but more pertinently, there was praise for Graham's tactics, and Adams's superb performance.

'There was a heroic defiance with Tony Adams leading not only by example but with a constant dialogue of encouragement and cajoling,' wrote Steve Curry in the *Daily Express*. In *The Times*, Rob Hughes wrote, 'This was a victory for the pace, power, and collective spirit of English football. Arsenal have achieved through organisation what England failed to do, prove themselves the equal and more of foreign opponents.'

With Graham Taylor's England failing to qualify for the 1994 World Cup, Arsenal's success in reaching the final was afforded slightly more praise and congratulation than normal.

The odds were stacked at 3-1 against Arsenal before the final. Not only was Wright suspended but John Jensen, who had excelled against PSG and Torino, was injured, as were Keown (who would have been assigned to man-mark Gianfranco Zola) and Hillier, leaving the Gunners down to their bare bones.

The difference between Arsenal and Parma couldn't have been starker. The north Italian club, managed by Nevio Scala, had only recently risen to prominence after being bankrolled by the Parmalat conglomerate. Scala revealed, 'My bosses expect us to play in a certain way. The directors want to be entertained. They're also willing to pay big money for the best players which the club can attract, but they expect us to win in style.'

Whether that was a subtle dig at Arsenal's yeoman-like qualities on the pitch and cautious business approach off it is debatable, but Graham's almost myopic mission to bring a European trophy to Highbury after 24 years was about to reach its conclusion.

In his autobiography, he explained, 'It took my undivided attention in the 1993/94 season. I saw it as a challenge to my tactical perception and I spent hours studying videos and scouting reports and making secret trips to watch the opposition. I felt like a field marshal making battle plans.'

The message conveyed directly to his troops? 'Don't let Parma play. Don't give them a minute,' explains Davis. Graham's dossiers highlighted the liveliness of Parma's three-man midfield – with Tomas Brolin as an attacking midfielder, Pin on the right and Crippa out left, and Zola and Asprilla in a dazzling forward line. The resourceful Scala was adept at switching his players; occasionally pulling Zola back into midfield and bringing on substitute Melli if required.

The story got around among the Arsenal players that Parma somehow 'weren't up for it'. The source of these rumours remains unclear. 'We heard that some of their players felt that a physical battle was somehow "beneath them",' commented Steve Bould after the final. True, veteran Belgian midfielder Georges Grun did say, 'Technically, we are superior to the English and should be able to win it even if Arsenal are a physically strong team,' but he was only encapsulating what the English media were saying anyway.

Brolin was alleged to have uttered the words, 'No Wright, no problem', but this has never been proved and the player denies it.

'Perhaps there was a bit of negative body language before the kick-off, maybe the odd things we'd got to hear they'd said in the media – but nothing I can put my finger on,' admits Davis.

Asprilla later recalled, 'None of us took Arsenal for granted, not for a second, because we had seen what'd they'd achieved against PSG.'

In the tunnel before the match, the Italian team was a study in concentration with Brolin stony-faced, the normally ebullient Asprilla bouncing a ball up and down, his eyes fixed on the wall, and Zola hopping nervously from foot to foot. None of the Parma players appeared distracted or unfocused at all.

The inevitable conclusion about Parma's apparent 'fear' of facing Arsenal is that the story was fanned by someone within the club itself, to invoke the fortress mentality which had served Graham so well down the years. If so, it worked perfectly. Arsenal – the underdogs – were facing a bunch of Serie A prima donnas who had been offered £150,000 a man to retain the trophy. The stage was set for an unforgettable occasion.

The early stages of the match were dominated by Parma. Brolin put Asprilla through at the gallop and as the leggy Colombian prepared to pull the trigger, only a desperate Steve Bould lunge denied him. Soon afterwards, a Benarrivo cross was headed on to the roof of Seaman's net by Brolin, then the Swede crashed a shot against the inside of Seaman's post and it rebounded to safety. Arsenal appeared likely to crumble, but crucially, Parma didn't score.

'Had Tony Adams not taken command at that point,' recalls Davis, 'I think we would have struggled. He got around to everyone to remind them of their role. Steve Morrow needed to get tighter on Zola, and

Ian Selley and I had to close down Crippa and Pin, who were a good double act down the middle.'

On 17 minutes, a misplaced clearance by Parma skipper Minotti fell to Smith, who chested it down and rifled in a shot from just outside the box past keeper Bucci. Smith's goal supply might have dried up since the arrival of Wright but he proved that on the big occasion he could still grab the goals that really mattered.

He recalls, 'I felt I played one of my best ever games for the club. I was back as the leading striker, and I had more room to operate, without Ian in the team.' A magnanimous Wright admitted afterwards, 'I was delighted that "Smudger" scored that goal, because when I arrived, I took away everything he had.'

Somehow, Arsenal were 1-0 up, and although Zola twisted past Bould and his shot forced a fine save from Seaman, the Gunners stood firm. Parma's customary passing game was broken up by Adams and Bould, later nominated man of the match by no less an authority than *Gazzetta dello Sport*.

'Sometimes, you have a period in the game where if you don't score, you sense that it just isn't your day, and I got the impression that when Parma didn't break us down in that first half, they started to think that way,' explains Davis.

Morrow, Selley and Davis ensured that the supply line to Asprilla and Zola was cut, leaving Parma's front two increasingly isolated. Asprilla later commented, 'Arsenal's work rate was astonishing. Morrow – he was one, and the little man – Selley – I kept thinking, "When are you two going to stop running?" They never did.'

The Parken Stadium had almost been annexed by Arsenal fans, who outnumbered their Italian counterparts 4-1. Before the game, and at half-time, Arsenal's stadium announcer Paul Burrell hijacked the PA system and endlessly pumped out the season's adopted theme, the Pet Shop Boys' 'Go West', with the lyrics reworked to 'One-nil to the Arsenal'. By the early second half, with Graham warning his side at the break that they were defending too deep, Parma's stars began to lose heart. 'Tell-tale signs were there,' recalls Selley. 'Asprilla and Brolin began to glance at one another uneasily, and Parma looked niggly. Asprilla and Crippa were booked for kicking out. They looked a bit desperate.'

Not so Arsenal, drilled impeccably by Graham. Although Crippa volleyed over a good chance late on and Melli's shot was correctly ruled out for offside, Parma couldn't disentangle themselves from Arsenal's midfield web. Patrick Barclay summed up Parma's plight in *The Observer* as 'artistry ensnared in mean machine'.

To show just how tightly drilled the Arsenal players were, Morrow later described the 'absolute fear' he had of allowing Parma to attack. When the final whistle went, Graham jumped straight into Adams's arms. His trusty lieutenant had again been magnificent and the pair of them had some closure on the Benfica debacle at last.

Ridiculed after being torn to shreds by Marco Van Basten at the 1988 European Championship, Adams had enjoyed success on the European stage. 'We settled down and stifled them,' Graham explained. Aware that Parma boss Scala had made reference to 'negativo' in his press conference he added, 'My team may not be everyone's favourites, but we win trophies. It's not all about who a manager picks, but more about how he asks his team to play.'

Scala later admitted, 'Arsenal deserved to win, showed how to control our system of play and to me they are the least typical English team I have seen.' And Parma were arguably the most atypical Italian side Arsenal could have faced in that era – aside from AC Milan.

In *Gazzetta dello Sport*, Scala was joined by Cesare Maldini and Giovanni Trappatoni in praising Graham's tactical thinking. 'He has shown clarity of thought. He problem-solves his way through European games. I admire George Graham hugely,' admitted Trappatoni. Graham, meanwhile, still grumbled about the English media's obsession with 'tittle tattle and gossip, rather than the football. Continental football writers are so much more knowledgeable and talk about the real issues surrounding the game,' he argued.

It was an ironic statement. Even as Adams lifted the Cup Winners' Cup, and the Parken Stadium once again thronged to 'One nil to the Arsenal', Graham's hull had already been fatally breached by tip of the iceberg revelations about illegal payments from the Pal Lydersen and John Jensen transfers.

Following an investigation by Danish investigative journalist Hans Christian Blum, TV reporter Henrik Madsen approached Graham at the London Colney training ground two weeks before the Cup

Winners' Cup Final and asked, 'Mr Graham, do you know Rune Hauge? Have you ever taken money from him?' Graham normally tried to ignore the press, but this time, he strode towards Madsen, said, 'Those are very serious allegations,' and security removed the journalist from the premises.

Nothing more was said until the *Evening Standard*'s allegations in November but Graham – to all intents and purposes – was already sunk. The enemy had broken through the gates. 'GEORGE KNOWS', read a banner in Copenhagen. But not even the seemingly all-powerful Graham could have foreseen what was coming next. It was remarkable how quickly events were about to unravel.

Graham wasted little time in the close-season to assure Arsenal fans that he was 'aiming for the title' once again but now there was an obvious credibility gap opening up between what he promised and what was delivered.

'I spoke to him a while after the win against Parma,' recalled Brian Woolnough, 'and he was deluding himself. He talked about winning the European Cup, but on the other hand ranted about star players and inflated wages, and claimed he wouldn't change his style. Arsenal were light years from winning the Premier League. George's managerial approach had had its day. The Cup Winners' Cup victory only just papered over the cracks.'

The 1994 World Cup had been a feast of attacking football, and Bergkamp, Brolin, Overmars, Baggio and Batistuta were all strongly linked with a move to Arsenal. Even the normally reserved Graham entered into the spirit of things, promising his players 'a World Cup signing that will blow your mind'.

Stefan Schwarz – a neat and effective performer in Sweden's midfield – arrived for a £2m fee, but hardly created a frisson of excitement in N5. Within a few months, Schwarz told the Swedish press, 'George Graham's tactics don't appeal to me at all,' and he only stayed for a season.

Davis recalls, 'He was expected to be creative, but also to cover the defence. He couldn't do it all, and he became unhappy.' Graham's judgement – and willpower to rebuild the team – was fading. After Copenhagen he had praised the contributions of Davis and Smith, acknowledging that Davis 'remains our most gifted midfielder' and that Smith's fine display 'shows that we need more than just Ian Wright up front'.

Although the Gunners were linked closely with QPR striker Les Ferdinand and Leeds midfielder Gary McAllister, who were possible replacements, they opted to stay with their respective clubs, and Davis and Smith – both in their 30s – only played a handful of matches between them in their final season at Highbury due to injuries and loss of form.

Chris Sutton's £5m transfer from Norwich to eventual 1995 Premier League champions Blackburn revealed how much top players now cost. 'Had George splashed out for any of those players, it would have sent out a statement of intent,' explains David Hillier. 'That was what was needed to turn Arsenal back into genuine title contenders, but that sort of outlay was never going to happen with George in charge.'

By November, Arsenal were floundering in lower-mid-table, and behind the scenes, Graham had already made a secret deal with the board to leave the club at the end of the season.

The macabre events of 'Black November' speeded up the whole process. Sandwiched between a woeful defeat at Leicester City, and a gutsy goalless draw with Manchester United, two cataclysmic stories broke. Taking a break from investigating the Tories' Euro rebels, and John Major's divided Cabinet, the *Daily Mirror* turned its attentions to Paul Merson. 'I'M HOOKED ON COCAINE' ran the headline. Underneath was a shocking picture of the gloomy and unshaven-looking striker, who had obviously reached the end of the road.

The harrowing account of how alcohol, drugs and gambling pushed Merson to the edge is described in his autobiography *Rock Bottom* but the revelations, although stunning, were also unsurprising. For several years, with Paul Gascoigne playing in Italy, Merson was the *enfant terrible* of the English game.

His tale of woe – rightly or wrongly – didn't reflect well on Graham. The player's ballooning weight and palpable lack of fitness meant he had been a virtual passenger in the team for too long. Over the last 20 years, a raft of stories have since emerged from the Arsenal dressing room of him wearing bin liners at training to 'sweat out' the night before, and of Merson and Adams sucking polos to hide the smell of alcohol from their manager. It suggested that Graham was never quite as all-seeing as he would have liked to believe.

Two days later, the Graham scandal finally exploded. Playing it cool, the *Sunday Mirror* announced that 'a top Highbury official' received a large sum of money from the Jensen deal in 1992. Those early stories were shrouded in rumour and counter rumour, littered with buzzwords like 'sweeteners', 'kick-backs', 'unsolicited gifts' and of course 'bungs'.

When the mist cleared, all routes led, staggeringly, to Graham, who had received two 'kick-backs' from Norwegian agent Rune Hauge. The first was a payment of £140,500, allegedly his cut from the Lydersen deal, and the second was for £285,000, supposedly his take from the Jensen signing.

The board had found out about the payments in August but Graham only told them after he realised Hauge's tax returns were being investigated. For many, that was sufficient evidence to label Graham 'the sleaze manager'.

Graham begged to differ, insisting that although he had been naive to accept Hauge's 'gift', that's all it was – a gift. A Premier League inquiry was set up, tasked with revealing its findings in February 1995.

During an uneasy peace, Graham – whose immaculate dress sense prompted AC Milan president Silvio Berlusconi to liken his appearance to that of a Mafia don – saw the empire he had meticulously built crumble. This was a Tony Soprano meltdown. A Vito Corleone decline. The white knight who had ridden to Arsenal's rescue nine years earlier was now forever tainted. 'All those years when he'd been so tight over our contracts, and then we find out he's been lining his own pockets. I could barely look him in the eye after that,' explains one ex-player.

It was the perfect story for the ravenous tabloids, who were convinced that sleaze was everywhere – in politics, the city, and football. Major's disastrous 'back to basics' policy had backfired and the press exposed the likes of David Mellor and Neil Hamilton as being less than honest. In the city, they had investigated insider dealing with Nick Leeson's activities at Barings Bank the main story.

With so much money sloshing around due to Sky it was inevitable that the press would investigate tales of illicit payments in football. And of course, Graham – the man who had so often spoken to the press through clenched teeth – was at the eye of the storm.

Mike Langley explained, 'George always felt that he was made a scapegoat, but even he admits he'd been naive. Of course he would be targeted by the media afterwards. They'd got the story and wouldn't let it go. George had been spikier and spikier down the years with the press. Some journalists felt a sense of relish in pursuing the story.'

Graham attempted to stem the tide by splashing £5m on forwards John Hartson and Chris Kiwomya, plus winger Glenn Helder. It remains a bizarre episode – given that he was sacked a fortnight later – and raises the question of why the board hadn't encouraged him to invest in new talent in the close-season. It is a question which has never been satisfactorily answered, but suggests the board – right up to the last minute – were actually unsure as to whether to dismiss him. Although none of the new signings made a lasting impact at Highbury, he was finally acknowledging that more pace, strength and width was required up front. But it was far too little, far too late.

Financial irregularities aside, Graham's time at Arsenal was over. First Division side Millwall, Graham's former club, dumped Arsenal out of the FA Cup at Highbury and events had now turned almost full circle. The side required as much internal surgery as it had when he took over nine years earlier. The most tactically astute Arsenal manager since Chapman was – shockingly and suddenly – gone.

When any dictator falls, their image disappears quickly. Graham's waxwork dummy in the museum was moved into storage and his greeting to visitors was replaced by a message from Bob Wilson. Official publications abruptly stopped mentioning his name, although in the issue for the home match with Nottingham Forest – the day on which he was dismissed – he had noted, 'Rumours of my impending departure have been proved somewhat premature.'

- - - - -

Graham's legacy is tainted. When he attended the 125th birthday celebrations for the club at the Emirates Stadium in December 2011, he received a distinctly cool reception. Yet here was the manager who proportionately won more trophies per season than Wenger, Mee and Chapman, whose tactical nous drew plaudits from abroad, who moulded the legendary back four, and whose impact at the club gave a significant proportion of the 60,000 crowd for the Everton game some of their best Arsenal memories. By the time he departed, Arsenal was a slick money-making machine with a turnover of over £23,. Success on the pitch had bred commercial growth. And that was down largely to him.

The ambivalence towards Graham isn't purely because of the bungs scandal, the fact he later managed Tottenham, or because Arsenal were in a poor playing state by the time he left. It is because despite the 'Rolls-Royce' team he had assembled by 1991 his judgement failed him, and Manchester United replaced Liverpool 'on their perch'.

Like Mee 20 years before, Graham was unable to rebuild a successful team and man-manage a new breed of footballer. It is ironic that Graham – so dismissive of much that was new in the Premier League era – remains the only top flight manager to have been found guilty of illegally pocketing the 'new money' which has poured in since the inception of the Premier League.

The travails of Merson and Adams also showed that he was powerless to intervene in the hedonistic lives of two of his young, Sky-moneyed stars.

The wars of attrition on the pitch – perfectly encapsulated by the Cup Winners' Cup Final victory in 1994 – happened because Graham moulded the team into an attritional unit. They were battles of his making. 'I like hearing the supporters singing "One nil to the Arsenal."' It makes me smile,' he claimed after the final whistle in Copenhagen. But Graham was turning a deaf ear to the crescendo of boos that regularly rang out when his team eked out single-goal wins in the league or worse, failed to find the net.

Ignoring the big European nights, and the one-off cup games, the staple diet was deadly dull. 'When George left, we could breathe again,' explained Adams in *Addicted*. 'It was like a strict schoolteacher not being there any more.'

It was the bitter end for Graham. But it was a new beginning for Arsenal.

# A Change Of Identity

'I'd never heard a manager in England talk about the game with such intellect and insight as Arsène Wenger. I thought straight away, "He'll take Arsenal to a new place."' Patrick Barclay, football journalist.

'The teams chasing us seem to me to be a bunch of also-rans. But appearances can be deceptive. I might live to regret that comment.' Alex Ferguson, March 1998.

FOLLOWING a juddering 3-0 loss at Old Trafford in March 1995, which left Arsenal deep in relegation trouble, caretaker manager Stuart Houston admitted, 'We were formless and shapeless. We seem to have lost our identity. Something has to change quite radically.' In his five-year spell at Highbury, it was the most incisive and pertinent comment the Scot ever uttered.

As Sky money poured in, Arsenal and Manchester United had travelled along increasingly divergent paths. Ferguson's team gobbled up trophies, reaped the financial rewards of the Champions League, and invested in players. Their youth policy, with Beckham, Scholes and the Neville brothers breaking through, was poised to bear fruit. And there was Cantona. As the Premier League went global, the charismatic Frenchman was a marketing man's dream, and added to United's allure.

Arsenal seemed to be on a path to nowhere. The epic European Cup Winners' Cup semi-final victory over Sampdoria in April 1995 proved a welcome distraction from the travails of a dismal league campaign. The back four appeared to be on its last legs. The midfield lacked any creative spark. Even Ian Wright couldn't bail out this lot. When Arsenal lost the final to Real Zaragoza courtesy of former Tottenham player Nayim's freak goal, it was the final insult.

The departing Paul Davis commented, 'The team needed a massive overhaul and the club needed a huge lift.' It was about to get one. The day after the Zaragoza defeat, the tabloids claimed that Arsenal were tracking Inter Milan's Dennis Bergkamp.

Initially, solicitor Mel Goldberg hawked the Dutchman to Kevin Keegan's Newcastle, but Keegan opted to sign Les Ferdinand instead. Bergkamp was then offered to Aston Villa but the prospect of living in Birmingham didn't appeal. Only then did Goldberg approach Arsenal vice-chairman David Dein to see if the Gunners wanted him. Initially Dein declined, claiming Arsenal did not want to break their wage structure, but Dein knew they couldn't remain hamstrung by this forever.

The fact Bergkamp was offered to Arsenal almost as an afterthought showed he was the antithesis of what the Gunners were during that period. Both Newcastle and Villa, along with Tottenham, his favourite childhood team, were seen as far more stylish and aesthetically pleasing – more *Bergkamp* – than Arsenal in the summer of 1995.
But he signed on the dotted line on 20 June, resplendent in his new Arsenal top. The £7.5m transfer prompted a raft of cheesy headlines, none more so than *The Sun*'s 'HELLO KAMPERS – Den for Hi-de-Highbury'. The aura surrounding him was quite unlike that of any player who had joined the club since the glamour signings of the late 1920s and early 1930s. A fortnight later, midfielder David Platt arrived at Highbury. His cumulative worth in transfer fees had reached £22m. Splashing a big wedge on the pair was the ultimate statement of intent, proof for supporters that the club was poised to ditch the functional, down-at-heel veneer which blighted Graham's later teams. These were glamour signings, spearheaded by Dein, who now took the lead on transfer negotiations.

Bergkamp became a talisman almost without even kicking a ball. His arrival (probably more by accident than design) coincided with the BBC1 documentary *Dreaming Of Ajax*, presented by Gary Lineker. It had been commissioned in the wake of Graham Taylor's England side failing to qualify for the 1994 World Cup and the introspection that followed.

Viewers saw first-hand the type of holistic training a young Bergkamp would have enjoyed at his first club. Twenty-odd years ago, before the Premier League went global, the Dutch cerebral, all-encompassing approach to the game wasn't especially widely known about. Bergkamp's arrival would prove to be a revelation in a raft of ways for both his new club and English football.

Midfielder Steve Morrow recalled, 'He was utterly different to anything we'd seen before. He was all about poise and grace. He was an absolute perfectionist in every way. He'd arrive early for training, sometimes half an hour or so, just to feel ready. He'd expect his training kit to be spotless. He had phenomenally high standards. We had an exercise where we'd fire crossfield balls to one another.

'He'd bring the ball down and control it in one movement. He messed it up once out of 20 repeats, and insisted on repeating the whole set of exercises over again, until he got it right. That was the hallmark of the man.'

He was a perfect new signing for a club anxious to rid itself of its 'sleaze' tag. Happily married to Henrietta, the Dutchman's clean-living lifestyle – he virtually abstained from drinking alcohol – was in marked contrast to the antics of several members of Arsenal's first team. In his book, Bergkamp expressed amazement that his new team-mates drank such vast quantities of beer. 'It makes no sense to work so hard, and then drown it in alcohol,' he has since said.

He is referring to the notorious Hong Kong tour in 1995 where Tony Adams, Ray Parlour and Chris Kiwomya ended up in court after Parlour threw a bag of prawn crackers into a taxi driver's open bonnet, and was chased by the club-wielding cabby. Bergkamp was humble too. He recalled in his book seeing his name up in capitals on Ceefax on the television in his hotel room, 'I'm on teletext. Me! They must rate me here.' Ominously for Bruce Rioch, appointed manager a fortnight earlier, he had been third favourite for the job behind Bobby Robson and Arsène Wenger, but on the face of it at least the former Bolton boss fitted the bill perfectly.

He had impressed neutrals with the way he instilled a high-energy passing game at Bolton, who had recently knocked Arsenal out of the

FA Cup and who had just gained promotion to the Premier League. He made it known that he preferred his players to be settled with a family and enjoying quiet evenings in rather than falling out of nightclubs. Platt and Bergkamp were ideal Rioch players, both arriving with squeaky clean labels. One of Rioch's tasks – if he was to move the club decisively in the right direction – was to fumigate the stench of alcohol from the club, but this was easier said than done.

Adams compared the atmosphere in the dressing room after Graham's dismissal to that of a rowdy classroom entirely lacking in discipline. In a sense it's difficult to see Rioch as anything other than an earnest, hard-working supply teacher at the mercy of a group of rowdy, self-absorbed pupils, until a more respected figure arrived. Adams felt resentment that Rioch had taken over 'my club' and later confessed, 'I wasn't there for Bruce' as he sank further and further into a destructive alcoholic cycle. Merson was preoccupied with overcoming his own addictions, which he'd confessed to some months earlier. Glenn Helder admitted to 'gambling most of what I had away'. David Hillier had recently been prosecuted after stealing two holdalls from an airport.

The team had seemingly mutated into a living, breathing *Viz* cartoon. There was beer guzzling in the evenings. To and from games, there were pie and chocolate eating competitions. On the coach. Farting and belching contests. Gurning challenges. One player developed a temporary twitch when his face went into spasm after pulling too grotesque a face.

The players shoved sweets and chocolate into their mouths to get their sugar levels back up after matches, and when they were stuffed they would spit them at each other. This was the state of the club Bergkamp walked into in 1995, and the reality of what Rioch inherited. *Animal House* meets *Men Behaving Badly*. Carry On Arsenal.

~ ~ ~ ~ ~

Dressing room distractions aside, Rioch began to implement a passing game at Highbury. 'You could break my aims into two distinct areas,' he informed me. 'Firstly, I wanted goals scored from all over the pitch, rather than concentrating on one player to get them. Secondly, I wanted the ball played out skilfully from defence and knocked around in midfield – with less reliance on balls over the top.'

Rioch set the ball rolling at least, but couldn't sort out the dearth of creativity in midfield. Platt was certainly not the solution. Rioch's early midfields were a hotchpotch of journeymen and 'fillers'. A typical midfield consisted of Platt, Keown and Merson. A midfielder, an attacker and one defender. Ray Parlour flitted in and out of the team.

Platt was the right signing at the wrong time. He had previously flourished in teams playing with a lone striker, or ones which allowed him to move into 'the hole' behind the strikers. His trademark late gallops meant he was at his best playing between attack and midfield. Bergkamp also tended to function best in a slightly more withdrawn role.

In the opening matches of the campaign Merson pushed up from midfield, leaving the 'hole' too crowded. It was an issue that Rioch never fully addressed. He was duty bound to play both his new signings, and Arsenal's most skilful existing player, whatever the tactical quandary may have been.

There was much to admire during the 1995/96 season. There were two thrilling home victories – in the Premier League and Worthington Cup – against Keegan's Newcastle. High-octane, precision passing, and Wright's sublime finishes in both matches, secured a pair of 2-0 victories.

There was the rampant 3-0 destruction of Leeds at Elland Road with Merson and Wright in superb form, and a last-day fightback against Bolton at Highbury which enabled Arsenal to secure a UEFA Cup spot after finishing the season in fifth place.

Then there was Bergkamp himself. He had gone six games without scoring for his new club. 'Hartlefool – Bergy can't even score against 10 men' headlined the *Mirror*, after he failed to find the net against Hartlepool in the Worthington Cup. Dutch team-mate Helder recalled, 'It was fascinating to see the media reaction to Dennis during those early games. He set up the winner for Ian Wright at Manchester City. He set up another two during the Hartlepool game. It seemed to me a very English thing, to focus on him not scoring. The beauty of his game was in the build-up, the inter-play leading to the goal. For the English, it was about the end product. "Why hadn't Dennis scored? What's wrong in his head?" That was the gist of what they were saying.' Aside from the settling-in period, the tactics weren't quite right during those early games.

A frustratingly inconsistent performer, Helder was reintroduced against Southampton in order to 'give the team a bit more of an engine', as he explains. The Dutchman played a blinder, worrying the Saints' defence with his pace and cutting in from the flanks at will. Early in the first half Helder ripped down the left, crossed the ball, and Bergkamp cracked home a finely controlled volley. He later delivered the most exhilarating *coup de grace* in a 4-2 win. Cutting inside Saints defender Ken Monkou, he unleashed a thunderbolt from 30 yards which cannoned in off the post. 'It was stupendous. A beautiful, beautiful goal,' recalled Helder. 'Pace and power. Grace. Everything.'

Rarely, if ever, had a more iconic goal been scored by an Arsenal player. Like Charlie Buchan – several generations before – Bergkamp fought through early press criticism to stamp his mark upon the team. 'The man just had incredible vision,' explained Martin Keown. 'Dennis could size up and assess operations across the whole pitch, and make space for himself and others.'

At Tottenham a few weeks later, a marvellously silky, snaking move down the pitch – culminating in a glorious one-two between Bergkamp and Merson and the smoothest of finishes from the Dutchman – remains the everlasting vision of a game which Arsenal somehow contrived to lose.

There was a splendidly drilled goal at Barnsley in Arsenal's 3-0 win during an almost biblical downpour in the Worthington Cup, and a sublime double against Aston Villa in the semi-final at Highbury in that competition. He netted the winner against Manchester United in an October league game after stealing in behind Denis Irwin and slipping the ball past Peter Schmeichel. But this team was a work in progress.

Those stellar Bergkamp moments were thinly stretched throughout the season. There were some joyless and foreboding days under Rioch. One was a spineless 3-1 reverse at home to bogey side Wimbledon, and a highly embarrassing FA Cup third round exit to Sheffield United.

Rioch lambasted the entire team in the press afterwards. In his next programme notes, he wrote, 'The skipper [Adams] played with the determination he always shows. I wish everyone had followed his example.' It emerged that he and Wright had had a heated half-time *téte-à-teté* in the dressing room. Following another row with Wright after a 2-1 home defeat to Everton, the striker handed in a transfer request. Rioch accused him of being a 'Charlie Big Potatoes' and Wright was unhappy that the service to him was insufficiently direct.

Adams sustained a long-term knee injury after Christmas. No one to keep the troops in order. Perhaps Rioch's sliding doors moment – where history looked one way but went another – was the second leg of the Worthington Cup semi-final at Villa Park. Dwight Yorke's double had secured a 2-2 draw at Highbury and in the second leg Gareth Southgate man-marked Bergkamp. He did a sterling job. In the dying seconds, Nigel Winterburn's crunching left-footed shot shaved the outside of the post and flew wide. Arsenal were out on away goals.

Rioch cursed his luck. Had Winterburn scored, Arsenal would have reached Wembley where they would have faced an impotent Leeds United, who were swatted aside 3-0 in the final. Rioch would have emulated George Graham by winning a trophy in his first season. Upon such tiny margins hinge managerial careers – perhaps.

The arguments continued behind closed doors. John Hartson – whom Rioch never rated – claimed to have been treated 'like a dog'. Rioch kicked over a water dispenser after a 1-1 draw at Blackburn, which flooded the players' feet. He struggled to cope with the idiosyncracies of his players, admitting to feeling like 'Marje Proops'.

Yet counselling skills were prerequisite if he was to be successful. Players' personal demons needed to be exorcised, and egos needed to be massaged. All the time, the toxic personality clash with Wright rumbled on. 'There he was, a manager who'd never been in the top flight, put in charge of a dressing room full of internationals,' Wright later commented.

Several first-teamers got sick of Rioch espousing the virtues of his Bolton players, including striker John McGinlay. 'Who the fuck is John McGinlay?' barked Wright on several occasions. The saga of Rioch's unsigned new contract rumbled on into the close season. He did eventually sign one but was fired two week later.

He had been linked with several stars from Euro 96 – Alan Shearer, the de Boer twins, Edgar Davids and Gary McAllister. 'All of them would have moved us in the right direction,' he argued. No stellar signings arrived. At the September AGM, it was claimed that Rioch had spent too long prevaricating over potential transfers, making

David Dein look a fool throughout Europe. Rioch kept quiet. It was a horrendous mess.

Peter Hill-Wood later commented, 'Bruce gave us a list of players but you cannot sign world class players if their clubs won't sell. In a way, it's an impossible task that he set us.'

Rioch claimed, 'I couldn't win at Arsenal. I discovered they'd always wanted Arsène Wenger, even before I became manager. David Dein and he were good friends. The problem was that he was under contract in Japan, so Arsenal had to wait for another year. But for me, it was always just a matter of time.'

The right man in the wrong decade? Possibly. Joe Lovejoy wrote in *The Independent*, 'The skulduggery which brought Graham down meant that Rioch took over a job with very different parameters to that of any of his English counterparts.' The power within Arsenal lay with Dein – the *de facto* chairman – from whom Rioch had become increasingly isolated.

Wright revealed that he nicknamed Rioch 'Dagenham' because he was 'only a couple of stops short of Barking', but he deserves better than to be lampooned. Dein claimed there was never a rigid plan to turn Arsenal into a more 'total' side when Rioch took the helm, no insistence on a more 'continental' style. That being the case, Rioch deserves huge credit for gradually implementing a new style at Highbury of his own volition.

Dixon and Winterburn confirmed that Rioch urged them to throw off their defensive shackles and display a more attacking outlook. Keown – often on the end of Rioch's verbal tirades – explained, 'Bruce played me in midfield because he had little other option, but he helped me read the game better and look at the game holistically.'

But Rioch – conservative, traditional and parochial – was never going to be the revolutionary to steer the ship into uncharted waters. His continental connections were precious few. He spoke in a clipped, regimented manner. He didn't have progressive views on training techniques or diets, or new age thoughts about stadium or training ground designs.

Nonetheless, he did make his mark and laid down a partial blueprint, but just as when Dave Sexton handed over the coaching reins to Don Howe back in the late 1960s, it took someone else to change the course of Arsenal's history.

The outgoing manager claimed that the grand plan had always been to bring in Wenger, and it was to the Grampus Eight manager that the club now turned. Rioch was correct. Wenger had been on Dein's radar for at least eight years. In the late 1980s, the up-and-coming AS Monaco coach made regular trips to see games around Europe, and on one of his visits to Arsenal the Frenchman got lost in the bowels of Highbury, ending up in the Ladies' Lounge.

None other than Barbara Dein, the vice-chairman's wife, came to his rescue, taking him to meet her husband David. The two men struck an immediate rapport. Dein took Wenger along to a friend's dinner party where the continental guest endeared himself to everyone during a late-night game of charades and impressed Dein with his savvy asides, his intelligence and humour. Dein told Alex Fynn, author of *Arsenal: The Making Of A Modern Superclub*, that he straight away regarded Wenger as 'one for the future'.

Dein saw a kindred spirit in Wenger. Just as Wenger was utterly absorbed in his work, travelling far and wide to watch matches in different parts of Europe, so Dein (who admitted to looking in the shaving mirror each morning and saying to himself, 'Get a winning team') scoured the globe to improve the facilities at Highbury (his regular visits to the US reaffirmed his belief that all English clubs should modernise their stadia), scouting networks, and training facilities.

As luck would have it, Dein had a yacht moored at Antibes on the Côte d'Azur, a couple of miles down the coast from Monaco. By the early 1990s Dein began to watch Monaco matches at the Stade Louis II on a regular basis, enjoying dinner with Wenger after matches. As Arsenal began to decline in the latter years of Graham, Dein began to think that if the club were ever to reinvent itself then Wenger could be the man to spearhead the revolution.

This was still some years off but Dein was able to see at close hand the initiatives which Wenger used to turn Monaco, who had been struggling, into a powerful force in France, and which he has since deployed in north London. Jean Luc Ettori recalled, 'We wanted someone to get into our heads, in a positive way. Arsène did that, and instilled some of his natural confidence.' His tactics at Monaco, as they are at Arsenal, were for his players to impose themselves collectively on their opponents. Ettori added, 'He was never going to adapt himself to the opposition. He was never going to instruct his players to stop the opposition. That simply isn't his way, then or now.' Never was a truer word spoken, for better or worse.

Dein saw that Wenger turned upside down Monaco's training techniques. Wenger insisted on short, intense sessions, which were timed (virtually) to the microsecond. Former Monaco striker Mark Hateley explained, 'You're working the areas that you need to work: your mind, your body, your feet, quick thinking.'

Then there were also the physical audits of the players, the plethora of specialists, and the development of scouting networks across the globe. Players were made fully aware of the coach's almost messianic views concerning drinking and eating. Hateley recalled, 'Healthy, fresh food and produce only. Drink in absolute moderation.' It wasn't entirely revolutionary, but rather like Chapman in the 1930s, Wenger was a highly astute assimilator and adapter of ideas.

Even when Wenger opted to coach Grampus Eight in Japan he never veered far off Dein's radar, and in the turbulent summer after George Graham's sacking Dein officially recommended Wenger to the board. The Wenger option appeared too much of a risk, particularly given that only one foreign coach, Dr Josef Venglos, had managed an English team at that point (Aston Villa), with little success.

Even when Bruce Rioch became Arsenal's new boss, Wenger's influence could be felt as he recommended to Dein that signing Inter Milan striker Dennis Bergkamp could help revamp the Gunners' playing style. A year later though, amid the chaos emanating from Rioch's sacking, the Arsenal board agreed to Dein's insistence that, if the club was really to move into the 21st century, it had to take a punt on 'Arsène Who?' as the *Evening Standard* headline soon described him.

He was unveiled to the Arsenal crowd in *Big Brother* style on the Jumbotron screens before the Sheffield Wednesday game at Highbury. It wasn't inspiring. The acoustics were so poor that the only decipherable comment was, 'Let's win tonight.' For 45 minutes, table-topping Wednesday led through an Andy Booth goal before Wenger, watching via the new-fangled internet (quaintly described as the 'information super highway' by the club in press releases) instructed caretaker manager Pat Rice to send on the new signing from AC Milan, midfielder Patrick Vieira, all 6ft 3in of him, to replace Ray Parlour. It was a hugely symbolic substitution in several ways.

It was a Frenchman replacing an Englishman. Guile and power replacing limited talent, although in time Vieira's galvanising presence would have a hugely positive impact on Parlour's hitherto lacklustre form. Here was a new-age midfielder whose short, accurate passing induced terror in Wednesday's previously well-organised back line. In the *One Nil Down* fanzine, Mike Collins commented, 'The muscular strength of Mickey Thomas was there, as was the speedy box to box athleticism and the subtle vision and touch of Paul Davis.'

Always looking for colleagues to link up with, the former AC Milan man's debut was arguably the most memorable since Wright had joined the club five years earlier. Platt pulled Arsenal level and a tornado-like hat-trick from Wright gave Arsenal a 4-1 win. The midfield had for so long been Arsenal's problem area, cluttered with plodders and earnest destroyers.

Vieira recalls, 'I felt as if I slotted in right away. Lots of people told me that the Arsenal midfield was weak, but that they had a strong defence and a strong attack. I agreed with them about the attack and the defence. I gave Arsenal more options in midfield. It clicked right away.' Vieira's signature demonstrated the almost faultless nature of Wenger's judgement during his formative days at the club. His knowledge of European football meant he knew that Vieira, a virtual unknown to English fans, wasn't enjoying his experience at AC Milan.

Tellingly, Vieira admits, 'Clubs at that time weren't making signings like the one which took me to Highbury. There wasn't the in depth knowledge of the second level of the European game. I mean – everyone knew about big stars like Klinsmann and Bergkamp – but they didn't know about players like me who were below the radar. Only Arsène did, at that time. He did what no one else was doing, and tapped into markets no else was.' Why did Vieira join Arsenal? 'Because of Arsène Wenger, because of the potential of the club, and because really Bergkamp's signature raised Arsenal's profile. All those things rolled together.'

Vieira's arrival at Highbury was instantaneous, more effecting than Bergkamp's. Midfielder Steve Morrow explained, 'Patrick was gangly and ungainly, but as a midfielder, there wasn't much he couldn't do. His height meant that he was a presence in the opposition's box, and an excellent defensive screen back in ours. He gave us a new dimension, and a fresh perspective in games.'

Wenger told the *Evening Standard*, 'He reads the game well. He has quick feet, he's a good passer and a strong defender. I think Milan will realise they made a mistake in letting him go.'

What Bergkamp and Vieira both had in common was the fact that neither had enjoyed their Italian sojourn. At different times, both commented on the 'impersonal' feel of Italian football, in contrast to the more homely Highbury environs.

At Selhurst Park against Wimbledon, filling in in defence after both Adams and Bould suffered head injuries, Vieira surged forward and delivered an inch-perfect slide-rule pass to Wright (who was later punched in the face by Vinnie Jones) and Wright slipped the ball into the net. A box-to-box midfielder. An enforcer. A footballer who could turn defence into attack in the blink of an eye.

Keown recalled, 'When Patrick arrived, you could see straight away what we'd missed for several years in midfield. He wasn't perfect, but he has to be described as a revelation anyway.'

Brick by brick, Wenger dismantled Arsenal's resolutely English edifice. His overhaul of the training regime saw the players stretch, stretch and stretch some more. The sessions were shorter and far higher octane. Tony Adams may have been suspicious of Wenger's 'schoolteacher' image, but Dixon and Winterburn, written off on numerous occasions prior to the Frenchman's arrival, found themselves feeling a good deal more energetic, which was important because Wenger wanted them to maintain their sojourns into the opposition half which they had begun under Rioch.

The post-match sweets and chocolate went. 'They used to eat Mars Bars and Milky Ways,' laughs Vieira. 'Arsène confiscated them. For a few weeks, they'd sing, "We want our chocolate back," but Arsène would just smile and say nothing.' The steamed chicken and broccoli anecdotes are now well worn. 'After a while at least, I think we were allowed to have some mustard or lemon sauce on them. It tasted better then,' recalled Vieira.

Wenger had famously scoffed at the England team's pre-match tomato soup/spaghetti bolognese dinners at Euro 96, claiming, 'All that kind of thing gives you is wind.' Then there was the alcohol issue.

'One beer is OK. More is a problem,' he said, and stopped the players' lounge stocking alcohol. But the drinking didn't stop overnight. As Chris Lightbown wrote in the *Sunday Times*, 'He knows how to drain a bath without discarding the baby.'

Eight months after Wenger took over, Ray Parlour recalled Bould ordering 35 pints in a bar in one go for seven English players on the 1997 close-season tour while the French contingent smoked cigarettes in a coffee shop across the road. 'How are we going to win the league this year? We're all drunk, and they're all smoking,' thought Parlour. Such bonding sessions wouldn't be tolerated by the chaste Wenger regime any longer though.

The dressing room remained overwhelmingly English in Wenger's formative days, with its pranks and tomfoolery. 'Ray Parlour would sneak up behind you and pull your shorts down,' recalled Vieira.

'Ray taught me lots of English swear words. He was always trying to get me into trouble and repeat them,' recalled midfielder Remi Garde. Vieira added, 'Ray mocked Arsène's accent, and Arsène would smirk at him and say, "Are you joking with me, Raymond?"'

In contrast to the almost monastic feel to the Milan dressing room, at Highbury 'the ghetto blaster was booming. Ian Wright would be pumping away, swinging his shorts around his head, often dancing in just his socks,' admitted Patrick Vieira. 'Remi Garde and I would look at one another as if to say, "What kind of madhouse is this?"' Steve Morrow recalled Dennis Bergkamp's bewilderment when Ian Wright suddenly leapt 'like some crazed creature onto the windscreen and pulled these crazy faces at the team as the driver carried on with Wrighty stuck to the windscreen'.

But the gradual fusion of English and continental talents made for some stellar moments on the pitch during the early months of Wenger's reign. There was Wright's fine double against Blackburn on Wenger's debut, and the intense 3-1 win over Tottenham in the lashing rain. With five minutes remaining, Adams rampaged forward to volley home. Minutes later, Wright's long cross was collected by Bergkamp, who seemed to control the ball and curl it home in the same movement. He slid to his knees in the mud, screaming to the clouds. Patrick Vieira recalled, 'We were so powerful and passionate. People began to take notice.'

Wright slipped in a late winner against Newcastle after Arsenal had gone down to ten men following Adams's sending-off. Paul Merson, gushing about 'the incredible belief Arsène has given me', temporarily returned to the type of form he had displayed during the 1990/91 title-winning season.

Dead wood was shipped out: Helder, Kiwomya, and McGoldrick, all hangovers from the dark days of the Graham era, went. So did Hartson, for £4m, to West Ham. Merson, whose form had faded in the new year, signed for First Division Middlesbrough. His departure prompted claims that Wenger wanted rid of the English influence.

Sixteen years later, Merson confessed that Wenger actually wanted him to stay but that he left because he could double his wage in the north-east, which 'would come in handy for my gambling'. The truth will always come out eventually.

In came striker Nicolas Anelka, bought for a pittance – £500,000 – from Paris St Germain. Wenger knew that a major decision loomed. Although Wright remained Arsenal's prime goal-getter, his form was becoming increasingly listless for long periods and his behaviour more fractious. It was arguably the first 'big call' of Wenger's Arsenal tenure: how to bring the curtain down on Wright's Arsenal career without incurring the wrath of the player or supporters. But whereas Rioch tried to forcibly erode Wright's power base, Wenger was more subtle, introducing Anelka to the equation and letting nature take its course.

Arsenal grabbed a UEFA Cup spot by finishing third. It had been a fine first season for Wenger's Gunners, although the team's disciplinary record was becoming a major concern with yellow and red cards dished out aplenty. Ultimately Arsenal had fallen short against their main title rivals, and Wenger admitted that reinforcements were needed if the club was to launch a title bid in 1998, 'We need more power and strength in midfield and more pace on the wing.'

It had been six years since Arsenal last won the title and Adams suggested to Bergkamp, 'Dennis, isn't it time you won something here?' Wenger meanwhile, spoke of the challenge which lay ahead. 'Sooner or later, we have to use our strengths to defeat the champions, who will be our main threat.' Manchester United and Alex Ferguson lay in wait.

Wenger invested heavily in the squad during the summer of 1997. *Loaded* had recently dubbed football 'the new rock n roll' and the merchandising revolution, especially replica shirt sales, reached its height. *The Times* labelled Islington as 'arguably the most desirable part of London', aided by the fact that new Prime Minister Tony Blair had just sold his pile there for a tidy profit.

It was also helped by the screening of Nick Hornby's *Fever Pitch*, with Colin Firth in the lead role. Hornby has always denied that the book or the film had any impact on gentrifying football, or Arsenal. But with their burgeoning 'global village' populated by glamorous foreign signings and a cerebral, multilingual new manager, *Fever Pitch*'s release was certainly a timely (if fortuitous) piece of marketing.

It helped that Firth, who had sprung to fame in BBC's *Pride And Prejudice*, modelled the club's classic early-70s kit throughout the film, and sales in club retail outlets rocketed. That retro shirt quickly became a fashion accessory. For the first time since the early 1930s, Arsenal were regarded as 'hip'.

Monied – courtesy of director Danny Fiszman's cash injection – Arsenal were upwardly mobile and increasingly European in their outlook at a time when budget airlines and the cost-cutting internet deals (the club had just launched its own website) made foreign travel more accessible, and foreign Arsenal fans from France and Holland began to flock to Highbury. Arsenal were *à la mode*.

A few weeks into the new season, *Marie Claire* readers were asked to vote on the best-looking Premier League footballer. Three Arsenal players – Bergkamp, Overmars and Petit – finished three, four and five in the poll behind Ryan Giggs and David Ginola, who was about to be substituted by Tottenham boss George Graham with alarming regularity.

In the grand scheme of things the *Marie Claire* poll didn't matter. Nor did the fact that Wright was being touted as a chat show host, that Emmanuel Petit spoke to highbrow magazines about his love of French poetry, and that Adams was now taking piano lessons. But in one sense it was important because it proved that Arsenal were revamping themselves rapidly.

Tony Blair's advice that businesses should indulge in 'global interfacing' was taken at face value by Arsenal. In a rather scattergun summer spending spree, the new arrivals hailed from a variety of European countries. Petit, Gilles Grimandi and Christopher Wreh all played in France, Marc Overmars in Holland, Alberto Mendez in Germany, Luis Boa Morte in Portugal, Alex Manninger in Austria and Matthew Upson in glamorous Luton.

Overmars had won the European Cup with Ajax and was the speedy winger Arsenal had craved since Limpar departed three years earlier. Monaco's Petit was known mainly to followers of the French game. 'I knew that Manu would be a superb signing,' recalled Vieira. 'He could tackle, he could distribute the ball and he could add weight either up front or back in his own defence. Some saw Manu as a mirror image of me in terms of ability. That was a compliment, although I was more of a box to box player than him.'

Wenger predicted that Overmars 'will give us a faster engine this season. He will increase the tempo of our matches, as we were a bit slow at times last year.'

Overmars speaks in reverential tones about Wenger. 'I'd snapped my cruciate ligament whilst playing for Ajax, and there were some who doubted that I'd ever be the same player again. It did set me back slightly and knock my confidence, but Arsène was very encouraging. There were several signings at that time who'd had setbacks in their careers of different kinds. I think that we all had points to prove. We were a very determined and motivated group.'

Overmars is likely referring to Vieira's and Bergkamp's challenging Italian sojourns, and the tragedy suffered by Petit when his brother Olivier died on the football pitch, which he admitted had affected his focus.

At the beginning of the 1997/98 season Adams and Wenger challenged the players to fulfil themselves. Whether it was Wenger suggesting to his skipper that this time he could win the title 'sober', Adams insisting that his fellow defenders could win the title 'playing the Wenger way', or Wenger telling Wright that he could break the Arsenal goalscoring record and win a league title, each player had their own personal goals, and their own demons to exorcise.

A rose-tinted view of the campaign distorts the season into a procession of awesome Arsenal moments: Bergkamp's barely-credible early season form, with his mind-boggling hat-trick against Leicester at Filbert Street and magnificent double against Southampton, Wright grabbing the club's all-time goalscoring record against Bolton at Highbury, Arsenal's storming finish to the season from late March onwards confirming the emergence of Anelka...the fabulous day at Highbury when Arsenal thrashed Everton 4-0 to win the title in front of their own supporters. All under the tutelage of a beguiling, multilingual manager.

Yet as Vieira recalls, 'People tend to remember only the great parts. They're not too interested in the bits which don't go so well. Really, we had a great spell for the first two months, but didn't click again until March onwards. What kept us going in difficult spells was our team spirit. Our victories over Manchester United were pivotal. So was our conversation at the Christmas party in late 1997. I'd say it was the point at which we properly became a team.'

Even in the early part of the campaign, there were periods when the team looked disjointed. Wenger allowed Wright his moment in the sun, at which point his form declined rapidly. In a number of matches from October onwards he became a virtual passenger in games, until injury ruled him out in January. It was a natural process with Anelka taking Wright's place in the team and, arguably, Arsenal wouldn't have prevailed with their increasingly static record goalscorer in the team in the New Year.

Anelka's early performances lacked consistency and defences tightened on Bergkamp by late autumn. At Selhurst Park, the Dutchman grew frustrated at the close attention afforded to him by Crystal Palace's Hermann Hreidarsson and later over-protested a foul so much that he received a booking which saw him banned for three games. His form didn't hit those dizzy summer heights again that campaign.

Petit occasionally cut a frustrated figure in those opening few months and was sent off in a patchy goalless draw with Aston Villa. The Gunners fell to a 3-0 hammering at Derby and were undone at Hillsborough by Ron Atkinson's Sheffield Wednesday. But when they absolutely had to, Arsenal pulled it together against Manchester United at Highbury.

- - - - -

Matches between the two sides had always been feisty and combustible in the late 1980s and early 90s but there had been a mutual respect between the two Scots: Graham and Ferguson. Whatever the result, both men indulged in a spot of cosy post-match banter about vintage wines or malt whiskies. Ferguson even used details of Graham's handsome contract at Arsenal (the United boss claimed that in the early 90s, Graham was on double his salary) to lobby for a substantial pay hike at Old Trafford. When Graham departed Arsenal, Ferguson said he 'missed the camaraderie and the competition which existed between George and I and both our clubs'.

Such comradely feelings never existed between Ferguson and Wenger late last century. The first bit of verbal sparring between the pair came almost immediately Wenger stepped off the plane in September 96 when the Frenchman registered his annoyance that Ferguson was complaining about the crowded fixture list. In the United manager's words, it was 'a complaint about a complaint'. Ferguson countered, 'He's just arrived from Japan. What does he know about it?' Frosty and tetchy.

In fairness, Ferguson added, 'If Arsenal are successful over the next few seasons, he'll be in that boat too,' and Wenger did indeed spend a great deal of time over the next two seasons griping about playing 'Saturday, Wednesday, Saturday'. The two managers shared a glass of wine after the game, but Ferguson commented, 'Perhaps he should spend more time controlling Ian Wright's behaviour,' which went down like a lead balloon with Wenger.

The Gunners lost by a Nigel Winterburn own goal in Wenger's first visit to Old Trafford. Peter Schmeichel was accused of making a racist comment towards Wright. The FA didn't charge Schmeichel, claiming, 'It's very difficult to prove exactly what was said by viewing TV evidence.' When the two teams met at Highbury in the New Year, Arsenal lost again. The headlines once more surrounded Schmeichel and Wright.

Wright's late lunge on the Dane prompted a censuring by the FA. Things were becoming personal.

Ebullient Liberian striker Christopher Wreh was taken aback by the ferocity surrounding the November 1997 clash, 'About two weeks before the game, I had journalists asking us about United. About Beckham and Keane and Sheringham. And about Ferguson. It amazed me. Journalists wanted me to make comments which would stir things up, I think.

'Wenger always told us to make no comment. It was his way of taking the pressure off the players. I remember on the morning of the game at Highbury looking at a football sports supplement and it was all about the game, and a "face-off" between the two managers. Afterwards when I drove home there were copies of it strewn across the roads around the stadium. Ferguson and Wenger were staring at each other in the [mock-up] photo.'

As Arsenal took to the field, they trailed United by four points. The media was in general agreement that United would win and therefore open up a substantial lead in the Premier League race. With Petit and Bergkamp suspended, and Wright's form spluttering, the omens didn't look good. The atmosphere was rancorous. Schmeichel was hit by a flying bag of chips, thrown from the crowd. The Jumbotrons lingered for longer than usual on Ferguson, who ran the gauntlet of the abuse from the crowd.

Anelka rifled Arsenal ahead with a 20-yard drive which fizzed past Schmeichel at his near post. Vieira doubled Arsenal's lead with a vicious swerving drive from the edge of the box. 'It had a strange trajectory, but the spin on it deceived Schmeichel and it was a great sight to see it hit the net,' he explains. Less good news for Arsenal was that as Vieira slid to his knees in celebration, he tore knee ligaments. 'It wasn't the cleverest thing to do,' he admits.

Teddy Sheringham's brace made it 2-2 before half-time. After his second goal he kissed his shirt, and ran towards the North Bank laughing. The match reached its fulminating climax when David Platt headed in from a late corner, the ball perfectly bisecting the leaping Gary Neville and the crossbar. As Platt wheeled away, he motioned for his team-mates to follow, and they piled on top of him in celebration.

There was still time for United to pour forward in search of a late equaliser and for Wreh to miss, in his words, 'An absolute sitter. The ball came in late to me, but I flapped at the ball, and somehow dragged it wide when it looked easier to score.'

As the teams trooped off the Jumbotrons once again zoomed in on Ferguson. He spat his chewing gum out in disgust on to the turf and stomped off with his players. 'It was breathless out there. It gave us all a massive sense of achievement,' recalled Overmars, 'but we never got carried away.'

The victory didn't signal an upsurge in Arsenal's form. They lost at home to Liverpool, and then to Blackburn Rovers. Wright was heckled at the final whistle and when he remonstrated with fans in Avenell Road from the dressing room window, police were called. Wenger sent Adams, suffering from knee and ankle problems, on a month-long sabbatical in the south of France to regain fitness.

Press articles focused on the defence's age and fragility, and internal wrangles. In *The Observer*, Peter Robinson wrote, 'The great Arsenal back four, the buttress on which success was built, may at last be dismantled.' Others talked of the creaking *entente cordiale*. *The Mirror*'s Mike Walters suggested, 'Gallic subtlety is in danger of marginalising English grit.'

In *Addicted*, Adams admitted that several players reckoned Petit and Vieira were 'indisciplined 45 minute players'. There was a forthright team meeting and a follow-up debate at the Cafe Royal, where Adams, Bould and Keown put their grievances forward to Petit and Vieira.

'Tony and the others told Manu and me that they needed us to play for the full 90 minutes, and that we needed to protect them. Tony said that in the successful Arsenal teams he'd played in, the midfield had always protected the back four. Playing as individuals wouldn't get us anywhere. It was a very powerful speech and it stayed with me throughout my career at Arsenal. It reminded Manu and me of what was expected of us,' recalled Vieira.

It was a turning point, although it didn't feel like it. As the Christmas schedule approached, with the team beset by injuries, loss of form and suspensions, they found themselves 13 points behind United, although the floodlight failure at Wimbledon meant Arsenal had a game in hand.

Arsenal embarked on a monumental 26-match unbeaten run, and Vieira and Petit became the most devastating midfield partnership in the Premier League. Overmars recalls, 'If you asked any fan to remember the games in January that season, I bet they'd struggle. But that's not important, because although we played so well later in spring, we dug in and kept going in the winter. We were tougher than people thought.'

Arsenal scraped five points from deep-winter clashes with Leicester, Spurs and Coventry. Wright made his last meaningful impact in an Arsenal shirt in domestic cup matches. Due to injuries and suspensions, Wenger switched to a 4-3-3 formation, rotating any two from Vieira, Petit, Platt or Stephen Hughes to play alongside the massively improved Ray Parlour in midfield. Overmars was pushed further forward to join the attack.

It was an inspired decision, perfectly illustrated when the Dutchman slammed home two goals against Leeds in January. Despite this gradual upturn in Arsenal's fortunes, one Manchester bookmaker paid out early on United winning the title. Following a 1-0 victory away at Wimbledon, on the night United dropped two points against West Ham, Wenger claimed, 'I honestly believe we can do it. But then perhaps I'm a little crazy.'

Arsenal trailed United by nine points with three games in hand, meaning punters could back Arsenal at odds of 7-2. Crazily, if the Gunners could prevail in their Old Trafford experience in late March, there was even a chance they could complete the Double. But that was highly unlikely.

The United v Arsenal match was a patchwork of drama and near misses. It was also the day on which Overmars came of age in an Arsenal shirt. He recalled, 'I was told to use my pace, and cut inside and cause damage when possible, and to be as direct as possible.'

In the first half, Overmars sliced through the United defence twice. On one occasion, defender John Curtis appeared to bring down the Arsenal man. No penalty was awarded. The second time, he scythed past Curtis, only to blast the ball into the side netting as Schmeichel crashed in. 'On another day, I could easily have had two by half-time, and the game could have been over,' shrugged Overmars.

At the other end, Manninger made last-ditch saves from Andy Cole and Ole Gunnar Solskjaer. The United crowd grew restless. The 1,500 travelling Arsenal supporters got louder and louder. Vieira and Petit nullified United's midfield threat, which didn't go unnoticed by Ferguson.

The winner was a classic fusion of old and new. Petit delivered a long, probing pass, Anelka flicked on the header, and Overmars galloped on to the ball, dashed forward 20 yards, and slipped his shot under Schmeichel. 'I put my head down, ran as fast as I could, and placed it. The whole process was done with in a flash,' recalled Overmars in typically concise style.

'Arsenal will slip up. You can be assured of that,' insisted Ferguson. They didn't. Vieira recalled, 'We decided that from then on, we weren't going to let it slip.' Arsenal nabbed three 1-0 victories on the bounce, giving Wreh his chance to carve out a name for himself with the winners against Bolton in the league and Wolves in the FA Cup semi-final. Wreh explained, 'I think that once we'd got past those games, we could really open up and enjoy ourselves.'

And enjoy themselves they did, winning 5-0 at home to Highbury bogey team Wimbledon, and marauding past Blackburn 4-1 away at Ewood Park when an impromptu snowstorm necessitated the need for an orange ball in the second half. There was the 3-1 win at home to Newcastle with Anelka's double topped off by Vieira's thunderous shot from 30 yards. 'I never hit a goal so straight and true,' he explained.

There was also the obligatory backs-to-the-wall 1-0 victory, courtesy of a Petit goal just as the going got tough. On this occasion it came against Derby, with happy echoes of those vital single-goal wins from the Bertie Mee and George Graham eras. And when it really mattered, Arsenal turned on the style at home to Everton in their last match of the season.

Rightly, it is Adams's half-volley from Bould's chipped pass — thrashed in to make the score 4-0 — which for many Arsenal fans remains their abiding memory of the club captain. Once Graham's hard-drinking, tough-tackling lieutenant, he had evolved into Wenger's thoughtful, ball-playing, tough-tackling lieutenant.

Following the 2-0 win against Newcastle at Wembley which secured the club's second Double, Lee Dixon claimed, 'This surpasses anything we have done in the past.' That may be subjective, but given the style in which the team won the Double he may well be correct.

The dynamos behind the Everton and Newcastle wins? Overmars and Petit. Now in full flow since early spring, Overmars was simply unstoppable once he had skipped ahead of his man. He scored twice against Everton, roaring forward again and again, and once against Newcastle. And Petit, badly injured against Everton following a reckless tackle, constantly extinguished Newcastle's attempts to fight back in the FA Cup Final.

'Manu and I were frustrated because it was quite a slow game in the heat,' recalled Vieira. 'Perhaps a few months earlier, we'd have pushed forward and been impatient and reckless. But we learned how to stay in control, and not to panic. We'd learned so much, so quickly as a whole team.'

It was the manner of Arsenal's play which was such a sea change, and which drew plaudits from a bewildering array of sources. On the 1998 title run-in the home crowd at Oakwell broke into spontaneous chants of 'ole' every time an Arsenal player received the ball in the Gunners' 2-0 win over Barnsley, and formed a guard of honour when the away team's bus departed. George Graham's sides often used to slink away, with boos ringing in their ears. Newcastle manager Kenny Dalglish, so grudging in his praise of Graham's team a decade or so before, remarked, 'Arsenal have been the best team by a country mile this season. I've enjoyed watching them, and they are fitting champions.'

In an era of global saturation coverage, Arsenal's makeover was completed during the summer in the World Cup finals. Bergkamp's beautifully executed goal against Argentina, an aesthetic delight, won him the BBC's goal of the tournament award. When Vieira threaded through a glorious ball for Petit in the dying minutes of the final against Brazil, the ponytailed Frenchman neatly slotted his shot past Claudio Taffarel to make the score 3-0. 'It was an incredible few months,' admitted Vieira. 'After winning the league and then the World Cup, you think to yourself, "Anything is possible."'

After France's victory, the tabloids showed a photograph of the two Frenchmen embracing on the turf. 'ARSENAL WIN THE WORLD CUP' boomed *The Sun*. With all that had happened in the last few months under Arsène Wenger, it certainly felt like it. From the humdrum, reactionary outfit of just three years earlier, Arsenal had morphed into a side which had set the benchmark for other clubs to aspire.

# Invincible?

*'That era had to be the best time of all for Arsenal fans. The football we played often seemed to be off the scale. It was a privilege to play in that side.' Robert Pires, speaking in 2007.*

*'I think you can say that the 2003/04 season was probably the last time that it was all about the football and just the football. After that it became about other things, like worries about money, and questioning where the team was heading.' Gilberto, speaking in 2008.*

IN THE four fallow seasons that followed Wenger's first Double, his main challenge was to settle on his favoured formation up front. There were numerous subtle tactical shifts. The 1998 formation – Wenger's classic Mark 1 Arsenal side – adhered to the core strength of Herbert Chapman's teams, the counter-attack. The defence, or the Petit–Vieira midfield axis, broke down the opposition's moves and shifted the ball to the fast-running Parlour, or turbo-charged Overmars, who then fed Wright, Anelka, or Bergkamp. It was about pace, precision, and incision. The 1998/99 vintage, without the poaching instincts of a predator like the departed Ian Wright, played to the strengths of the ultra-direct Nicolas Anelka.

At times in 1998/99, the style of performance was even better than that of the previous season. After Christmas, Anelka and Bergkamp – the latter's slide-rule passes to the Frenchman a master class in inch-perfect precision and timing – often dovetailed to devastating effect. Anelka's hat-trick in the 5-0 destruction of Leicester was arguably his finest performance in an Arsenal shirt, although the increasingly listless Frenchman couldn't summon up the *joie de vivre* to smile.

There was also the jiggery-pokery displayed by the new signing from Inter Milan, Kanu. After the Nigerian's winning goal against Derby in the FA Cup quarter-final, *The Times*'s Matt Dickinson wrote that he 'tiptoed through the flying tackles with a grace and guile that should not be possible with a basketball player's physique'. His telescopic legs, soft shoe control and adroitness at dummying opposition defenders and goalkeepers left many defences befuddled in his early Arsenal displays, never better illustrated than his back-heeled goal in the 6-1 destruction of Middlesbrough, or his sublime flick of the ball over the head of Tottenham's Luke Young and devastating finish in Arsenal's 3-1 win at White Hart Lane in May.

'Kanu was a conjuror. A magician,' recalled Edu, 'but I did sometimes get the impression that he didn't always know what the end of his trick would be.' And so it proved. Kanu was rather too singular for his own good. He wasn't really a target man. He wasn't a predator in the box, and he lacked pace. Wenger also seemed unsure as to where to slot Kanu in the team. Kanu often seemed perplexed as to his best position too, and the situation was never fully resolved during his five years at the club.

It wasn't quite enough though, and Arsenal were pipped to the title by Manchester United, and defeated by Alex Ferguson's team in the FA Cup semi-final replay at Villa Park courtesy of Ryan Giggs's outstanding solo goal.

A key reason was Arsenal's conservative approach in the transfer market. Two experienced players, David Platt and Ian Wright, departed and weren't replaced after the 1998 Double. The hot favourite to replace Wright was Dutch striker Patrick Kluivert. The stumbling block proved not to be the reported £10m fee, more Kluivert's demand for around £60,000 per week. Despite hiss keenness on moving to Highbury, chairman Peter Hill-Wood announced the deal would not be taking place. 'Books have to be balanced, and why should a club go dangerously close to financial suicide for the sake of signing a player short term?'

It was an odd statement. Kluivert had just turned 22. Given that Arsenal would have a guaranteed six extra matches to play in 1998/99 due to Champions League commitments, and that Bergkamp wouldn't fly to away games in Europe, Arsenal seemed underprepared.

It was becoming a prerequisite that for a successful season both in Europe and domestically, teams needed four strikers in the squad. Arsenal had only three, Bergkamp, Anelka and Wreh, and Wreh barely figured at all from then on. Arsenal made a sluggish start to the campaign in which they failed to score in four consecutive early league matches. Bergkamp looked out of sorts and Anelka looked increasingly disaffected as the campaign had worn on.

Arsenal racked up the goals in the latter stages of the season but failed to score in ten of their league matches. Patrick Vieira says, 'In our position, United would probably have gone for him [Kluivert] and it would probably have worked for them. Arsène was very creative when it came to who he signed, thinking about how the player could be adapted to the team's needs, like Thierry, rather than just throwing money around. Sometimes a club maybe has to go for it, like we probably should have done with Kluivert. Alongside Kanu, Bergkamp and Anelka, he'd have given us an edge.'

After Anelka departed in the close-season to Real Madrid, left-footed Croatian striker Davor Šuker came in the opposite direction for £3.5m, but his speed of thought around goal couldn't compensate for the loss of Anelka's speed of foot. Šuker never gained a regular place in the starting line-up.

Wenger spent another £10m on Juventus forward Thierry Henry, with whom he had worked at Monaco when Henry was a youth team striker. Henry had spent an unhappy season stranded out on the wing in Italy. Wenger told him that he wanted to bring him into a more central position. Keen to distance himself from the outgoing Anelka, Henry said, 'Nicolas lives his life and I live mine.' Henry made a stuttering start to his Arsenal career, partly because Wenger seemed unsure as to precisely what his best forward line was. In those first few months, Henry suffered from minor thigh and hamstring strains. Often, he was used as a substitute.

Henry confessed that his performance against Liverpool, in a game that Arsenal lost 2-0, was the worst of his career. He missed several chances against Bradford City. Wenger rotated Kanu, Šuker, Henry and Bergkamp, trying to work out which combination worked best. Henry netted his first Arsenal goal against Southampton at The Dell in September, swivelling and crashing in his shot from 25 yards out. His celebration was more one of relief than anything else. He later told Philippe Auclair, 'It takes time to relearn how to move, to bend your run and find the right angle to score goals.'

Freddie Ljungberg also struggled to find his feet after moving from Swedish club Halmstads a year before. Gradually, Henry pulled it together, using his pace to eviscerate the Derby defence in a late-November 2-1 win. Injuries to Kanu and Bergkamp aided Henry's cause as Wenger was forced to deploy him as a central striker. He got more robust too, holding off Chelsea's Marcel Desailly to score in a 2-1 home win in May. Overmars recalls, 'Thierry took a little time to find his feet partly because the forwards were being churned all the time.'

Some of the most sublime Henry/Kanu moments came in the UEFA Cup where Arsenal scored 21 goals in eight games to reach the final. Henry and Kanu were in majestic form during the 5-1 hammering of Deportivo La Coruna at Highbury. 'The defences weren't of such a high quality,' explains Vieira, 'and once we got our necks in front, Thierry and Kanu could relax a bit more. It helped Thierry get his bearings at the club, I think. Some of the angles those two worked in games were astonishing, and then you had Dennis who was such an unorthodox thinker too.'

Arsenal's forwards continued to shape their moves. At Stamford Bridge on 7 September 2000, Arsenal fought back from two goals down to draw 2-2 at Chelsea. One of the goals was hugely significant but sadly for Brazilian left-back Sylvinho, it wasn't his stupendously swerving 25-yard blockbuster that had positively fizzed its way past Cudicini. Dazzling though that strike was, Henry's goal was a symbol of what was to come. From a flicked chest pass by Bergkamp, Sylvinho slipped the ball down the inside-left channel to Henry, who took one touch with his left foot and then swerved the ball round Cudicini with his right. It became Henry's signature Arsenal goal but despite a second high-scoring campaign for the Frenchman, no silverware was forthcoming.

There appeared to be an embarrassment of riches up front with Sylvain Wiltord joining early in the season for £15m from Bordeaux. But the team appeared to have become 'specialists in failure' before the phrase was even coined. There was a lacklustre loss to Galatasaray in the 2000 UEFA Cup Final and they were mugged by Liverpool in the dying minutes of the 2001 FA Cup Final.

'As the English say, that Liverpool match was daylight robbery,' recalls Vieira. 'Incredible, incredible.' Vieira lamented the departure the previous summer of Petit to Barcelona, and at times Arsenal's midfield looked lightweight.

Like Kanu and Ljungberg, new signing Robert Pires had been frustratingly inconsistent, often disappearing entirely from matches. Tony Adams reckoned Arsenal needed another leader at the back – or a 'big game defender' as he called it. Henry suggested that Arsenal needed a poacher up front. Arsenal got their 'fox in the box' – Everton's Francis Jeffers. Sol Campbell joined from Tottenham Hotspur and grew more influential in central defence as the season went on. Giovanni Van Bronckhorst added depth in midfield. Pires reflected, 'The big difference in 2001 was that no one left and rocked the boat.' Vieira recalls, 'Sometimes it's about stability, and sometimes, you have a season where everyone seems to click. And that's what happened.'

⌣ ⌣ ⌣ ⌣ ⌣

Arsenal began the new campaign under something of a cloud. Vieira was strongly linked with a move to Old Trafford where Ferguson planned to play him alongside Paul Scholes. Several sources have confirmed that Ferguson had every intention of taking Vieira north but Arsenal refused to enter into discussions with the champions. Ferguson had already spent over £50m on midfielder Juan Sebastian Veron and striker Ruud van Nistelrooy. Journalist Steven Howard wrote in *The Sun*, 'There could be no greater loss of face or admission they are second best than allowing the heartbeat of their team to be ripped out and transplanted into the chest of the very team they are spending millions on trying to catch.'

Vieira stayed, despite allegedly telling a friend, 'I'm off,' with Real Madrid also prepared to offer a huge sum for his services. With Henry warning that the gap between Arsenal and United 'was far too big for anyone at Highbury to be happy with', the campaign began with Arsenal's rivals firm favourites to retain their crown. 'I feel that it will be all about who's recruited most effectively,' explained Wenger.

United had sold Jaap Stam in the close-season, a move which Ferguson later admitted was 'my biggest mistake in the transfer market'. He wasn't adequately replaced. Meanwhile, Arsenal's addition of Tottenham captain Campbell, though highly controversial, proved a masterstroke in a team where the longevity of Martin Keown and Adams was on the wane. 'It took a while for me to realise what a good signing he [Campbell] was,' recalled Pires. 'At first he wasn't fully fit, but once he got his confidence back, he became more dominant, and he was very quick over a few yards.'

Doubts were raised about Arsenal's ability to deliver up until late November. When Leeds beat Arsenal 2-1 at Highbury in their opening home match, Ian McGarry wrote in the *Daily Mail*, 'If Arsène Wenger's side is to do better than their second place of the past three years, they will have to show far greater character than this.' They squeezed through their Champions League group without gaining a single point on their travels to Schalke, Panathinaikos or Mallorca.

In *The Observer*, Andy Dunn suggested Henry was 'ever so jolly putting Premiership journeymen to the sword, but a moody absentee when the going gets tough in Europe'. In Greece, Henry had to be restrained by police while remonstrating with the referee after Arsenal's loss. Against Newcastle at Highbury following a 3-1 home defeat, Henry turned on Graham Poll, leaving visiting manager Bobby Robson to comment, 'A lot of people around Highbury have got to learn how to lose.'

Newcastle went top after their win, with Liverpool, Leeds, Arsenal and United firmly in the hunt. Arsenal were by no means infallible in that part of the season – Pires recalls the sense of 'bewilderment after we lost 4-2 to Charlton after we had 25 shots on target and they had nine'. But piece by piece the Gunners were getting it together, individually and collectively.

Ashley Cole, having warded off competition from Sylvinho, began to look the part at left-back. Campbell, who had looked rusty and slightly overweight in his early days at Highbury, got through his stern initiation test at White Hart Lane unscathed as Arsenal drew 1-1. And Henry proved that, on his day, he could get the better of any team in the Premier League, perfectly illustrated when he scored a dramatic late winner at home to Aston Villa to give his team a 3-2 win that barely seemed possible given their shambolic first-half performance.

In the dying minutes of their Champions League tie with Juventus, Bergkamp, introduced by Wenger supposedly to kill the pace of the game, took a pass from Ljungberg. Bergkamp turned one way and then another, then back again, before flicking the ball over a defender to the Swede. One delicate chip later and Arsenal had their finest European goal of the season in their 3-1 win.

The Bergkamp/Ljungberg combination proved potent. At Anfield, Ljungberg slammed home the winner after fine work by Pires down the left. 'There was nothing in particular that we worked on in training, Freddie and me, or Freddie and Dennis, but we all shared the collective vision of how the game should be played,' explained Pires. 'Under Wenger, you could do nothing but. When you play with team-mates week in and week out, and you're settled and happy, you start to get a sense of telepathy about what the other will do. It's a very powerful experience when it happens.'

Ljungberg and Bergkamp's telepathic understanding reached a perfect pitch at just the right time of the season. It was slide-rule, geometric precision, that picked the lock of defences which had done their level best to slam the back door firmly shut. On Easter Monday, Ljungberg slipped the ball home against Tottenham after the Dutchman's fine-tuned pass, and the underrated Lauren scored the winning penalty to put Arsenal two points clear with a game in hand.

Ljungberg was in the right place again against Ipswich and West Ham, all courtesy of Bergkamp passes. Pires recalled, 'Freddie had an injury of his own, but then when I injured my knee, he slotted in well on the left flank, where I'd been playing. At the end of the season, he was flying. When a player is in form like that, you just let them fly, and fly.'

On a foul night at the Reebok Stadium, with Arsenal smelling silver polish, Bergkamp delayed his killer pass, and then delayed it some more, waiting for Ljungberg to make his move. Surrounded by a forest of Bolton defenders' legs, the Dutchman threaded the ball through the eye of a needle. With precision timing Ljungberg seized the pass and slammed the ball past goalkeeper Jaaskelainen. Bergkamp picked out yet another sumptuous pass on the stroke of half-time and Wiltord put Arsenal 2-0 up.

Four days later they defeated Chelsea at the Millennium Stadium in the FA Cup Final. It was a scrappy affair but goals by Ljungberg and Parlour, both expertly curled past Cudicini, were the difference between the two London clubs. Now all the Gunners needed was a draw at Old Trafford and a third Double would be theirs.

It wasn't until the mid-noughties that the Ferguson/Wenger relationship turned seriously prickly. But as the two clubs prepared to lock horns in May 2002 there was definitely needle in the air, probably because Ferguson knew that his team wouldn't emerge on top from this skirmish. Any verbal jibes from Old Trafford were batted firmly back. 'We've played the better football since the turn of the New Year,' insisted Ferguson. Wenger's response? 'Everyone thinks they have the prettiest wife at home.'

In Michael Crick's excellent *The Boss: The Many Sides of Alex Ferguson*, he suggests that Ferguson believed Wenger might have been making a dig at his wife Cathy. Ferguson appeared desperate and short-tempered before the game.

He had been railing all season at suggestions that Arsenal had got more bang for their buck from their summer signings, and when asked by football journalist Neil Custis in the lead-up to the Arsenal game about Juan Sebastian Veron's future, Ferguson declared, 'Veron's a great player. Yous are fucking idiots' to the assembled press corps. But aside from Wenger mischievously saying, 'What are all those little asterisks for?' when he read the transcripts of Ferguson's expletive-filled rant at the press, he barely mentioned the United boss at all publicly or privately.

'In all the time I was at Arsenal,' recalls Edu, 'Wenger never once mentioned him [Ferguson] in team talks. There was rivalry between the two clubs, sure, but it never became a case of him using Ferguson's words to motivate us.' Was the team aware of Ferguson's words prior to games? 'Yes of course, but we were made aware of them by journalists, not Wenger.'

On 2 May, Arsenal travelled to Old Trafford and won 1-0. In his autobiography, Roy Keane described it as 'men against boys'. 'Roy's comment is maybe a bit generous,' explains Vieira, 'but it was a fantastically controlled display.'

United fought for every ball, as would be expected. Scholes and Phil Neville were booked. So was Keane, for his late challenge on Vieira, but aside from a Veron free kick and a Scholes effort the home side were held easily at bay.

The midfield pairing of Edu and Vieira stayed firm and although Campbell and Keown had some worrying moments, Arsenal created the two best chances of the game. In the opening minutes, Wiltord's goalbound shot was deflected over, but midway through the second half, with United committing more men forward, Wiltord and Ljungberg broke in tandem. The Frenchman fed the Swede, whose scampering run and shot was pushed into the path of Wiltord by Fabien Barthez. Wiltord was on hand to slam the loose ball past his international colleague.

Arsenal had done it without arguably their three best performers – Henry, Bergkamp and Pires – starting the game. 'We'd been written off at different times, and we were questioned as to whether we'd win anything under Wenger again,' recalled Vieira.

After the match, Arsène Wenger said, 'This is an unbelievable feeling…we wanted there to be a shift of power and to bring the Premiership trophy back home to Highbury is fantastic.' But although there was further glory to come, there was no permanent power shift to north London.

The early signs of financial restructuring had been visible since the 1997 AGM, when the board announced that a feasibility study was being launched into the possible redevelopment of Highbury – a stadium with a 38,000 capacity that was, in Brian Glanville's words, 'a bad joke'. There were conversations about building options in the Kings Cross area and off the M25 in Hertfordshire, but when the club revealed that Champions League games would be played at Wembley for the 1998/99 campaign that gave a fairly clear indication of where their thinking lay.

Arsenal tabled a £125m bid for the ground in late 1997 with Dein and Fiszman keen to push the deal through. By May 1999, the option to remain at Highbury had fallen through and so did the Wembley bid due to the Wembley licence limiting the number of games which could be held there. Broadly speaking, the Wembley option proved a success with the ground being sold out for each of the Gunners' three group stage matches, although Arsenal's European displays in 1998/99 were insipid. Later that year, the *Daily Telegraph* suggested that Arsenal, within eight years, would be playing football in Hertfordshire, Bedfordshire, or Buckinghamshire, casting serious doubts over whether 'the soul of the club can possibly survive in the future'.

Incredibly, the answer to this knotty and seemingly insurmountable problem lay on Arsenal's doorstep – quite literally. Arsenal fan Antony Spencer, who ran major West End retail estate consultancy Anthony, Green and Spencer, was keen to keep the club as close as possible to Highbury. In late 1999, using a London A-Z and a CD, he started investigating possibilities. He recalled, 'Arsenal were looking at greenfield sites, and I was looking at brownfield sites. I am a dyslexic, so have always been a bit of a lateral thinker. I was in my boardroom, looking at a map of the area, and I just saw this big triangle of land staring back at me. It was Ashburton Grove. Pretty much a stone's throw from Highbury. It was a Eureka! moment for me. I superimposed a picture of Wembley onto Ashburton Grove and it fitted in there perfectly.'

Over the next few days, Spencer, convinced this down-heeled industrial site really could be Arsenal's future home, brought a team of experts to the site to check the viability of the plan and also discovered it was earmarked for regeneration.

Spencer realised that not only could a new stadium be constructed there, but that the whole project could bring thousands of jobs to the borough and help regenerate the area.

When Spencer informed the board that the site was just 500 yards away from Highbury, there was a sense of disbelief among all those present but over the next few years, the project took shape. It came at a cost though.

⌣ ⌣ ⌣ ⌣ ⌣

'By around the 2002/03 season, we all knew about the money situation,' admitted Edu. 'When you've got United spending £50m on Veron and Van Nistelrooy, and then £30m on Rio Ferdinand, and we spend around £6m [total] on Gilberto and Pascal [Cygan], you know where the whole thing's going. It became so important just to keep the squad together.'

World Cup winner Gilberto Silva joined the squad to work in tandem with Vieira. The Frenchman – promoted to the role of skipper following the departure of Tony Adams – refers to Gilberto as 'the wall' and in time, the Brazilian would be as potent a midfield force as Emmanuel Petit.

Arsenal began the campaign in devastating form, winning seven and drawing two of their opening nine league games. Their 4-1 win at Leeds, with Kanu and Henry in scintillating form, was one of the finest victories of the Wenger era. An irresistible 4-0 victory away at Dutch champions PSV Eindhoven almost beggared belief with Arsenal's superb counter-attacking moves ripping the Dutch side's defence to shreds.

But the Gunners' all-consuming self-belief was mistaken for arrogance, particularly after Wenger was misquoted as claiming that his side could go through the league season unbeaten. 'When you lose only three games, as we did last season, I set a target to do better. What can I say to the players? Do I set a target to do worse?' retorted Wenger. A mocking *When Saturday Comes* front cover encapsulated the perception of Arsenal at the time. Pires tells Kanu, 'We're absolutely brilliant,' and Kanu responds, 'And so modest too.'

After 17-year-old Wayne Rooney grabbed a late, late winner for Everton at Goodison Park in October, a dangerous combination of brittleness and aloofness crept into Arsenal's persona. Perhaps it was due to the hype which surrounded Henry. Twenty minutes into a match at Highbury against Tottenham in November, he ran from just inside his own half, outpaced the entire Tottenham midfield, sidestepped Matthew Etherington and slammed the ball past Kasey Keller. Henry celebrated by running virtually the whole length of the pitch, screaming like a madman at anyone who cared to look at him, and slid to his knees in front of the Spurs fans, who responded, in Edu's words, 'by indicating that they thought he should go and fuck himself'.

'I think I read that over 100 million people had seen that match on satellite television around the world,' explains Edu. 'Shortly afterwards, he began appearing in the Renault Clio ads, and became linked with the Va Va Voom catchphrase.'

Wenger labelled him 'the best player in the world'. Subtly, Henry's on-pitch demeanour was changing when things didn't go his way. 'At his worst, he is sulky, sloppy, simpering… Maybe he and his team-mates should settle for the ugly tap-in or ragged rebound,' wrote Russell Kempson in *The Times*.

Brian Woolnough recalled, 'Several of my colleagues reckoned that Arsenal had become too precious. In Wenger's opinion, defeating Arsenal was almost like defiling a piece of fine art. Arsenal were about aesthetics and beauty, with all their foreign artisans. They didn't like being touched or impeded. Henry would throw up his hands, and Vieira would lose his temper and remonstrate. The feeling was that Arsenal refused to play "ugly" and score "ugly goals".'

In other words, there were no 'fox in the box' style goals – and Francis Jeffers was failing to integrate himself into the side. 'It was difficult for him [Jeffers],' recalls Gilberto, 'because his strengths really didn't fit in with the way Arsenal played. Wiltord was the nearest thing we deployed to a "poacher". But he was very versatile. Arsène's team played in a particular way, and that didn't really include a traditional striker like Jeffers.'

In the increasingly personality driven world of the Premier League the press had long been obsessed with the individual foibles of Arsenal's players, ever since the start of the foreign 'invasion'. Bergkamp; increasingly susceptible to colds and muscle cramps from May 1998 onwards. Steadfastly refusing to fly. Nicolas Anelka; professing to be 'bored with London' before his £25m move to Real Madrid in the summer of 1999. Emmanuel Petit; ('I'm not an animal, I am a human being') claiming that English referees had 'a vendetta' against him before he and Overmars departed for Barcelona in the summer of 2000, a year after Anelka jumped ship.

French truculence increased as English influence waned, so the tabloids claimed. Bould and Winterburn departed. Adams, Dixon and Keown weren't always regular starters. 'Journalists were obsessed with whether the French players got on OK with the English boys,' admits Edu, the Brazilian who joined in early 2001. 'I pretended I didn't understand what they were asking me. Anyway, at least it made a change from them asking me about my passport,' he laughs.

Earlier in the season, Wenger labelled his side 'the best team in Europe at the moment'. Such grandiose claims didn't go down well at Old Trafford, and United were able to comfortably defeat Arsenal

2-0 at home in November, eventually whittling down the Gunners' supposedly unassailable lead at the top of the table to take the title in May.

Wenger didn't remain ultra-cool. He ripped his tie off in frustration as Bolton set about his team at the Reebok, fighting back from 2-0 down to grab a draw which effectively killed off Arsenal's title challenge. Wenger prowled the touchline tetchily as he saw both Lauren and Ljungberg kicked out of the contest, joining Campbell and Vieira on the sidelines. With Dixon and Adams no longer around, Arsenal didn't like it 'up 'em', apparently. All of this at a time when the building work on the new ground stalled due to the Royal Bank of Scotland refusing to underwrite the project.

In many ways, the Bolton match was a turning point. Wenger began to come across as a seriously bad loser, defending Campbell to the hilt despite TV evidence that his centre-half deserved a red card after elbowing Manchester United striker Ole Gunnar Solskjaer in the throat during the sides' 2-2 draw at Highbury in April. By now, he and Ferguson were barely on speaking terms and much was made of Wenger's refusal to pen his counterpart a letter of congratulation after United won the title. Ferguson always made a point of dropping a line to the title-winning manager at the end of the campaign. 'I am not a great writer,' Wenger told *The Telegraph*'s Henry Winter.

Wenger's Arsenal still got to Ferguson though. Ferguson caricatured London as a cliquey environment in which the seat of power, the Football Association (David Dein was vice chairman), the refereeing Headquarters and Arsenal were conspiring against his club. With the Gunners' planned move to Ashburton Grove, Arsenal would soon draw in another 20,000 well-heeled punters, with the aim of matching United's spending power. Ferguson often seemed needled by his capital rivals. After his side's 2-0 FA Cup defeat to the Gunners in February, Ferguson kicked a boot in frustration at David Beckham for failing to deal effectively with the attacking threat of Ashley Cole. Beckham needed stitches in his wound.

Arsenal retained the FA Cup with a narrow 1-0 win over Southampton, thanks to Pires's goal, but as Vieira commented, 'That couldn't make up for blowing the title.' Neither could it make up for another hugely frustrating exit from the Champions League in the

New Year. In late February 2003, the always erudite Martin Samuel wrote in *The Times*, 'There comes a moment in the development of a team when it cannot stand still. It has to take another step up the ladder or go backwards. To advance, Arsenal must make an impact in Europe this season. If they do not, the consequences could be far reaching.'

The gist of what Samuel said was that each year, the challenge for Arsenal's superstars lay more and more in the Champions League.

'This was our fifth campaign in the Champions League,' explained Edu. 'We believed it was now time for Arsenal to make its mark.' Going into the crucial second phase group clash match with Roma at Highbury, the Gunners knew that victory against the bottom-placed club in Group B would virtually guarantee qualification for the quarter-finals. It should have been straightforward given that Totti was sent off after only 20 minutes for attempting to thump Martin Keown.

Arsenal were often at their showboating worst, squandering several chances to make the game safe after Vieira put Arsenal ahead and moving the ball about to one another in ornate triangles. They pushed further and further forwards when they only needed to protect their lead. While Arsenal maintained their quest for a perfect goal, Roma's Emerson kept things simple and spotted Cassano drifting away from Cygan. Cassano slammed home his shot to make the score 1-1.

Arsenal flapped around in the final minutes desperately trying to win the game but Roma dug a defensive ditch that the Gunners were never going to penetrate. 'We played right into their hands,' admits Gilberto. 'We committed too much when we didn't need to early on, and then we panicked when we still had plenty of time to win the game. Even Roma, who weren't a great team, were able to vary their tactics. We couldn't. We only knew how to play one way.'

In other words, there was no Plan B. Similarly naive tactics had been deployed at home in draws against Valencia and Ajax, games which Arsenal should also have won.

At the Mestalla in 2001 they nervously chased the game when a draw would have taken Arsenal into the semi-finals. They went out to two John Carew goals. Wenger blamed Valencia's time-wasting tactics for his side's defeat but the truth was that Arsenal had simply been outmanoeuvred and outfoxed in their second phase games. 'Arsenal are a great team,' explained Roma manager Fabio Capello after their Highbury clash, 'but it's fairly easy to predict what they might do next.'

But no one could have predicted what Arsenal would do next, during the 2003/04 season. It was to be a glorious campaign, but poignant and bittersweet too.

The 2003/04 campaign can be scrutinised in much the same way as historians view the mythical golden summer of 1913 – the final blissful days of a peaceful Europe before the spectre of conflict blotted out the sun. One can wallow in the moment and focus solely on the heavenly football served up by the 'Invincibles' during the campaign or one can adopt a more circumspect approach, scanning the horizon for impending storm clouds.

Other tomes luxuriate in Pires's gravity defying winner against Liverpool at Anfield, or the miraculous intricacies of Vieira's goals at White Hart Lane. The raison d'étre of this book is to investigate the giddy blend of high points and turning points of that season.

A new force was rising in west London. Chelsea splashed approximately £90m on new players during the close-season, including Claude Makelele, Adrian Mutu and Juan Sebastian Veron. Other signings, the likes of Damien Duff, Wayne Bridge and Joe Cole, had previously been linked with Arsenal. Now Chelsea were buying them up at inflated prices once Roman Abramovich arrived in July.

'I think it is a shame for football, as sanity was being restored to transfer fees,' remarked Wenger. All of this came at a time when Arsenal pulled up the drawbridge and spent a combined £4m on defender Philippe Senderos and goalkeeper Jens Lehmann, who replaced the released David Seaman.

Chairman Peter Hill-Wood went public in the *Evening Standard* and beat out what would become a familiar tune, 'The stadium has not affected the transfer budget. We have tried to keep the two budgets apart.' Hill-Wood made no mention of Chelsea's new-found wealth but, after discovering that the Blues had signed Cole and Veron, Wenger commented, 'Chelsea must buy a new team coach as well then. To get everybody on. When you have money you can buy. It is as simple as that, but it looks to me that it won't be the end.'

It certainly wasn't, but the huge churn in players at Chelsea worked to Arsenal's advantage and for the time being at least, the focus remained almost solely on the football. The Gunners made a flying start to the campaign, winning their opening three games.

Although hardly an uplifting experience, Arsenal's clash with Manchester United at Old Trafford in late summer was pivotal in many ways. Still smarting from Campbell's four-match ban after his sending-off the previous May (Alex Ferguson described Arsenal's decision to appeal the ban as 'nauseating and absurd') and with the side's behaviour under the microscope following Francis Jeffers's dismissal against United a few weeks before in the Community Shield, which marked the end of the striker's Arsenal career, the match was a tetchy one from the start.

Arsenal did a good job of containing United for 80 minutes before Vieira was sent off after kicking out at van Nistelrooy following the Dutchman's foul on him. After van Nistelrooy missed a last-minute penalty he was jostled by several Arsenal players, including Parlour, Lauren, and Keown, who jumped with glee in front of the United striker.

United's players were markedly restrained at the end of the 0-0 draw, in contrast to the Old Trafford brawl some 13 years before. 'Whether this was right or wrong, this was pent-up. There was a team aggression towards him [van Nistelrooy],' explained Keown. 'He was involved in an incident with Patrick Vieira shortly before the penalty, when he took a dive, feigned injury and Vieira was sent off. It felt like the last straw…we'd had enough of him and any respect went.'

In the tunnel afterwards, Vieira threatened to put van Nistelrooy 'down properly'. Wenger wanted his players to fight the subsequent misconduct charges but was overruled by a board anxious to stop, once and for all, the team's indiscipline. Vieira, Cole, Keown, Parlour and Lehmann were all punished but Wenger continued fighting his team's corner all the same.

Wenger described the whole episode as 'trial by Sky TV' and another example of 'Arsenal against the world'. Edu recalls, 'Arsène was very defensive of us. He urged us to keep our cool, but it was a balancing act, because if you are wanting to win the title, you must be combative, but avoid disciplinary problems too.' Gilberto describes 'van Nistelrooy-gate' as 'regrettable in many ways, but it served its purpose, because it bonded the players, and showed that we were on Patrick's side and the manager was on our side'.

Wenger had invoked the spirit of George Graham's Arsenal and it's notable that Keown and Parlour, the last of Graham's lieutenants left at the club, were in the thick of it. The team's discipline improved significantly after the United clash with only Keown and Cole sent off during the remainder of the season. And of course, van Nistelrooy's missed penalty, thundered against the underside of Lehmann's crossbar, meant that Arsenal remained unbeaten, and escaped Old Trafford with a point.

Towards the end of the season, Wenger told ITV's Gabriel Clarke that of all Arsenal's matches that season, the United game was the one that would live longest in his memory. 'We got a point against the champions with a lot of trouble around. It was a turning point.' Not for Wenger, then, any of Henry's stellar goals, or marauding Pires runs. Rather, a team in unison, and the image of a snarling, vein-popping Keown – the oldest Gunner in town – behaving disgracefully.

For purists, the defining fixture might just be Arsenal's November liquidation of Inter Milan in the San Siro. In *Arsenal: 100 Greatest Games* Jem Maidment ranks the match at number two, second only to the 2-0 win at Anfield in 1989. It was certainly one of Arsenal's most stunning results in their history – especially as Inter had swatted Wenger's team aside so effortlessly at Highbury two months previously.

The Gunners needed to win to get their Champions League campaign back on track. After 25 minutes on a miserable Milan evening, Cole and Henry interchanged passes and the Frenchman side-footed the opener. Oddly, Arsenal's huge win was partly as a result of the 'Chelsea effect'. Inter striker Christian Vieri was at loggerheads with the board who had sold Crespo to Chelsea at the start of the campaign. 'They might as well just sell me today. They clearly have no ambition,' Vieri declared on the eve of the Arsenal match.

It didn't prevent Vieri equalising for his side, courtesy of a massive deflection off Campbell, but his refusal to celebrate and the fact that Cannavaro and Javier Zanetti had also criticised the club showed that Inter's players were hardly in a positive frame of mind for the match.

Ljungberg prodded home Henry's pass to make it 2-1 early in the second half but it wasn't until the final nine minutes that Arsenal really lacerated Inter's defence, with Henry, Pires and Edu scoring to make it 5-1. It was a truly remarkable scoreline with Wenger declaring afterwards, 'Not in my wildest dreams could I have predicted a result like that.'

The next morning, *Gazzetta dello Sport* declared, 'Henry umilia l'Inter'. The Frenchman's second goal, when he crossed the halfway line, twice teased defender Javier Zanetti and found a yard of space before firing the ball past Toldo, was indeed ravishing, but as Edu recalled, 'What we did was astounding, but their heads dropped the minute Thierry scored the third. We deserved everything we got from the match, but Inter collapsed in a way that you wouldn't see from an English club in such circumstances. I'm not referring to the scoreline necessarily. Any side can be hammered. I'm referring to the lack of fight in Inter.'

It was a joyous romp; a rare example of Arsenal fulfilling Wenger's (occasionally) myopic wish that they impose their game on European sides – whoever the opposition. But in Europe at least, it was a one-off and not a trend setter.

Arsenal were certainly able to do that at a domestic level as the increasingly messianic Henry demonstrated on an almost weekly basis in the Premier League. There was a match-winning goal against Chelsea at Highbury, plus sumptuous doubles against Wolves on Boxing Day and Manchester City and Southampton early in the New Year, and peerless free kicks against Charlton and Blackburn. He also played a key role in his team's almost regal 5-1 win in the FA Cup at Fratton Park, where Portsmouth fans serenaded the Arsenal team with chants of, 'Can we play you every week?'

Henry swirled in a wondrous goal against Manchester United in the side's draw at Highbury in late March. It left the Gunners seven points ahead of United with eight games remaining. Ferguson correctly predicted, 'Arsenal will win the league now. You can count on that. They're a fabulously gifted side.' His follow-up comment, 'It will be their next three games which define them,' proved uncannily accurate, and in many ways at least, an indication of what would unravel over the next decade.

A rather tame Arsenal lost the FA Cup semi-final to United at Villa Park just a week later. Matches between the two were becoming ever more visceral with hostilities now starting in the tunnel. Prior to the Highbury game there had been an odd moment (preserved on YouTube) where Keane is told by Vieira to 'smile man'. Keane responds, 'I'd be smiling if I were 12 points clear, but we're not.'

Henry and new signing Jose Antonio Reyes – snapped up from Sevilla – were rested from the starting line-up, and this appeared to hand the initiative to United. Arsenal had their chances. Edu lobbed his effort against the crossbar, Kolo Toure's shot was excellently saved by Roy Carroll, and Pires drove wide. But Paul Scholes not only slammed home United's winner, he also eliminated Reyes from the game with a late tackle. 'I instructed my players to get at the Arsenal team,' revealed Ferguson afterwards. 'There's nothing wrong with that.'

Arsenal finished 15 points ahead of United but their record against the Red Devils in head-to-head encounters during that era showed they rarely got the better of Ferguson's side, and that United, although perhaps less artistic at that time, knew which Arsenal players could be bullied into submission.

Four days later, Arsenal faced Chelsea in the second leg of the Champions League quarter-final at home having grabbed a 1-1 draw at Stamford Bridge in the first leg. It was their fifth clash of the season, and so far, Arsenal had emerged from all of them unscathed. The Gunners' first meeting with the newly minted Chelsea took place at Highbury in October 2003. Edu put Arsenal 1-0 up with a deflected free kick but Crespo curled home an exquisite equaliser, and for a while it seemed that the Blues were poised to gain their first league victory at Highbury for 13 years. But a second-half error by Carlo Cudicini allowed Henry to knock home Arsenal's winner.

In the FA Cup in the New Year, Mutu put Chelsea ahead before two excellent goals from Reyes gave Arsenal a 2-1 success. Arsenal's relentless charge towards Premier League glory saw them win 2-1 at Stamford Bridge with goals from Edu and Patrick Vieira.

Wenger appeared to have a sense of unease about the prospect of meeting Chelsea in the Champions League. 'I hope we don't get them,' he confessed to a reporter before the draw had even been made. It was an odd thing to say, given that Arsenal hadn't lost at home to Chelsea since John Bumstead grabbed the winner back in 1990.

Wenger was prickly, too, about Alex Ferguson's hinting that he put money on a Chelsea victory at Highbury in the return leg. 'I pay no attention to what Ferguson says. Why does he not think we will win that match?' asked a tense Wenger.

The mood in the Arsenal camp was that it was a case of now or never in Europe. Edu recalls, 'Claudio Ranieri had his team really fired up, and in a sense, Chelsea had none of the baggage that Arsenal have when it comes to the Champions League. They could just come and prove themselves. Chelsea had some great players, and it was always the case that on a one-off occasion, they could do us some damage.'

Vieira says, 'That was the time to do it [win the competition]. You have to fulfil your potential, your destiny or accept that things must change. After the first leg, it was in our hands, too. It was all set up for us because we had the advantage of the away goal.'

Arsenal played the first half at a thunderous pace. In *Thierry Henry: Lonely At The Top*, Philippe Auclair singles out those 46 minutes as Arsenal's finest passage of play in the entire 2003/04 campaign. They pinged the ball around with almost hypnotic relentlessness. Makelele and Lampard closed down the Arsenal players at every opportunity, which seemed to make the home side play at an ever more furious tempo. Reyes caused mayhem down the left flank. Pires cut in at will. Henry made several coruscating runs at the heart of the Chelsea defence.

Did Arsenal need to play at such an obscenely high tempo? Gilberto explains, 'The mood was that we could kill Chelsea off if we got at them prior to the break. It wasn't in our make-up to sit back, let them come at us, and draw them in. We weren't that type of side.'

In the 37th minute, Arsenal went for the jugular. Pires set up Henry, whose shot was blocked in the Chelsea area. Henry then clattered in an effort which grazed goalkeeper Marco Ambrosio's post. Reyes's inch-perfect cross found Pires, whose header skimmed the side netting. Chelsea survived and Eidur Gudjohnsen could even have given them the lead.

But nine minutes later, Reyes slotted home the opening goal after Henry's shot was again blocked. Highbury erupted and Vieira reflects, 'It was probably the best sustained half of football I saw from us that season.'

Chelsea weren't finished. Like Muhammad Ali in Zaire in 1974, who had been forced to adopt his 'rope-a-dope' tactics in the opening rounds of the 'Rumble in the Jungle' while George Foreman subjected him to savage assaults, they had spent most of the first half swinging in the rigging as Arsenal's hurricane force attacking left them battered and bruised.

But they weren't beaten and in the second half they came off the ropes. Ranieri replaced Scott Parker with the quicker Jesper Gronkjaer at half-time and as Arsenal tired in the second half, Gronkjaer became more influential. Arsenal had punched themselves out but like a headstrong child they tried to play in the same manner as they had in the first half. 'We should have slowed the game down,' admits Edu. 'We only needed to keep the scoreline as it was.' Gaps appeared in Arsenal's rearguard, and Wenger opted only to use one substitute – Bergkamp for the jaded Henry – when he could have deployed two more. It was another example of how the initiative had been tossed away.

Chelsea then landed their knockout punches in rapid succession. Makelele hammered a speculative 30-yard drive at Jens Lehmann, who spilled the ball. Lampard slotted home and it was 1-1. The fatigued Gunners were like distance runners who had gone off too quickly, and ran out of steam in the latter stages. They failed to rally and with six minutes remaining, Bridge and Gudjohnsen played a one-two, to put the English defender clean through on Lehmann. Bridge made no mistake as he slotted the ball home, it was 2-1 to Chelsea and Arsenal were out of Europe.

In his excitement on the touchline, Claudio Ranieri almost self-combusted. The 2,000 Chelsea fans, wedged in the far corner of the Clock End, surged down the steps to salute Bridge as he ran towards them in celebration. Chelsea had got the Arsenal monkey off their backs. In so doing they had exposed the fact that there was no Plan B in Europe for Arsène's Arsenal, who once again had failed to dictate the pace of the game.

The unstoppable blue tidal wave, powered by Abramovich's petrodollars, had finally swept over Arsenal's defences, although Ranieri's side were beaten in the semi-finals. In the midst of Arsenal's superb league campaign, the balance of power had shifted.

⌣ ⌣ ⌣ ⌣ ⌣

Critics suggested that Arsenal's season was poised to blow up in their faces, perhaps allowing Chelsea to sneak in on the blind side. The forthcoming Good Friday clash with Liverpool in the Premier League took on huge significance.

During the first half, Arsenal's performance was poor. Goals by Michael Owen and Sami Hyypia put Liverpool 2-1 up at the interval, the reply coming courtesy of a supposedly half-fit Henry, suffering from back trouble. Gilberto recalls, 'Wenger's team talk was very focused. He reminded us that despite our recent setbacks, we still had the chance to win the Premiership title. But in order to do so, we had to sort out the next 45 minutes.'

The Gunners destroyed Liverpool with a dazzling second-half display and Henry's second goal – a slaloming run from just inside the opposition half which made the score 2-2 – prompted Wenger to comment, 'That shows just how priceless Thierry is to us. I think that we can go on from here and win the Premiership.'

Vieira recalls, 'Beating Liverpool 4-2 helped us get over what had happened against Chelsea. It cleared our path to win the title, and focus on the job in hand, which was now to ensure that we went through the season unbeaten.'

Seven days later, Leeds United, whose win 12 months earlier at Highbury had prevented Arsenal from winning the title, were crushed 5-0. Henry's four-goal haul even had the opposition drooling. Leeds defender Michael Duberry recalls, 'I'd never seen anything quite like Thierry's display that night. He was like a machine. Electrifying – like he was on a higher plane. Every time he received the ball, he burnt us off. It was a horrible season for Leeds that year, but I made a beeline for him afterwards because sometimes you just have to accept that what you've seen is exceptional.'

Arsenal clinched the title at White Hart Lane following a 2-2 draw with Tottenham and on 15 May, after 25 Premier League victories and 12 draws, they defeated relegated Leicester City 2-1 at Highbury to earn their 'Invincibles' tag, a title first bestowed on Preston North End's title-winning side from 1888/89, with Vieira scoring the winner.

After the final whistle, Arsenal fans threw Wenger a t-shirt which had been mocked up by Manchester United fans. The logo on it read 'COMICAL WENGER' (he was pictured with a Frank Spencer-style beret on his head), and he was saying, 'I think we can go the whole season unbeaten.' Wenger paraded it around Highbury.

Gilberto recalled, 'We didn't feel pressure going into the game, but we did feel a huge responsibility. This was our chance to do something which can only ever be equalled, and never beaten. Arsène Wenger is acutely aware of the traditions of the club, and he reminded us that this would be our chance to become – in a footballing sense – immortal. When the final whistle went, it was a fantastic feeling. Ours was a record which will be remembered and talked about throughout the world for years to come.'

Amid the red-and-white ticker tape celebrations, one knotty issue remained. Press leaks suggested that the players would have swapped the unbeaten league record for European success. Understandably, they remain coy on the issue. Edu explains, 'We're talking hypothetically. What we did in the Premiership in 2003/04 was astonishing. Arsenal players still glow with pride just thinking about the whole Premiership campaign. On the other hand, it is also a fact that in the modern era, players feel the urge to prove themselves on a European stage.

'Put it this way, if we're talking about emotional reactions, I was as crushed by losing to Chelsea that night as I was elated by remaining undefeated all season. Sometimes, you need some time to bask in what you have achieved.'

Gilberto says, 'Every player would look at the issue differently. Each season with Arsenal, every Champions League failure hurt more and more. But this was also my first title – so that feeling of joy outweighed any disappointment I felt about [losing to] Chelsea.'

Vieira remained sanguine about the whole thing, answering my question about whether the 'Invincibles' team could be classed as 'truly great' in the following way, 'I don't believe that what we achieved that season in the league will ever be done again, especially not with all the competition between the leading six teams. We all look back on the "Invincibles" side as a marvellous one. To be a captain of that team, in that season, is my finest achievement as a player.'

The Frenchman skilfully evaded my question, in much the same way that Wenger did when asked the same question by Oliver Holt in May 2004. Wenger responded, 'Someone wins the Champions League every year but what we have achieved is even better…it's history.'

Whatever the soundbites, there remains a sense of annoyance that the team couldn't have gone the distance in the Champions League

– while they still possessed the required mojo. Arsenal's achievement certainly made them, in one sense, 'IMMORTAL' as the *Sunday Mirror* claimed. In the Premier League sense they were also 'UNBEATABLE, UNTOUCHABLE and INVINCIBLE' as one of the banners at the Leicester game proclaimed. But they certainly weren't invincible in Europe. Vieira commented, 'We've got to learn how to defend better. Otherwise we run the risk of being left behind in Europe.'

Arsenal's 'Invincibles' can't be mentioned in the same breath as the Liverpool, Ajax and Bayern Munich sides of the 1970s, the AC Milan team of the early 1990s, or even Manchester United's Treble-winning team of 1999 because there were no back-to-back titles, and no European trophies to put in the cabinet.

The side's loss to Chelsea in the Champions League proved, as Martin Samuel had predicted a year earlier, that whatever pomp and ceremony surrounded them, Arsenal circa 2004 were a 'busted flush' in Europe.

～ ～ ～ ～ ～

Football is also about living the moment and in the league, Arsenal proved themselves to be a cut above the rest in 2003/04. The team played an exhilarating brand of football which remains the most potent and fluid ever seen in N5, and was admired across the globe. To go through an entire league season unbeaten – something which none of Arsenal's rivals have achieved – remains a monumental, unique and unforgettable achievement, one which left an indelible mark in English football history.

The season of the 'Invincibles' was a watershed moment for both the Gunners and for football as a whole. It was as good as it ever got for Arsène's Arsenal. Chelsea were now on the march. during the close-season and beyond, as David Dein memorably commented, they 'drew up in their tanks outside our boardroom, and started firing £50 notes at us,' led by their brash new commander in chief, Jose Mourinho. 'I think Arsenal are a top club, but not a top, top club,' claimed the outgoing Porto manager. 'To be so, you have to win this competition [the Champions League]. They always play the same way. It's makes them beautiful to watch – but it's also their weakness.'

Arsenal's defensive walls would soon be further eroded by the barrages emanating from Stamford Bridge.

# And Mercury Orbited The Sun 32 Times...

*'One day if I write a book, I'll tell everyone why finishing fourth for all those seasons was so important.' Arsène Wenger, speaking in August 2014.*

*'This has got to be the springboard for a new era of Arsenal success.' Mikel Arteta, speaking in May 2014.*

WHEN did Arsenal cease to be 'invincible'? Literally, it was in October 2004, when Manchester United defeated them 2-0 at Old Trafford to end the team's unbeaten league run after 49 games. For want of a better phrase they freaked out after the defeat, and tabloids busied themselves for weeks afterwards attempting to identify the player who threw the slice of pizza at Alex Ferguson, which hit him directly in the face.

The Gunners' ire focused mainly upon Rooney, whom the Arsenal players believed had dived over Sol Campbell's foot to win the penalty which van Nistelrooy converted. 'He knew, I knew and by the end of the game everyone watching on TV also knew,' claimed Campbell. 'I refused to shake his hand at the end. He cheated.' Edu recalled, 'The atmosphere was really tense. Wenger was absolutely fuming.'

In his most recent autobiography, Sir Alex Ferguson claimed, 'It seemed to me that losing the game scrambled Arsène's brain.'

But psychologically, it wasn't until Sunday 30 January 2005, when the *News Of The World* printed an article claiming that Chelsea manager Jose Mourinho, chief executive Peter Kenyon and Arsenal left-back Ashley Cole had met in the Royal Park Hotel in Lancaster Gate that the fact the club's star was waning became incontrovertible.

The events at Old Trafford could be put down to sheer bad luck, or a questionable refereeing decision in awarding United a penalty. But Cole – the London-born boyhood Arsenal fan who had only recently stated, 'I think if you ask the top players in the world and in the Premier League they would love to play for Arsenal. Who wouldn't want to play for Arsenal?' – being tapped up by newly-moneyed Chelsea for a transfer across the city, and attending a meeting of his own free will? This was something else entirely.

Chelsea had already made several offers in the region of £50m for Thierry Henry over the previous few months. David Dein's firm response was, 'He's not for sale at any price. If we sold him we would weaken our team, strengthen the opposition, and demoralise our manager, our coaching staff and our supporters.'

Henry simply reaffirmed his desire to stay at Arsenal but when the club's hierarchy discovered that the meeting with Cole had indeed taken place, their mood changed from one of defiance ('We shall launch a full and thorough investigation into what has happened,' insisted Dein) to one of eventual incredulity. Wenger said, 'I'm amazed they didn't just hold the meeting in the middle of the M25 and have done with it.'

The Cole saga – the player continued to protest his innocence – rumbled on for the best part of 18 months. Eventually, Cole was found to be in contravention of Premier League rules, and was fined £100,000 for the meeting with the Chelsea contingent. Whatever soundbites were uttered by the club or the player, things could never be the same again.

Four days after the *News of the World* scoop, Cole played in the Arsenal team which lost 4-2 at home to Manchester United. It was the last visceral 'blood and thunder' league clash between the two sides, who had turned the Premier League into a virtual duopoly.

Keane and Vieira nearly came to blows in the tunnel after the Irishman accused the Arsenal skipper of bullying Gary Neville. Twice Arsenal took the lead through Vieira and Bergkamp, but United hit back through Giggs, Ronaldo (twice) and O'Shea, and won 4-2. Keane clattered into Vieira. Rooney trash-talked Pires and referee Graham Poll. Arsenal fans goaded Rooney throughout. Ferguson fumed at Vieira's behaviour in the tunnel.

But for the sixth league clash in a row between the two sides Arsenal had failed to beat United and the loss effectively eliminated the Gunners from the title race. Chelsea romped away with the title. The world of the 'Invincibles' was being rocked off its axis.

A reckless 5-4 win at White Hart Lane ('A scoreline like that suggests it's not a proper football match,' sniffed a scornful Jose Mourinho) showed that the defence was a less than secure edifice, and there were clear signs that several of Wenger's most trusted players were starting to flag.

Robert Pires and Freddie Ljungberg struggled to impose themselves on matches, their overall effectiveness never entirely the same after they sustained serious knee and hip injuries respectively back in 2002. Pires recalled, 'Even a five per cent drop in effectiveness can make a big difference.' Then there was Vieira, who admits, 'I should have got closer to Neil Mellor' before the young Liverpool player curled in an outrageous late winner for his team at Anfield in November.

On occasion, Wenger appeared perplexed and befuddled by Chelsea, waging of financial warfare, 'When you see a club who make a loss of £80m, and it doesn't matter to them, you feel there is no logic needed in the way they conduct their business. It is very difficult for any club to cope with that kind of competition. It is troublesome. It disturbs the market.'

It was a similar reaction to that of McLaren's Ayrton Senna, who said of the Williams team's all-conquering FW14B car, 'This kind of electronic warfare means races are no longer proper races, for most drivers.' Senna soon joined the 'enemy'. Wenger was always resolutely opposed to Chelsea's new modus operandi.

He had nothing but contempt for the 'lack of financial logic' which they displayed. 'Chelsea don't have to say, "If we buy a player for £5m, then we have to sell a player for £5m."'

Instead, Wenger preferred to put his faith in his younger players; Senderos, Eboue, Fàbregas and Reyes. Once more, Reyes had the shit kicked out of him against Manchester United back in October. He had told *The Times*'s Chris Hatherall, 'It was the hardest match I have played in England and the referee should have stopped the violence of the Manchester United players.'

The Neville brothers' treatment of him was vicious, intimidating and blatant. It worked. They had eliminated what they saw as Arsenal's main threat and Reyes was substituted after 70 minutes. He was rebuked by team-mates. 'He was told that public complaints about United gave them the upper hand,' explains one of his former colleagues. 'He never did like the physical side of the game.'

There was the predictable gnashing of teeth as Arsenal tumbled to another Champions League exit at the hands of Bayern Munich ('While lessons in European football seem wasted on a team that remains unable to learn…' lamented Matt Lawton in the *Daily Mail*) in a 3-2 aggregate win for the Germans, and Arsenal finished a distant second in the title race.

The statistics were alarming. Arsenal gained 83 points, five more than Wenger's team had racked up during the Double triumph of 1998. Chelsea, relentless and remorseless under Mourinho, were shifting the goalposts, in every sense. But Wenger's Mark 2 team dug deep to enjoy one final fling against old adversaries.

~ ~ ~ ~ ~

After the 'Invincibles' season, Wenger commented, 'I enjoy the feeling of fulfilment when I feel the team has deserved its success.' Judging by his beatific grin at the end of the 2005 FA Cup Final, undeserved success against United was a more than acceptable alternative. Dogged defending (*The Times* nominated Arsenal defender Philippe Senderos as man of the match with a score of 8/10), a packed midfield (Fàbregas, Vieira and Gilberto stood firm throughout), goalkeeping heroics (Jens Lehmann made crucial saves from Rooney and Scholes in normal time and saved Scholes's penalty in the shoot-out), 'lucky' or 'boring' prefixes in tabloid reports, and the Millennium Stadium sound system belting out a tinny version of 'One Nil To The Arsenal'; the 'windfall final' was reminiscent of the club's cup triumphs a decade before.

Short of John Jensen joining the midfield fray at some point in the second half, or Paul Merson indulging in a spot of mock lager-swigging after Vieira dispatched his winning penalty, this was as close to a George Graham-style win as one could get.

With Henry injured, Bergkamp was left up front to forage on his own. Wenger, the high priest of stylish football, claimed, 'I thought, "OK, for one day let's just try to get what we want at any price. And it worked."' Sort of. Reyes and Pires contributed precious little to proceedings, and Lauren and Cole were both given a torrid afternoon by Ronaldo and Rooney. *The Times* awarded the Arsenal starting XI a total score of 59, compared with United's cumulative 69. It truly was that one-sided, although Arsenal did finish as the stronger team.

Vieira chuckled at the memory of one of Arsenal's narrow escapes. 'Ruud van Nistelrooy headed goalwards – and you think, "This might be it." Then somehow Freddie Ljungberg gets his head to the ball and it hits the crossbar and stays out. Had Freddie ever headed a football before? Probably not! At that point, you think to yourself, "This might just be our day."'

Wenger had almost stumbled upon the prototype of the 4-5-1 formation which he deployed in the Champions League during the following season. It represented the team's first tentative move towards a more flexible approach. Intriguingly, Wenger had hinted in a recent Canal Plus interview that he was prepared to utilise a sweeper system in the following year's Champions League, admitting that 'a slower pace of game is required'.

Vieira recalled that after the Bayern Munich defeat a few months before, senior players met to discuss tactics. 'It was always very hard for us to snap out of Premiership mode – quick, quick pace – and adapt our style to the more possession-based Champions League. There was also the issue of luck. You have to enjoy a degree of this to be successful in Europe.' As the victory in Cardiff proved, luck was the one thing Arsenal seemed to have in abundance.

They also had stout hearts as Lauren, Ljungberg, Van Persie, Cole and, finally, Vieira dispatched five perfectly-taken penalties past United goalkeeper Roy Carroll. Wenger admitted, 'I am not really convinced that you have to play like that always. I wouldn't be happy playing every week like that.'

But Arsenal supporters didn't care, and neither did Vieira, who recalled, 'It was an uncharacteristic win for us, but good too, because sometimes a team needs to win with spirit and determination to prove to itself that it's a united group.'

Vieira, who fired home his winning kick with customary coolness and aplomb, never kicked another ball for the club.

The 2005 'windfall final' – won against a United team which had just been taken over by the Glazer family – was Wenger's 497th match in charge of Arsenal. Another 513 games would pass before his team lifted silverware again in 2014.

A plethora of websites, the most prominent of which was www. sincearsenallastwonatrophy.co.uk, were built in the intervening period and browsers were furnished with some useful facts. Twenty-seven of the Arsenal players who departed the club post-2005 won a combined 83 trophies elsewhere. Twenty-seven of the league's 92 clubs won trophies – increasing to 52 if one includes promotion play-off trophies. And Mercury orbited the sun 32 times.

A total of eight years, 11 months, 26 days, 38 minutes and 20 seconds elapsed between Vieira's spot-kick and the referee blowing his whistle at Wembley at the end of Arsenal's game with Hull City at Wembley in 2014.

Not that anyone was counting of course.

- - - - -

The precise contents of Wenger's much vaunted 'summer war chest' (by now a stock phrase among tabloids) were a mystery. Arsenal's only major close-season signing in 2005 was Alexander Hleb while Patrick Vieira departed to Juventus.

Once upon a time, the Gunners would likely have moved for Michael Essien to replace the departed Frenchman, but the Ghanaian midfielder ended up at Chelsea. Gilberto explains, 'Patrick's departure was a huge loss. It did give Cesc [Fàbregas] the chance to break through, but I don't think I'm being too controversial by saying that Arsenal have never replaced Patrick's leadership since then.'

Player by player, the squad was being trimmed. Kanu and Wiltord had gone a year before. Edu headed off to Valencia in Spain, recalling, 'The cloth was being cut because of the financial shortfall with the Emirates Stadium. The club always said that it [the move] wouldn't affect the transfer budget, but it was uppermost in everyone's minds.'

With his side clad in blackcurrant for the final Highbury campaign, Wenger initially spoke optimistically about his belief, 'Arsenal have a very good chance of landing the title this season at Highbury.'

However, the crunch Highbury games lost their sting. After an impressive start against Chelsea, with Robin van Persie's goal being ruled out and Henry hitting the post, the Blues won 2-0 – completing a league double over Arsenal that season. The annual fight club with United – such a combustible contest in recent times – fizzled out into a tame 0-0 draw. It was partly due to Vieira's absence. 'Patrick would spark us and give us that physical edge,' recalled Gilberto. 'Without him, we were a less combative side.'

In Europe however, Arsenal became more robust and workmanlike, and more adept at altering the tempo of the match to suit the occasion. With the pace and incision of Pires and Ljungberg fading, and Bergkamp playing only sporadically in his last year at Highbury, much of the 'preening peacock' element of Arsenal's game had gone.

That wasn't necessarily a bad thing. They still had Henry and new signing Hleb was frequently deployed by Wenger to lend an element of surprise to matches away from home.

Following early-season injuries to Ashley Cole and Lauren, Wenger drafted in Emmanuel Eboue and utility man Mathieu Flamini in the full-back positions. Gilberto recalled, 'Mathieu was basically a defensive midfielder, and Eboue back then was quite cautious about pressing forward. When it came to the knockout stages in Europe, that helped us. The defence was more of a unit, and we were more content to sit and wait and choose our pace, rather than go out at a million miles an hour. It was a more methodical way of playing.'

Arsenal cruised through their qualifying group containing Thun, Ajax and Sparta Prague, conceding just two goals in the process. Wenger launched his experimental 4-5-1 formation against Ajax in the final group stage game. Arsenal didn't concede, drawing 0-0.

Wenger stuck with the plan in the New Year when his team was drawn against Real Madrid in the last 16. The Galacticos may have been a little jaded but the Gunners, mired in sixth place in the Premier League, were hardly in a healthy position either. In Madrid,

Arsenal's defence remained rock solid with Flamini and Eboue playing a marvellously controlled game. Ljungberg, temporarily transformed back to his 2001/02 form, Reyes and Henry carved out early chances for one another, but the half-time score remained 0-0.

After half-time the pendulum swung in Arsenal's favour. Fàbregas nudged the ball to Henry in the centre circle, and the Frenchman – on cruise control – surged past Ronaldo's half-hearted tackle and Gravesen's lunge. After motoring past Guti and Ramos, he slipped the ball past Casillas. Arsenal's young upstarts had come to the Bernabeu, where Madrid were used to pummelling teams into submission, dictated the pace of the game, and emerged as 1-0 winners.

The Spanish giants – not at their best but still boasting the collective talents of David Beckham, Zinedine Zidane and Roberto Carlos – were expected to make a strong comeback in the return leg. Pires recalled, 'We were able to play a much more passing-based game, and when we could, we launched counter attacks against them. As Patrick said, you need some luck in Europe, and we got ours at Highbury when Jens Lehmann saved from Raul, and then Raul hit the post with the goal at his mercy.' Arsenal edged through 1-0 on aggregate. 'Fortune favours the brave,' said Wenger afterwards.

Arsenal had reached the stage from which no Gunners side had ever progressed before, and drawing Juventus meant the quick return of Vieira to Highbury. Arsenal wore down Juventus by playing a fast tempo passing game. Pires recalls, 'We never allowed them a second on the ball. We were able to impose an English style of play on them, and it was almost unheard of for anyone to do that to Juventus. We judged the occasion and the mood right.'

Five minutes before half-time, Pires stunned Vieira by tackling him sharply on the left and tucked the ball inside to Henry. The French striker rolled a through pass to Fàbregas, who side-stepped Thuram to open the scoring. Henry made it 2-0, guiding the ball home despite Hleb's pass falling slightly behind him.

Philippe Auclair claims that by now, Arsenal had entered an age of 'Henry dependence'. Certainly he was the prime outlet up front, but in Europe at least the rest of the team marshalled operations effectively in order to provide him with those chances. Increasingly, Henry was playing with his back to goal. This was a more defensive side, and Henry had to wait to bring his team-mates into the game. The goalless draw in Turin, which confirmed Arsenal's passage to the semi-finals, was another highly impressive example of intermittently slowing down and then increasing the rhythm of the match to peg the Juventus backline.

Arsenal eked past the obdurate but unfancied Villarreal in the semi-finals. Kolo Toure's single goal at Highbury – the last European match staged at the stadium – was the only score of the tie, with Arsenal following that up with a battling 0-0 draw in Spain.

Accused of fielding another negative line-up, Wenger laughed and told journalists, 'You try and get Ljungberg, Fàbregas and Hleb to play as defenders.' The three had little choice but to fall back, prompting Kevin McCarra to write in *The Guardian*, 'Last night, too jittery to follow their natural instincts, they acted as if they really did yearn to be spoilers.'

The question remained as to whether this Arsenal team, playing so out of character, could spoil Barcelona's chances in the Champions League Final in Paris. It is hard to fathom what else Arsenal could have done to win the game that night. The defence coped manfully with Ronaldinho and Eto'o for the first 75 minutes, despite having goalkeeper Jens Lehmann sent off so early. The saddest sight of the night was seeing Pires sacrificed so that substitute custodian Manuel Almunia could enter the fray.

Pires confirmed, 'The hurt I felt. It wasn't an easy substitution for him [Wenger] to make of course, but at the time, it felt like I wasn't being valued or trusted anymore.'

Nonetheless in the early stages, Eboue drove hard down the right and crossed for Henry, whose effort was saved by Barcelona keeper Victor Valdes. Campbell headed his team into an unlikely lead, which they held until late strikes by Eto'o and Juliano Belletti. Henry had previously had another great opportunity to put Arsenal 2-0 up. Slipped through by Hleb, he drove his shot hard at Valdes. Henry admitted, 'I didn't make the difference. I'd be the first to say that. I've got two big chances. I always have the feeling that I've let my team down if I haven't made a difference.'

It was a disorientating time at Arsenal. A few days earlier they had played their last game at Highbury, pinching fourth spot from

Tottenham with a dramatic final-day win over Wigan Athletic. Pires, Bergkamp, Campbell and Cole were about to depart. Reyes (once described by Rob Smyth in *The Guardian* as 'a man who can take them to another level, because he appears unafflicted by the choking pressure that does for Henry') was farmed out on loan to Real Madrid. The press speculated that Henry was poised to join Barcelona.

The least Wenger-like Arsenal team had come close to finally landing Europe's prize. Tactically they had been virtually flawless throughout the whole competition. 'I felt we were very unlucky. It often seems unsatisfactory when a player explains that a team lost because they were unlucky. On another occasion, Thierry would have taken at least one of those chances, and we'd have been less tired with 11 men not ten,' recalled Gilberto.

The departure of Cole to Chelsea in the summer was hugely damaging. Cole's autobiography *My Defence* may be staggering in its pomposity ('Arsenal hung me out to dry, using me as a scapegoat to get back at Chelsea'), crassness (was he really going to elicit sympathy from Arsenal fans when he wrote, 'When I heard Jonathan repeat the figure of £55k, I nearly swerved off the road. "He's taking the piss Jonathan?"') and self-justification (he couldn't work out why Arsenal fans sang Thierry Henry's name after the Champions League Final and not his, despite being found guilty of a cloak and dagger meeting with Chelsea). But *My Defence*, written while he was still an Arsenal player, didn't always reflect well on the club either.

In the *News Of The World*, Martin Samuel suggested that for a left-back, Cole had ideas above his station. But Cole's gripe – that as a homegrown player he wasn't being paid as much as bought players – was an age-old frustration held by the likes of Charlie George, Liam Brady and Michael Thomas.

Given the rarified financial atmosphere in which top-flight footballers operate, he probably was irked that the club downgraded their initial offer of £60,000 a week. His claim that the Arsenal dressing room was becoming an increasingly divided and morose environment was ill thought-out – disloyal even – but hardly incorrect, as events proved.

His departure showed that Arsenal were a selling club, unable to hold on to a player who had professed, 'My heart and soul was tied to

Arsenal with a fisherman's knot.' It heralded an era of insecurity and fragility at Arsenal, much like the immediate post-Brady/Stapleton era 25 years before. Through the crescendo of abuse he received during every subsequent clash with Chelsea, Arsenal fans – frustrated with their own club's lack of investment – were simply indulging in a spot of transferred rage. It was easier to lambast Cole's treachery in leaving Arsenal than it was to openly criticise the management of the club he left behind. Gilberto explained, 'Once you lose someone who's been nurtured through the club like Ashley, it starts to tear out the heart and soul of a club. Things aren't the same again.'

Cold-blooded arithmetic was now the order of the day. Arsenal received £5m plus William Gallas for Cole. Wenger warned, 'We can no longer afford to spend huge money on signings. Not in the short-term, at least.' As Arsenal prepared to move to the Emirates Stadium, it seemed more of a poignant farewell to a bygone era, than actively embracing a new one.

Between 2004 and 2012, Arsenal bought and subsequently sold a raft of players who remained, as the current parlance goes, 'hungry'. Robin van Persie (to Manchester United), Emmanuel Adebayor, Samir Nasri, Kolo Toure (to Manchester City), Alexander Hleb (to Barcelona), and Mathieu Flamini (to AC Milan). Cesc Fàbregas (to Barcelona) and Ashley Cole, graduates from the youth team, went too. Only Cole and Toure won title medals at Arsenal. None of the others did. 'That's a string of top players who might reflect that their time at Arsenal was wasted,' laments Gilberto.

Hampered by waiting for the multi-million-pound windfall from the sale of Highbury Square, and saddled with hastily completed stadium and kit sponsorship deals, the club was effectively treading water. All except for the 2007/08 campaign, when the story could have been so, so different.

⌣ ⌣ ⌣ ⌣ ⌣

Thierry Henry, increasingly injury prone and erratic, departed during the 2007 close-season for around 24 million euros following his waning influence in his final Arsenal campaign. He appeared more irascible in that final season, and increasingly self-indulgent, as his post-goal celebratory dances with Emmanuel Adebayor suggested. Yet to suggest that Henry should have been jettisoned after the Paris final, and perhaps more pertinently, following his heroics in the final Highbury match with Wigan, is to be wise after the event. Wenger was dismantling the 'Invincibles' team with almost bewildering speed. Of the regulars from just three seasons before, only Touré remained a fixture in the side. Lehmann's and Gilberto's cards were marked.

Yet the post-Henry landscape wasn't as barren as the harbingers of doom had predicted. Shorn of experience (and on average, three years younger, two stone lighter and three inches shorter than the 'Invincibles'), Wenger's 'baby Gunners' remained unbeaten for the opening 21 games of the season. Some of the football in that spell was heavenly. At times, it was a 2004-style return to 'Wenger-ball'. Arsenal piled up the goals in late summer, picking off Tottenham at White Hart Lane with clinical precision, and outplaying Harry Redknapp's emerging Portsmouth side at the Emirates Stadium. The team could – literally – pulverise also-rans. Following a Theo Walcott-inspired 7-0 obliteration of Slavia Prague in the Champions League, Sam Wallace wrote in *The Independent*: 'The Englishman in the most lustrous attacking football team in the country finally got his chance to sparkle last night and his two goals gave English football something it could cling to.' After a 5-0 thumping of Derby, Henry Winter wrote enthusiastically in *The Telegraph* about 'the rise and recovery of Abou Diaby, following his horrific leg break against Sunderland 16 months before.'

Arsenal could also tough it out when they needed to. Under William Gallas's more abrasive captaincy, they fought back to draw 2-2 with United; Gallas himself grabbed the late equaliser. 'It was like playing one of George Graham's sides out there at times,' remarked Ferguson. Presumably, he meant that as a compliment. Arsenal held out to win 1-0 against Chelsea. Gallas headed the winner. They fought back at home to complete the league double over Tottenham. Nicklas Bendtner scored the winner with his first touch after coming on as substitute. 'I look on this group as my third generation of players at this club,' claimed Wenger proudly. 'Hopefully they can deliver for themselves and the fans.'

In midfield, Fàbregas and Flamini were developing a potent partnership, with Rosický and Hleb adding width and pace. On the wings were Gilberto, Lassana Diarra – a spiky and versatile summer addition from Chelsea – and Diaby. Up front, the Eduardo–Adebayor partnership began to flourish. The Gunners' last act of 2007 had been to wipe the floor with Everton at Goodison Park, with the dextrous, left-footed Eduardo notching his first two league goals. The only concern was that Robin van Persie, injured while playing for Holland in October, was recovering slowly, and wasn't due back until March.

In the January transfer window, Arsenal were linked strongly with former striker Nicolas Anelka – plying his trade at Bolton – for a sum of around £15 million. The club passed on the opportunity to sign the mercurial Frenchman, possibly because of the manner of his departure eight years earlier, but the rumours were that Arsenal, increasingly desperate to balance the books, baulked at the fee. Arsène Wenger said, 'In my opinion we have four top strikers at the club. I don't need a fifth.' A journalist at a press conference posed the question: 'You already have van Persie out injured. What happens if Adebayor or Eduardo gets injured too?' 'In that case, Nicklas Bendtner will step in,' came the swift response. Anelka, meanwhile, headed to Stamford Bridge.

The question of Diarra's departure to Portsmouth remains open to conjecture. The player has since admitted that he left Arsenal 'too quickly', and the club suggested that Diarra's advisers wanted assurances that their man would be given playing time in the second half of the season, which Arsène Wenger refused to do. Off he went to the south coast, where he won the FA Cup. Given Flamini's excellence as a defensive midfielder, it would be churlish to suggest that Diarra would have been a better option, but what if, with Arsenal fighting on all four fronts, Flamini had got injured or needed a rest? Wenger also pointed out that he had Gilberto at his disposal, but the Brazil star's pace had slowed dramatically over the last few months. So, with Wenger unwilling to fight a running battle with the occasionally abrasive Diarra, he was allowed to leave for £5.5 million. Arsenal's parsimony, and unwillingness to take a speculative approach in the transfer window, cost them dear.

Arsenal galloped through most of January, before being thumped 5-1 by Tottenham in the League Cup semi-final second leg. With Wenger rotating his squad, it became clear that Nicklas Bendtner operating as a lone striker wasn't a viable option. Only the introduction of Adebayor as a second-half substitute sparked the Gunners into any kind of life at White Hart Lane, and by then it was too late. It was the same sorry story at Old Trafford on 16 February, when United scored four without reply in the FA Cup fourth round tie. Arsenal were overrun in midfield and blunt in attack; the lack of real depth in the squad clear for all to see. Fàbregas told a Spanish magazine, 'I'm getting exhausted.' Flamini revealed: 'My hamstrings feel tight.' In truth, both could have done with a rest. Diarra would have been an ideal replacement.

Arsenal maintained their impressive league form with a 3-1 win at Manchester City, with Adebayor and Eduardo 'dovetailing to absolute perfection' in the words of Arsène Wenger. If only the season could have ended there, with the Gunners five points clear at the end of February with 12 matches to play. Instead, the wheels came off during that infamous 2-2 draw at St Andrew's. Eduardo broke his leg. 'It derailed the whole team,' confirmed Gilberto. 'You didn't have to see the actual injury to be affected by what had happened to him.' Eduardo admitted, 'I think what happened [to me] threw the players. We suddenly drew four games in a row. Previously, those are matches we most likely would have won.' Arsenal conceded a late equaliser after Gael Clichy's lapse in concentration saw Birmingham awarded a penalty. Adebayor and Bendtner, who'd already had a set-to at White Hart Lane ('Nicklas showed me the finger, so I headbutted him,' recalled Adebayor), showed a distinct lack of chemistry in the second half which saw them miss a glorious opportunity to net the winner. Gallas sulked on the pitch after the Birmingham game. 'There were two Arsenal players who showed leadership in the aftermath of Eduardo's injury,' recalled an Arsenal player from that team. 'One was Mathieu [Flamini]. The other was Gilberto. Gallas didn't help us.' Touré admitted, 'Me and Gallas…we didn't talk to each other at all.' Not even during matches. Gallas, the gravel-voiced grouch, reckoned Touré was too soft. Touré reckoned Gallas was too abrasive. The team's soft underbelly was finally being exposed.

Arsenal drew against Aston Villa, Wigan and Middlesbrough. Without Eduardo's tricks or van Persie's guile, the attack looked blunt. What Arsenal would have given for Anelka, who was now providing assists aplenty for Chelsea by early March. As United and Chelsea overhauled the Gunners at the top of the league, attention turned to the Champions League quarter-final with Liverpool. Arsenal were unlucky in the first leg at the Emirates. They drew 1-1, but should have won a penalty when Hleb was dragged back by Kuyt. Bendtner inadvertently blocked Fàbregas's shot. In the second-leg match at Anfield in April, Diaby clubbed Arsenal ahead after a beautiful interchange of passes between Hleb, Flamini and Fàbregas. Adebayor's goal seven minutes from time, following Walcott's inspired run, appeared to have put Arsenal in the final, but they collapsed defensively immediately afterwards.

Flamini pulled up lame, and missed the rest of the season. The Frenchman who would have been an ideal young replacement was now on his way to Wembley with Redknapp's Portsmouth. On the following Saturday, Arsenal lost the crunch match at Old Trafford 2-1 despite dominating the first half. In the second half, United steamrolled Arsenal's midfield, as the Gunners seized up. The problem in Wenger's opinion? 'We lacked a little bite in midfield, and a little pace up front.'

The team rallied after Old Trafford, but it was too little, too late. Most damningly of all, the jungle drums beat louder and louder as rumours grew that both Flamini and Hleb had been 'tapped up' prior to the team's famous Champions League win away to AC Milan. It wasn't idle gossip. Hleb's agent Claudio Vigorelli claimed they'd simply left the team hotel for an ice cream prior to the San Siro game, but such a claim seems fanciful given that Hleb's proposed move to Inter was circulated in the press during the days that followed. Flamini's refusal to sign a new contract rumbled on. He would depart to AC Milan at season's end. The birds of prey were circling above the club. Within a few months, Adebayor was also strongly linked with a move abroad. 'Not everyone was fully focused on the job in hand,' claimed Gilberto. 'There were too many distractions both within the dressing room, and outside.' Gilberto left.

Arsenal should have won the league that year. They finished in third place on a massive 83 points, four points behind United, having lost just three league games all season. The goalposts moved again. Manchester City joined the billionaires' club, with their wealthy

Arab owners, and quickly began to sniff around Arsenal's players. Adebayor and Touré went to the Etihad in 2009 for a combined fee of £40 million. Adebayor claimed, 'Arsène Wenger told me that I had to go, because Arsenal had no money.' Kolo Touré admitted, 'One of me or Gallas had to go. It was me. And Arsenal needed the money.' With Chelsea and the Manchester clubs financially doped up to the eyeballs, finishing in the top four – always the bottom line in Wenger's opinion – would prove to be a massive challenge. Especially as Tottenham now had Arsenal firmly in their sights.

At times over the next few years it seemed entirely possible that Wenger could be swept away at key moments. Some Arsenal fans called for his head at the end of the disastrous 2-1 defeat to Birmingham in the 2011 Carling Cup Final, a loss which Wenger admitted "left everyone at the club crushed." Following the 8-2 humiliation at Old Trafford in August 2011, Alan Hansen warned in *The Telegraph*, 'One more defeat like this and Wenger could be history.' Walcott admitted, 'It's a humiliating day, my worst in football. There was no shape, no team spirit.' Ferguson expressed sympathy for his old rival – never a good sign. It was like the time he sold Wenger defender Mikael Silvestre back in 2008. Presumably Ferguson rated neither Silvestre nor Arsenal by then.

Nasri and Fabregas left a few days before the Old Trafford defeat. It seemed ominous for the club and after damaging defeats at Tottenham (2-1) and Blackburn (4-3) – away fans at Ewood Park could clearly be heard chanting at Wenger, 'You don't know what you're doing' – football writer Patrick Barclay commented on Sky's *Sunday Supplement*, 'I can see Arsenal in a relegation scrap, the way they're going.'

The worrying thing was, none of the panellists disagreed with Barclay, and he wasn't taken to task by Gunners fans for his comments either. 'In Arsène We Rust' said one banner at the Blackburn match. There was a mad 'Supermarket Sweep' purchasing spree prior to the transfer window slamming shut, which brought Mikel Arteta and Per Mertesacker – among others – to the club.

The Black Scarf movement mobilised, protesting against being priced out of the Emirates Stadium, fed up with the spin emanating from the club, and frustrated that the vast sums paid out for tickets weren't being reinvested in the team.

Social media suggested Wenger had lost his touch and that tactically, he was a myopic dinosaur. He stood accused of preventing Andrey Arshavin, who had begun his Arsenal career with so much zest, from playing his natural game. He was lampooned on YouTube as the man who couldn't zip up his coat, and who freaked when Arsenal didn't get their way. By the time Arsenal were slaughtered 4-0 in Milan in the Champions League and lost 2-0 to Sunderland in the FA Cup – both defeats within four days of one another – the 'You don't know what you're doing' chants resurfaced. This time, Wenger's position genuinely seemed under threat.

Trailing fourth-placed Tottenham by ten points, Arsenal faced the biggest north London derby of recent years on 26 February 2012 at the Emirates Stadium. This, more than any other game was the ultimate 'House of Cards' match during Wenger's reign. Lose this one, and the game might really have been up. Emmanuel Petit insisted, 'These players are fragile, they can sink. They are peacocks in the middle of a farmyard. Pull your fingers out, guys.'

Arsenal players were instructed not to talk to the press in the lead-up to the game. Walcott recalled, 'There was a piece written in one of the newspapers suggesting that of our starting XI, only Robin would get into the Spurs side. That hurt, but none of us commented on it.'

On a beautifully mild day in early spring, Tottenham fans were in full voice in and around Arsenal tube station, taunting their Arsenal counterparts about the Gunners' Kentish roots.

'North London is ours, north London is ours, fuck off back to Woolwich, north London is ours.'

Outside the away fans' entrance, a small group of Spurs fans carried a mini mock-up coffin with the inscription 'AFC – RIP' emblazoned across it. Tottenham's keyboard warriors were also crafting their verbal barbs on assorted Spurs chatrooms. 'Let's annihilate these clowns. Let's bomb Arsenal back to the stone age,' read one comment. 'In all seriousness, Arsenal are so poor at the moment that if we get one or two early goals, we can batter these mugs. The tide is about to turn in north London,' read another.

With 34 minutes gone, Tottenham were two goals up courtesy of Saha and Adebayor. Arsenal seemed to be on the edge of the abyss.

Then a 28-minute miracle (with a 15-minute interval in the middle) happened, where Arsenal struck back to disembowel Tottenham.

The pivotal moment of the match was van Persie's equaliser just before half-time, where he used his refined touch and stunning awareness to curl the ball past Brad Friedel with that sublime left foot of his. In the second half, Arsenal were rampant, with Rosický and Walcott injecting fear into the heart of Tottenham's ragged rearguard. Walcott's brace of goals, both coolly dispatched past Friedel, were remarkable given that Wenger later admitted to pondering whether to substitute him at the break as his first-half display was so wretched.

Tottenham supporters evacuated the away end almost as soon as Rosický made it 3-2, leaving the ground with sarcastic chants of 'Harry for England' and 'Mind the Gap' chants ringing in their ears.

This was a truly extraordinary display of character, one which prompted Arsenal to win seven league games on the bounce and come close to a sensational second-le g comeback against Milan in the Champions League.

Arsenal's epic fightback (and Tottenham's staggering collapse) at the Emirates turned the season around. In the end, both clubs finished in the top four. Arsenal nabbed third but due to Chelsea winning the Champions League, Tottenham's fourth-place finish wasn't sufficient to bag them a place at Europe's top table.

A year later, when asked if Tottenham could be regarded as Arsenal's chief rivals, both in terms of geography and threat, Wenger shrugged, 'I suppose if you look at the league table this year and last, then the rivalry is no longer just geographic.'

Arsenal's 2-1 defeat at White Hart Lane in March 2013 once again left them on the brink. They were five points behind fourth-placed Chelsea and seven adrift of Tottenham. Spurs manager Andre Villas-Boas claimed that, given Arsenal's recent capitulation to Bayern Munich in the Champions League, the Gunners were 'on a negative spiral in terms of results'.

Arsenal's porous defence, with skipper Thomas Vermaelen culpable for Aaron Lennon's goal, was the architect of its own downfall. Walcott conceded, 'The Tottenham matches are ones which we dare not lose, because Spurs are right on our tails. We're all aware that if we drop out of the top four, it will be doubly hard to ever get back in.'

After the defeat at White Hart Lane, no less than three broadsheets – *The Guardian*, *The Telegraph* and *The Times* – barked out the phrase 'POWER SHIFT'. Remarkably, that never happened because Arsenal dropped their misfiring captain Vermaelen from the starting line-up and embarked on a fine unbeaten run until the end of the season.

'We spoke on the training ground about what needed to happen,' explained Alex Oxlade-Chamberlain. 'We needed to tighten up, ensure that we didn't concede in the first instance, and make sure that we exploited the opposition for weaknesses.'

Hardly the most revealing comment ever, but it showed that new assistant manager Steve Bould's influence was beginning to be felt after reports earlier in the campaign that he was being marginalised by the manager.

By June, chief executive Ivan Gazidis confirmed that 2014, long vaunted as a sort of promised land by the Arsenal board, was indeed the year when the club could begin to 'use our financial artillery in the transfer market'. With Emirates continuing as the stadium sponsor and a kit deal agreed in principle with Puma, Gazidis estimated that it would lead to an annual revenue increase of around £70m, meaning that Arsenal had the fiscal power to compete with Manchester United.

For the first time in eight years Arsenal looked to add talent, not cash in on their best assets. It wasn't easy. Their pursuit of Luis Suarez ended in embarrassment, and the club prevaricated for so long over Gonzalo Higuain's proposed move from Real Madrid that Napoli, flush with the money they received from Edinson Cavani's transfer, signed him instead.

'Arsenal haven't been in at the kill for a top player for too long,' a European 'super-agent' informed me in typically cut-throat style. 'Since they last won the league in 2004, the world has changed, and the feeling in the game is that Arsenal prevaricate just when a deal seems to be in the offing. It comes down to inexperience, and a certain level of naivety. Possibly even arrogance.'

The approach for Suarez was not just about Arsenal landing the player, it was about fundamentally altering the perception of the club from being muddling middleweights to serious big hitters. The

£40,000,001 bid simply made Liverpool more intransigent, giving various former Reds players including Phil Thompson the chance to mock the Gunners. 'Fair enough that he wants Champions League football,' he said on Sky TV, 'but don't go to Arsenal.'

With Flamini returning as the only recognised signing in the 2013 close-season, Arsenal fans urged Wenger and the board to 'spend some fucking money' throughout an opening-day loss to Aston Villa. In the nick of time, with the transfer window poised to slam shut, the Gunners swooped for Real Madrid playmaker Mesut Özil for £42m. Only Lionel Messi could come close to Özil in the number of assists he provided for colleagues. When new signing Gareth Bale was unveiled on the Bernabeu pitch, the Real Madrid supporters still sang Özil's name.

He was handed the number 11 shirt but, given his classic 'number ten' playmaker qualities and the headlines his transfer garnered, there were obvious similarities with the capture of Dennis Bergkamp in the summer of 1995 by Bruce Rioch. Arsenal were an entirely different proposition after he arrived. The club had made a statement of intent, and shown they meant business. Bergkamp oozed class and immediately added a shimmering of quality to the team. Özil arrived with none of Bergkamp's baggage. Whereas the Dutchman had been criticised for his Inter displays, Özil was regarded as La Liga's most savvy performer. On the face of it, Özil was Bergkamp – and then some. Bergkamp said of Ozil: "It's about the first touch. If the first touch is right you create more time for yourself. And when your head is up you always create more possibilities to give a pass. He does that all the time."

The league season showed that, on its own, Özil's arrival did not beget a title-winning side – far from it – but like Bergkamp's arrival helped lure Vieira, Petit and Overmars to Highbury, the galvanising presence of Özil has already helped lure in Barcelona's Alexis Sanchez, who commented shortly before joining Arsenal in June 2014, 'It will be an honour to play alongside players like Mesut Özil, who is rightly regarded as one of the world's best players.' Potential signings now looked at the club as one which means business.

Ivan Gazidis likened the modern transfer market to 'the Wild West', but Arsenal appeared to be finally cutting through the gun smoke and adding top players to the squad. 'It's wonderful of course that we have added a player with the talent of Özil to our squad,' explained Wenger in September 2013, 'but what everyone connected with the club is hungry for is a trophy.'

Arsenal led the table for much of the 2013/2014 season but were undone largely by some gruesome hammerings on their travels – going down 5-1 at Liverpool, 6-3 at Manchester City, 3-0 at Everton and 6-0 at Chelsea in what was Wenger's 1,000th game in charge. On such occasions Arsenal's tactical naivety often beggared belief, as did another season where key players including Walcott, Ramsey, Oxlade-Chamberlain, Podolski and Özil spent significant chunks of time on the sidelines.

Hopefully the appointment of Shad Forsythe, a highly regarded fitness coach with the German national team, will bear fruit over the next few years. There was also a lingering frustration about Wenger's steadfast loyalty to Nicklas Bendtner and Abou Diaby, who both – for differing reasons – contributed little of note during the season. 'Wenger's loyalty is his key strength and also his main weakness,' claimed Vieira.

But there was also much to savour with Aaron Ramsey's emergence as a potent midfield force, and – sporadically – Özil's deliciously smooth forays up the pitch. And with Mercury poised to orbit the sun for the 33rd time since they last won a trophy in 2005, Arsenal finally broke their duck at Wembley.

Perhaps the spirit of George Swindin arranged for Arsenal to be drawn at home from the third round to the quarter-final (Author's note: If you don't understand the reference to Swindin, you haven't been reading chronologically), but if so the notoriously hard-nosed former Arsenal keeper handed the club some tough assignments.

The Gunners played extremely well to defeat Tottenham, even though Walcott – who gestured '2-0' to Spurs fans as he departed the action – was stretchered off with a knee injury, and eased past a gutsy Coventry City team in round four with a hefty 4-0 win.

A full-blooded encounter saw Wenger's men edge past Liverpool in a controversial clash. Eight days after being hammered 5-1 at Anfield, goals from Oxlade-Chamberlain and Podolski put Arsenal through, although Liverpool protested long and hard that the former had brought down Suarez in the area late on.

In the quarter-finals Arsenal brushed aside an unusually downbeat Everton side to reach the semi-finals for the first time since 2009. Lying in wait were holders Wigan Athletic, conquerors of Manchester City in the quarter-finals. 'This is the sort of game which I know Arsenal sides often struggled with in the past,' admitted Oxlade-Chamberlain, showing a fine awareness of Arsenal's past travails against less-fancied teams.

The Wembley clash with Uwe Rosler's side was no different. Rosler had sent Wigan out with the message, 'You have absolutely nothing to lose. They, on the other hand, have everything to lose. Disrupt Arsenal.' And they did with their hard-pressing game preventing the Gunners from getting into any sort of rhythm. Oxlade-Chamberlain admitted, 'For long periods, Wigan suffocated us. It was hard to think clearly and impose our game on them.'

The defence looked jittery and on 59 minutes, the rickety-looking Mertesacker upended the lively McManaman. Gomez put Wigan a goal up from the penalty spot. Wenger's decision to substitute Podolski and bring on Giroud was met by a crescendo of boos by Arsenal supporters, and it was only with around 15 minutes to go that the team began to make inroads on Wigan's defence. Sagna hit the post and Gibbs went close before, with 83 minutes gone, Mertesacker scrambled home Oxlade-Chamberlain's wayward shot. Relief.

The game meandered into extra time and penalties. On a rain-soaked Wembley day, Fabianski proved to be Arsenal's hero in the shoot-out, saving both of Wigan's first two kicks. 'As we saw in the 2005 final, sometimes, you have to win ugly. A win is a win,' admitted Wenger, sounding remarkably like George Graham. And with Wenger desperate to finally win silverware at almost any cost, that probably wasn't a bad thing.

⌣　⌣　⌣　⌣　⌣

The day of reckoning – 17 May 2014 – was finally here. As had been the case with the semi-final against Wigan, the FA Cup Final against Hull City was a match which Arsenal dared not lose.

'Twitter will dissolve into an anti-social media as crowing rivals pile in. The years of hurt will stretch to a decade. The choke's on Arsenal. The favourites know the high price of failure,' warned Henry Winter in *The Telegraph*. One of the 'Invincibles' – Gilberto – commented, 'There's absolutely nothing which can beat the feeling of lifting silverware. Without trophies, for all the money and the status, there's nothing to connect you to the fans – not at a club like Arsenal. The team has to win today.'

Such high stakes couldn't prevent Arsenal from the most calamitous of starts. After four minutes, James Chester diverted in a skewed shot. Four minutes later Curtis Davies rammed the ball home after Stephen Quinn's shot was tipped away by Fabianski. Mertesacker recalled, 'There was nothing else to do but try and keep our heads, and fight back. There wasn't a grand tactical plan.'

Those crazy eight minutes encapsulated much of what had been awry at Arsenal for years; a lack of leadership at the back, serious jitters on the big occasion, and an inability to learn from past mistakes.

But Arsenal's fightback also espoused their good points. Santi Cazorla – whose form hadn't been up to the standard of his first season at Arsenal – curled home a spectacular free kick on 17 minutes. Ramsey, back from a long-term injury a few weeks earlier, probed and tried to carve out openings. Koscielny, at least, tried to cajole his colleagues, although Giroud was displaying the type of insouciance which occasionally frustrated supporters. Özil pushed more down the flank. Hull's Tom Huddlestone proved a constant menace.

On 71 minutes, Arsenal's pressure told as Koscielny bundled the ball home following a header by Sagna and it was 2-2. Arsenal attempted to grab a late winner. Giroud's stinging shot was saved by McGregor in the Hull goal and Sanogo hit the side netting. Cazorla was denied what appeared to be a clear penalty.

In extra time, Giroud hit the bar and Ramsey went very close before, finally, the ghosts of recent failures were exorcised. Wenger had given a clear indication that he was going for broke when he substituted Cazorla and Özil, two players who would have taken penalties in a shoot-out, and replaced them with Wilshere and Rosický.

With a copse of Hull players on the edge of their area, Wilshere nudged the ball forward to Sanogo, who lost control. Giroud gained possession in the box, ran towards the touchline and back-heeled into the path of Ramsey, who drilled the ball home with the outside of his right foot to make the score 3-2.

The Welshman thoroughly deserved to join the likes of Lambert, George, Sunderland and Linighan in the pantheon of Arsenal's dramatic late FA Cup Final winners. There was a huge outpouring of relief as Ramsey was hotly pursued by Gibbs and Wilshere, in front of the jubilant Arsenal fans, before skidding to a halt flat on his back. For a few seconds he lay still, grinning and looking up at the clear blue sky.

There was still an opportunity for Aluko to take advantage of Fabianski's rush of blood and pull his team level; he missed by a few inches. The final whistle went soon afterwards. Wenger's players gave him the bumps and soaked him in champagne. He didn't exactly look comfortable ('It's not really the boss's kind of thing,' admitted Walcott) but when it was a smiling Wenger's turn to lift the FA Cup a few minutes later, he immediately looked around nine years younger – give or take five days or so.

Maybe it reminded him that Arsenal's *raison d'être* shouldn't be simply to finish fourth in the Premier League each year. As the joyous scenes at Wembley, and the impromptu pitch invasion at the screening of the match at the Emirates Stadium proved, there's far more to football than that. At the victory parade, the players were almost overcome by the sheer relief and joy at finally breaking the trophy hoodoo.

Wenger confirmed that he would be signing a new contract which will take him beyond the 20-year milestone at the club, thereby giving him the opportunity to do what no other Arsenal boss has achieved – or been allowed to do; bring more success to Arsenal after a lengthy fallow period.

Several questions remain: can Wenger purchase and integrate the required reinforcements in midfield and attack, and, most importantly, successfully alter the team's tactics in crunch domestic and European matches?

Can all the main protagonists be kept fit throughout the season? Did the Özil signing really herald the start of a golden era, or will it simply be regarded as a flashily ephemeral transfer in years to come?

Will the win against Hull City be the springboard for a sustained era of Arsenal success like the 1930 victory over Huddersfield? Or, like the 1979 FA Cup Final triumph over Manchester United, remain a false dawn in the club's rich history?

Only time will tell.

# Select Bibliography


Ackroyd, Peter, *Charlie Chaplin* (Chutter & Windass, 2014)

Adams, Tony, with Ridley, Ian, *Addicted* (Harper Collins, 1998)

Allison, George, *Allison Calling: A Galaxy Of Football And Other Memories* (Staples Press, 1948)

Andrews, Mark, *The Crowd At Woolwich Arsenal FC* (Hamilton House, 2012)

Astaire, Simon, *Sol Campbell – The Authorised Biography* (Spellbinding Media, 2014)

Attwood, Tony, *Making The Arsenal* (Hamilton House, 2009)

Attwood, Tony, with Kelly, Andy and Andrews, Mark, *Woolwich Arsenal FC: 1893–1915, The Club That Changed Football* (Hamilton House, 2012)

Auclair, Philippe, *Thierry Henry: Lonely At The Top* (Macmillan, 2013)

Azulay, Bernard, *Arsenal All 4-1* (Mainstream Publishing, 2004)

Azulay, Bernard, *Arsenal On The Double* (Mainstream Publishing, 2002)

Bagchi, Rob and Rogerson, Paul, *The Unforgiven: The Story Of Don Revie's Leeds United* (Aurum, 2009)

Barclay, Patrick, *The Life And Times Of Herbert Chapman: The Story Of One Of Football's Most Influential Figures* (Weidenfeld & Nicolson, 2014)

Ball, Alan, *It's All About A Ball* (WH Allen & Co, 1978)

Barnes, Walley, *Captain Of Wales* (Stanley Paul, 1953)

Barrett, Norman, *The Daily Telegraph Football Chronicle: A Season By Season Account Of The Soccer Stories That Made The Headlines From 1863 To The Present Day* (Ted Smart, 1993)

Bastin, Cliff with Glanville, Brian, *Cliff Bastin Remembers* (The Ettrick Press Ltd, 1950)

Bergkamp, Dennis with Winner, David, *Stillness And Speed* (Simon & Schuster, 2013)

Bower, Tom, *Broken Dreams: Vanity, Greed And The Souring Of British Football* (Simon & Schuster, 2003)

Brady, Liam, *So Far So Good…A Decade In Football* (Stanley Paul, 1980)

Brown, Deryk, *The Arsenal Story* (Arthur Barker Limited, 1972)

Brown, Jim, *Huddersfield Town: Champions Of England 1923–26* (Desert Island Football Histories, 2003)

Buchan, Charles, *A Lifetime In Football* (Phoenix, 1955)

Chapman, Herbert, *Herbert Chapman On Football* (Garrick Publishing, 1934)

Crick, Michael, *The Boss: The Many Sides Of Alex Ferguson* (Simon & Schuster, 2003)

Cropley, Alex with Wright, Tom, *Crops The Alex Cropley Story* (Luath Press, 2013)

Eastham, George, *Determined To Win* (Stanley Paul, 1964)

Evans, Richard, *The Wenger Code, Will It Survive The Age Of The Oligarch?* (GCR Books, 2012)

Ferguson, Alex, *Managing My Life My Autobiography* (Hodder and Stoughton, 2000)

Ferguson, Alex, *My Autobiography* (Hodder & Stoughton, 2013)

Finn, Ralph, *Arsenal Chapman To Mee* (Robert Hale, 1969)

Fisher, Keith, *Arsenal Greats* (Sportsprint, 1990)

Francis, Mike, *You Little Beauty – The Gooner 1987–1989* (Sporting Editions, 2000)

Fynn, Alex and Guest, Lynton, *Heroes And Villains: The Inside Story Of The 1990/91 Season At Arsenal And Tottenham Hotspur* (Penguin, 1991)

Fynn, Alex and Whitcher, Kevin, *Arsenal The Making Of A Modern Superclub* (Vision Sports Publishing, 2011)

Fynn, Alex and Whitcher, Kevin, *Arsène & Arsenal: The Quest To Rediscover Past Glories* (Vision Sports Publishing, 2014)

Giller, Norman, *Billy Wright: A Hero For All Seasons, The Official Biography* (Robson Books, 2002)

Glanville, Brian, *Famous Football Clubs: Arsenal* (Convoy Publications, 1952)

Graham, George with Giller, Norman, *The Glory And The Grief* (Andre Deutsch, 1995)

Greaves, Jimmy, with Giller, Norman, *Taking Sides: The Ten Greatest Football Teams* (Sidgwick & Jackson, 1984)

Groves, Perry with McShane, John, *We All Live In A Perry Groves World: My Story* (John Blake, 2007)

Hapgood, Eddie, *Football Ambassador* (Sporting Handbooks Limited, 1945)

Harding, John, *Alex James, Life Of A Football Legend* (Robson Books, 1988)

Hardy, Lance, *Stokoe, Sunderland And '73: The Story Of The Greatest FA Cup Final Shock Of All Time* (Orion, 2009)

Heatley, Michael and Welch, Ian, *The Great Derby Matches: Arsenal Versus Tottenham. A Complete History Of The Fixture* (Dial House, 1996)

Hills, David (ed), *Arsenal: 20 Defining Matches* (Guardian Shorts, 2012)

Inglis, Simon, *Charles Buchan's Football Monthly: Arsenal Gift Book* (Played In Britain, 2007)

James, Gary, *Joe Mercer OBE Football With A Smile* (James Ward, 2010)

Jennings, Pat, *Pat Jennings: An Autobiography* (Willow Books, 1983)

Joy, Bernard, *Forward Arsenal: Seventy Years Of Football* (Panther, 1950)

Keane, Roy, *Keane The Autobiography* (Penguin Books, 2003)

Kelly, Stephen, *Back Page Football: A Century Of Newspaper Coverage* (Aurora Publishing, 1995)

Kelsey, Jack, *Over The Bar* (Stanley Paul, 1958)

King, Jeff and Willis, Tony, *George Graham, The Wonder Years* (Virgin, 1995)

Knighton, Leslie, *Behind The Scenes In Big Football* (Stanley Paul, 1950)

Kuper, Simon, *The Football Men: Up Close With The Giants Of The Modern Game* (Simon & Schuster, 2012)

Kurt, Richard, *Red Devils: A History Of Man United's Rogues And Villains* (Prion Books, 1998)

Lawrence, Amy, *Proud To Say That Name: The Marble Hall Of Fame, Arsenal's Greatest Games* (Mainstream, 1997)

Lees, Andrew and Kennedy, Ray, *Ray Of Hope: The Ray Kennedy Story* (Penguin Books, 1993)

Macdonald, Malcolm, *Malcolm Macdonald, My Autobiography* (Arthur Barker, 1983)

Maidment, Jem, *Arsenal 100 Greatest Games* (Hamlyn, 2005)

McLintock, Frank with McNeill, Terry, *That's The Way The Ball Bounces* (Pelham Books, 1969)

McLintock, Frank, *True Grit, The Autobiography* (Headline, 2005)

Maxwell, Tom, *The Fabulous Baker Boys: The Greatest Strikers Scotland Never Had* (Birlinn, 2013)

Mercer, Derrick (ed), *The Twentieth Century Day By Day* (Dorling Kindersley, 1999)

Merson, Paul, with Harris, Harry, *Rock Bottom* (Bloomsbury, 1996)

Merson, Paul, *How Not To Be A Professional Footballer* (Harper Sport, 2012)

Murray, Scott and Walker, Rowan, *Day Of The Match: A History Of Football In 365 Days* (Boxtree, 1998)

Neill, Terry, *Revelations Of A Football Manager* (Sidgwick And Jackson, 1985)

O'Leary, David with Miller, Harry, *David O'Leary, My Story* (Mainstream, 1988)

Page, Simon, *Herbert Chapman, The First Great Manager* (Heroes Publishing, 2006)

Pardoe, Rex, *The Battle Of London: The Full Story Of The Rivalry Between Spurs & Arsenal From The 1880s To The 1970s* (Tom Stacey, 1972)

Ponting, Ivan, *Arsenal Player By Player* (Hamlyn, 1998)

Powter, David, *Arsenal FC: The 25 Year Record* (Soccer Books Limited, 1997)

Rees, Jasper, *Wenger The Making Of A Legend* (Short Books, 2003)

Rippon, Anton, *The Story Of Arsenal* (Moorland Publishing, 1981)

Rivoire, Xavier, *Arsène Wenger, The Biography* (Aurum, 2007)

Robertson, John, *Arsenal* (Hamlyn, 1985)

Sammels, Jon with Oxby, Robert, *Double Champions Playing The Arsenal Way,* (Arthur Barker Ltd, 1971)

Sharpe, Graham, *Free The Manchester United One: The Inside Story Of Football's Greatest Scam,* (Robson Books, 2003)

Shaw, Phil, *The Book Of Football Quotations* (Mainstream Publishing, 1999)

Simmons, John and Simmons, Matthew, *Great Brand Stories Arsenal: Winning Together: The Story Of The Arsenal Brand* (Cyan Books, 2006)

Simpson, Paul and Hesse, Uli, *Who Invented The Stepover? And* Other *Crucial Football Conundrums,* (Profile Books, 2013)

Smith, Bruce, *Arsenal Fact File, The Ultimate Arsenal Fan's Stats Book* (Virgin, 2000)

Smith, Denis, *Just One Of Seven* (Know The Score Books, 2008)

Soar, Phil, *Tottenham Hotspur: The Official Illustrated History* (Hamlyn, 1997)

Soar, Phil and Tyler, Martin, *Arsenal: The Official Centenary History Of Arsenal Football Club: 1886–1986* (Guild Publishing, 1986)

Spurling, Jon, *All Guns Blazing: Arsenal In The 1980s* (Aureus, 2001)

Spurling, Jon, *Highbury: The Story Of Arsenal In N5* (Orion, 2006)

Spurling, Jon, *Rebels For The Cause: The Alternative History Of Arsenal Football Club* (Mainstream, 2004)

Spurling, Jon, *Top Guns: Arsenal In the 1990s* (Aureus, 2001)

Stapleton, Frank, *Frankly Speaking* (Blackwater Press, 1991)

Storey, Peter, *True Storey: My Life And Crimes As A Football Hatchet Man* (Mainstream, 2011)

Stubbs, David, *Charlie Nicholas: The Adventures Of Champagne Charlie* (Boxtree, 1997)

Studd, Stephen, *Herbert Chapman Football Emperor* (Souvenir Press, 1998)

Taylor, Stewart, *Stuck In A Moment: The Ballad Of Paul Vaessen* (GCR Books, 2014)

Tibballs, Geoff, *FA Cup Giant Killers* (Collins Willow, 1994)

Tossell, David, *Bertie Mee: Arsenal's Officer And Gentleman* (Mainstream, 2005)

Tossell, David, *Seventy-One Guns: The Year Of The First Arsenal Double* (Mainstream, 2002)

Tueart, Dennis with Spurling, Jon, *Dennis Tueart: My Football Journey* (Vision Sports Publishing, 2011)

Ure, Ian, *Ure's Truly* (Pelham Books, 1968)

Vaeth, Joseph, *Graf Zeppelin: The Adventures Of An Aerial Globe Trotter* (Frederick Muller, 1959)

Vieira, Patrick, *Vieira My Autobiography* (Orion Publishing, 2005)

Wall, Bob, *Arsenal From The Heart* (Souvenir Press, 1969)

Ward, Andrew and Williams, John, *Football Nation, Sixty Years Of The Beautiful Game* (Bloomsbury, 2009)

Weaver, Graham, *12-0 To The Arsenal (And A Goal In Injury Time)* (Mainstream, 1998)

Welch, Ian, *Arsenal v Spurs: Classic North London Derby Games* (Haynes Publishing, 2012)

Welch, Julie, *The Biography Of Tottenham Hotspur* (Vision Sports Publishing, 2012)

White, Jim, *Premier League A History In 10 Matches* (Head of Zeus, 2013)

Whittaker, Tom, *Tom Whittaker's Arsenal Story* (Sporting Handbooks Limited, 1957)

Wilson, Bob, *An Autobiography* (Pelham Books, 1971)

Wilson, Bob, *Bob Wilson My Autobiography, Behind The Network* (Hodder And Stoughton, 2003)

Wilson, Jonathan, *Inverting The Pyramid: A History Of Football Tactics* (Orion, 2008)

Wilson, Jonathan and Murray, Scott, *The Anatomy Of Liverpool: A History Of Liverpool In Ten Matches* (Orion, 2013)

Winner, David, *Brilliant Orange, The Neurotic Genius Of Dutch Football* (Bloomsbury, 2000)

Wozencroft, Sean, *Cardiff City's Greatest Games: The Bluebirds; Fifty Finest Matches* (Pitch Publishing, 2013)

Wright, Ian, *Mr Wright: The Explosive Autobiography Of Ian Wright* (Harper Collins, 1996)

**Newspapers, Periodicals, and Fanzines**
*All Sports Weekly*
*Arsenal Echo*
*Athletic News*
*Daily Dispatch*
*Daily Express*
*Daily Graphic*
*Daily Mail*
*Daily Mirror*
*Daily Star*
*Evening Standard*
*Evening Times*
*Football Monthly*
*FourFourTwo*
*Gazzetta dello Sport*
*Glasgow Evening News*
*Goal!*
*Gooner*
*Highbury High*
*Huddersfield Examiner*
*Hull Daily Mail*
*Islington Daily Gazette and North London Tribune*
*Kentish Independent*
*Manchester Guardian*
*Match Of The Day Magazine*
*North London Press and St Pancras Gazette*
*Observer*
*One Nil Down*
*Southampton Echo*
*Sunday Evening Telegram*
*Sunday Pictorial*
*Sunday Post*
*Sunderland Echo*
*The Blizzard*
*The People*
*The Times*
*West London and Fulham Times*
*When Saturday Comes*

**Websites**
guardian.co.uk
arsenalinsider.com
arsenal.com
independent.co.uk
guardian.co.uk
thearsenalhistory.com
blog.woolwicharsenal.co.uk